Robert J. Mockler, PhD

# Multinationa[l]
# Manage[ment]
## *An Integrative E[ntrepreneurial]*
## *Context-Speci[fic] [Pr]ocess*

*Pre-publication*
REVIEWS,
COMMENTARIES,
EVALUATIONS . . .

"**B**ob Mockler is one of the outstanding original thinkers and writers in the field of strategic management. His non-textbookish approach provides significant value for the forward-thinking professional in the field. He provides practical, buzzword-free knowledge for the reader. One merely needs to scan the list of acknowledgments for his latest book, *Multinational Strategic Management,* ranging from Warren Buffet to Charles Schwab to Peter Senge to Jack Welch, to realize the league in which Mockler plays. His worldwide perspective is reinforced by his contacts and activities in Italy, Russia, China, Costa Rica, and elsewhere.

The book recognizes that one cannot limit strategic management to a domestic playing field; today's (and certainly tomorrow's) field of application is worldwide, cross-border, and technologically related. Managing in this environment is not easy and requires entrepreneurial skill, strategic thinking, and the correct 'bag of tools,' as Mockler describes them. The diverse set of contingencies faced by such managers is the focus of this book, and it delivers on its promise. This book is invaluable for strategic managers and professionals at all levels, and essential reading for MBA students in particular."

**L. A. Digman, PhD**
*U.S. Bank Professor of Management,*
*University of Nebraska–Lincoln*

*More pre-publication*
## REVIEWS, COMMENTARIES, EVALUATIONS . . .

"There are many books on strategic management but there are very few that cover the field with specific emphasis on global corporations. As the former chair and CEO of a *Fortune 100* multinational corporation, I see the entire book as a valuable addition to management strategic thinking. I especially find the concepts on interpersonal interaction in multicultural management extremely meaningful for U.S. corporations entering international markets or foreign companies entering the U.S. market. Having taught business school seniors since my retirement, I am sure this would be an excellent textbook for the future managers of global corporations."

**Eugene J. Sullivan, MBA**
*Chairman Emeritus,*
*Borden, Inc.*

"I highly recommend Dr. Mockler's *Multinational Strategic Management: An Integrative Entrepreneurial Context-Specific Process* to anyone working in or teaching a course in the multinational management area. The book provides, to all levels of international managers and teachers of multinational management courses, detailed guidance in building strong cross-border businesses and managing cross-cultural diversity in a wide range of business situations. The book has a very practical 'how to do it' perspective, as well as a sound theoretical structure."

**Dorothy Dologite, PhD**
*Professor of Computer*
*Information Systems,*
*Zicklin School of Business,*
*Baruch College,*
*City University of New York*

"Dr. Mockler's latest work, replete with recent and relevant examples, reminds us once again of the harsh reality that there is no single formula for the successful management of the modern enterprise. He then gives us the good news, which is that there is a process that with care and diligence can work. His context-specific process is the only one I have ever seen that puts sound management principles, common sense, and awareness of one's environment into a formalized structure that is easy to understand and would benefit any leader, manager, or entrepreneur."

**Mory Katz, MBA**
*Chairman and CEO,*
*Direct Response Corporation,*
*White Plains, New York*

International Business Press®
An Imprint of The Haworth Press, Inc.
New York • London • Oxford

# Multinational Strategic Management
*An Integrative Entrepreneurial Context-Specific Process*

# INTERNATIONAL BUSINESS PRESS®
Erdener Kaynak, PhD
Executive Editor

New, Recent, and Forthcoming Titles:

*Privatization and Entrepreneurship: The Managerial Challenge in Central and Eastern Europe* by Arieh Ullmann and Alfred Lewis

*U.S. Trade, Foreign Direct Investments, and Global Competitiveness* by Rolf Hackmann

*Business Decision Making in China* by Huang Quanyu, Joseph Leonard, and Chen Tong

*International Management Leadership: The Primary Competitive Advantage* by Raimo W. Nurmi and John R. Darling

*The Trans-Oceanic Marketing Channel: A New Tool for Understanding Tropical Africa's Export Agriculture* by H. Laurens van der Laan

*Handbook of Cross-Cultural Marketing* by Paul A. Herbig

*Guide to Software Export: A Handbook for International Software Sales* by Roger Philips

*Executive Development and Organizational Learning for Global Business* edited by J. Bernard Keys and Robert M. Fulmer

*Contextual Management: A Global Perspective* by Raghbir (Raj) S. Basi

*Japan and China: The Meeting of Asia's Economic Giants* by Kazua John Fukuda

*Export Savvy: From Basics to Strategy* by Zak Karamally

*Strategic Networks: The Art of Japanese Interfirm Cooperation* by Frank-Jürgen Richter

*Export-Import Theory, Practices, and Procedures* by Belay Seyoum

*Globalization of Business: Practice and Theory* by Abbas J. Ali

*Internationalization of Companies from Developing Countries* by John Kuada and Olav Jull Sørensen

*Guanxi: Relationship Marketing in a Chinese Context* by Y. H. Wong and Thomas K. P. Leung

*Multinational Strategic Management: An Integrative Entrepreneurial Context-Specific Process* by Robert J. Mockler

*New Product Development: Successful Innovation in the Marketplace* by Michael Z. Brooke and William Ronald Mills

*Economic Dynamics in Transitional Economies: The Four-P Governments, the EU Enlargement, and the Bruxelles Consensus* by Bruno S. Sergi

# Multinational Strategic Management
## *An Integrative Entrepreneurial Context-Specific Process*

Robert J. Mockler, PhD

International Business Press®
An Imprint of The Haworth Press, Inc.
New York • London • Oxford

Published by

International Business Press ®, an imprint of The Haworth Press., Inc., 10 Alice Street, Binghamton, NY 13904-1580.

Cover design by Anastasia Litwak.

**Library of Congress Cataloging-in-Publication Data**

Mockler, Robert J.
    Multinational strategic management : an integrative entrepreneurial context-specific process / Robert J. Mockler.
       p. cm.
    Includes bibliographical references and index.
    ISBN 0-7890-1474-2 (alk. paper)—ISBN 0-7890-1475-0 (alk. paper)
    1. International business enterprises—Management. 2. Strategic planning. I. Title.

HD62.4 .M626 2002
658.4'012--dc21

2001045681

114916

Dedicated to the late Colman M. Mockler,
former Chief Executive Officer of The Gillette Company,
brother and mentor of the author,
one of business's truly great leaders,
and an extraordinary human being.

# ABOUT THE AUTHOR

**Robert J. Mockler, PhD, MBA,** is Joseph F. Adams Professor of Management at St. John's University Tobin Graduate School of Business. He is the director of the Strategic Management Research Group and its Centers of Case Study Development and of Knowledge-Based Systems for Business. Dr. Mockler is a widely published author and an international lecturer, consultant, investor, and teacher of MBA courses. He has received national awards for innovative teaching and has been a Fulbright Scholar.

# CONTENTS

# Preface

Multinational strategic management is best understood when viewed from the perspective of an individual manager in a specific firm working to win in a highly competitive market.

## *A RAPIDLY CHANGING, HIGHLY COMPETITIVE CONTEXT*

The rate and magnitude of change in today's global competitive environment is not expected to slow. In fact, multinational competition in most industries is expected to increase over the next decade. Very often the old rules no longer apply (Maitland 2000; Mandel 2000).

For example, in mid-2000, France Telecom announced that it was buying British cell-phone operator Orange PLC for $46 billion (Reed et al., 2000), and Deutsche Telekom bought controlling interest in Matav, the dominant telecom in Hungary (Eddy and Waters 2000). These were only the latest of many mergers, alliances, and acquisitions (Cane 2000) that were expected to have a major impact on global telecommunications firms not only by causing but also by forcing major earnings losses. This trend also forced larger firms, such as AT&T (United States), France Telecom, Deutsche Telekom (Germany), Telefonica SA (Spain), and Nippon Telegraph and Telephone Corp. (Japan), to acquire new partners, cut prices, and create new alliances to remain competitive (Andrews 2000; Baker and Capell 2000; Shillingford 2000; Vitzhum 2000).

Hoechst AG, a German chemical and pharmaceutical company, underwent a major transformation in the mid-1990s, motivated by a maturing market, restrictive labor practices, environmental activism, and tax problems in Germany. By late 1999, Hoechst had sold twelve businesses—all except two based in Germany—and acquired four companies—all outside Germany. These moves reduced Hoechst's labor force in Germany from 80,000 to 45,000. Its purchases of U.S. pharmaceutical firms increased its U.S. sales to 33 percent of total company sales in 1996, up from 6 percent in the late 1980s. Although these moves hurt short-term profits and sometimes failed, they helped shift emphasis from low-profit chemical to high-profit pharmaceutical businesses. The firm also appointed a Brazilian and an American to its nine-member board as part of its internationalization strategy.

Such changes, made in response to global competitive pressures and the open markets created by a unified European market, were contributing to unrest and uncertainty in Europe. Further instability was created in 1999 by economic problems in Asia and Russia. These problems had a negative impact on many multinational firms and led some countries to reintroduce market controls. Although opportunities for multinational businesses are great, uncertainty, diversity, new technologies (such as the Internet), and rapidly changing environments indicate that winning will not come easily and skillful management is needed to survive, prosper, and win.

This book is designed to overcome a major problem in today's educational systems arising from rapid change: "the rampaging speed with which recent information media and technical innovation has given us a new view of the world has far outstripped our educational system's ability to prepare us" (Burke 1997, p. x). To meet this challenge, educational systems have a "new commitment to offering broader perspectives that enable people to deal with complexity and uncertainty, act with wisdom, build powerful social relationships, and master entrepreneurship skills" (Denning 1997, p. 267).

This book aims to help users *learn how to handle these needs*. It goes beyond simply describing these needs and explaining how others meet them. It provides help in learning how to manage complex diversity when working alone and with others, and how to act purposefully. In this sense, it is a nonprescriptive, nonformula text, which makes use of systematic strategic management processes and structures, but only selectively as appropriate for individual situations, and always in conjunction with creative and often unstructured entrepreneurial thinking and action.

## AN INTEGRATIVE, MANY-DIMENSIONAL PROCESS

This book is not based on any single "approach," not only because the diverse multinational environment is changing rapidly, but also because multinational strategic management requires many approaches which are integratively used *depending on the situation involved*. In keeping with this segmented but integrative perspective, the discussions in this text are often segmented for explanation purposes, in the same way sports are often learned by focusing on different aspects or parts of the sport during training. As in sports, however, strategic management is, in practice, an integrated process that uses whatever approaches are appropriate for the situation involved. The discussions in this book should be viewed within this balanced, segmented, and integrative perspective.

For many readers, this perspective is initially confusing. A reader instinctively longs for a single right approach or magic bullet, but that rarely exists. Instead, many good approaches exist. The reader's task is threefold:

- To acquire and enhance skills in entrepreneurial contingency thinking and action
- To learn more about the processes and commonly used "bag of tools" (and where possible develop new ones)
- To acquire increasingly greater skills in integratively using combinations of these tools in creative entrepreneurial ways appropriate for handling specific situations

The material presented and discussed in this book is designed to help readers accomplish this multifaceted task.

## THE INTENDED READERSHIP

Although this book provides an overview of how international business works, its primary focus is to provide an introduction to *leading and managing* enterprises that operate across national borders, whether they are called multinational (operating in many countries), international (operating between nations), or global (operating worldwide). In this book, the term "multinational enterprise" is used interchangeably with these other terms.

Drafts of this book have been used to support executive training workshops, as well as full semester and compressed graduate and advanced undergraduate university business programs in Italy, the United States, Russia, China, and Latin America. The complete text has been translated into Chinese. Portions of it have been translated in Russian.

The book has proved useful in introducing readers at all levels to integrative decision making from the entrepreneurial perspective as is found at successful multinational companies such as: General Electric and Intel (U.S.); Nestlé, Carrefour, Benetton, and Groupe Danone (Western Europe); Bacardi (Latin America); and News Corporation (Australia).

Because this book is designed to introduce readers to basic strategic management practices, it can be used in any country as a text in any undergraduate or graduate business policy course which covers international applications. Such an international focus is a major American Association of Colleges and Schools of Business (AACSB) accrediting agency objective.

## MEETING THE CHALLENGES OF MANAGING ACROSS NATIONAL BOUNDARIES AND CULTURES

This book has many distinguishing features. First, it provides a way to meet the needs of multinational managers by initially focusing on common frameworks. Chapters 1 through 4 introduce the multinational business environment and review basic strategic management processes, especially integrative, creative, and unstructured entrepreneurial contingencies that provide common frameworks for strategic management decision making and action domestically and multinationally.

Applications in multinational tasks, activities, and situations of these and other familiar common contingency frameworks (such as organizational and behavioral processes, global products and services, telecommunications/information systems technologies, finance/accounting systems, and strategic alliances) are explored in Chapters 5 through 9 in a variety of multinational situations at the enterprise-wide, business unit, and operational levels. These chapters also explore specific problems involved in synergistically managing differences, diversity, and change in different situations.

A second distinctive feature of this book is that it describes how managers actually balance the diverse aspects of multinational management. It focuses on the job of balancing, for example, the global aspects of multinational management with responsiveness to local situation factors in different firms and countries. Acquiring entrepreneurial and integrative skills needed to achieve this balance (action) is as important as knowing what to do and how it should be done (planning).

The book's chapters describe how leaders and managers do this balancing and reconciling not only when planning (Chapters 2 and 4), but also when putting in place the functional enabling operations involved in carrying out plans and managing operations (Chapters 5 through 12). Chapters 13 and 14 provide integrative strategic management perspectives.

A third distinguishing feature is that the book is essentially experience based. Although basic theory development and research was important to this book's development, its basic themes and orientation come from the experiences of the author, his associates, and multinational companies.

This book's fourth distinguishing feature is that it treats the topic from an individual manager's decision-making and action viewpoint. In this sense, it presents readers with an opportunity to develop their skills by experiencing a variety of multinational management situations of growing diversity and complexity much as they would on the job.

A fifth distinguishing feature of this book is that it deals with multinational management on three levels:

- Surviving and prospering in the present competitive environment
- Anticipating, adapting to, and generating ideas that manage and exploit change over the intermediate term more rapidly than competitors
- Leading and creating change across industries and markets

# Acknowledgments

I wish to thank my many associates and friends in business who helped me: Krister Ahlström (former President and CEO, Ahlstrom Corp.), Warren Buffet (Chairman, Berkshire Hathaway), Manuel Cutillas (Chairman and CEO, Bacardi Ltd.), Michael Eisner (Chairman and CEO, Walt Disney), Jack Eyman (former General Manager, Rohm and Haas China, Inc.), Roberto Goizueta (former Chairman and CEO, Coca-Cola), David Hussey (David Hussey & Associates), Raymond Lane (former President and CEO, Chrysler Corp.), Ernest Micek (former Chairman, President, and CEO, Cargill, Inc.), Rupert Murdoch (Chairman, News Corp.), David Puttruck (President and CEO, Charles Schwab & Co., Inc.), Joseph Saggese (Chairman, President, and CEO, Borden Chemicals), Donald Schneider (President, Schneider National), Peter Senge (Director, MIT's center for Organizational Learning), Roberto Servitje Sendra (Chairman, Groupo Industrial Bimbo), Don Tapscott (Chairman, Alliance for Converging Technologies), Jack F. Welch, Jr. (former Chairman and CEO, General Electric), Alfred Zeien (former Chairman and CEO, Gillette), and Lorenzo Zambrano (Chair and CEO Grupo Cementos Mexicanos— Ccmex).

My thanks are also extended to my many professional friends and associates and to my graduate students who contributed to the development of this book at St. John's University (New York and Rome), at Bocconi University (Milan, Italy), at the state universities in St. Petersburg and Moscow (Russia), at Renmin and Tsinghua Universities (Beijing, China), and at the Universidad Internacional de Las Americas (Costa Rica). I also want to thank my many workshop participants around the world who used drafts of this book (and its accompanying supporting materials) and so helped me make it a more useful teaching and learning tool.

# PART I:
# INTRODUCTION

# Chapter 1

# An Integrative Entrepreneurial Process

The United Nations (UN) has defined *multinational enterprises* as enterprises which own or control production or service facilities located outside of the country in which they are based. A multinational business operates in more than one country, a domestic business in only one country.

Each country in which a multinational enterprise operates has a distinct economic, political, legal, cultural, industrial, and competitive market context. Businesses must be responsive to this diversity, especially when integrating their different operations. Achieving integration in a multinational firm involves maintaining a balance between capturing global efficiencies and responding to local differences, a task which requires both creative innovative entrepreneurial unstructured approaches as well as systematic structured ones.

Whatever the approach, the ability to change, whether abruptly or over time, has become a critical factor in successful multinational management.

## *AN ENTREPRENEURIAL PERSPECTIVE*

Rapidly changing markets, and resulting market dislocations and discontinuities, are not a new phenomenon. From the beginning of time, entrepreneurs and entrepreneurial managers have found ways to profit from often unanticipated rapid changes within marketplaces. In fact, they welcome them—and at times create market dislocations because others become confused and see chaos when faced with such dislocations, and so in this way create opportunities. In contrast, aggressive entrepreneurs think positively about ways to exploit change and profit from the opportunities accompanying rapid change.

In many ways, today's business environment is similar. The major forces creating change are different of course:

- the digital revolution, the knowledge explosion, globalization of business, worldwide deregulation and privatization, increased pace of change and reduced cycle time, convergence of industries and less well-defined industry boundaries, the Internet and its growing links with expanding mobile telecommunications, disintermediation caused by the Internet, more competitor cooperation, sensitivity to ecology and other social forces, and overabundance of capital.

Even though the circumstances have changed, entrepreneurial and innovative contingency perspectives, such as the process shown in Figure 1.1, are still needed.

A dramatic example of the entrepreneurial perspective described previously is found in the Peter O'Toole movie, *The Lion in Winter,* in the scene where he creates chaos and then remarks in reply to Katharine Hepburn's question:

HEPBURN (*ELEANOR*): "What's going to happen?"

O'TOOLE (*HENRY II*): "I've no idea. I'm winning. I know I'm going to win. I just don't know what will happen."

O'Toole as King Henry II of England makes the point that at times a leader can even go so far as to create dislocations because it confuses most people, enabling an opportunist to in a sense "buy cheap and sell high," if he or she approaches it entrepreneurially and innovatively. The late Colman Mockler, former CEO of Gillette, described this leadership vision in this way: "I know exactly the kind of company I envision; I just don't know precisely what it will look like."

"Creative Destruction" is also not a new concept. The world has often experienced it and it is part of basic economic theory, as noted by Joseph Schumpeter, among others (Fisher 1999). It is a social, economic, and literary phenomenon. The steam engine, the telephone, the radio, the airplane, the television, and the computer were all new forces that led to dramatic and uncertain changing times (Barringer 2000). The Internet is just one more in a long series of these new disruptive challenges which entrepreneurs have faced and eventually mastered and exploited.

Jack Welch, the former CEO at General Electric (GE) was an early advocate of the creative destruction approach, creating crises (like O'Toole as Henry II in *The Lion in Winter*)—for example, by reorganizing GE, reducing the layers of management, and laying off over 100,000 people. He then worked through the chaos he created and successfully renewed GE, which in 2000 was among the largest and most admired companies in the world (Colvin 2000). His objective was entrepreneurial, to stretch the potential of the firm, even though his firm was very large (Hurst 1995; Slater 1999; Stewart 1999; Waters 1999).

Welch's major talents included his ability to define patterns or strategic guidelines (structures) that channel and stimulate innovative and entrepre-

FIGURE 1.1. A Basic Emergent Entrepreneurial Contingency Process

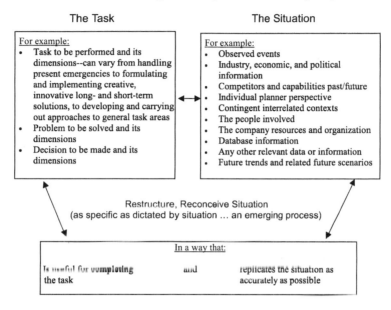

The Task           The Situation

For example:
• Task to be performed and its dimensions--can vary from handling present emergencies to formulating and implementing creative, innovative long- and short-term solutions, to developing and carrying out approaches to general task areas
• Problem to be solved and its dimensions
• Decision to be made and its dimensions

For example:
• Observed events
• Industry, economic, and political information
• Competitors and capabilities past/future
• Individual planner perspective
• Contingent interrelated contexts
• The people involved
• The company resources and organization
• Database information
• Any other relevant data or information
• Future trends and related future scenarios

Restructure, Reconceive Situation
(as specific as dictated by situation ... an emerging process)

In a way that:

Is useful for completing the task     and     replicates the situation as accurately as possible

neurial actions without inhibiting often unstructured individual initiative. Planning, for him, was something everyone did, not just top management. Welch's other talents were his charismatic leadership and his ability to change.

An entrepreneurial perspective is needed to deal with the many disparate forces existing today, such as globalization, deregulation, the knowledge explosion, and digitalization—especially the Internet—which provides instant access to a global marketplace. The entrepreneurial fever appears to be a worldwide phenomenon (Fleming 2000; Spindle 2000). At the same time, a systematic structured perspective is also needed to formulate and implement strategies.

Balancing diverse multinational forces while dealing with the demands of rapidly changing and highly competitive multinational markets creates major challenges for managers. Meeting these challenges often requires "breaking the mold," or as Marcus Buckingham describes it, breaking the rules (Buckingham and Coffman 1999). For example, in 1999, Unilever, the Anglo-Dutch group that makes much of the world's detergent, took twenty young managers—average age thirty-two—and set them loose for six months to examine trends and identify opportunities. The group questioned many traditional ways of thinking about brands and consumer buying motivation. The studies led to a dramatic shift of brand strategy; Unilever reduced to 400 the number of brands it would focus its resources on and let the remaining 1,200 brands find their own level of sales or eventually disappear (Cowell 2000; Willman 1999).

As seen from Unilever's, GE's, and other companies' experiences, managing the challenges presented by the multinational market requires cognitive skills to understand what is (and may be) happening in those markets, entrepreneurial skills to respond to and exploit rapid changes innovatively, and leadership and management skills to balance the many diverse elements using both structured and unstructured approaches.

## THE MULTINATIONAL STRATEGIC LEADERSHIP AND MANAGEMENT PROCESSES

As used in this book, *leadership* refers to envisioning the future and leading an enterprise by developing strategic frameworks, putting enablers in place, and energizing, guiding, and motivating others. *Strategic frameworks* and their related *values, strategies,* and *visions* generally define important aspects of the envisioned enterprise: they are action patterns intended to integratively guide how a firm allocates its resources and so are the basis of *action plans. Management* involves managing the activities involved in formulating and implementing strategies and their related action plans. Because the management discussed in this book is done within a strategic perspective, it is called *strategic management.* Strategic management encompasses both leadership and management, since individual leaders and managers may perform both leadership and management activities.

Based on company experiences described throughout this book, it is possible to identify various multinational strategic leadership and management processes. The familiar linear process shown in Figure 1.2 is a specific application of the one shown in Figure 1.1. Figure 1.2 outlines a common sense systematic *contingency* approach as applied to the task of formulating enterprise-wide strategies multinationally and then implementing them: systematically examine situation restraints, creatively and systematically formulate and evaluate alternative solutions, make a decision, and take action as appropriate for each situation.

When a Chinese entrepreneur started his small conglomerate, each venture was built on:

- The *analysis* of external (market, customer, and competition) and internal (financial and other resources) situation factors

- The *formulation and evaluation* of possible alternatives given future conditions
- The *development of specific strategies and action plans,* the *synthesis*
- The skillful *implementation*—management of making each venture work given the individuals, organizations, and external market conditions involved

FIGURE 1.2. The Multinational Strategic Management Process: A Linear Situational Overview

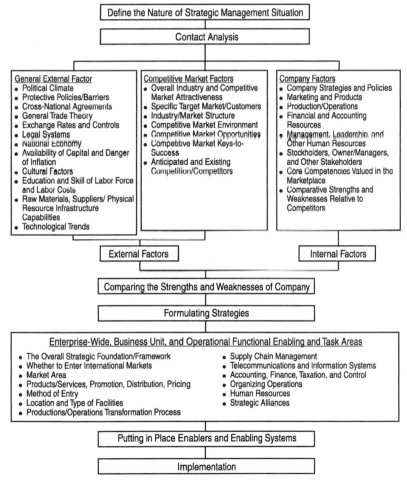

The viewpoint of this book is that entrepreneurial and systematic approaches to formulating and managing strategic frameworks in today's rapidly changing markets have always been used by entrepreneurs and niche players, approaches described in general in Figures 1.1, 1.2, and 1.3. The major differences arise from the speed of continuing change and the current ability (because of worldwide electronic infrastructures, easier access to knowledge, deregulation, and huge capital reserves) of much larger firms, and many individuals and firms with different size resource bases, to do it domestically and globally.

The basic general skills needed are the age-old ones of analysis, evaluation, synthesis, and communication/action (Dauer 1996), applied to, and balanced with, creative, unstructured entrepreneurial approaches, combined with conceptual thinking, associative reasoning, and practical "get the job done" skills (Whittington 1999). The specific management tools used, some of which are indiscriminately called "models," are contingent both on the type of situation and specific situation requirements.

The first step in dealing with rapid change in business now, as in the past, is to *think positively*. For example, the Internet can be a huge opportunity, not a threat, for the entrepreneur who embraces change. In April 1998, Jay Walker started Priceline.com, an Internet service which allows users to set their own prices for airline tickets; a year later his share was worth $1 billion (Weber and Petersen 1999). It was clearly an effective strategic business model, timed perfectly to meet a then market need; several years later the market shifted and Priceline.com was having problems and working to formulate new strategies (business models).

During the *situation study* (that is, studying how a situation works), the *analysis* involves decomposing the new and existing forces (identifying components) and evaluating their impacts (their relationships to present and future success). This involves searching for clues to future market trends affecting *opportunities* and *keys to success* (Slywotzky et al.1999). A similar situation analysis is needed of the investor or company involved, and creative ways in which his or her or its resources can be reconceived and reapplied in light of the new force. This is an indispensable step in tailoring strategies to the specific situation requirements.

The situation study includes *relationship evaluations,* evaluations which explore the ways new forces can be exploited at the enterprise-wide, strategic business unit, or operational level. This *opportunity search* continues within the perspective of the specific company and market under study. During this phase, *preliminary ideas* about possible alternative strategies and strategic plans are formulated, using one's own and others' business experiences and one's own thinking about the situation (Slywotzky and Morrison 1997, and Brown and Eisenhardt 1998, for example). These syntheses are initially treated as hypotheses to be studied further.

FIGURE 1.3. Strategic Management: Multinational and Domestic

**The Focus: An Emergent Entrepreneurial Leadership Process**

**The Process**

1. *Strategic Vision/Mission:*
   "I knew exactly what kind of company I envisioned; I just did not know precisely what it would look like." Precise definitions, in other words, often emerge over time, through the experiences involved in doing it.

2. *Strategic Guidelines:*
   This is the map, the path, the planned steps. The secret here is KISS—"Keep It Short & Simple." That means one page written, five minutes oral, maximum length.

3. *Implementation:*
   "Doing whatever was necessary to get the job done, within well-defined general moral, legal, ethical, and policy guidelines." This often involves reconciling and balancing diverse, conflicting, and often paradoxical forces, on a continuing basis, in a complex and rapidly changing competitive market environment.

**The Activities**

- Creating an overall vision (values, mission, strategic focus on core competencies, opportunities in future) and strategic framework (the guidelines or map). Specific strategies and strategic plans (enterprise-wide and in business units and functional areas) often emerge over time, through the enabling systems and processes.

- Activating, energizing, putting into place, and monitoring enabling systems and processes, such as: functional area operations; telecommunications/information systems; accounting and finance systems; organization and business structures, processes and cultures; and strategic alliances.

- Nurturing and enabling human resources and processes through: organization development; understanding cultural diversity; staffing, training, and communication; and effective flexible leadership and integrative management at all levels.

- Ensuring that a core management staff (with appropriate interpersonal, communication, entrepreneurial, and management skills and potential) is in place and functioning.

- Communicating and implementing the strategic framework, as well as the cultural benchmarks that are needed to enable the core management staff to translate the desired vision into action. The actual process involves superior visionary and pragmatic leadership appropriate for both the managers and people/groups involved in the situation.

- Leaving managers relatively free to manage, and pushing decision making as close to the customer as possible, but intervening where appropriate to make certain that integrative activities are operating efficiently and effectively to achieve the company's strategic short- and long-term objectives.

FIGURE 1.4. Strategic Management Process Cycle

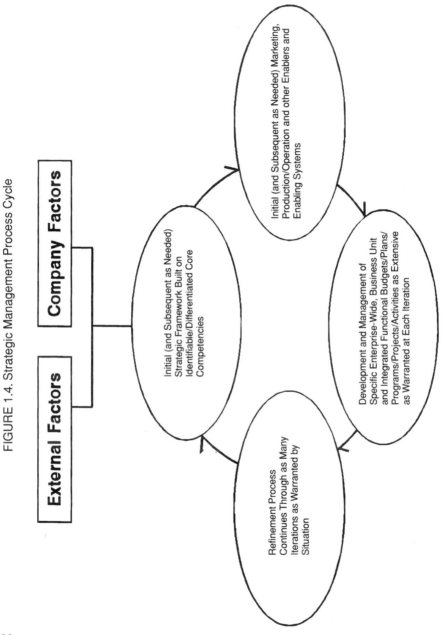

External Factors

Company Factors

Initial (and Subsequent as Needed) Strategic Framework Built on Identifiable/Differentiated Core Competencies

Initial (and Subsequent as Needed) Marketing, Production/Operation and other Enablers and Enabling Systems

Development and Management of Specific Enterprise-Wide, Business Unit and Integrated Functional Budgets/Plans/ Programs/Projects/Activities as Extensive as Warranted at Each Iteration

Refinement Process Continues Through as Many Iterations as Warranted by Situation

As alternatives are formulated and evaluated, the *structured synthesis phase* involves more detailed systematic planning at the operational, strategic business unit, and enterprise-wide level for the immediate, intermediate, and long-term time frames. The exact form of this strategic structure or framework will depend on the situation.

The *action phase* involves formulating specific action plans, putting in place enablers, and communicating and managing the strategy and plan implementation systematically and innovatively. Interpersonal skills are needed for effective implementation.

This four-phase process—getting to know the situation, the opportunity search, the structure synthesis (three time frames, three business levels), and action—provides a theoretical framework for understanding and doing strategic management, as does the required cognitive and behavioral skills inventory—thinking positively, analysis, evaluation, synthesis, and interpersonal (leadership and management) skills.

The linear process outlined in Figure 1.2 is only one aspect of strategic management, however. Figure 1.3 outlines the processes and activities involved in strategic management from another perspective. Both of these models are useful for understanding and explaining basic relationships and are useful systematic, structured ways to organize thoughts. They do not replicate all the realities of strategic management, however, because people do not always think linearly in sequential steps, nor does the world always act in a systematic, nonchaotic way. The processes involved in formulating and implementing strategies are often emergent, iterative ones through which solutions emerge over time, as shown in Figure 1.4, or are introduced explosively through creative destruction. Strategic management, therefore, involves balancing and integrating structured and unstructured approaches both when formulating and implementing strategies.

In the 1990s, Citibank was emphasizing *consumer* banking, with the strategic objective of eventually having most of its business in that segment. During 1996, its strategy in the *commercial* banking area, therefore, was a holding strategy. As Citibank rapidly expanded in dramatically changing emerging markets worldwide and as populations became more affluent, its CEO had a wait-and-see attitude toward commercial banking. He was prepared to listen to what emerging trends indicated over the coming years was the best balance of customer markets—even if it meant gradually getting out of the large-company commercial banking business.

In Europe, Airbus Industrie, founded in 1969 and backed by a consortium of the governments of Great Britain, France, Germany, and Spain, had been primarily a marketing operation that sold planes manufactured jointly by the four partners. Faced with changing market requirements as emerging countries, such as China, became more active both as customers and competitors, and as competition with Boeing intensified, Airbus revamped its enterprise-wide strategy through very difficult extended negotiations with its four partners (Rossant 2000).

At other times, solutions occur swiftly and creative destruction (the ultimate unstructured approach) produces major discontinuities, as at GE, Unilever, and other firms described throughout this book. Managers may also break molds by creating new future markets instead of just trying to anticipate them.

Although described as phases, the process is not necessarily linear or structured. Depending on the situation, it could be unstructured as well as contingent, sometimes emergent and sometimes abruptly discontinuous and creatively destructive, iterative, exploratory, circular, and generally continuous.

These and other experiences suggest that the ability to create solutions in response to specific situation factors (as described in Figure 1.1) and to skillfully carry out solutions can be as important to success as using popular planning techniques, such as matrix and SWOT analysis (discussed in Chapter 2), or other systematic structured approaches to strategic management, such as those described previously.

## *FORMULATING STRATEGIC FRAMEWORKS WITHIN DIFFERENT TIME PERSPECTIVES*

The emergent entrepreneurial contingency processes outlined in Figures 1.1 and 1.4 and the related linear ones in Figures 1.2 and 1.3 can be observed at work in strategy formulation and the related strategic framework activities shown in Figure 1.5.

Three perspectives of winning strategic frameworks and their related strategies in rapidly changing competitive markets shown in Figure 1.5 are discussed in this section. The first is:

- knowing existing markets and managing to meet their needs to survive and prosper over the short term.

Threshold strategies are needed to meet existing and anticipated near-term competitive market needs, thus enabling competing in a given market. This basic survival process involves traditional, structured, and analytical thinking to determine how things work and how the situation can best be handled with available resources. Entrepreneurial thinking and action are also required to handle day-to-day operations and respond quickly to changing market conditions. Dell Computer did this in Germany and France by using direct selling. Since many readers of this book will be students (graduate and undergraduate) of international business, it is necessary to empha-

FIGURE 1.5. Strategically Focused Management: The Strategic Framework

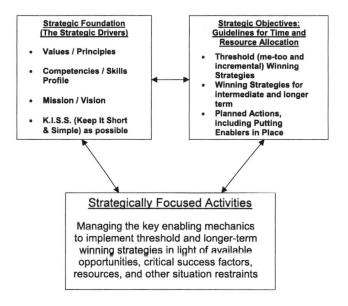

size the importance of establishing a thorough knowledge base of the markets, competition, and company under study. Chapter 4 describes this systematic structured analysis.

Although it is important to deal with the existing situation, managers should avoid being limited to a short-term perspective. Looking to the future and responding to changing needs rapidly, innovatively, and improvisationally is also important. This requires formulating strategies that enable winning against the competition in critical areas of the value chain. A second perspective, then, involves

- anticipating, generating, and adapting ideas often involving known or emerging technologies in a way that manages and exploits change over the intermediate term more rapidly than competitors.

This perspective involves formulating strategies for developing emerging business and new ways in which to differentiate or distinguish a firm and its products from the competition and to continue to renew this differentiation. It requires envisioning situations from multiple perspectives by studying the impact of differing future scenarios, ideas, and viewpoints. The situation should be analyzed from a broader context of all related technical, organizational, and individual perspectives in a search for ways to "break the mold." Intel did this by increasing the pace of new product introductions.

Coca-Cola's former CEO Roberto Goizueta formulated such a winning strategy in the 1980s when he invested in formerly independent bottling firms, a move which broke with past industry practices. This move enabled Coke to control its value chain and pricing, and expand rapidly overseas by buying its way into markets such as Venezuela where it purchased PepsiCo's distributor and overnight temporarily achieved an 85 percent market share until Pepsi countered with major investments in new plants, alliances, distribution systems, and advertising (Colitte 1999).

Citibank exploited new markets by using advanced technology to anticipate and meet consumer needs worldwide. For example, in 1998, Citibank announced a new online banking and investment service which was introduced in late 1999 (Beckett 1999). In contrast, managers at a major Swiss bank talked about such forward thinking, but when questioned about introducing branchless banking, the Swiss bank managers assured that the Swiss would not accept that. Although they paid lip service to new strategic perspectives, such as those of Jack Welch, Roberto Goizueta, Rupert Murdoch, and other business leaders, the Swiss bank was slow to initiate steps to meet emerging customer needs.

The Internet revolution has had a major impact on strategic management decision making, creating many opportunities and problems. For example, Barnes & Noble booksellers has had to adapt its retail-only enterprise-wide strategy to the major moves of the direct-selling Amazon.com, which has developed a new direct-to-consumer Internet strategic business model (Hof et al., 2000). Merrill Lynch (stockbrokers) has had to redefine its enterprise-wide strategy to respond to the online success of Charles Schwab discount brokers. The Toys "R" Us, Inc. multinational retail chain moved to start its own online selling firm in response to newly-formed eToys' online successes during the 1998 Christmas season. Initially, eToys had a greater market value than the much larger Toys "R" Us, though eToys eventually had severe problems (Bannon 2000, 2001). Beginning in 1999, Oracle Corporation, a worldwide computer software firm, was betting its future on a variety of new Internet strategic initiatives (Greene and Rocks 2000).

Furthermore, business leaders have to look beyond the immediate and intermediate future and explore what can be expected to happen and be made to happen years from now (Oliver 1999). This requires

- sensing, anticipating, and knowing how to handle the longer-term future and, if necessary, creating new markets and industries built on a company's existing or newly developed core competencies and strategic capabilities.

Studies have identified trends expected to dominate business in the future. For example, Wind and Main (1998) believe that marketplace emphasis is shifting from capital to knowledge, producer to consumer, Atlantic to Pacific, Japan to China, international trade to electronic commerce, computers to Internet, and money to people. As for organizations, emphasis appears to be shifting from mechanistic to organic, engineering to ecology, corporations to individuals and networks, horizontal and vertical to virtual integration, and business processes to cultures. As for individuals, emphasis is shifting from hard work to hypereffectiveness, faith to hope, security to uncertainty, current to future careers, and loyalty to courage.

This book provides many examples of how these trends affect formulating and implementing winning strategics. For example, in 1997 Hewlett-Packard (HP) was promoting a global information infrastructure to allow consumers to utilize digital devices using telephones, faxes, and printers. This global strategy enabled HP to develop and sell an array of its communications and computer products. This infrastructure also provided other manufacturers with a common framework for developing new common communication channels and new products equipped with computer chips. In a sense, HP was working to create a new market, a major strategic management task. The Internet has accelerated this development because it enables new products and computers to be integrated more easily. Intel and other firms, including France Telecom and IBM, have introduced simple, limited purpose computers, so-called "information appliances," which enable broader use of computers and the Internet (Manchester 1999).

In 1999, C. Michael Armstrong, AT&T's chairman, had the long-term vision of creating a company that sells every communications service American consumers and businesses could possibly want—not only phone services, but also video and high-speed data connections. He also wanted to own the wires that carry those services. He realized that to achieve that vision he would require hundreds of billions of dollars, face enormous obstacles, it would take many years, and that he would face competition at that level because MCI Worldcom also had similar aspirations (Kupfer 1999; Reinhardt, Yang and Crockett 1999). He also faced the merger of AOL/Time Warner, a company with content and access to homes worldwide (Schiesel 2000). A similar situation is developing in Europe as telecommunications firms race to form major multimedia communications and content enterprises (Boudette and Delaney 2000).

These and other experiences show how a strategic leader can go beyond anticipating and responding to the perceived long-term future. It is often necessary to attempt to "create" the future (Belasco and Stead 1999). Many firms are aggressively exploring "real option" scenarios involving how the Internet and other digital technologies will be changing traditional industry relationships, for example, by bypassing intermediaries and selling directly to customers which is discussed in Chapter 6. Many new industries are expected to be created based on these so-called "digital" forces (Downes and Mui 1998).

Making strategies work in the future requires creating an enabling environment, as shown in Figures 1.2, 1.3, 1.4, and 1.5, because a manager cannot possibly anticipate and plan for all the changes that can occur in rapidly changing worldwide markets. Planning this enabling environment includes studying such areas as the organization's structure and culture, telecommunication and information systems, financial and accounting systems, functional operations, and human resources (communications, staffing and training, and leadership and management). Strategic alliances are also key enablers today because the complexities of today's multinational markets require such alliances to extend a company's reach and knowledge and experience depth rapidly (Mockler 1999). Such an environment is needed to enable the formulation of specific operating plans, to carry out plans, and respond to the changing circumstances that inevitably arise even in well-planned situations. Effective day-to-day leadership and management are equally critical to success. Chapters 5 through 14 are concerned with these critical enabling multinational strategic management tasks, decisions, and actions.

Although strategic frameworks and related visions, strategies, and plans are important, *what* needs to be done in general to meet the needs of changing and diverse competitive environments is not the main concern of managers. Business leaders such as Jack Welch and Al Zeien have described it (Slater 1999; Zeien 1995), and others, such as Helmut Maucher, former CEO of Nestlé, have written books about it (Maucher 1994). Rather, managers need to know *how to act in their own specific situation* in a rapidly changing environment when implementing strategic frameworks. They may be familiar with basic entrepreneurial processes, quick to analyze, evaluate, synthesize, communicate, and act, they may be familiar with their main strategic management jobs, but what they need is help in putting these processes to work in their own job (Maitland 2000; Pfeffer and Sutton 2000).

## THE PROCESSES AT WORK: IMPLEMENTING STRATEGIES

Identifiable strategic frameworks and other common frameworks such as computer information and telecommunications technologies, global or world products, and common contingency/entrepreneurial thinking processes can contribute substantially to success when working across cultures and nations. Success also depends on creatively breaking molds and continually balancing and managing the specific human, business, and cultural factors in specific situations (Mitroff 1998). This is often not a simple task.

Anheuser-Busch encountered such a situation in the mid-1990s, when it found itself in the middle of a trademark dispute with the small Czechoslovakian brewery Budejovicky Budvar. These two breweries signed an agreement in 1911, which allowed the Czech brewery to use the Budweiser name in Europe and the (former) Soviet Union. In its efforts to establish Budweiser as a global brand, Anheuser-Busch attempted to invest in and even buy the small Czech brewery. However, every attempt made, such as building a cultural center and giving scholarships or even negotiating a new brand agreement, failed. The main reason was that the small brewery was not willing to give up its charm, profits, and superior-tasting product to the American brewery giant. They wanted to preserve their cultural and local identity and flavorful beer, two very important characteristics for any European brewery. In addition, the Czech company realized that they did not need Anheuser-Busch, but Anheuser-Busch needed them—a very powerful strategic position. Moreover, other European breweries are getting involved in attempting to block Anheuser-Busch's international expansion into Europe. The American Brewer is still looking for other ways to settle this trademark conflict (Perlez 1995).

Anheuser's immediate task was to determine how to solve its problem, given the specific people, markets, cultures, and other situation factors. The state-owned Czech brewery was profitable and might be sold to its managers. In addition to taking conciliatory local action, such as offering to buy substantial amounts of raw materials from other Czech enterprises, Anheuser pursued legal action and undertook marketing steps designed to expand its "Bud" presence in Europe (Calbreadth 1997; Hays 1999). Nike ran into a similar problem when a Spanish court ruled that a local apparel manufacturer owned the rights to use the Nike name on sports apparel sold in Spain (Tran 1999).

The solution in such situations is *contingent on* effectively and efficiently responding to and managing the factors in that situation—hopefully by going beyond compromise to find or improvise a "third," better, unexpected synergistic solution. Strategic management is a context-specific, contingency discipline; therefore, finding practical—not theoretical—entrepreneurial solutions appropriate for a situation is often all that matters when trying to survive and prosper.

For example, Dell Computer's performance in Europe by 1993 was dismal when it used retail sales channels—the usual way of selling in Europe. In an effort to increase sales, Dell defied the commonly accepted guideline, that is, that success formulas often are not able to be successfully transferred across national and cultural boundaries. Using its U.S. selling method, Dell began selling direct in France and Germany. As a result of "breaking the mold," Dell's sales in France and Germany rose five times faster than European personal computer sales in 1996, and Dell doubled its market share (Ascarelli 1997). Dell successfully used the same selling approach in China (Chowdhury 1999).

Creative entrepreneurial, even improvisational and innovative thinking and action are important to successful multinational management, at all levels of an enterprise.

In another situation, the threat of possible U.S. trade sanctions against Chinese textile imports had a minimal impact on many firms because of swift entrepreneurial action. The threat did not bother a garment firm in the city of Wenzhou, China, for example, because markets in China were booming enough to absorb all of its production (Faison 1996). Another Chinese firm simply shifted its production to a partner in the Caribbean and accessed the United States in that way.

In the mid-1990s, major problems in Russia were handled in another innovative way by many entrepreneurial Russian businessmen:

Once a prominent factory owner in the Volga River city of Saratov, Mr. Alexander V. Skorynin says he long ago grew disenchanted with Russia's high taxes, bureaucratic headaches, and violent crimes against executives. So three years ago, he decided to follow thousands of other rich countrymen to Russian capitalism's home away from home, the Mediterranean island of Cyprus.

Russian expatriates there are insuring themselves against the uncertain politics in Russia. Using Cyprus as a place to manage their money and keep up their trade and business contacts with the rest of the world, these Russians operate in a dynamic and growing economy free of many of the constraints that plague businesspeople back home.

By 1996, Russians had registered 7,000 offshore companies in Cyprus (Nelson 1996; "Survey" 1998). By 1999, the number of new Russian businesses there was increasing rapidly (Banerjee 1999). These experiences reflect the entrepreneurial spirit that enables survival anywhere in the world, regardless of the speed of change, amount of diversity, and intensity of competition.

Many feel that such an entrepreneurial approach works for individually-owned small firms, but is not effective in larger firms. Jack Welch, former CEO of GE, set out in the early 1980s to prove these skeptics wrong. Welch sought to create the body of a large company with the soul of a small company, possessing such cultural traits as self-confidence, simplicity, and speed. As this small-company culture emerged, GE became a "boundaryless" firm that has sought to constantly renew and exhilarate itself with consistent learning. By 1998, GE was the largest and the third most-profitable publicly traded company in the world. Welch engaged in "creative destruction," involving over 100,000 layoffs in the early 1980s, in order to quickly break old habits and set the stage for change. At the same time, Welch masterfully managed individual and organizational resources to stimulate maximum people involvement in achieving his new visions. A description of how Welch and GE top executives did this, in their own words, is given in Figure 2.4 in Chapter 2 and in Chapter 11. Motivating and managing human resources effectively is always an essential implementation success factor.

If Welch could do all this in a huge, diversified firm such as GE, it can be argued that other large firms could mount comparable programs suited to their own firms and their own competitive markets (Welch, Fresco, and Opie 1996). Hundreds of small and medium-sized firms have undertaken similar programs worldwide. Many executives are emulating the *essence* of what Welch and others have done in instilling the entrepreneurial spirit into their company cultures (Landers 2000). Success depends on balancing creative, unstructured approaches with structured ones in a way that is suitable to the industry, market, and individual firm.

## MANAGING DIVERSITY IN A BALANCED WAY

A key aspect of multinational strategic management is managing diversity in a balanced way. For example, the growing number of television channels in Europe has sparked a rise in homegrown television production. American shows initially dominated the European market; as costs rose and tastes changed, money was moved into local programming. In the early 1990s, for example, Radio Television Luxembourg, a European cable TV channel, spent only $220 million on locally produced shows; this number rose to $750 million six years later, with only $280 million spent on American shows (Tagliabue 1996). Although many European shows are still American-inspired and American shows are popular, the most popular shows in the European market are no longer solely American.

As a result, American and European television producers have formed a wide range of joint ventures in an attempt to synergistically balance American and European technologies, cultures, stories, and actors/actresses. There seem to be few universal success formulas, and only a fluid, rapidly changing, entrepreneurial international approach in this industry. A similar situation exists in the motion picture industry.

Multinational managers often face culturally diverse, complex situations which require integrative strategic management. Such pressures are increasing with the rapidly growing globalization of business. These managers need to reconcile, balance, coadapt, improvise, lead, and manage diverse, conflicting, and paradoxical forces in a way that is suitable to individual situation needs. At the same time, they need to strive to do this in a way that synergistically exploits the advantages of global operations and integrates these diverse activities within a firm's strategic framework.

For example, multinational managers are at times advised to "Think globally, act locally." For most people, this phrase presents an unclear, unresolvable paradox which fails to answer the key question, "How do I balance stability and adaptability, global and local needs, structured and unstructured leadership and management, traditional and digitalized value chains, regulated, deregulated, and transitional economies, and other seemingly conflicting forces in *my* situation?" In response to this paradox, Coca-Cola, which was experiencing major profit problems in early 2000, changed their strategy to "Think local, act local" (Daft 2000). This book focuses on these balancing challenges that are increasingly faced by individual business managers.

### THE USEFUL BUT LIMITED ROLE
### OF ADAPTIVE COMMON FRAMEWORKS

The balancing of structured and unstructured perspectives in multinational management requires using common structures or frameworks without overusing them. This book grew out of the author's and others' experiences in dealing with the paradoxes, conflicts, and diversity encountered when working both within and across cultural and national boundaries both domestically and multinationally (Overell 2001). Surviving and prospering led to a continuing search for common frameworks that enabled working effectively and efficiently in many countries and cultures.

Many business managers have actively sought common global links, that is, common frameworks that enable national and cultural differences to be accommodated while at the same time taking advantage of the synergies created when differences are integratively reconciled.

> McDonald's is an example of this so-called "glocal" approach [Barboza 1999]. It presents itself as a "multilocal" company by emphasizing local ownership and modifying its products slightly to meet local cultural demands. This has led to the fact that not only localities, but also entire countries share in the success of McDonald's whose supplies of meat, potatoes, and bread for the entire Central European region, for example, is provided by Poland [Friedman 1996].

Coca-Cola, Toyota, McDonald's, Honda, Rolex, Fiat, Rolls Royce, and Gillette are just a few of the many firms that have built global reputations for brand names and products. At times, however, these firms, like McDonald's, have encountered resistance to global brands—as in France (Daley 2000; Graham 2000)—and have tried to adapt to local differences. For example, in 1998 Coca-Cola's local soft drink "Thumbs Up" outsold Coke in India by a margin of 4 to 1. In China, Coke introduced a fruit-flavored soft drink called "Smart," in Turkey, a pear-flavored drink, a berry drink in Germany, and a local sports drink in Belgium (Echikson and Foust 2000). Gillette has had similar experiences (Mockler 1994-1999).

When Honda Motor Company made its Accord auto larger for the U.S. market, sales fell in Japan and Europe where smaller cars are preferred (Tagliabue 1998). Honda responded by creating a flexible bracketed frame for its 1998 models, which allows the automaker to shrink or expand the overlying car without using a different frame (by far the most expensive part of a new car). Both Ford and General Motors were planning to use common frames (or platforms) to develop different models for different countries in the late 1990s. In essence, Honda solved a major industry problem: how to create a world car that could be cheaply adapted to different country market needs.

Many retailers and mail-order companies, electronics firms, global telecommunications companies, airlines, advertising agencies, accounting firms, and others have been working to identify and further a growing trend toward a more unified global community, which at the same time is rich in local diversity and requires flexibility and adaptability to meet diverse and rapidly changing needs. Rupert Murdoch, chairman and owner of a 30 percent controlling interest in the Australian-based News Corporation, provides another example of this trend (Gunther 1998). His firm's strategic objective is:

> to marry the News Corporation programs with the means to distribute them . . . to own every major form of programming—news, sports, films, and children's shows—and bring them via satellite or TV stations to homes in the United States, Europe, Asia, and South America. (p. 93)

Such a global or whole-world perspective (for example, worldwide telecom technology) that accommodates local diversity (for example, local programming) can help multinational firms more easily and cost effectively capture the efficiencies arising from a global approach, while at the same time helping managers to respond creatively and rapidly to national and cultural differences and the increasing speed of competitive multinational market changes.

In addition to global telecommunications, brands, and products, other common global frameworks exist. Advances in computer information systems technologies, for example, are furthering this trend towards a locally diverse, globally unified world community. This is evident in such strategic innovations as the Cable News Network (CNN) which provides worldwide and local news coverage, and the growing use of the Internet, a worldwide flexible and adaptable computer communications system.

Al Zeien, former CEO of The Gillette Company in 1999, provides an example of the way his company's global manufacturing operations have been affected by sophisticated computer systems:

> Let me give you an example of a global company as it works in the computer age. You are all probably familiar with the Atra cartridge, which is a small razor blade shaving cartridge that we sell. About six months ago our computer optimization program was saying we really shouldn't continue to be supplying those Atra cartridges to the Australian market from our manufacturing operation in Melbourne, Australia. There was a cheaper way the computer identified in just one hour. How are we supplying Atra cartridges to the Australian market today? The steel comes from Yusugi on the west coast of Japan. It goes from there to Rio de Janeiro where it is processed into blade steel. It is then shipped out into the Atlantic Ocean and up the Amazon River 1200 miles to Manaus, also in Brazil, where the plastic molding takes place and the blade steel is mounted into the cartridge, what we call a naked cartridge. Back out to sea, it goes to Singapore and there it is packaged and shipped to our Melbourne warehouse. Ladies and gentlemen at this time that is the lowest cost way to supply cartridges to Australia. Believe it. (Zeien 1995)

Gillette's experiences with the global manufacturing of its Atra cartridge show how common frameworks (in this case, global products and advanced computer information technology) are used to balance differences across national/cultural borders (in this case, capabilities, facilities, costs, and needs in Japan, Brazil, Singapore, and Australia) effectively and efficiently.

Entrepreneurial contingency thinking processes have also provided useful common frameworks that allow national and cultural boundaries to be crossed more easily and effectively, especially when working with individual managers in multinational enterprises. For example, a Chinese entrepreneur starting a small conglomerate in Beijing exhibited many basic entrepreneurial skills and thinking patterns common worldwide:

- He developed five different "deals," ranging from a joint venture with a local municipality which was privatizing a small chemical plant to a trucking firm working under long-term supplier contracts.
- In each venture, he first focused on studying customer markets (from immediate and longer-term perspectives) and their needs, his available financial resources, and other contingent situation requirements. He then skillfully executed the plans by doing whatever was necessary to make them work in each market.

Without any formal business training, this entrepreneur demonstrated considerable ingenuity in overcoming day-to-day obstacles. For example, he coaxed municipal officials to relinquish control of captive companies, obtained distribution channels and financing, and closed deals. His overall approach to managing and making his diverse enterprises grow was the *common entrepreneurial contingency process framework* in evidence throughout this book. This process, outlined in Figure 1.1, is found worldwide in successful businesses. The Chinese entrepreneur's approach was supported by his mastery of the behavioral skills needed to entrepreneurially handle both crises and the inevitable day-to-day customer and operating problems.

When investors from the state of Georgia (U.S.) explored building on their successful U.S. experiences with cellular telephone networks in the early 1990s, their initial strategy was to find a major city in a former Soviet country with poor phone service. They first considered Moscow, but found little interest there in their small venture. They later investigated and received a better reception in Tashkent in Uzbekistan, a city which fit the desired strategic market profile. After spending $500,000 of their own money on research, the investors created a financial package in phases (for example, they eventually found some Pakistani investors who wanted to participate). Once the joint venture was formed, they spent several years introducing the business into Tashkent and overcoming a series of seemingly insurmountable local problems. By 1996, the U.S. investors had increased their initial investment fortyfold (Guyon 1996).

As seen from this and other experiences discussed in this book, strategic management is many things—iterative, contingent, sometimes emergent, and sometimes abruptly discontinuous, innovative, and entrepreneurial— not guided solely by universally applicable management principles and practices.

## *CONTINGENCY PROCESSES: A POWERFUL, WIDELY USED COMMON FRAMEWORK*

In a practical way, the common framework approaches provide an international bridge that enables work to be done more easily and quickly across borders. They also provide a mechanism for reconciling, handling, and using cultural differences. Although it is useful to employ common frameworks for crossing cultural boundaries, such approaches cannot solve all problems because not all people adapt to them and cultural differences can have a major impact on a decision situation. Differences often can be better handled if common links are emphasized and common working frameworks, such as the ones shown in Figures 1.1 and 1.2, are used.

*Contingency theory,* an emerging theory which involves situation-specific decision and action processes, has been labeled the "It All Depends" theory. This chapter has described some familiar *contingency processes,* which can be useful common frameworks in formulating strategies at both the enterprise-wide and operational levels when dealing with different cultures.

## *SUMMARY*

Figure 1.1 is considered by many to be a universally applicable "tool" of strategic management in business. It is ultimately common sense or "street smarts," which enables us to constantly stay tuned to our environment and our own strengths and weaknesses, and to also develop a canny sense of how to work successfully through the situation at hand—all within the context of objectives. The processes described in this chapter are not magic formulas: they are systematic descriptions of familiar and commonly used contingency ("It All Depends") processes in today's rapidly changing multinational business environment.

The core entrepreneurial contingency processes replicated in Figures 1.1 through 1.4 go beyond traditional analytical processes that attempt to find a single solution and obtain consensus based on existing and past situation factors. They provide a systematic, yet flexible and adaptive way to view existing factors from multiple perspectives ("what-if" scenarios, for example), explore future assumptions, question assumptions and solutions through examining and reconciling differences, and consider broader contexts and longer-term horizons as approaches are tried and tentative solutions formulated.

Many aspects of the balancing and integration involved in multinational strategic management have been covered in this chapter. Effectively meshing global and local perspectives is a continuing job, as is synergistically integrating diversity in a way that creates new and better solutions when dealing with the many decision tasks and activities involved in multinational strategic management (see Figure 1.6). The interplay of planning and doing requires managers to have their "head in the air" and "feet on the ground." Building future visions must be balanced with the present realities involved in getting things done and putting visions to work successfully. Finding the mix of approaches appropriate for each situation also requires balancing cognitive, behavioral, visionary, and practical techniques and tools. It requires balancing meeting the needs of speedy response to a rapidly changing environment, with doing the time-consuming work needed to get things done successfully (Claxton 1999).

The following chapters discuss these aspects of integration from a balanced entrepreneurial perspective. This perspective can help readers go beyond the experiences of others and develop their own approaches to, and solutions for, their specific situations. In doing this, readers can learn how to

FIGURE 1.6. Multinational Strategic Management: Selected Decision/Task Areas

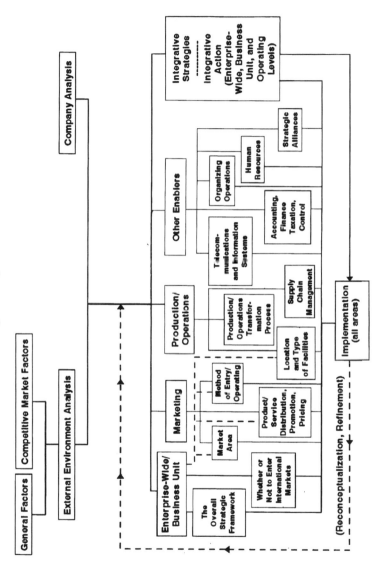

Copyright © 2002 by R. J. Mockler

independently teach themselves and draw their own conclusions—that is, how to be their own "teacher," their own "boss." This "learning how to learn process" is described in Chapter 14.

## *REVIEW QUESTIONS*

1. What is a multinational enterprise? What is the difference between a multinational enterprise and a domestic business?
2. What is strategic management and in what ways, if any, does it differ in a multinational firm and in a domestic firm?
3. In what ways do leadership and management activities differ? In what ways are they both related to the strategic management job?
4. What are the key challenges faced by business managers in rapidly changing multinational markets? Why and in what ways has speed become important to winning against the competition in business?
5. What are some "global" frameworks that can affect the success of a multinational enterprise? In what ways are they necessary and useful in operating successfully in a multinational environment? Cite examples of how they help reconcile country-to-country differences.
6. What are three time frames of strategic planning? What is needed in each to create and maintain a competitive advantage?
7. What are some potential problems facing a multinational enterprise when trying to balance global integration with meeting local needs? What are some possible solutions to these problems?
8. In what ways is the entrepreneurial process outlined in Figure 1.1 essential to effective multinational management? Give examples.
9. Discuss the role of innovation and creativity in multinational strategic management.
10. Discuss the similarities and differences in multinational strategic management in different size firms.
11. Based on company experiences, in what ways is strategic management an "emerging" process?
12. According to Wind and Main, what characteristics are expected to dominate future businesses, organizations, and individuals?
13. Discuss some of the problems involved in balancing the different forces at work in the rapidly changing multinational competitive market environment.
14. Describe ways in which common contingency frameworks can help to manage multinational cultural differences in business. In what other ways are these common contingency frameworks, especially those involving entrepreneurial thinking and action, critical enablers in effective strategic leadership and management?

## *EXERCISES*

1. Search the business literature you are familiar with and look for examples of companies and business leaders who "broke the mold" and developed new ways of doing business. From these observed experiences, formulate guidelines that might help you to do something similar in the future in the professional area in which your work.

2. Search the business literature you are familiar with and look for examples of companies and business leaders who were faced with specific problems that significantly affected their business' survival. Describe how one such company/leader successfully met the challenges. Compare that experience with one that failed. Formulate any guidelines you feel may be helpful in future situations that you may face.

3. Review recent periodical articles of your choice and write a report on company experiences dealing with how telecommunications and information systems have changed the outlook of companies and the way companies are changing to meet the new needs and standards. For example, in *Fortune* (September 30, 1996) the article "Software Hardball at Microsoft" discusses how CEO Bill Gates planned to overthrow Netscape as the leader on the Internet. In *The Wall Street Journal* (November 4, 1998, pp. A1, A14) George Anders' article "Some Big Companies Long to Embrace Web But Settle for Flirtation" discusses how companies want to do more business online but worry about the negative impact on their long-time sales and distribution channels. Compare and discuss the implications of these or other experiences familiar to you. You might examine Ethan Allen's (the furniture store) solution to this potential conflict in James Hagerty's "Ethan Allen's Revolutionary Path to Web," *The Wall Street Journal,* July 29, 1999, pp. B1, B12.

# Chapter 2

# An Enterprise's Multinational
# Strategic Framework

Successful enterprises and leaders most often have a general vision. Jack Welch's vision at GE involved large and small company integration. Rupert Murdoch's vision at News Corporation involved an integrated media empire, whether in a single enterprise or in related ones (Hansell 2000). Both of these strategic visions were discussed in Chapter 1.

This chapter and the rest of this book discuss the different ways in which these general strategic concepts are translated into strategic frameworks, strategic plans, enabling structures, action, and eventually profits through effective management in a variety of multinational company and market situations. This chapter focuses on formulating strategic frameworks, which provide an overall integrating perspective for all the tasks, decisions, and activities shown in Figure 1.6 and discussed in the following chapters.

During the early 1980s, Mitsubishi Motors Corporation, Japan's youngest automaker which faced heavy competition in Japan (its primary business area), considered European and U.S. expansion. However, it faced aggressive competition from experienced local companies in both target markets, as well as from larger successful multinational companies such as Honda and Toyota. Necessity dictated that it diversify into Asia, a newly emerging market, where competition was less intense at the time.

What was born out of necessity initially turned into great good fortune for Mitsubishi. In the mid-1990s, auto sales boomed as fast as local economies in Asia. South Korea's gross domestic product soared 300 percent since 1989, and car ownership went up 500 percent to 74 million. Some 500 new cars were hitting Bangkok's traffic-choked streets daily, and the Asian market was expected to become as big as the European or North American markets. In spite of its major core competencies—a huge network of relationships in Asia and its wide product mix designed to match the varied Asian car buyers' tastes, Mitsubishi encountered major problems in the late 1990s as competition increased at home and the Asian financial crisis worsened (Bremmer, Thornton, and Kunii 1999).

The concept of a "Strategic Framework," outlined in Figure1.5 (p. 13), can vary in its details by company and by management level, depending on the situation. At a minimum, a strategic framework usually includes a statement defining the kind of enterprise envisioned in terms appropriate for the situation—for example, more general in some diversified volatile industries and firms and more specific in stable narrowly circumscribed ones.

Strategic frameworks can be formulated at many levels in a firm. *Corporate* or *enterprise-wide strategies* provide long-term general guidelines or patterns for action. *Strategic business unit (SBU) strategies* are for businesses which serve a uniform, identifiable set of customers and have a well-defined set of competitors. When an enterprise consists of a single-business unit, an SBU strategy *is* the enterprise-wide strategy. This chapter focuses on these two strategic levels. *Functional* or *operational strategies,* the third level, involves enabling areas discussed in Chapters 5 through 13. Developing such frameworks requires integrating systematic, disciplined approaches with entrepreneurial creativity, as noted in the Preface and Chapter 1.

Although the discussion is divided into three management levels, these levels are not always distinct in practice. The levels are often blurred because each is formulated as part of a continuing process, outlined in Figure 1.4 (p. 11), which builds on continuing situation context analyses such as those described in Chapter 4.

Because of the rapidly changing multinational business context, an outside-in (external-focused), as well as an inside-out (company-focused) perspective is helpful when formulating strategies. Enterprise-wide strategies may initially be stated in fairly general terms. As business activities are studied in detail, more information is gathered, competitive circumstances change, and functional/operating strategies and plans are formulated and carried out, more precise strategic frameworks are developed within the different time perspectives discussed in Chapter 1. This is why strategic frameworks are said to "emerge," as shown in Figure 1.3, (p. 9).

At GE, for example, strategy formulation has been a continuing process. In 1980-1981, GE believed that a firm had to be number one or two in its industry, since at that time market-share leadership did produce profits. By 1986, GE translated market share into a more productive position, because its large customers were pushing for lower prices. By 1991-1992, GE moved to creating customer services and solutions because there was overcapacity in its businesses. In 1999, GE and Jack Welch moved to make the Internet and digital commerce its number one strategic management priority including both Internet and intranet (internal company Internets) applications throughout the company (Marsh 2000). Its long-term strategy in general terms, then, was to be *flexible in responding to anticipated changing customer requirements.* Ford Motor Company announced in 1999 that it would extend its business scope to consumer products and services, first by diversifying into services related to cars such as renting, financing, repairs, leasing, and insurance (initially through acquisitions), and then later into other consumer products and services areas.

New technologies, especially the Internet, have modified the concept of strategy by shortening time frames in many industries, and so have had a major impact on strategic management. The increase in the speed of change often requires rapid strategy shifts, or creating new strategies—in a sense throwing out the rule book (Maitland 2000). At times, this discourages formulating precise strategic plans, and has led firms, such as Microsoft, to appear to have no strategy, except for general guidelines on how to aggressively explore everything to stay ahead and win.

This so-called "perpetual" strategy process continually gathers information on all business areas. This information is used to explore future trends (competitive intelligence), as well as to create new operating plans and take actions based on emerging strategies, as has been done at GE over the years.

## ENTERPRISE-WIDE SITUATIONS

Enterprise-wide strategic management refers to decision making and action involving the enterprise as a whole, not just a single business unit within the enterprise. Mitsubishi's decision to diversify into Asia was such a decision; additional company experiences are described in the following sections.

### The Strategic Framework: Company Experiences

The experiences of Jack Welch provide an example of the process at work in developing and implementing a strategic framework at a successful, large, diversified firm. A five-page "To Our Shareholders" statement from Welch and his vice-chairmen describes the formulation and articulation of their strategic vision of GE and how they put it to work (Welch, Fresco, and Opie 1996). The *enterprise-wide vision* was:

> What we wanted was a hybrid, an enterprise with the reach and resources of a big company—the body of big company—but the thirst to learn, the compulsion to share and the bias for action—the soul—of a small company. (p. 2)

The *supporting values* and *principles* included developing an open environment, friendly toward the seeking and sharing of new ideas, self-confidence, simplicity, speed—boundaryless individual entrepreneurial behavior in a large company context. The statement covers *redefining those businesses GE is to be involved in*. The statement, which appeared in GE's 1995 Annual Report, describes how Welch and his managers translated their new

---

### General Electric Company from 1995 Annual Report

To Our Shareholders

Your Company had a terrific 1995—a record year by any measure.

- Revenues rose to $70 billion, up 17%.
- Global revenues increased 34% to $27 billion.
- Earnings were $6.6 billion, up 11%.
- Earnings per share of $3.90 were up 13%.
- Seven of our 12 big businesses produced double-digit earnings increases.
- The quarterly dividend was increased 12%—the 20th consecutive year of dividend increases.
- We repurchased $3 billion of our stock, increased our buy-back program from $5 billion to $9 billion, and extended it though 1997.

This performance was recognized by the market, which rewarded GE investors in 1995 with a total return of 45%.

As strong as the year was, we did not achieve two of what we call "stretch" performance targets: operating margins and inventory turns. Over the last three decades, our highest corporate operating margin hovered around 10%, and our inventory turns around five, so in 1991 we set two "stretch" targets for 1995: 15% operating margin and 10 turns. 1995 has come and gone, and despite a heroic effort by our 222,000 employees, we fell short on both measures, achieving a 14.4% operating margin and almost seven turns. But in stretching for these "impossible" targets, we learned to do things faster than we would have going after "doable" goals, and we have enough confidence now to set new stretch targets of at least 16% operating margin and more than 10 turns by 1998.

The hottest trend in business in 1995—and the one that hit closest to home—was the rush toward breaking up multi-business companies and "spinning-off" their components, under the theory that their size and diversity inhibited their competitiveness. The obvious question to General Electric, as the world's largest multi-business company, was "When are you going to do it?" The short answer is that we're not. We've spent more than a decade getting bigger and faster and more competitive, and we intend to continue.

*Breaking up is the right answer for some big companies. For us it is the wrong answer. "Why" is the subject of our letter to you this year.*

Our dream, and our plan, well over a decade ago, was simple. We set out to shape a global enterprise that preserved the classic big-company advantages—while eliminating the classic big-company drawbacks. What we wanted to build was a hybrid, an enterprise with the reach and resources of a big company—the body of a big company—but the thirst to learn, the compulsion to share and the bias for action—the soul—of a small company.

Here's how we went about it.

*(continued)*

*(continued)*

Changing the Hardware

**No. 1 or No. 2—or Fix, Sell or Close**
The Foundation for our future was to be involved in only those businesses that were, or could become, either number one or number two in their global markets. The rest were to be fixed, sold or closed. We made this decision based on our observation that when a number-one market-share business entered a down cycle, and "sneezed," number four or five often caught galloping pneumonia. Consistent with this view, we divested, in the eighties, $10 billion worth of marginal businesses, and made $19 billion of acquisitions, to strengthen the world-leading businesses we wanted to take with us into the nineties.

**Delayering**
While we were restructuring the businesses, we also changed the management hardware at GE. We delayered. We removed "Sectors," "Groups," "Strategic Business Units" and much of the extensive command structure and staff apparatus we used to run the Company.

We cleared out stifling bureaucracy, along with the strategic planning apparatus, corporate staff empires, rituals, endless studies and briefings, and all the classic machinery that makes big-company operations smooth and predictable—but often glacially slow. As the underbrush of bureaucracy was cleared away, we began to see and talk to each other more clearly and more directly.

As the Company moved through the eighties, the businesses grew increasingly powerful. Freed from bureaucratic tentacles, and charged to act independently, they did so, with great success. Corporate management got off their backs, and instead lined up behind them with resources and support.

Changing the Software

**Self-Confidence, Simplicity, Speed**
As the big-company body was developing, we turned from changing its hardware to the infinitely more difficult task of changing its software—toward creating, in GE, the spirit and soul of a small company.

Most successful small companies possess three defining cultural traits: self-confidence, simplicity and speed. We wanted them. We went after them.

**Self-Confidence**
We began with a theory of the case that valued self-confidence as the absolutely indispensable ingredient in a high-performance business culture. Self-confident people are open to good ideas regardless of their source and are willing to share them. Their egos don't require that they originate every idea they use, or "get credit" for every idea they originate. We began to cultivate

*(continued)*

*(continued)*

self-confidence among our leaders by turning them loose, giving them independence and resources, and encouraging them to take big swings. The inevitable surge of self-confidence that grows in people who win leads to another and natural outgrowth: simplicity.

### Simplicity
Self-confident people don't need to wrap themselves in complexity, "businessese" speech, and all the clutter that passes for sophistication in business—especially big business. Self-confident leaders produce simple plans, speak simply and propose big, clear targets.

The boldness that comes from self-confidence, and the clarity that comes from the simplicity, lead to one of the small company's greatest competitive advantages: speed.

### Speed
Simple messages travel faster, simpler designs reach the market faster, and the elimination of clutter allows faster decision making. All this happened in the upper echelons of GE. We saw the leadership come alive with energy, excitement and the crackle of small-company urgency.

### Involving Everyone
The challenge then became to involve everyone—to spread our new openness into every corner of our Company; to give every one of our 222,000 employees what the best small companies give people: voice. We were running out of models at this point, and moving into uncharted territory—at least for big companies—and so our next move, the centerpiece of culture change at GE, was one we had to invent ourselves. We called it Work-Out.

### Work-Out
Work-Out was based on the simple belief that people closest to the work know, more than anyone, how it could be done better. It was this enormous reservoir of untapped knowledge, and insight, that we wanted to draw upon. Across GE today, holding a Work-Out session is as natural an act as coming to work. People of disparate ranks and functions search for a better way, every date, gathering in a room for an hour, or eight, or three days, grappling with a problem or an opportunity, and dealing with it, usually on the spot—producing real change instead of memos and promises of further study. Everyone today has an opportunity to have a voice at GE, and everyone who uses that voice to help improve things is rewarded.

### Management Selection
It was at Work-Out sessions that it became clear that some of the rhetoric heard at the corporate level—about involvement and excitement and turning people loose—did not match the reality of life in the businesses. The problem was that some of our leaders were unwilling, or unable, to abandon big-company, bit-shot autocracy and embrace the values we were trying to grow. So

*(continued)*

*(continued)*

we defined our management styles, or "types," and how they furthered or blocked our values. And then we acted.

Type I not only delivers on performance commitments, but believes in and furthers GE's small-company values. The trajectory of this group is "onward and upward," and the men and women who comprise it will represent the core of our senior leadership into the next century.

Type II does not meet commitments, nor share our values—nor last long at GE.

Type III believes in the values but sometimes misses commitments. We encourage taking swings, and Type III is typically given another chance.

Type IV. The "calls" on the first two types are easy. Type III takes some judgment; but Type IV is the most difficult. One is always tempted to avoid taking action, because Type IV's deliver short-term results. But Type IV's do so without regard to values and, in fact, often diminish them by grinding people down, squeezing them, stifling them. Some of these learned to change; most couldn't. The decision to begin removing Type IV's was a watershed—the ultimate test of our ability to "walk the talk," but it had to be done if we wanted GE people to be open, to speak up, to share, and to act boldly outside traditional "lines of authority" and "functional boxes" in this new learning, sharing environment.

**Crotonville**
Throughout this process of change—much of it wrenching and all of it new—our Management Institute at Crotonville, New York, served as a forum for the sharing of the experiences, the aspirations and, often, the frustrations of the tens of thousands of GE leaders who passed through its campus. It was the glue that held things together as the process of change took hold.

With the new culture in place, Crotonville has become a vehicle for learning and sharing the best practices that can be found anywhere around the globe. Leaders return from these intense courses to their businesses prepared to put these new ideas quickly into action. Entire classes are regularly sent to Europe or Asia, to wrestle with specific potential opportunities. After data gathering, and intense Work-Out style discussion, each class returns and presents recommendations directly to the top 35 officers of GE, who act on them—often on the spot. Crotonville combines the thirst for learning of academia with an action environment usually seen only in small, hungry companies.

**Boundaryless Behavior**
These changes in the culture of our Company—the profound and pervasive effect of Work-Out and the steady reduction of Type IV management—developed a fresh, open, anti-parochial environment, friendly toward the seeking

*(continued)*

*(continued)*

and sharing of new ideas, regardless of their source. It also encouraged looking outside the traditional boundaries that shackle thinking and restrict vision. Ideas around the Company quickly began to stand or fall on their merits—rather than on the altitude of their originators.

An endless search began for best practices—for ways of getting better, faster. Meetings around the Company that used to consist of self-serving "reports" and windy speeches became interactive forums for disseminating new ideas and the sharing of experiences. A whole new behavior has invigorated and freshened this century-old company.

We've seen the emergence of true small-company phenomena; dreaming, which is at the heart of those "stretch" goals we mentioned earlier; and constant celebrations of milestones toward those goals—even if we occasionally don't quite get there. We describe our emerging culture by an awkward but descriptive name: "boundaryless." It is the soul of our integrated diversity and at the heart of everything we do well. It is the small-company culture we've been after for all these years.

The sweetest fruit of boundaryless behavior has been the demise of "Not-Invented-Here" and its utter disappearance from our Company. We quickly began to learn from each other: productivity solutions from Lighting; "quick response" asset management from appliances; transaction effectiveness from GE Capital; the application of "bullet-train" cost-reduction techniques from Aircraft Engines; and global account management from Plastics—just to name a few. At the same time, we embarked on an endless search for ideas from the great companies of the world. Wal-Mart taught us the direct customer feedback technique we call Quick Market Intelligence. We learned New Product Introduction methods from Toshiba, Chrysler and Hewlett-Packard, an advanced manufacturing techniques from Amercan Standard, Toyota and Yokogawa. AlliedSignal, Ford and Xerox shared their insights into launching a quality initiative. Motorola, which created a dramatically successful, quality-focused culture over a period of a decade, has been more than generous in sharing its experiences with us.

**Stretch**
"Stretch," which we mentioned earlier in connection with inventory turns and margin goals, simply means moving beyond being as good as you have to be—"making a budget"—to being as good as you possibly can be: setting "impossible" goals and going after them. Crucial to stretch is the trust that grows in a boundaryless organization, as self-confident people come to know that it is the quality of their effort toward achieving the "impossible" that is the ultimate measure.

**Compensation**
To reinforce the boundaryless and stretch behavior taking root across the Company, we adapted our compensation system. When we began our journey in the eighties, about 400 of the senior people in GE received stock

*(continued)*

*(continued)*

options. Today, 22,000 individuals, at all levels, have options, and thereby have a clear financial incentive for driving total Company performance by doing everything they can to help their colleagues in their own, or another, GE business.

Today, stock option compensation, based on total GE performance, is far more significant than the salary or bonus growth associated with the performance of any individual unit or business. This aligns the interests of the individual, the Company and the share owner behind powerful one-company results.

A New Kind of Company
What we have described is the creation of a new kind of company—one that has, and uses, all the strengths of a big company while moving with the speed, hunger and urgency of a small company.

While the excitement, speed and growing confidence can be felt all across GE, its accelerating performance can be quantified as well.

In the first five years of the eighties, as we divested, invested, and restructured our array of big, leading business, GE returned to its share owners about $850 million a year in dividends.

Through the following five years, ending in 1990, as the effect of Work-Out took hold across the Company and small-company values began to flourish, we returned nearly double that—about $1.4 billion in annual dividends—and repurchased $2.6 billion of stock.

During the past five years, as boundaryless behavior has taken hold, and the best practices we shared have taken effect, we've returned to share owners about $2.3 billion a year in dividends and repurchased an additional $5.5 billion of our stock.

The pace continued to accelerate in 1995 when $5.9 billion impacted share owner value—$2.8 billion of it in dividends, and $3.1 billion supporting the equity by stock repurchase.

The GE Board of Directors has approved an additional $6 billion of stock repurchase through 1997. That, and our performance objectives in the current global economic environment, should permit us to maintain or increase the $6 billion level of share owner support each year, through dividends and the repurchasing program.

Moving from about a billion dollars of share owner support in 1985 to $6 billion in 1995 say more than any of the words we've written about the new GE, and its new look to investors.

*(continued)*

*(continued)*

Once this big, diverse Company is looked at for what it has become—an accelerating earnings and cash engine—its performance is much easier for investors and analysts to judge. Those who follow GE are increasingly aware that there are very few individual hits or misses of sufficient magnitude to alter the trajectory of a Company moving toward the $100 billion revenue level in any reasonable global economic scenario. By focusing on the scale, breadth and growth of our Company, rather than on the "event of the day"—whether it be a hit or miss, from locomotives to TV programs—investors should look beyond the headline—to the bottom line.

Growing Rapidly into the Next Century
As the millennium approaches, this Company will pick up the pace, as it brings to bear its enormous financial, technical and human resources in support of its big businesses as they move to sieze five of the biggest growth opportunities in our history: Globalization, New Products, Information Technology, Installed-Base Service and Quality.

**Globalization**
Approaching joint venture partners, and even sovereign states, as multi-business teams, sharing country knowledge, and capable of assembling supportive financing packages from GE Capital, our globalization is accelerating. Global revenues over the last 10 years have increased from 20% of the Company's total to 38% today—and, somewhere around the millennium, we expect the majority of GE revenue to come from outside the United States.

**New Products**
The sharing of new product introduction techniques, developed both inside and outside GE, is compressing the cycle of learning and executing, and is already producing a torrent of new products, from jet engines to turbines to washing machines to TV shows.

**Information Technology**
The enormous leverage of information technology, combined with our culture of learning and sharing, creates a tremendous opportunity, both internally—with better inventory control and shorter order-to-remittance cycles, for example—and externally—with remote diagnostics in medical imaging and just-in-time inventory replenishment for our customers.

**Service**
Improving the profitability of our customers through technology upgrades of the enormous installed base of GE equipment—scores of thousands of jet engines, locomotive, turbines and CT scanners, for instance—is an enormous growth opportunity for us and a profit opportunity for our customers.

**Quality**
Already equal to or better than our competitors—quality at GE will be taken to world-leading levels, providing us with yet another competitive differentiate.

*(continued)*

*(continued)*

Our openness to learning, our ability to share across the Company and our bias for speed, as well as the generosity of Motorola and others in sharing their techniques with us, will bring GE to a whole new level of quality in a fraction of the time it would have taken to climb the learning curve on our own.

This is a Company focusing on huge growth opportunities as we look to the millennium—a GE that renews itself constantly, exhilarates itself with speed and freshens itself by constant learning.

*We are a Company intent on getting bigger, not smaller—a Company whose only answer to the trendy question—"What do you intend to spin off?"—is "cash"—and lots of it."*

Two significant events occurred within a couple of weeks of each other as 1995 ended and the new year began. The first was the 100th anniversary of the Dow Jones Industrial Average and an invitation from Dow Jones to GE to open the market with them on the year's first trading session. The reason we were invited to "ring the bell" was because we are the only surviving company of those in the original Dow Average. We celebrated that occasion, but thought "surviving" an anemic adjective, inadequate to the vibrancy of our Company and the promise of its future.

There was a glimpse of that future in the second event, in that two-week time span, when NBC and Microsoft, a company synonymous with the future, announced they were joining in two exciting new information ventures. The juxtaposition of those two events provides a nice snapshot of GE—a Company with a legendary past, humming powerfully in the present, with its greatest days always ahead.

Thank you for supporting us.


John F. Welch, Jr.
Chairman of the Board
and Chief Executive Officer

Paolo Fresco
Vice Chairman of the Board
and Executive Officer

John D. Opie
Vice Chairman of the Board
and Executive Officer

February 9, 1996

vision into action in GE's twenty-plus business units. *Planned action steps* and activities included "management selection"(staffing) consistent with the new values and mission, "delayering" the organization structure to eliminate the layers separating managers and workers, "work-out" sessions during which managers and workers put the new values and mission to work, the elimination of 100,000 job positions, and leader involvement in the process at all levels. This was the creative destruction phase. The statement also discusses GE's strategy for rapid growth during the next century: globalization, new products, information technology, service, and quality. These activities led to GE becoming one of the largest and most profitable and respected publicly held companies worldwide. This statement of GE's enterprise-wide strategic framework is one of the most articulate ever published. It reads like a guide on how to transform a firm into a modern multinational firm (Slater 1999; Waters 1999).

The process of strategic change at GE generally follows the outline of key activities given in Figures 1.3, 1.4, and 1.5:

- *Formulating the concept of an enterprise.* At the enterprise-wide and business unit level, this involves studying the environment to determine the strategic vision and mission, as well as to create an overall strategic framework, including strategic guidelines for action, as shown in Figures 1.3 and 1.5. Specific strategic plans often emerge over time.
- *Establishing, activating, energizing, and monitoring enabling systems and processes.* These include functional operations (marketing and production); telecommunications/information systems; organization and business structures, processes and cultures at all levels; accounting, finance, and control systems; and strategic alliances.
- *Leading and managing enabling human resources and processes.* This is accomplished through understanding cultural diversity, and by staffing, training, and communicating effectively throughout an enterprise.
- *Exercising entrepreneurial initiative.* This involves creating and sustaining an entrepreneurial enterprise culture that encourages people to do whatever is necessary to get the job done within the enterprise's strategic frameworks in response to rapidly changing competitive market conditions.

This book focuses on these tasks/activities, which are the essence of multinational strategic leadership and management.

Although GE's approach is admired and imitated worldwide (Landers 2000), developing and imitating strategic frameworks varies considerably, depending on differing company and marketplace needs. Unlike GE, many firms' published strategic frameworks are more limited in scope (Abrahams

1995). For example, as shown in Figure 2.1, Ciba-Geigy Corporation's mission statement provides only a brief summary of its mission, vision, and beliefs and as such is not an enterprise-strategic framework, but only one segment of it. Very often, the public and internal versions of a company's mission statement differ in detail, since operating information is often proprietary. Each firm presumably considers its versions appropriate for the company and the purpose its public and internal statements are designed to fulfill.

Enterprise-wide strategic frameworks for smaller companies operating in limited markets with well-defined product lines are often shorter and more specific than GE's and may resemble strategic business unit (SBU) frameworks. Enterprise-wide and SBU frameworks ideally both define the business(es) and products/services a company or business unit is, intends to be, or is engaged in, and often identifies how those products/services are distinguished from competitors'. Other identified aspects may include customer type, relevant technology, diversification, and management culture. Any strategy formulated should be achievable and supported with strong core competencies, since strategy formulation cannot be separated from implementation.

Although more general, like SBU strategies, enterprise-wide strategies attempt to focus on a distinct set of capabilities that a company can excel in and that are (or can be perceived as being) of special value or importance to a particular market segment. As one expert defined it (Davidson 1995, p. 80):

> Competitive success follows from focusing every element of an organization on a strategic vision. Achieving that requires the development of superior competence, or the ability to excel, in a set of *distinctive* capabilities that have *special* value to a *particular* part of the marketplace.

In other words, focusing on existing, as well as anticipated market needs, and continually coming up with new ways to meet them in key-to-success areas, and with the needed resources to do this, is a major way to outperform competitors. Matching internal resources and capabilities (existing and potential) with external market requirements and opportunities (existing, future and created ones)—so-called resource-based planning—is critical to success. Studying what competitors are doing now and might do in the future is also an important aspect of this external perspective. Because core competencies often can be imitated and surpassed by competitors, it is necessary to continually renew and reinforce them, and develop new ones, and to formulate new winning strategies based on these. The pressure is to create new opportunities and stretch the organization beyond its present limits.

FIGURE 2.1. Ciba-Geigy Corporation Mission Statement

### Statement: Our Vision

*By striking a balance between our economic, social, and environmental responsibilities we want to ensure the prosperity of our enterprise beyond the year 2000.*

### Responsibility for long-term economic success

We aim to generate appropriate financial results through sustainable growth and constant renewal of a balanced business structure, so that we justify the confidence of all those who rely on our company—stockholders, employees, business partners and the public.

We will not put our long-term future in danger by taking short-term profits.

### Social Responsibility

Ciba is open and trustworthy toward society. Through our worldwide business activities we wish to make a worthwhile contribution to the solution of global issues and to the progress of mankind. We recognize our responsibility when turning new discoveries in science and technology into commericial reality; we carefully evaluate benefits and risks in all our activities, processes and products.

### Responsibility for the Environment

Respect for the environment must be a part of everything we do.

We design products and processes to fulfill their purpose safely and with as little environmental impact as possible. We use natural resources and energy in the best possible way to reduce waste in all forms. It is our duty to dispose of all unavoidable waste using state of the art technology.

**Industry Category:** Chemicals

**Corporate Description**

Ciba is a leading worldwide biological and chemical group, based in Switzerland, dedicated to satisfying needs in healthcare, agriculture and industry with innovative value-adding products and services.

**Number of Employees:** 87,480 (worldwide) as of 1993

*Source:* Ciba-Geigy Corporation (1999). Annual Report, 1993.

Effective business leaders such as Jack Welch reinforce these ideas daily as they ask employees such questions as:

- What does your global competitive environment look like?
- In the last three years, what have your competitors done?
- In the same period, what have you done to them?
- How might your competitors attack you in the future?
- How might you leapfrog them?
- What kinds of products/services will customers need in the future?
- What are you doing to meet their anticipated or perceived needs?

This example of leadership in action directly links top management with line workers and helps them focus on significant strategic directions, thus making the organization part of the process. According to Ken Iverson, former Chairman of Nucor Corporation—a $3.8 billion firm he led from near oblivion to become America's third-largest steel firm—such direct communication links are essential to effective leadership (Iverson and Varian 1998).

Strategic frameworks, both as defined explicitly in published or unpublished statements and as developed implicitly within a firm, can also specify how to achieve or make enterprise missions, strategies, and objectives work. As such, they can be a linking mechanism that helps convert enterprise-wide strategies into plans and action, as seen in the GE example. At a minimum, they provide general guidance as to what resources are needed, how to allocate resources, the kinds of planned steps appropriate for achieving objectives, and how to manage and lead.

Because enterprise-wide strategic frameworks and the statements communicating them are context-specific, they may vary widely from firm to firm. For example, because Welch's statement (GE 1995 Annual Report) includes the history and justification for what he was doing at GE for the general public, it is longer than many. Many companies have produced single page summaries of strategies and values (Blanchard and O'Connor, 1997; Blanchard and Waghorn, 1997; Kotter 1996). For smaller firms, these may be similar to SBU strategies discussed as follows.

For example, another much smaller start-up company proposed by two young professionals (a Costa Rican and an American) had the following strategic objective:

> To establish a privately-owned Web site for the tourist industry in Costa Rica which would provide detailed information on tourist attractions in Costa Rica (for a fee from the service providers) and which would be available worldwide. This site would be extended to overseas companies providing tourist services to Costa Rica (again for a fee). Eventually the venture would provide selected noncompetitive tourist services for a commission.

This objective was supplemented by detailed plans in each of the operational areas critical to success—the marketing plan.

Another firm encouraged each manager and employee to develop their own version for their level, which they could then discuss among themselves and with their managers. One firm reduced its strategic framework to a small card carried by each employee:

> Our employees have a partnership relation to their customers, suppliers, shareholders, and other employees; this necessitates responding rapidly to customer's needs as to what, where, when, and in the way they want their service, as well as the need to be alert to what the competition is doing and to develop ways to better them.

As with many enterprise-wide strategic frameworks, this one emphasizes the role of partnerships. Such liaisons may exist among employees or with competitors, stockholders, suppliers, customers, and financial sources, as well as other industry and market participants. This brief summary statement suited the company, even though its annual sales were over $1 billion, because it was a wholesaler/supplier of pharmaceutical products to retailers with a well-defined product line and function. Another enterprise had a brief statement of its overriding strategy printed on the back of all of its managers' business cards.

The exact length of a statement—ranging from the GE five-page letter to the business card summary—is dictated by the situation requirements. In many instances, shorter statements are extremely effective, since they make communicating and remembering strategic frameworks easier. John Kotter and Ken Blanchard recommend less than a page for a strategic foundation (including values, which are important to fostering employee trust) and less than a page for the *planned actions,* followed by a summary outline of *activities done* or *being done to achieve objectives* (Blanchard and O'Connor, 1997; Blanchard and Waghorn, 1997; Kotter 1996). These three steps are part of a general process, given in Figure 1.5 (p. 13), which is as applicable to corporate planning as it is to personal planning.

Effective strategic frameworks are based on a thorough knowledge of the market, industry, and firm involved, as described here and in Chapter 4. They also require the visionary thinking described in the discussions of IBM, Hewlett-Packard, Oracle Corporation, Microsoft, and other firms in this chapter and in Chapters 1, 5, and 14. Firms and their organizations especially need to be flexible and adaptable to market changes, such as the strategic management opportunities and threats created by the Internet. For example, the experiences of Microsoft, which in the late 1990s strategically refocused its operations on the Internet, are described in Chapter 14.

### General Types of Enterprise-Wide Strategies

This section describes some of the more common enterprise-wide threshold, intermediate, and longer-term strategies found in business. Many enterprise-wide *diversification strategies* have proved effective. *Concentric diversification* occurs through expansion into related product areas, such as the Taiwanese firm Acer did in computer-related product areas and businesses related to its core competencies. This has been called a "lily pad" approach. It can be likened to a clever frog that jumps to the nearest lily pad so that it can still hop back to safety if the new perch starts to sag.

*Multinational expansion* is another kind of concentric diversification. Groupe Danone, a French firm led by Franck Riboud, had a strong stable of brand-name products including Dannon yogurt, LU cookies, Evian spring water, and Kronenbourg beer. With only 15 percent of its sales outside Western Europe—versus 55 percent for rival Nestlé—it desperately needed to tap Asian and Latin American markets to build economies of scale and offset mature, cutthroat markets in the European Union. To expand overseas, in 1996, Riboud initiated deals such as: a Chinese venture to produce milk-based drinks, a 33 percent stake in South Africa's largest dairy company, and a cookie operation in Brazil. In 2000, he moved to strengthen Danone's presence in North America by attempting (unsuccessfully) to buy Nabisco Holdings Corporation (U.S.) (Woodruff 2000). In keeping with its strategy to become a global brand, like Nestlé, Danone planned to launch a new mineral water, labeled Dannon, in the United States to make *multiple use of its global brands*. Danone spent more than $5 billion on global acquisitions and expansion during the 1990s.

*Conglomerate diversification* occurs when growth is achieved through expansion into areas unrelated to a company's current business. Wayne Huizenga used this strategy when, after his success in waste management, he moved into the videotape rental business and subsequently expanded Blockbuster Video overseas.

A common enterprise-wide *concentration strategy* involves *vertical integration*. For example, in the 1980s, Coca-Cola began investing in its bottlers because this strategy was profitable (20 percent return on capital), gave Coke some control over pricing and distribution, and was a key to building overseas markets. Concentration strategies may also involve *horizontal growth,* as when Guiness PLC., a British brewer, acquired other beer and spirits producers and in 1997 merged with Grand Metropolitan PLC, a large distiller.

Another popular enterprise-wide strategy is *spin-offs*. This is done by distributing (spinning off) stock in a subsidiary to its stockholders or through creating a partially public subsidiary (PPS) by selling stock in a subsidiary—either through an initial public offering (IPO) or through breaking up a firm into segments. In 1999, Telefonica SA, Spain's dominant tele-communications firm, brought together all its media-linked assets (football broadcasting rights, digital TV, cable and conventional TV networks, radio and print media, and Internet services in Spain and Latin America) into a single new firm which was to be partially spun off in a market flotation (Burns 1999;White 2000). Spin-offs are often used as part of a strategic *refocusing* or *transformation* strategy. For example, in 1999,Tomkins PLC, a UK conglomerate, considered a combination of strategies (spin-offs, management buyouts, and stock sales) to narrow its business focus to automotive and building products through "demerging" its baking and foods division and its lawnmower and bicycle division (Marsh 1999). In 1999, Vickers PLC, a UK engineering firm, was refocusing its operations to marine-related equipment through the selling off of its Rolls-Royce and Bentley luxury car units and buying of marine-related firms (Fleming 1999).

A spin-offs' success varies by firm since it can depend on how it is managed. Often, spin-offs stimulate entrepreneurial growth in a business unit, but they do not solve all problems, because value is created, if at all, in the real work of business.

Many of these strategies are used in situations requiring restructuring as part of *turnaround* strategies. These can involve *simultaneously building on the past, while breaking with it* (Aeppel and Ansberry 2000; Hamel 2000). For example, as with so many other businesses, in early 2000, Deutsche Bank AG was struggling to prosper in the Internet marketplace, especially in its German retail banking operations. The Internet was expected to canni-balize conventional banking channels and lead to drastic reductions in profit margins in already weak retail banking operations in Germany, a major strategic management problem. Its proposed strategy was to build a virtual market across Europe in all areas and seek local partners for its German retail business (Andrews 2000). In early 2000, as part of this strategy, it announced its merger with Dresdner Bank (Rhoades and Portanger 2000).

Many types of generic enterprise-wide and SBU strategies are found in multinational businesses. These generic strategies emerge in a wide variety of ways in specific firms, so that considerable creative ingenuity is needed to pursue them effectively. In addition, innovative firms worldwide are constantly creating new enterprise-wide strategic approaches.

For example, the Internet has created a new competitive environment which has changed customer buying habits, as well as their expectations about product adaptability, speed of change, convenience, geographic reach, comparability, price, and service. Several Internet-related strategy formulation experiences are discussed in the following section.

The abundance of capital and nimble local competitors have also created opportunities and problems, as McDonald's discovered when it planned to double the number of outlets worldwide in three years (it took thirty years to build its existing outlet base) and found that some store sales fell in countries such as Argentina during this period due to aggressive local competition. Such developments have forced many firms to search for new strategic approaches and ways to break traditional molds.

### Intel: A Creative Multidimensional Strategy Mix

Intel Corporation produces microprocessors (chips) for computers. The industry is fast-growing and changing rapidly. Some commentators point to Intel's strategic success formula as being *time-paced, producing new products faster than competitors, and timing their introduction to produce maximum profits.* In fact, Intel's success is based on a broader strategic capability—to change *(adapt to or lead change)* in many areas (enterprise-wide, SBU, and functional) as competitive success factors change: "A mindset that allows for *continuous reinvention* in many areas in the face of success" (Slywotzky and Morrison 1997, p. 190).

By systematically and continuously *focusing on customer needs,* Intel has moved through a series of new strategic initiatives over the years. In the late 1960s, when competing with a much stronger Motorola, Intel focused on end users of its products and on *building on its past successes.* To do this, Intel introduced a customer support campaign showing customers how to use its microprocessors as solutions to customers' problems. For example, Intel helped Ford develop Intel micro controllers for its autos, and by 1983, Ford was using them in over a million cars annually.

Intel extended this *customer solutions* approach in the 1980s and focused on showing how its products could help customers like IBM get to market more rapidly with newer faster computers. To support this move, Intel *reduced product development time* from two years to one year, and so outperformed competitors in making new faster microprocessors; this also discouraged imitators. Intel also began development work on new products earlier: as a product replacement was being developed, development of the next generation product to replace it was begun.

Intel also had the courage and foresight to embrace *product refocusing— to drop major product lines that it felt would not be profitable* in light of competitor market dominance and competition. During the 1980s, it dropped its DRAM (dynamic random access memory) chip business; in 1999 it exited the market for high-end graphic chips (Takahashi 1999). In this way, Intel pursued a strategy which combined a *systematic review of the competitive market and its customers* with a strategy based on *building on Intel's major core competencies.*

Another strategic step taken by Intel was its move to make motherboards, the guts of a personal computer. This gave it greater control of its then primary market, personal computer manufacturers, and helped the firms who dealt with Intel to get to market faster than competitors. This enabled Intel to *move further down the value chain* in creating and maintaining markets. In the 1990s, Intel went further and began *promoting its name to the final consumer,* the computer user. The campaign, entitled "Intel Inside," encouraged computer makers to use Intel microprocessor products by creating end-user preferences for Intel products. As with Coca-Cola, Intel's strategy had moved closer toward management of the entire value chain, though in a much different way. Another strategic move by Intel, in an effort to discourage competition, was to continually *pursue legal action* against any and all competitors, former employees, semiconductor manufacturing plants, venture capitalists, and even customers for alleged patent infringements (Jackson 1997).

In 2000, Intel was again striking out in new strategic directions as a supplier of semiconductors for networking gear, information appliances, and PCs. In addition, Intel was focusing on e-commerce, consumer electronics, Internet servers, and mobile phone markets. For example, it introduced a new family of chips for the networking and communications gear that zips data through the Internet, it opened a $3 billion Internet services center for other firms, and began producing information appliances (Reinhardt 2000).

In all cases, Intel appears to have made use of a systematic structured approach to market analysis by focusing on the industry value chain and the customer. In creatively building on this, Intel used a variety of *innovative strategies* to *meet and beat competition* initially (short-term), then to *anticipate competition* in key areas and proactively surpass them in dramatic ways (intermediate term), and finally to *change competitive market structures and relationships* (long-term). In contrast, Microsoft's approach (described in Chapter 5) appears to have pursued a more chaotic unstructured planning process.

### Innovatively Going Beyond the Obvious and Breaking Molds: Enterprise-Wide Brand Strategy at Unilever

In late 1999, Niall Fitzgerald, cochairman of Unilever, reported results of market trend studies in regard to usage of detergents. These studies showed that consumers no longer wanted soap powder, they simply wanted clean clothes without the mess associated with using washing machines. Fitzgerald said:

> In 15 years very few people in the world will be using products to clean their clothes. There will be services which do it, in different ways and to different levels of sophistication and cost. [Willman 1999, p. 2]

This was but one of the many ideas that Unilever was exploring in its Project Foresight. For the project, Unilever assigned a group of twenty young managers—average age thirty-two—to spend six months exploring new marketplace trends and new ways to deal with them. One major outcome of the project was a change in brand strategy. Unilever decided to focus on its 400 major brands—those that provided 90 percent of its revenue (Cowell 2000). It planned to devote most of its marketing resources to developing these brands. Unilever's experiences using a similar strategy in Brazil raised sales by half and increased margins 1 percent. As for the other 1,200 existing brands, some had no future and were dropped, others were harvested but faded away over time, and still others survived and prospered without the marketing support, but with lower costs and so increased profits.

Whether or not you agree with Unilever's brand decision and the reasoning underlying it, this experience illustrates some of the ways businesses go about breaking with past molds—another example of creative destruction—in an effort to deal with a rapidly changing multinational environment.

## STRATEGIC BUSINESS UNIT (SBU) SITUATIONS

The strategic framework for SBUs is usually narrower in scope and more specific than at the enterprise-wide level. The SBU strategic framework would cover some or all of the following: the strategic foundation; size and scope of the operation; strategic thrust; kind of products or services sold and delivered; customer service quality and image; product/service brand identification and image; breadth of the product/service line; functions performed by the company; distribution outlets; customer market served; geographic market served; ownership; and financial targets. The following discussions of the strategic frameworks of several firms explore how enterprise-wide and functional/operational factors impact on SBU strategic framework formulation. An SBU strategic framework also defines planned activities needed to carry out an enterprise-wide strategy.

### Background Studies

Studies of current and future *industry and market structures* as well as of *industry and market attractiveness* and related *opportunities and keys to success,* such as those described previously and in Chapter 4, are needed when formulating SBU as well as enterprise-wide strategies. Other key external factors involve *competitors* and *customers,* as GE's Jack Welch made clear in the focused questions he asked continually about how each employee was working to meet market pressures and needs. Internal factors include resource strengths and weaknesses. Ideally, this process results in identifying a firm's *core competencies* and how a firm can differentiate itself from competitors. As noted in Chapter 4, these studies go beyond systematically analyzing existing environments to creatively and innovatively studying future circumstances and trends and ways they might stimulate thinking about new winning strategies, as was done at Unilever. One additional key factor considered in SBU strategy formulation is the enterprise-wide strategic framework.

### Formulating Business Unit Strategies and Strategic Plans: UPS and FedEx in China—A Study in Contrasts

Federal Express Corporation (FedEx) and United Parcel Service of America, Inc. (UPS), both U.S.-based worldwide express mail and cargo delivery service firms, have used different strategies for their operations in China (Blackmon 1998a; Blackman and Brady 1998).

FedEx's approach was to use the same strategy it had used successfully in the United States. It purchased its own air routes. In1989, it bought Flying Tiger Line Inc. for $888 million for its Asian routes (especially its Japan-China link), and in 1995 spent $67.5 million to purchase the only operating authority permitting a U.S. cargo carrier to fly directly into China at that time from Evergreen International Aviation Inc.. The company intended to add twenty cities a year to its delivery network. In time, in more than a dozen major cities in China, FedEx's operations, trucks, and uniformed employees resembled those in the United States. In 1998, FedEx held 13 percent of the express market share, with the largest share (30 percent) being held by DHL International Ltd., a long-established Brussels-based company. In early 1998, FedEx announced its first quarterly loss on international operations, due largely to the high costs of its Asian network and the Asian economic crisis.

In contrast, UPS used a conservative growth strategy. It operated in only three cities initially, Beijing, Shanghai, and Guangzhou. Its deliveries were made in brown trucks by drivers with brown uniforms, as in the United States, but UPS did not operate its own aircraft. Rather, it used other carriers; this limited the logistics services it could offer. UPS concentrated on mail and small package delivery, instead of less profitable air cargo.

UPS also believed that China was a major express freight market with expected growth of 20 percent per year, but it also understood the risks one of which included a volatile Asian market that in 1998 was going through a severe recession. Consistent with its image and history, UPS built relationships throughout Asia in a quiet way, in contrast to FedEx's aggressive advertising and promotion. UPS felt that it could expand as the market grew, and that it was too risky and too early to put an expensive network in place as FedEx had done. In 1998, UPS had less than a 5 percent market share in China, but overall, its profits were strong (Blackmon 1998c).

It is still too early to predict which strategy will be more successful when faced with such a changing market and strongly entrenched competitor—DHL. The differing strategies were consistent with the corporate cultures of both FedEx and UPS, were reasonable ways to deal with different market segments, with long-term profitability as the primary objective.

## DEVELOPING THE SPECIFICS OF STRATEGIC FRAMEWORKS: THE SYNTHESIS

At both the enterprise-wide and strategic-business-unit levels, strategic frameworks, strategies, and strategic plans are developed continually as the action plans are formulated and carried out, operations are managed, and competitive markets change. The process involves forming and evaluating alternatives, making tentative plans, and revising and refining them over time where appropriate.

Long-term planning, as the experiences of GE, Intel, and Microsoft show, does not necessarily lead to a specific, inflexible, long-term plan. Rather, in a rapidly changing and highly uncertain market, firms are often inclined to first think in terms of "real options," or possible alternatives, a scenario-planning approach which explores possibilities, and enables both speed and agility. The objective of these alternatives is to develop a flexible base for future action, providing a firm with the possibility to move in different directions as markets change, while reducing the risks (Coy 1999).

The following sections discuss additional experiences that firms have had when formulating enterprise-wide, SBU, and functional strategic frameworks. Different ways of adapting general strategic management processes to individual situations, as well as additional specific approaches available to refine strategic frameworks and to identify the activities and planned action steps required to implement strategic frameworks will be explored. The strategies described are not intended as magic formulas that are directly useful in every situation; they are designed only to stimulate creative thinking when formulating and evaluating specific strategies in your own situation.

### Gaining a Competitive Edge: Other Non–Internet-Related Company Experiences

As with Intel, many companies encourage *continuous product innovation.* For example, the 3M company requires that each year between 25 percent and 30 percent of sales come from products developed within the past four years, though, as 3M found, such a strategy is not sufficient in itself to maintain superior growth (Deutsch 1999). SMH, which makes Swatches, used a *brand pyramid approach,* as did GM, with products ranging from lowest to highest priced.

Disney, the entertainment giant, makes money through *multiple use of its major products/brands,* such as its animated characters, on a wide range of products from theme parks, to films, to T-shirts and watches. This approach involves capturing *cross-business synergies.* The French cosmetics giant, L'Oreal, has a *brand portfolio* strategy, which maintains a growing mix of internationally known brand names, such as Maybelline cosmetics, Ralph Lauren fragrances, and Redken hair care products.

Adaptability is often enabled in a cost-effective way by following a *common platform approach,* which can be adapted in different markets. Honda Motor Co. was able to produce cars for different markets by developing a single frame or platform, the most expensive part of an auto, which could be used for different size cars (large in the U.S., small in Europe and Asia). Electrolux, the Swedish white goods company, was also moving towards a common product platform strategy in 1999 (Burt 1999).

Many firms *focus on niches.* For example, Germany's BMW automaker has successfully used a niche strategy—contrary to the auto industry's general belief that "size does matter." BMW focuses on luxury cars priced from $24,000 to $95,000, where operating margins are relatively higher.

Southwest Airlines (U.S.) was able to *find profitable new niche opportunities by looking at substitute industries* (Kim and Mauborgne 1999). Southwest understood that for short-haul destinations, the automobile was a substitute for flying. Southwest focused on why people fly (to save time) and why people drive (to save money). It then created its market by making its fares very low, making its flights faster by creating point-to-point flights, and using secondary airports (cutting average flight time because of reduced taxi time, fewer gate holds, and less stacking). It "broke the mold" by ignoring normal industry competitive factors such as meals, designated seats, central airports (with detours through hubs), and multiple classes of seats— all considered indispensable to those whose thinking was locked into past molds. *Breaking with conventional wisdom* also explains how Home Depot (U.S.) gained the insight to create the "do-it-yourself" market, and how Kinepolis, the Belgian cinema group, transformed European cinema with megaplexes.

The winning strategies discussed thus far are related to what a firm can do to *create value* by focusing on where the opportunities (profits) are, *especially through creating value for customers,* the so-called *EVA (economic value added) strategic focus* (de Kluyver 2000). This approach also focuses on how these profits can be achieved through *differentiating a firm from its competitors in a dramatic way* and enabling it to go *substantially beyond meeting threshold success requirements* in their market.

This discussion has covered only a small sampling of the many strategies that can be developed to win against the competition in specific critical profit areas of the value chain, and so need to be defined within the strategic framework. The previous discussion also explored ways to stimulate thinking about alternatives through innovative structured competitive market analysis.

### Gaining a Competitive Edge: Internet-Related Company Experiences

The Internet revolution is one of the most widely written about current business forces driving change. Its impact on strategic management has been felt in all kinds of businesses, not just Internet businesses, and at all management levels (Wilder and Kolbasuk-McGee 2000). The following section covers alternative, winning, Internet-related strategies at operational, strategic business unit, and enterprise-wide levels for different time frames (immediate, intermediate, long-term):

- *More effective selling and servicing at lower costs*—Charles Schwab & Company, a financial brokerage firm, has a strategic focus that involves making it easier for customers to do business with it at costs lower than the competition's, by automating order entry (through the Internet most recently), and financial advice. Schwab uses new Internet technology to create these values for its customers. This initially helped differentiate Schwab from the competition, which quickly followed Schwab's lead. Reduced ordering costs enabled setting commissions below the competition, a threshold competency needed to compete in the discount brokerage business. In the words of one observer, "Schwab bet the farm on low-cost Web trading and in the process invented a new kind of brokerage firm" (Schonfeld 1998, p. 24). Later, it was the first brokerage firm to introduce it into England.
- *E-commerce in banking*—In 1997, Citigroup formed e-Citi, an online bank with 1,000 employees which emulates everything Citigroup does. To fulfill its new mission, in 1999 e-Citi introduced versions of Citibank's Direct Access online retail-banking services with new features for savings and checking accounts, bill payment, stock trades, and credit-card transactions every quarter. It also expected to introduce new brokerage and insurance products, as well as corporate banking services. In addition, Citigroup was working on using expanded cellular phone access distribution channels (Violino 1999). In July 1999, American Express announced that it too was starting an online bank, while Bank One was creating a separate competing online bank. In 2000, Deutsch Bank AG (Germany) announced that it was spending $1 billion on online services, merging with Dresdner Bank AG (Germany), and spinning off both companies' branch operations (Rhoades and Portanger 2000).
- *More effective selling to businesses*—Dell Computer has a Web page for each corporate customer who leases PCs from Dell, using the Internet to improve service, save servicing costs, and facilitate pulling together products from suppliers. Nearly $2 billion of its sales (16 per-

cent of total revenue) was processed online in the late 1990s (Slywotzky et al., 1999, Chapter 11).

- *The corporate intranet*—The Ford Motor Company has an internal company internet (intranet) that is consulted by 80 percent of its connected employees daily. Human resources uses the intranet to *communicate new job postings, update benefit information, calculate merit pay increases, and review employees and supervisors. Each auto or truck model has its own Web site to facilitate design, control, and planning.* According to Ford's former CEO, Jacques A. Nasser, the internal web is the backbone of Ford's business today (Kerwin, Stepanek, and Welch 2000).

- *Streamlining the supply chain*—Pitney Bowes, the postage meter company, has *extended its electronic data interchange (EDI) and enterprise resource planning (ERP) links with suppliers by using Web sites to link suppliers, even very small ones, to its EDI and ERP systems.* Using "VendorSite" software, suppliers can check Pitney's inventory of their products, Pitney's planned needs, and other ordering and delivery information.

- *Coordinating finance*—Cisco Systems, a major networking software firm, gets 73 percent of its customer orders over the Internet. Employees can make all of their travel arrangements and file their expense reports over the Web, and the same goes for big and small purchases and hiring decisions. Its financial systems are equally sophisticated. On a daily basis, company management can call up, for example, company revenues, margins, orders, discounts given on these orders, and top ten customers for the previous day, and the system enables the company to close its books each quarter in two days, instead of ten—the earlier record. Such a system enables management to detect changes in market conditions almost instantly (Donnelly 1999; Slywotzky et al., 1999, Chapter 11).

These examples show not only the *breadth of change* but also the *depth of change* resulting from the Internet. Early on, managers in these firms recognized the strategic management impact of the Internet and moved forward resolutely to exploit its potential. A strategic management decision, combined with entrepreneurial drive, was all that was needed to start the process.

Making it work? Again the process is simple in concept: "A little demystification: How well the Web (and the Internet) works for a company depends on old-fashioned smarts and elbow grease. It isn't glamorous at all" [Brown, 1999, p. 112]. He adds that Web success and the amount of detail-orientation and planning put into it are positively corelated. In addition, successful e-businesses are those that know how to create new online tools and businesses.

In other words, skillful entrepreneurial persistence is what wins. As for how to do it in your firm, you can study the companies that have done it, such as those discussed previously. These include older (Ford), and newer (Schwab) firms, from a wide range of industries, that have adapted business practices in different ways to take advantage of Net technology without necessarily redoing their whole business model. Since the Internet affects different businesses in different ways, the strategy for dealing with its impact and the changes it generates varies.

For example, Chris Gent, Chairman of Vodafone AirTouch PLC in the UK, made alliances with and/or bought several hundred billion dollars worth of Internet companies in an effort to build the first worldwide major Internet company using wireless devices—a risky but potentially rewarding strategy (Baker and Capell 2000a,b). Richard Branson, head of Virgin Group PLC in the UK, first developed a mobile phone service in November 1999 that had 300,000 subscribers four months later, and then moved in a major way into the Internet business. Virgin had no prior experience in either mobile phones or Internet services (Sorkin 2000).

However, the previous company strategic management experiences are only selected examples designed to stimulate thinking about new strategic directions in light of changing competitive markets. Each reader will also have their own experiences to draw upon when searching for creative solutions. Winning strategies and related core competencies can be identified at the enterprise-wide, SBU, or functional levels.

Such strategies and core competencies are essential to a firm's ability to remain competitive in the future and so are a significant part of the strategic framework. Winning competitive edges based on core competencies shift constantly as competitors mimic and surpass rivals' competencies. A company, therefore, continually seeks to renew existing competencies and competitive edges, as well as create new ones.

The strategies discussed previously are not magic formulas that can be mechanically transferred to different firms in different industries. Each situation requires its own solution. Reviewing success stories of others can, nonetheless, stimulate creative thinking about one's own situation. Therefore, they are useful in helping find solutions, not necessarily in providing specific solutions.

Winning strategies built on such comparative analyses can involve three time frames. First, they can involve reacting to competitor moves and winning today, such as Intel did when it focused on stimulating customer usage of its products and getting out of the DRAM business. Second, they can also involve building enabling mechanisms for winning in the future, as GE did in its organization structure and Intel did in reorganizing its research and development operation to decrease product development time. Third, these winning strategies can involve creating new markets, as Intel's new microprocessor applications did. These strategies may involve changing market structures to create new profit opportunities, as Intel did. They can even involve looking further into the future and creating new visionary products and services, as Intel did in the household products area. They may also involve strategies at three levels of a company: the enterprise-wide, strategic business unit, and operational levels.

### Quantitative Strategic Goals

When formulating strategic frameworks, strategies are eventually translated into precise quantitative targets, such as: sales projections, both in the aggregate or as a percentage of market share (market position); return-on-investment targets; cash-flow goals; acceptable risks; operating margins; and firm ownership and control limitations. Translating strategic targets into specific quantitative goals is a key step in translating strategic objectives into enabling operating plans. The specifics, however, will depend on the situation. The following is the way one major company stated their financial objectives:

- To preserve stakeholders' equity
- To increase earnings an average of 11 percent per year
- To earn a return on book equity of 12 to 15 percent per year
- To pay out 30 to 40 percent of earnings each year in dividends to stockholders
- To maintain a sound financial position, which would enable the company to borrow on the most favorable terms available in world markets
- Where goals are not met, to meet or exceed the performance of comparable companies in the industry

In all instances the long-term success of strategies is ultimately measured by financial performance figures.

### EVALUATING ALTERNATIVES

Evaluating strategies and strategic plans can involve both quantitative and qualitative measures. Profitability measures are discussed in the following section, as are competitive and comparative quantitative measures. One useful qualitative evaluation tool is to write scenarios of probable competitor responses. An example is provided in Table 2.1. In preparing these, it is often helpful to assign one person the task of role playing the thoughts and actions of each competitor and of becoming an expert in thinking like their assigned competitor.

The comparative competitive evaluation analysis, shown in Table 2.2, involves comparing a firm's strengths and weaknesses with competitors' in

TABLE 2.1. Competitive Scenario Analysis and Evaluation Oil Services Company Situation, Most Likely Actions

| Competition | What Competitor Might Do | Probability (%) | Reasons for Probability |
|---|---|---|---|
| Competitor A | Try to develop a similar product | 75 | • Vast resources<br>• Market leader<br>• Already produces similar products that are well-known in the industry |
| Competitor B | Try to develop a similar product | 70 | • Has extensive engineering services and equipment<br>• Has 50 years experience |
| Competitor C | Undecided, will wait to see what happens | 70 | • Has only 5 years experience |
| Competitor D | Will not try to develop a similar product | 95 | • 95% of their business is selling a natural resource product |
| Competitor E | Try to merge our company | 50 | • Small company<br>• High-quality reputation |
| Competitor F | Can go either way: wait and see what happens, or develop a similar product right away | 40 | • Large company<br>• Has power to control prices<br>• Has the engineering and equipment capabilities |

## Planner B's Analysis

| Scenarios | Competitor A | Competitor B | Competitor C | Competitor D | Competitor E | Competitor F |
|---|---|---|---|---|---|---|
| Do nothing | 3 | 3 | 6 | 3 | 1 | 3 |
| Copy/improve new product | 6 | 6 | 5 | 1 | 8 | 6 |
| Try to buy or merge with us | 4 | 4 | 1 | 1 | 5 | 7 |
| Dirty tricks | 3 | 5 | 1 | 4 | 1 | 1 |
| Wait/see | 8 | 8 | 7 | 10 | 3 | 9 |
| Become our customer | 2 | 8 | 1 | 2 | 8 | 1 |

*Note:* Scale of 1-10
10 = Strong Possibility of Scenario Occurring
1 = Little Possibility of Scenario Occurring

critical success factor/opportunity areas. This tool helps identify the core competencies that need strengthening or further exploitation. Throughout, the evaluation is based on the study of the key situation requirements.

Another tool used for smaller, limited-scope firms is a decision matrix. An example of one is shown in Table 2.3. The matrix gives a structured view of the major alternatives within each strategic decision area affecting a firm's future.

Alternatives are often evaluated in stages, as for example at GE.

Additional formal tools and techniques used in evaluating alternative strategies are discussed in the following section.

TABLE 2.2. Comparative Evaluation of Competitor's and Company's Strengths and Weaknesses in Key-to-Success and Opportunity Areas

| | Competitor Groups | | | Compare Weight* | |
|---|---|---|---|---|---|
| | Company A | Big Three | Little Six | (1) | (2) |
| **a. Products** | | | | | |
| *Standardized* | | | | | |
| 1. Resources/price competitive | Weak | Strong | Weak | − | 0 |
| 2. Mass market presence | Strong | Strong | None | 0 | ++ |
| 3. Brand/quality reputation | Strong | Strong | ? | 0 | + |
| *Specialty* | | | | | |
| 1. New product capability | Strong | Good | Good | + | 0 |
| 2. Market Intelligence | Strong | Weak | Good | ++ | + |
| 3. Flexible production/organization | Strong | Weak | Strong | + | + |
| 4. Market access/presence | Strong | Strong | Good | 0 | + |
| 5. Brand Recognition | Strong | Strong | Good | 0 | + |
| **b. Outlets** | | | | | |
| *Chains* | | | | | |
| 1. Strong store relations | Strong | Strong | Good | 0 | + |
| 2. Chain buyer relations | Strong | Strong | ? | 0 | + |
| 3. Wide product line | Strong | Strong | Weak | 0 | ++ |
| 4. Promotional incentives | Strong | Strong | Good | 0 | + |
| *Independents* | | | | | |
| 1. Distribution cost control | Weak | Strong | ? | − | ? |
| 2. Strong store relations | Strong | Strong | Good | 0 | + |
| 3. Appropriate product line | Good | Good | Good | 0 | 0 |
| 4. Promotional incentives | Strong | Strong | Good | 0 | + |

*Note:*This is the result of comparing the strength of the company under study with the strength of each competitor group. For example, if the company is rated strong and the competitor weak, the rating would be ++. Where the company is strong and the competitor group strong, the rate would be 0.

TABLE 2.3. Decision Chart (Segment)

| Kind of Decision | Alternative I | Alternative II | Alternative III |
|---|---|---|---|
| Services Provided | Specialize in custom programming and modification services including Year 2000 and euro efforts<br><br>Support and maintenance services including desktop support, software maintenance, and network management | Maintenance and support services including desktop support, software maintenance, and network management<br><br>Systems integration services | Consulting and training services<br><br>Systems integration services<br><br>Custom programming—concentrating on Year 2000 and euro efforts<br><br>Minimal focus on desktop support and network management which require large capital outlays |
| Technology (Expertise and Knowledge in providing services around these technology areas) | Broad mix of technologies including client/server systems, networks, and the Internet/Intranet | Concentration on new cutting-edge technologies, such as client/server systems and the Internet | Broad mix of technologies including client/server systems, networks, and the Internet/Intranet |
| Customers (Clients) | Government sector | Commercial sector | Commercial and Government sectors |
| Geographic Markets (Expansion Opportunities) | Capture the US Federal market and Europe and Australia | Capture domestic markets and maintain international revenue from Europe | Continue expansion both domestic and international. Primarily focus on new expansion in Europe, Australia, and former Soviet Union states |

## FINANCIAL ANALYSIS
## AND EVALUATION TECHNIQUES AND TOOLS

In diversified companies, it is useful to continually examine the economic and financial value of each business segment's contribution to the enterprise as a whole. This provides one measure in deciding where to allocate and reallocate resources.

Uncertainties arise, however, since economic and financial (quantitative) analysis and evaluation deal with assumptions. The likelihood that a specific event will occur is uncertain. Evaluations are most often based in part on qualitative judgments, so it is usually best to view them only as estimates of the future outcomes. For example, when evaluating a proposed diversification strategy it can be useful to study the financial impact of different product strategies given different assumptions about political, economic, and competitor future actions (scenarios). This gives a specific measure of the relative value of alternatives and assists in deciding where to allocate limited enterprise resources.

Two of the many types of economic and financial analyses and evaluations will be discussed here: profitability analysis and evaluation; and resource allocation and portfolio management. The discussion is necessarily brief; the subjects are covered extensively in economic analyses texts, workbooks, and courses.

### *Profitability Analysis and Evaluation*

A business activity creates value when its return exceeds the cost of capital. The cost of equity capital is the risk-free cost of borrowing money (for example, U.S government treasury bill rate) plus an additional amount to take into account the risks involved in the business activity under study (risk premium). The risk premium is calculated by multiplying the estimated volatility of a business by the general capital market rate less the risk-free rate. For example, in the electric utility industry the cost of equity capital at a given time would be:

| | |
|---|---|
| .5 | (its estimated level of volatility at the time) |
| | times |
| 5% | (the capital market borrowing rate at the time of 9% minus the U.S. treasury rate at the time of 4%) |
| | plus |
| 4% | (the treasury bill rate) |

*Cost of equity capital:* $.5 \times 5\%$ (9% minus 4%) + 4% = 6.5%

In doing a financial evaluation of alternatives, the alternative's *projected rate of earnings* is estimated and compared to the *cost of equity capital*. For example, an electric utility did a financial simulation of costs and revenues of a proposed investment in England. The simulation showed a projected 8.5 percent return on equity using what was judged to be conservative estimates of economic and market trends. The cost of equity capital was 6.5 percent at the time, yielding a favorable 2 percentage point spread for the investment.

Whether a firm is expected to be profitable in the future is reflected in the firm's market value. For example, when a firm is profitable (return on equity exceeds cost of equity capital, a positive spread) and the corresponding net present value of the discounted cash flow is positive, growth would contribute to creating value at a compounded rate. If a firm that has borrowed money earns more than it pays in interest on the borrowed money and also generates excess cash flow, the firm is creating value.

If the market believes a firm has the ability to continue to create value in the future, the *m*arket value (for example, the stock exchange listed price) will generally be greater than the *b*ook value—that is the market/book (m/b) ratio will be greater than 1. The market value is also affected by the rate at which profits are reinvested and by the number of years a firm has been consistently profitable. One measure of the attractiveness of a business enterprise, therefore, is m/b value. For example, if a firm's market value is lower than its book value, then the market may not expect the firm to grow and create value in the future. Computing the m/b ratio is one way to establish a value for a prospective diversification opportunity.

Various other financial measures can be used to evaluate alternative diversification proposals and SBU worth, including:

* The projected growth rate
* Expected cash generated
* Rate and amount of reinvestment of profits
* The time period of the equity investment
* The discounted cash flow value over that time period
* The amount of equity investment required

Such financial analyses are necessary and are one key factor in making diversification (as well as divestiture) decisions.

### Resource Allocation and Portfolio Management

Some managers prefer to view SBUs as a portfolio. An analysis can be done to compare the profitability of a firm's SBUs to each other, to other firms in their market, and to proposals for acquiring or starting new SBUs. As such, it is a measure of an SBU's contribution to overall profitability.

Identifying underachievers, especially in relation to competitors and competing investment alternatives, helps target SBUs needing attention. Other portfolio tools useful in analyzing and evaluating businesses are: the life-cycle matrix, the industry attractiveness/business strength matrix, and the growth/share matrix (Buzzell and Bradley 1997; Hax and Majluf 1996; Hess and Miller 1993). Such matrix analyses are used to suggest possible generic strategies to consider when allocating resources among existing product lines or businesses. For example, the following alternatives might be considered, based on such analyses:

- *Build aggressively.* This is recommended when the business is in a strong, highly attractive, fast-growing industry, and management wants to build share as rapidly as possible. This role is usually assigned to an SBU early in the life cycle, especially when there is little doubt as to whether the rapid growth will be sustained.
- *Build gradually.* This is recommended when the business is strong in an attractive, moderate-growth industry and management wants to build share, or when rapid growth exists but there is doubt as to whether it will continue.
- *Build selectively.* This is recommended when a business is well-positioned in an attractive industry and wants to build share where it feels it has or can develop strength.
- *Maintain aggressively.* This is recommended when a business is in a strong position in a currently attractive industry, and management is determined to maintain that position.
- *Maintain selectively.* This is recommended when either the business is in a strong position in a less attractive industry, or the business is in a moderate position in a highly attractive industry. In this instance, management will want to exploit the situation by maximizing the profitability benefits of selectively serving where it best can do so, but with minimum additional resource deployment.
- *Prove viability.* This is recommended when the business is in a less-than-satisfactory position in a less attractive industry. If the business can provide resources for use elsewhere, management may decide to retain it, but without additional resource support.
- *Divest-liquidate.* This is recommended when neither the business nor industry has any redeeming features. Barring major exit barriers, the business should be divested.
- *Competitive harasser.* This is recommended when a business is in a poor position in an attractive industry in which competitors with a good position in the industry also compete with the company in another industry. The role of competitive harasser is to sporadically or continuously attack the competitor's position, not necessarily with the

intention of long-run success. The objective is to distract the competition from other areas, inhibit them from revenue business, or use the business to cross-parry when the competition attacks an important sister business of the strategic aggressor.

These are suggested perspectives, not recommended actions. They are designed to stimulate thinking about alternatives at the enterprise-wide or SBU level. They should be balanced with the many other strategies discussed earlier and in the following sections and chapters.

## ENABLING FUNCTIONAL /OPERATIONS SITUATIONS

As more precise strategies evolve over time, the strategic management process extends into operating areas. These areas are enablers which help to refine enterprise-wide and SBU strategic frameworks as functional area strategic frameworks are developed and as SBU and enterprise-wide strategies are implemented.

The principal enabling functional areas, which are discussed in the chapters noted in parentheses, are:

- Marketing and production/operations (discussed in Chapters 5 and 6)
- Telecommunications/information systems (discussed in Chapter 7)
- Finance and accounting (discussed in Chapter 8)
- Organization structure, processes (business and human), and culture (discussed in Chapter 9)
- Human resources (discussed in Chapters 10 through 12)
- Strategic alliances (discussed in Chapter 13)

## INTEGRATIVE STRATEGIC MANAGEMENT AT TOYOTA

Formulating an enterprise-wide strategic framework, and developing and implementing related SBU and functional strategic frameworks, plans, and programs can be a complex process. For example, in 1998, Toyota Motor Corporation (Japan) was in the process of implementing a $13.5 billion expansion designed to make Toyota a global automotive leader by the year 2004 (Bremmer, Thornton, and Kunii 1997). Doing this involved:

- Shaking up the firm's insular, consensus-driven culture
- Extending Toyota's edge in high-speed, flexible car making
- Pursuing perhaps the most aggressive overseas expansion in automotive history

- Outflanking Detroit in emerging markets and going after the United State's "Big Three" automakers
- Using new designs to create excitement about the Toyota brand
- Cutting costs

Carrying out the strategy involved many supporting plans and actions. A restructuring of the design division, for example, led to the introduction of twelve new models in 1996, some of which were created in 14.5 months, less than half the time competitors needed. These new models led to major sales gains in the United States, and Toyota's new "Europe Car" was expected to be a major competitor in Europe's minicar segment. Its sturdy, simply designed, fuel-efficient Asian car, built with local parts, was expected to help Toyota become a market leader in Southeast Asia and eventually in China.

By creating manufacturing hubs (SBUs) in Asia, North America, and Europe, Toyota was able to exploit consumer trends quickly by customizing vehicles for regional markets: it could now rely on locally based suppliers and design teams to tailor vehicles to local tastes. It was also now able to rely on its network of cheaper dollar-denominated parts suppliers when the yen was strong and increase exports from home when the yen was weak.

Since 1995, Toyota has saved nearly $2.5 billion in costs, mostly by developing ways to use fewer parts and eliminating production waste. This was an astounding feat, considering how frugal Toyota was in the past. Yet, in 1997, Chairman, President and CEO Hiroshi Okuda ordered managers to come up with $800 million in extra cost savings every year for the foreseeable future.

Probably the toughest task at Toyota was changing the company culture. To make tradition-shackled Toyota more multinational in outlook, Okuda intensified his efforts to flatten the corporate pyramid at headquarters, to tether pay to performance rather than seniority, and to promote frustrated young managers. Many older executives were stripped of fancy titles and given narrower responsibilities to make way for younger executives. Okuda admitted, however, that it might take years to change the corporate culture. Programs to improve service and marketing were also being introduced and further organization changes were planned (Shirouzu 2000).

Another Toyota enterprise-wide strategy was to decrease the company's dependence on auto sales. To do this, Toyota invested in auto accessory and prefabricated-housing businesses, and increased its stakes in more than thirty broadcasting and telecommunications firms, financing subsidiaries, a dot.com cybermall, and major SBUs in golf courses and leisure boats; it has also considered making small aircraft engines (Thornton, Armstrong, and Kerwin 2000).

As seen from Toyota's experiences, enterprise-wide, SBU, organizational, marketing, manufacturing, and financial plans and actions can require intensive integrative leadership to succeed.

## SUMMARY

This chapter focuses on formulating strategic frameworks, which can vary in their details by company and by management level, depending on the specific situation. Strategic frameworks can be formulated at three different levels: corporate or enterprise-wide strategies providing long-term general guidelines; strategic business unit strategies defining customers, markets, and competitors; and functional or operational strategies involving enabling ideas discussed in Chapters 5 through 13.

Developing such frameworks requires integrating systematic, disciplined approaches, with entrepreneurial creativity. This chapter has described how such frameworks are developed, including tools for developing, evaluating, and deciding among alternative courses of action.

New technologies, especially the Internet, have modified the concept of strategy by shortening time frames in many industries, and have had a major impact on strategic management. The increase in the speed of change often requires rapid strategy shifts, or creating new strategies—in a sense throwing out the rule book (Maitland 2000). This so-called "perpetual" strategy process continually gathers information on all business areas. This information (competitive intelligence) is used to explore future trends, as well as to create new operating plans and take actions based on emerging strategies, as has been done at GE over the years.

## REVIEW QUESTIONS

1. Discuss the phases involved in formulating a strategic framework and the levels involved.
2. What factors are examined when developing a strategic framework? Discuss the different ways in which companies present and use their strategic mission or vision statements. Give specific examples: for example, Jack Welch's at GE compared to several others.
3. Describe some types of enterprise-wide strategies that companies have used successfully to gain a competitive advantage in the multinational market and discuss why they have worked.
4. Describe the essence of a business strategy and the ways in which it can articulate a multinational company's distinctive competitive edge. Give specific examples to support your answer.

5. Identify the phases of strategy formulation and implementation experienced by Mitsubishi or another firm of your choice.
6. Describe the strategic steps that Toyota took in its quest to become a dominant worldwide automotive leader by the year 2000.
7. Discuss some of the tools that are useful in evaluating both business unit and enterprise-wide strategies and describe the advantages and limitations of each.
8. Describe the concept of enablers and discuss how they are used in strategic management. Give examples to illustrate you answer.
9. Compare the different strategic approaches to the merging of computer and consumer electronics technology that Acer and Sony might use given that one company is mainly involved in computers and the other is involved in consumer electronics and entertainment.
10. Define "spin-offs" and the ways in which they might be used strategically by firms trying to refocus their operations.
11. Discuss strategic analytical and evaluation tools and techniques and ways that they might be useful at both enterprise-wide and SBU levels when formulating strategic frameworks.

## *EXERCISES*

1. Find information on a firm of your choice using sources such as periodicals, annual reports, and the Internet. Imagine that you are the CEO of that firm: (a) create a detailed strategic framework statement for shareholders, such as Jack Welch's statement for GE; and (b) develop an SBU strategic plan for expanding internationally.
2. Evaluate several of the alternative strategies for the same firm, using analysis and evaluation tools described in the chapter.

# Chapter 3

# Specific Decisions, Tasks, and Activities

This chapter describes additional multinational strategic leadership and management decisions, tasks, and activities, which are outlined in Figure 1.6 (p. 25).

Chapter 2 described a key phase of the multinational leadership and management process outlined in Figure 1.5 (p. 13), creating strategic frameworks. The tasks through which the strategic framework is refined and developed and through which strategic frameworks are carried out are described in the following sections.

## THE BASIC STRATEGIC DECISION TO GO MULTINATIONAL

A basic enterprise-wide task area involves a firm's decision to go multinational. Successful multinational businesses can experience enormous increases in sales and profits. Companies such as Philips Electronics, IBM, The Gillette Company, Coca-Cola, and many large Japanese and European companies report that 30 to 80 percent of their revenue comes from production, sales, and services outside their home country.

A study by *Fortune* indicates that worldwide investors value global firms more than domestic ones. From the United States to Europe to Japan, firms high in the rankings were those that had earned multinational recognition in the areas of technology, manufacturing, and consumer goods (Colvin 2000). Multinational expansion is a major force affecting business today.

Basic decisions about whether to begin or expand multinational operations, the size and speed of expansion, and the best way to do it, depend on individual company and market factors (Rangan 1999). Each firm has special requirements, resources, and methods of matching these firm factors with market opportunities. For example, the French company, Groupe Danone, spent billions on global expansion and acquisitions in the 1990s to offset mature, cutthroat markets in Europe (Tagliabue 1998; Toy 1996). In contrast, hundreds of firms in Japan, the United States, and other countries established or bought manufacturing facilities in Europe to qualify for reduced tariffs in the European Economic Community and to protect or expand their markets there.

Unocal Corporation, an $8 billion California-based oil firm operating mostly in California, sold its oil properties there and invested heavily in overseas oil exploration, transportation, production, and marketing because of difficulties encountered in competing against large oil firms in the mature United States market. In the late 1990s, the firm was expected to become a key regional competitor in countries such as Burma, Indonesia, Thailand, and the former Soviet republics bordering the Caspian Sea, with 70 to 80 percent of its business coming from overseas markets (Prasso and Armstrong 1997). Investment firms such as Merrill Lynch (United States) have moved aggressively into overseas markets because of maturing home markets, as have cigarette firms and hundreds of other firms in mature markets.

Many reasons can motivate firms to expand internationally. In general, Hollywood movie studios obtain more income from overseas operations than from North American operations. International airlines such as KLM (the Netherlands), British Airways (United Kingdom), Qantas (Australia), American Airlines (United States), and Lufthansa (Germany) have established strong competitive positions by operating worldwide networks through strategic alliances (Mockler 1999). Many advertising, legal, and consulting firms have expanded their multinational links because clients need integrated multinational services ("Lawyers Go Global" 2000; Owen and Peel 2000).

A firm's reasons for deciding to go or grow internationally are as varied as the ways to do it. Surviving, increasing sales, acquiring resources and expertise, cutting costs, diversifying into a significant and growing multinational business area, applying its expertise to new markets, serving and expanding an international customer base, or selling existing products in new markets are some of the reasons why firms compete multinationally.

A retail industry study, for example, identified two kinds of factors ("push" and "pull") affecting multinational growth (Davies and Finney 1998). "Push" factors included:

- Saturation of the home market or overcompetition
- Economic recession or limited growth in spending
- A declining or aging population
- Strict planning policies on store development
- High operating costs (labor, rents, taxation)
- Shareholder pressure to maintain profit growth
- The "me-too" syndrome in retailing

"Pull" factors included:

- The underdevelopment of some markets or weak competition
- Strong economic growth or rising standards of living
- High population growth or a high concentration of young adults

- A relaxed regulatory environment
- Favorable operating costs (labor, rents, taxation)
- The geographical spread of trading risks
- The opportunity to innovate under new market conditions

Already having a strong global presence does not guarantee success in a world where hypercompetition—the disruption of existing markets by flexible, creative, fast-moving firms—is becoming the norm. Survival and growth require taking advantage of a global presence by continually:

- Adapting to local competitive conditions, as Coca-Cola and McDonald's have done
- Exploiting economies of global scale, as Gillette did in manufacturing its razors
- Selecting the facility location where the firm has a competitive advantages, as Mitsubishi did with its auto parts and manufacturing plants in Asia
- Maximizing knowledge transfer, as Whirlpool did with its compressor technology (Govindarajan and Gupta 1998)

Home Depot, the world's largest home improvement retailer (1,332 stores), opened its first overseas location in Chile in August 1998 in partnership with Falabella, an experienced Chilean upscale department store chain. Home Depot decided to pursue overseas markets because of the maturing U.S. market and because of the many "pull" factors listed previously. Chile was chosen because of its expanding middle class and predictable free-market policies. In Chile, Home Depot trained and used local managers, adapted its product line to local conditions, and focused on one geographic area—the lower-and middle-class suburbs surrounding Santiago where construction rates were the highest (Krauss 1998).

Shortly after the store opened, however, the spreading world economic crisis hit Chile. Unemployment was expected to rise, the local stock market fell sharply, and auto and home sales were declining rapidly. However, these events were not expected to have a lasting effect on Home Depot's overseas expansion in Chile. By mid-1999, Chile's economy and stock market had begun to recover (Torres 1999), and the company expected to have five stores in Chile by the year 2001, even though short-term profits had been hurt.

In spite of problems in overseas markets, globalization is accelerating. For example, there have been mergers or acquisitions of billion-dollar firms such as: Vodafone Air Touch PLC (United Kingdom) and Mannesmann AG (Germany); MeritaNordbanken (Finish-Swedish) and Unidanmark (Denmark); and Citigroup (United States) and Bank Handlowy (Poland) (Baker and Capell 2000; Raghavan 2000; Wagstyl and Bobinski 2000). Similar activity has also increased in Asia as financial crises have led to bargain-basement prices for many firms. After focusing on domestic businesses for decades, NTT (Japan's largest telecommunications firm) moved aggressively in 1999 to expand internationally (Nakamoto 1999a).

The decision to go multinational has also been affected by the Internet. The Internet enables both large and small companies to extend the scope of their operations into foreign countries with relative ease and often with minimal costs. The implications of the Internet in multinational strategic management is discussed throughout the chapters in Parts Two and Three.

## KEY MARKETING
## AND PRODUCTION/OPERATIONS ENABLING TASKS

### Selecting a Market Area

A wide array of potential overseas markets exists. For example, the unified European market, established in 1992, may eventually exceed the United States in potential opportunities. Newly-freed Eastern Bloc countries, such as Hungary, the Czech Republic, and Poland, also present opportunities. In mid-2000, Deutsche Telekom announced that it had purchased controlling interest in Matav, Hungary's dominant telecommunications firm, and offered to buy controlling interest in Slovakia's fixed-line monopoly; it also had a stake in Croatia's main telecom firm and interests in Polish and Czech Republic firms (Eddy and Waters 2000). In the 1990s, Daewoo Motor (Korea) invested billions in Romania, Poland, the Czech Republic, the Ukraine, and Uzbekistan to establish a dominant position in these countries.

Markets in China, Australia, and other countries in the Pacific Rim also appear to have great potential for U.S. and European firms. However, there are problems, such as when several Asian countries reintroduced economic controls during the 1997-1998 Asian financial crisis, and when Chinese partners failed to fulfill contractual obligations, and when ineffective legal protection exists (Rosenthal 2000). With a population of more than 1.2 billion, China could become the largest opportunity area in the world, especially since the government overall appears to be supporting change ("China" 2000). Future opportunities appeared to be so great during the 1990s that $270 billion was invested by thousands of foreign firms in China, a situation which has resulted in major overinvestment ("Infatuation Ends" 1999). For example, auto firms rushed to build plants to the point where it was expected to be ten years before demand catches up to capacity. The large near-term losses due to overbuilding were expected to be eventually offset by long-term profits (Smith 1998). Although overall foreign investment in China and all of Asia dropped by more than 50 percent in 1998 and was expected to continue to fall through 1999, and some companies questioned China's real potential (Liu and Emerson 1999; Harding 1999a,b), many firms were still buying Asian businesses, some selling at huge discounts (WuDunn 1999). For example, in mid-2000, BP Amoco announced that it planned to invest $2 billion in China (Bahrem 2000), as China's economy appeared to be recovering (Leggett 2000). In 1999, there was also revised interest in investing in Japan, in spite of its major economic problems (Ullman 1999).

Another international future growth area is expected to be the former Soviet Union. Since its breakup in 1991, however, questions have arisen as to when and how that business potential might be realized. During the 1998 economic crisis in Russia, for example, experts estimated that it could take several decades before this potential might be realized, if ever (Banerjee 1999a; Rose and Michaels 1998).

Some of the key problems in investing in foreign countries are widespread crime and corruption, political unrest, political favoritism, a lack of contract protection, and a lack of guarantees that foreign firms will be able to repatriate their profits (Whalen and Bahree 2000). When Gillette negotiated to build a $50 million dollar razor-blade plant in Russia in 1990, for example, the outcome hinged on Russia's willingness to allow Gillette (the major shareholder in the new firm) to take profits out in hard currency. One solution was to allow Gillette to import its non-razor products produced elsewhere and pay for these purchases in hard currencies. Another problem in the former Soviet republics is increasing competition. For example, since the Soviet Union's breakup in 1991, over 300 new airlines have emerged and many local state-controlled firms have started ventures involving fast foods, real estate, high-speed trains, and a wide range of heavy industry and consumer businesses (King 1998). Despite the problems and new competitive initiatives, foreign firms are expected to continue investing in the former Soviet republics (Banerjee 1999b; Jack 1999).

Latin America also presents major opportunities. The Australian-based News Corporation, which in 1997 owned two satellite services (B Sky B (British Sky Broadcasting) in England and Star TV in Asia), announced in the mid-1990s the formation of a direct broadcast service in Latin America with three partners: Globo, the leading media firm in Brazil; Grupo Televisa, a giant Mexican broadcaster; and Tele-Communications Inc., one of the U.S.'s larger cable television operator. The partners' $500 million venture was designed to transmit 150 channels of sports, entertainment, and news programming to homes equipped with satellite dishes and digital receivers. Although the service had only one million subscribers initially, Rupert Murdoch, chairman of the News Corporation, believed that the service had a potential audience of more than 400 million. In the auto market, South American sales were expected to increase substantially over the long run, which is why Honda, DaimlerChrysler, Renault, and Ford were opening auto plants in Brazil in 1999-2000, in spite of a short-term 30 percent drop in auto sales in 1998 (Barham 1999; Romero 1999).

Problems were expected in South America, however, because of fluctuating economies and continuing violent crimes against multinational firms (Schemo 1998). In addition, opportunities varied from country to country and time to time. For example, by early 2000 the cost of doing business in Brazil dropped sharply, making Argentina's production comparatively uneconomical; as a result, dozens of Argentinean firms moved their plants to Brazil, which received $29 billion in foreign direct investment in 1999, while Argentina's unemployment rate rose to over 15 percent (Katz 2000).

Although generally a mature market, Europe represents an opportunity area for many companies. Rupert Murdoch, for example, has taken a major step to expand into Italy (Betts 1999) and is seeking other alliances in Europe, which he sees as a major growth area in telecommunications (Reed, Resch, and Ewing 1999).

Africa and India are other markets with enormous potential (Kristof 1997; "India" 1997). Due to economic and social problems, Africa's potential does not seem realizable in the near future, however (Bayart, Ellis, and Hibou 1999; Chabal and Daloz 1999). India also has many problems to overcome, especially major political uncertainties.

In turn, the United States presents major international opportunities for foreign firms. During a nine-month period in 1999, foreign firms spent more than $256 billion—more than double that of the 1998 period—to buy U.S. companies, especially high technology ones, to take advantage of the comparatively stable and favorable U.S. market (Deogun 1999). This trend continued in 2000, as companies such as Deutsche Telekom, Vivendi and Suez Lyonnaise des Eaux (French multiutility firms), UBS (a Swiss bank), and ING (a Dutch financial group) made billions of dollars of acquisitions of U.S. firms (Andrews 2000; Carreyrou 2000; McGeehan and Sorkin 2000; Owen, Iskander, and Taylor 1999). Many were successful in penetrating the U.S. market. For example, Corona beer, produced by Grupo Modelo of Mexico, in less than a decade, has become a global brand whose name recognition approaches that of Coca-Cola and Marlboro cigarettes. Clever marketing has made it the tenth largest selling beer in the United States (Tejada 2000).

Multinational investments are not without risks, however. In the mid-1990s, Sony took a $3.2 billion write-off on its investment in Columbia and TriStar Pictures, and Mitsubishi lost close to $2 billion on its investment in Rockefeller Center in New York. In 1997, Mitsubishi announced the write-off of $341.5 million in losses from its U.S. auto sales subsidiary (Bloomberg 1997; Rudolph 1994). In 1999, Brazilian construction magnate, Sergio Naya, was fighting to stave off foreclosure of his $40 million investment in

Florida (U.S.) real estate (Fritsch 1999) and Sony quit the cellular phone market in North America (Nakamoto 1999b).

These examples show why extensive decision situation analyses are required when making an overall strategic decision to go overseas and when selecting an overseas market. Situation factors which require analysis range from general country, area, and regional factors such as the political climate, national economy, exchange rates, and cultural climate, to competitive market and internal company resource factors. These factors and their impact on this decision are discussed in Chapter 4.

The decision as to which market to enter is often made simultaneously with management decisions in such areas as determining what product or service to offer, the entry/operating method to use, and the location and type of facilities.

### Basic Marketing Activities: Products and Services to Be Offered; Pricing, Distribution, and Promotion

This task area, which is discussed in Chapter 5, as with other enabling marketing tasks, can involve enterprise-wide, business unit, and functional levels. This area's underlying entrepreneurial focus, at the enterprise-wide and business unit planning levels, is on deciding how to differentiate products, services, or brands from those of competitors. It also includes identifying core company competencies—such as low pricing, wide or select distribution, and promotion—that can be used to build competitive advantages in multinational and domestic markets. In contrast, a key functional level decision in this area might be how to modify a product mix strategy to effectively meet local requirements.

Several strategies exist for identifying and marketing existing, new, or redesigned products or services when entering and competing in international markets. Many companies choose a *global* marketing approach to product design, selection, promotion, pricing, distribution, and packaging. Global strategies involve using the same products and/or marketing approaches in all countries served. A *multinational* or *market-by-market* approach is often needed, however, due to local circumstances. Distribution, pricing, and promotion mixes are highly dependent on local needs.

A *mixed strategy,* which combines some aspects of the global approach with whatever modifications are necessary to meet local requirements, is often used. A company marketing decaffeinated coffee, for example, might use a global company name, such as Nestlé, but modify the formula country by country to meet local tastes and government regulations. McDonald's used this approach when developing its *"glocal"* strategy in India. Beer companies use a different kind of mixed strategy, by promoting and distributing local and international beers in the same markets.

Major changes affecting strategic management have been occurring in this area with the Internet. The Internet enables businesses to sell products and distribute knowledge directly to consumers (e-commerce, B2C (Business-to-Customer) retailing, and news distribution, for example) and to businesses (called Business-to-Business—B2B—commerce), a process of disintermediation. The strategic management impact of the Internet on these and other marketing areas is discussed in Chapter 5.

### *Method of Entry/Operating*

Three major strategies used to enter and operate in an overseas market are discussed in Chapter 5: wholly-owned investment (buying an existing company or setting up a wholly-owned subsidiary); joint ventures/strategic alliances (buying a percentage interest in an existing company or entering into cooperative or partnership arrangements); and exporting products to a country. Alliances are becoming especially important in light of the growing need to build relationships that quickly transfer knowledge and expertise in response to rapidly changing market forces, for example, in the telecommunications and e-business areas. The specific approach used in individual situations depends on situation requirements.

### *Location and Type of Facilities*

Another primary multinational strategic decision involves the location and type of facilities in a chosen international location. This key production/operations and marketing management, business unit, and enterprise-wide management decision and action area is discussed in Chapters 5 and 6.

In 1984, Compaq located a plant in Scotland to serve the market in Great Britain. The Scottish location was chosen because of that country's lower labor costs and high unemployment rate. Another factor affecting the decision was the educational (technical schools) and business (electronics parts supply companies) infrastructure in the computer industry in Scotland. This location proved to be a wise choice after the formation of the European Community in 1992, as it gave Compaq a low-cost entry to the entire European market. Northern England and Scotland have continued to be prime locations for facilities in the 1990s.

### *Managing the Production/Operations Transformation Process*

The production/operations transformation process involves:

- Developing general planning directions: formulating overall production/operations strategies
- Creating the product or service: product and service design and development

- Developing facilities to produce the product or render the service: designing production/operations systems
- Producing the product or rendering the service: planning and managing the production/operations function

These tasks are discussed in detail in Chapter 6.

## SUPPLY CHAIN MANAGEMENT

### Critical Production/Operations Decision Areas

The supply chain, like the value-added chain, involves activities ranging from sourcing materials for manufacturing through delivering products to distribution channels and customers.

Sourcing refers to both sourcing and logistics activities. Sourcing refers to where and how a company obtains the raw materials, subcontracted components, and other goods and materials needed to produce goods and services. Basically, firms have two sourcing alternatives: company-owned or controlled plants (vertical integration) or other companies (outsourcing). In addition, materials may either be sourced in the country where it is needed, or from overseas. International logistics involve the design and management of a business process or system that controls the flow of materials and products into, through, and out of the company. Two phases of logistics are especially important to managers: materials management (the movement of raw materials, parts, and supplies through the firm), and physical distribution (the movement of the finished product to the customer).

Using overseas sources is an important strategy and, like most important strategies, is influenced by the length of supply lines, production costs and quality, inventory levels, local import and tariff regulations, and currency fluctuations. Many companies find such outsourcing very profitable and useful. GM, for example, has in the past had agreements with Japan's Suzuki Motor Corporation, Isuzu Motors Inc., and Toyota, as well as with South Korea's Daewoo Corporation, to procure parts for its U.S. production plants.

When making decisions, an international logistics manager, as described in Chapter 6, considers such factors as: inventory (order cycle time, customer-service levels, and strategic needs of the firm, such as protection against inflation and devaluation); transportation (transit time, cost, and government regulations); packaging (size, weight, and customer specifications); and storage (available space within each country or area, cost, and location).

Supply and value chains are changing rapidly with the growth of digital technologies, which enable for example, as discussed in Chapter 6, bypassing intermediaries and reducing transaction costs substantially by using the

Internet, a major strategic management shift (Deutsch 2000; Downes and Mui 1998).

### Telecommunications/Information Systems

Advanced technologies in telecommunications and computer information systems have been a major driving force in managing businesses multinationally. Company information systems need to be coordinated and consolidated globally, while also being responsive to local needs. To support such systems, telecommunications systems links, often using worldwide services such as the Internet, need to be developed to support worldwide information systems architectures and enable local firm computer systems to operate effectively and efficiently throughout multinational company operations. Creating these information systems and the supporting telecommunications links requires analyzing such factors as the business involved, resources available, the countries involved, human resource capabilities, and the competitive market. The specific decision and implementation activities involved in this area, as well as the strategic management impact of such new technologies as the Internet, are discussed in Chapter 7 and throughout this book.

### Finance, Accounting, Taxation, and Control

Tasks in the key areas of finance and accounting (discussed in Chapter 8) affect most multinational operations. Basic financial decisions include determining the means by which funds are managed, allocated, and used. Financial reporting about a firm's financial position is a major task in this area. Such decisions can involve whether to obtain financing through local sources, such as government loans and banks, or to finance outside the overseas local area. In many instances, basic financial strategies are dictated by the entry method—which can involve full or shared ownership—as well as by a company's financial condition and its policy regarding financing expansion through long-term debt, equity, retained earnings, or short-term borrowing.

The fact that many accounting standards differ from country to country makes the preparation of financial statements consistent with the general accounting principles prevalent in the home country a challenging task for multinational firms. For example, a U.S. firm normally must produce an annual consolidated statement of earnings showing all the firm's operations in U.S. dollars converted at current exchange rates. At the same time, overseas subsidiaries need earnings statements in local currencies for use in their home countries. Meeting the requirements of consolidated and local reporting for both internal and external control, taxation, and management purposes is a difficult task. Common accounting standards and software able to function across national boundaries are being developed, but change is slow in coming.

As discussed in Chapter 8, several factors besides exchange rates affect accounting strategies and systems. These include: the overall objectives and policies of the firm; the accounting systems of the parent company and subsidiaries; the structure of the enterprise (corporation, proprietorship, or partnership); the nature of the industry; the internal and external users of information (management, owners, employees, investors, bankers, tax authorities, and creditors); the local government and its policies and regulations regarding taxation and money transfer; the relationship between parent and subsidiaries; the availability of electronic transfer facilities through the Internet; local cultural attitudes; the nature and state of the economy; the level of competition; and international influences, such as global professional accounting standards and auditing practices.

### Organization Structure, Processes (Business and Human), and Culture

As discussed in Chapter 9, several factors affect the organization of multinational business, including language and other cultural differences, geographic distances, the people involved, the nature of the business, intensely competitive and rapidly changing markets, technological advances, and changing company strategies.

In the past, three types of organization structures were generally used: *global,* in which a firm treats overseas operations as delivery pipelines to a unified global market; *international,* in which a firm regards overseas operations as appendages to a central domestic organization; and *multinational,* in which a firm regards overseas operations as a portfolio of independent enterprises (Bartlett and Ghoshal 1991). Problems are encountered with all three options.

Changing worldwide competitive market conditions have led to reduced emphasis on organization structure and more emphasis on administrative and business processes and systems, communication channels, and interpersonal relationships and leadership. As a result, hybrid organization structures with their exact form tailored to meet specific situation needs have become more common.

Organizations being developed today strive to balance the need to maintain global efficiencies, allow responsiveness to different local needs, and enable the transfer of new knowledge rapidly among divisions. The key is flexibility and adaptability, as seen in the description of GE's enterprise-wide strategy in Figure 2.1 in Chapter 2.

Corporate culture has also evolved to meet changing market needs. For example, Coca-Cola went so far as to ban the words "domestic" and "foreign" from its corporate vocabulary in order to bolster the image of a single, global firm which expected 90 percent of sales to come from non-U.S. sources by the year 2001.

As in other multinational strategic management task areas, the final organization concept, or form, appropriate for a firm depends on the needs of the industry, company, people, and markets involved. The form almost always evolves and changes as market leaders and competitive market conditions change (Bartlett and Ghoshal 1991). For example, with the rapid growth of the Internet and other digital technologies, new organization forms and business processes are evolving. Organization is another major strategic management area substantially affected by the Internet, as discussed in Chapters 7 and 9.

### Human Resources (Interpersonal Interaction, Leadership and Management, Staffing and Training, and Communications)

The role of leadership and management is changing as organizations and the international markets in which they compete change. Balancing factors such as local responsiveness and global efficiencies requires strong leadership and management. As seen in the leadership/management tasks listed in Figure 1.6, such leadership clearly identifies strategic frameworks, communicates those frameworks and reinforces a corporate culture consistent with them, establishes adaptive enabling systems (accounting and finance, telecommunication/information (including electronic links), and organization operating areas), maintains a core management group which can translate that balance into day-to-day operations, and intervenes where needed to ensure that integrative activities are operating effectively and efficiently to achieve strategic short- and long-term objectives.

The many different leadership styles, manager selection and training programs, communication channels and tools, and management processes used to manage human resources in multinational management situations are discussed in Chapters 10 through 12.

### STRATEGIC ALLIANCES

Strategic alliances are joint ventures, partnerships, and other types of cooperative arrangements among businesses which involve a continuing active relationship over an extended period of time (Mockler 1999). They are based on common goals and interests which are difficult to fully define and which often change over time, as business needs change. As discussed in Chapter 13, the factors affecting strategic alliance success include: alignment of strategic frameworks; importance of alliance to competitive success of all partners; relative contribution of partners; clarity of definition of shared activities; conflict with other business areas of partners; available protection of proprietary knowledge; ability to precisely measure each partner's contribution; cost and difficulty of measuring and controlling activities and contributions over time; compatibility and adaptability of partners involved; comparable levels of worker and management knowledge and expertise of the people involved; major cultural differences; and many external factors such as government intervention and control, industry practices, local market and competitive differences, and government stability. Alliances are becoming especially important in the age of the Internet's ease-of-access across borders and the related telecommunications links, as discussed in Chapters 7 and 13.

### A Cellular Phone Venture in Tashkent

The experiences of a group of investors from the state of Georgia in the United States in creating a new venture in Tashkent, Uzbekistan, illustrate the dynamics of formulating and implementing a strategic framework in light of complex situation factors and multiple tasks involved (Guyon 1996). The investors' strategy was simple: use their experience with cellular phone franchises in the United States to start a similar venture in one of the former USSR states with a need for up-to-date communications services. The details of this successful venture's strategy were worked out along the way.

At first, the investors considered Moscow, but found little interest there in their small venture. At the suggestion of those with whom they negotiated in Russia during an exploratory visit in 1990, they next studied Tashkent in Uzbekistan, then the fourth-largest city in the former Soviet republics, since it fit their desired strategic market profile with its 2.2 million population and poor phone service.

The new venture, named International Communications Group (ICG), invited Uzbekistan's minister of communications to visit Georgia, where the partners showed him the South Carolina cellular systems. The investors also invited President Jimmy Carter to talk with their visitor. Another critical factor was that many large firms were uninterested in Tashkent and the new venture was the first to trust and believe in Tashkent's future.

On August 19, 1991, ICG formed a joint venture with the then Soviet republic of Uzbekistan, with the ownership split 45 percent for ICG and 55 percent for the Uzbeks. The Americans agreed to finance construction of the system, named Uzdunrobita. Soon after, Uzbekistan declared its independence from the USSR, and the Americans hastily persuaded the Uzbeks to reregister the venture from Moscow to Tashkent because of legal uncertainties.

Another problem was that Uzdunrobita had no working capital and the Americans had not raised money to buy equipment. Up to this time, ICG had spent $500,000 on travel, translation, and documents. To raise money, ICG sold more than 50 percent of its equity to a group of Pakistanis, for which the Americans got $2 million and a stake in a Pakistani pay-phone firm. They also raised some money by persuading Uzbek Air, the nation's airline, to buy $160,000 worth of phones and to give Uzdunrobita an office in Tashkent, a desk, a car, and several Uzbek staff members. The Uzbek government allowed the venture to use a dozen of its best engineers and computer software designers, as well as its best government expediters. Using $10 million in loans and equipment from Northern Telecom, Uzdunrobita expanded to eight Uzbek cities and planned to one day expand throughout the country.

Problems to overcome were many: personnel clashes had to be resolved, differences in accounting systems had to be understood and reconciled, and government contacts and family ties had to be nurtured and used to assure the venture's success. The U.S. partners were guided through these problems by their Uzbek partners, who suggested little touches such as giving free phones to Uzbekistan's president which eventually led to many government officials and agencies buying them. Commercial customers, such as a local import company, gladly paid $1,100 to buy a Nokia phone, since the decayed state of the local landline phone system (built in the 1920s) made it impossible to do business without it.

The partners had to adapt to dress codes, eating styles, language barriers, airlines with erratic service and doubtful maintenance facilities, and government steps to introduce new competitors in violation of the venture contract. Problems with hard currency conversion made the payment of dividends difficult.

After five years the venture appeared to have been a success. It turned its first profit in 1993, with revenues close to $50 million in 1996 (triple 1995), 7,000 subscribers, 224 employees, and an estimated value of close to $100 million, giving the Americans an estimated 40 times their original investment. Major companies such as Motorola, Inc., Telenor of Norway, and Northern Telecom were wooing the venture for equipment contracts, communications link-ups, and a piece of the company's equity.

## SUMMARY

When training for a sport, it is often necessary during the early stages of learning to segment the process into component activities that can be learned and practiced. In a similar way, this has been done in this chapter and in the following chapters to enable learning multinational strategic management. In real life, however, one must go beyond merely mastering techniques and learn to blend these segmented techniques creatively, as was done in the Tashkent situation. To perform successfully, one must practice putting techniques to work synergistically in an integrated way, as when performing a sport.

In multinational strategic management, considerable integrative thinking and action—at the enterprise-wide, business unit, and operating levels—are needed when formulating and implementing strategies. In a sense, the tasks outlined in Figure 1.6 are carried out within the integrated processes outlined in Figures 1.2, 1.3, 1.4, and 1.5. This integrated orientation is essential in multinational management for several reasons.

- First, the tasks in practice are often interrelated: when deciding on a method of entry, for example, one would consider financial, marketing, production, logistics, product, and people factors.
- Second, in each task area, a manager is involved in both planning and doing, as strategic considerations blend with operating activities, which in turn help give greater definition to strategies.
- Third, all of these activities must be carried out with their present and longer-term future implications, as well as the requirements of global efficiency, local efficiency, and rapid transfer of knowledge, in mind (Bartlett and Ghoshal 1991). Success depends not only on business plans and their execution, but also on the people and larger global and regional contexts involved in a particular situation.

Clearly, some sense of the concept of an enterprise-wide and business unit strategy or vision is needed. This involves understanding the ways in which a firm's products or services differ from those of competitors. These differences can include: brand perception; product characteristics, availability, performance, or customization; patent protection; service (quality, speed, or proximity); facilities; cost and price; available financing; or in any other core competency the firm has in performing functions in a critical area of the value chain in the competitive market in a superior way. As shown in the discussions throughout this book, many firms strive to create strategic differentiation through the use of the Internet in different ways. These factors can help define a significant kind of differentiated franchise or brand image a company has (or can establish and maintain) in the customer's mind.

Supporting services through a wide range of enabling marketing, finance, production/operations, technology, finance and accounting, organization, and other functional plans, programs, projects, and activities is needed to support strategic objectives. These mechanisms are often put in place as strategies are formulated. They are essential to maintaining the company's abilities to entrepreneurially anticipate and change and to create future markets in rapidly changing worldwide markets.

These capabilities may evolve over time as they become more defined, change with market changes, or emerge in response to anticipated new markets and rapidly changing trends in all firms. How the process unfolds in integrating tasks, decisions, and actions depends on the company, industry, and people involved.

The multinational firm, 3M, provides an example of this integrative process at work. In anticipation of the unification of European markets, the company brought together representatives of its twenty-three plants and forty divisions in Europe, formed teams, and developed plans to consolidate its European operations. Its first moves were to increase research and development, coordinate advertising and other marketing programs, and consolidate production. The result was a new, coordinated European effort. For instance, a new product—the Soft Scour cleaning sponge—was developed at 3M's French consumer products laboratory, manufactured in its Spanish plant, and marketed across Europe by 3M's British subsidiary. At the same time, local tastes were still accommodated.

## *REVIEW QUESTIONS*

1. List four key strategic leadership/management activities involved in carrying out the multinational strategic management job and explain what is involved in each activity.
2. What are enterprise-wide strategic concepts and how are they put into action? Give examples from the text and from your experiences and readings.
3. Describe the strategic framework developed and used by Jack Welch at GE. In what ways can it be adapted for use by other companies? In what ways is it unique to GE?
4. Why are strategic frameworks said to "emerge" over time in the multinational environment? Give examples.
5. Describe and discuss the reasons why companies go international.
6. Describe the critical factors that affect multinational market selection and give examples of how these factors have affected different company decisions.
7. Describe three major strategies used to enter an overseas market and give some examples of company experiences in using each.
8. Discuss what is involved in determining the need (and extent) to adapt global products to local markets.
9. Discuss the significance of telecommunications and computer information systems to success in multinational businesses.

10. Describe the critical factors affecting multinational production/operations management and give examples of how these factors have affected different company production/operations decisions.
11. Describe major organization approaches to multinational business and the ways in which human resources management affects the kinds of organization structures used. Give examples of situations which help explain why the emphasis has shifted away from organization structures. What are the keys to succeeding in today's highly competitive multinational environment?
12. Describe and discuss the integrative and adaptive nature of multinational strategic leadership and management.

## *EXERCISES*

1. Read recent issues of periodicals of your choice and find articles relating to:
   Enterprise-wide strategies. Prepare a written report detailing the strategies of different multinational companies and how they relate to concepts discussed in the chapter.
   Find a strategy that went wrong and one that was successful and write an explanation of why it did or did not work.
2. Read recent issues of periodicals and detail the experiences of companies relating to review question number four.
3. Prepare a written report describing the major opportunities and the critical factors affecting the success of a company looking to expand internationally.

# Chapter 4

# Structured Analysis of Rapidly Changing Multinational Situations

Multinational strategic management is a contingency process. Specific situation knowledge is, therefore, needed to perform all aspects of multinational strategic management.

Multinational management is affected by situation factors in many ways. For example, a newly-elected government in Mongolia in the 1990s moved to privatize 60 percent of state-owned firms, creating joint venture opportunities for multinational firms (Tomlinson 1998). In 2000, however, a communist government was elected, which slowed the progress of privatization (Kynge 2000b,c). In India, McDonald's adapted its products in response to cultural biases against meat by serving Vegetable McBurgers and McNuggets.

Key situation factors were considered when a Russian and two Americans, all in their twenties, proposed a sports/fitness center in Moscow. First, they studied the target market: there were an estimated 500,000 expatriates and wealthy Russians to support such a center, which in the United States serves a middle-class market. Capital was raised from outside Russia, since people who owe money in Russia often get murdered. The Russian partner was a key enabler in forging the government connections necessary to get equipment through customs without considerable expense and delays. The facility was designed to balance American and Russian cultures. Based on these situation analyses, the trio opened the Moscow gym in early 1997 (Specter 1997; Vitullo-Martin 1997).

The experiences of the cellular phone venture in Tashkent described at the end of Chapter 3 also shows the adaptive nature of multinational management in response to key situation factors.

This chapter gives an overview of the context analysis involved in acquiring and restructuring (reconceiving) knowledge needed for multinational strategic management decision making and action in the areas discussed in Chapter 3 and shown in Figure 1.6. This context analysis' relation to the strategic management process is shown in Figure 1.2 (p. 7).

Due to the wide range of situations involved, the process outlined is general and is just one effective way—not the only way—to model such analyses. Within this structured context analysis, a considerable amount of unstructured entrepreneurial and innovative thinking and action is required to gain the insights needed to win against competitors over the short-, intermediate, and long-term.

The following discussion is developed in four parts: general external factors; competitive market factors; internal company factors; and focusing on the future. The time and effort needed for a context study depends on the knowledge, training, and experience of the manager involved. The situation analysis begins with the external environment because an outside-inside orientation, which focuses on customers and competitors, is an effective way to stay in touch with rapidly changing markets, as opposed to an inside-outside perspective, which, while important, often overly emphasizes what a company is presently doing (Tichy and Charan 1999).

## CRITICAL FACTORS AFFECTING THE GENERAL EXTERNAL MULTINATIONAL ENVIRONMENT

Factors affecting multinational management are listed in the left-hand box of the context analysis section of Figure 1.2.

### Political Climate

*Political climate* refers to the general nature of a country's governing systems and practices. In Sweden, for example, the political climate is relatively calm and stable. In contrast, in Lebanon, mob rule, terrorism, and anarchy are prevalent.

Political systems can affect business in many ways. For example, in most countries, various government approvals are needed to do business. In some countries, such as England, this approval process is clearly established and can be pursued in an orderly fashion. In contrast, in developing countries, the process for obtaining approvals can be unclear, and often requires considerable knowledge of local customs and the people involved, as well as payoffs to well-positioned people.

In India, the Enron Development Corporation had to fight to save a $2.8 billion power plant project. Five months after Enron began construction, a newly elected government in the state of Maharashtra "repudiated" the contract that was negotiated with the previous local government and with the national government in New Dehli. The problem was resolved only after Enron made concessions and threatened to sue. In spite of the problems, Enron continued to build power plants and pipelines and to expand existing facilities. Its efforts even led India to change its laws on business arbitration (O'Reilly 2000).

The two most familiar political systems are democracy and totalitarianism. *Democratic* societies can range from decentralized systems, as in Canada, where the provinces have considerable power (for example, over trade treaty decisions), to countries such as the United States, where the central government maintains stronger control over the states (which still often are free to tax foreign income), to highly centralized governments such as those in Japan and France. Each type of democracy has some form of free-market economy, although that freedom is carefully circumscribed and directed in a variety of ways in some instances. For example, in the past, Japanese firms developed a wide range of interrelationships among themselves (called Keiretsus), often through cross-holdings of stock, which tended to lock out foreign firms, especially at the distribution and supply levels. This system is changing, however, as Keiretsus are beginning to dissolve in response to increasing competitive pressures and deregulation (Williams and Landers 2000).

*Totalitarian* systems can range from those that are religion dominated, such as those in the Middle Eastern Islamic countries such as Iran, to those that are secular and usually dominated by military power, such as in Cambodia, Haiti, and Iraq. Communism, a familiar totalitarian form, is experiencing a period of transition from a controlled to a hybrid form of free-market system in the former USSR, China, and elsewhere, which creates political uncertainty. For example, four routes were considered for pipelines to move oil from the Caspian Sea near Azerbaijan in late 1998. The most expensive route—through Turkey—was seriously being considered over cheaper routes through Iran and Russia where political risks were greater (Kinzer 1998).

In addition to responding to the political environment by adapting operations, businesses often become activists and start programs to bring about change. For example, steps including threats of trade sanctions were taken by the U.S. government in the 1990s to force the Chinese government to require businesses in their country to comply with international copyright law.

Many governments worldwide, including those in Albania, Brazil, the Baltic Countries (Estonia, Latvia, Lithuania), Egypt, India, Nigeria, Pakistan, Poland, Russia, Slovakia, and South Africa, are moving to create a favorable free-market investment climate ("Survey: Albania" 2000; "Survey: Baltic Countries" 2000; "Survey: Brazil" 1999, 2000; "Survey: Egypt" 2000; "Survey: India and Pakistan" 1999; "Survey: Indonesia" 2000; "Survey: Nigeria" 2000; "Survey: Poland" 2000; "Survey: Russia" 2000; "Survey: Slovakia": 2000; "Survey: South Africa," 1999).

Circumstances can change, however, as when governments reintroduced controls in 1998 in response to the Asian financial crises. Countries such as China are continually changing the ground rules. In early 2000, China abruptly forbade foreign magazines published in Chinese from using their famous names and logos (Rose 2000), and also introduced restrictive regulations for the Internet; both were major strategic limitations (Landler 2000).

## Protective Government Policies and Barriers

Governments can raise a wide range of selective nontariff barriers to restrain trade. These include:

- Subsidies, including low-interest loans, capital, and procurement preferences
- Import quotas
- Domestic preferences, including buying only domestically manufactured goods, shipping only on domestic flag ships, and offering preferential treatment in contracting for minority or other socially favored or disadvantaged domestic groups
- Customs and administrative procedures, including country-of-origin markings that raise costs, limited ports of entry, and arbitrary customs' valuations
- Technical and regulatory barriers, including license requirements, limited facilities, holding periods for selected goods, excessive standards and testing/inspection procedures, and distribution requirements

These barriers are sometimes created for economic and political reasons. Governments may wish to protect domestic industries or monopolies. After India agreed to allow imports of chicken parts, local producers complained and the government raised tariffs from 35 to 100 percent to protect local producers (Dugger 2000). Governments may desire to balance trade payments, maintain the domestic supply of goods, assure consumers of lower prices, provide consumer protection, or simply favor politically connected interest (even family) groups, as frequently occurs in Indonesia (McCawley 2000). The General Agreement on Tariffs and Trade (GATT) is the main negotiating body through which countries multilaterally reduce trade barriers and agree on simplified mechanisms for conducting international trade.

During the 1990s, there was a trend toward deregulation worldwide, accompanied by a major increase in privatization of government-owned firms. For example, Brazil has started to deregulate telecommunications, a program which will be complete in 2002. The program has not only forced local telephone firms such as Telefonica to substantially improve services, but also allowed firms such as Telecom Italia to compete in Brazil's mobile phone market (Barnham 1999; Chionna and Mockler 1999).

Still, problems exist. For example, Deutsche Bank (Germany) has had difficulty reaching its goal of being Europe's "Bank of Choice" because of political and cultural pressures. Instead of expanding through major hostile merger bids (which governments and country publics resist), or through opening up new branch networks, which it has tried in Italy (280 branches) and Spain (260 branches), the bank has been forced to use a variety of non-traditional expansion approaches. For example, in France it opened fifteen branches to serve wealthy customers, and in some countries it seeks well-established local partners to sell its products. Deutsche Bank is also exploring ways to set up cooperative bank holding companies that would allow local banks to remain independent while they participate in joint ventures with Deutsche Bank in select geographic and product areas (Harnischfeger 1999).

Even in the United States many protective barriers exist. For example, Internet retailers have found that individual states often place restrictions on online companies. For example, contact lens, music, automobiles, and wine e-tailers have all encountered state regulations and limiting law suits in their efforts to sell across state borders, a major strategic management planning limitation factor.

### Cross-National Agreements

Cross-national agreements affect businesses in many ways because they regulate commerce among nations. The most familiar agreements are the European Union (EU) and the Canadian-U.S. Free Trade Agreement (FTA), which was renamed the North American Free Trade Agreement (NAFTA) when it expanded to include Mexico.

In 1999, the EU was comprised of Austria, Belgium, Denmark, Finland, France, Germany, Greece, Ireland, Italy, Luxembourg, The Netherlands, Portugal, Spain, Sweden, and the United Kingdom. Some of the EU's goals have been to abolish intrazonal restrictions on the movement of goods, capital, services, and labor; establish a common external tariff; achieve a common agricultural policy; harmonize tax and legal systems; devise a uniform policy concerning antitrust laws; and supersede national currencies. NAFTA is designed to eliminate tariff barriers and liberalize investment opportunities in North America. The inclusion of Latin American countries would make this an even more powerful economic bloc. Latin American and African efforts to create regional trading agreements have been unsuccessful, but an Asian group of some form will probably emerge over the next decade. Another example of a cross-national agreement is the Organization of Petroleum Exporting Countries (OPEC), a producers' alliance organized in 1960 that effectively forced historic increases in crude oil prices. The drop in worldwide demand for crude oil and the increase in supplies from non-OPEC producers has greatly reduced OPEC's influence for a time, but a new cartel that includes Norway and Mexico in 1999 contributed to the doubling of oil prices. China's desire to join the World Trade Organization (WTO), another worldwide organization, led to many internal reforms in China to meet WTO standards (Cooper and Johnson 2000).

### General Trade Theory and Related Overall Economic Factors

An understanding of general trade theory can be helpful in identifying forces that affect a country's major economic choices.

Adam Smith developed a general trade theory called the *theory of absolute advantage,* which holds that consumers will be better off if they can buy foreign-made products that are cheaper than domestic ones. According to the theory, a country may produce goods more cheaply because of a natural advantage (for example, raw material availability or favorable climate) or because of an acquired advantage (for example, technology or skills).

Many other theories exist concerning the optimum economic configurations given a country's circumstances. For example, the *factor-proportions theory* holds that a country's relative endowments of land, labor, and capital determine the relative costs of these factors. These costs, in turn, determine which goods the country can produce most efficiently. The *product life cycle (PLC) theory* states that many manufactured products are first produced in the countries in which they were researched and developed (usually industrialized nations). Over the product's life cycle, production tends to become more capital intensive and shifts to foreign locations. According to the *country-similarity theory,* most trade today occurs among industrial countries because they share similar market segments.

The *theory of country* states that countries with large land areas are more likely to have varied climates and natural resources, and so are generally more self-sufficient than smaller countries. A second reason for greater self-sufficiency is that large countries' production centers are more likely to be located at a greater distance from other countries, raising foreign trade transportation costs. The *comparative advantage theory* states that total output can be increased through foreign trade, even though one country may have an absolute advantage in the production of all products. *Mercantilist theory* proposes that a country should try to achieve a favorable balance of trade (exports greater than imports) in order to receive an influx of gold. Finally, *neomercantilist* policy also seeks a favorable balance of trade, but its purpose is to achieve a particular social or political objective.

Understanding the forces underlying a country's economy and its impact is important for several reasons. For example, when Japan was developing a national trade strategy for foreign expansion and Brazil was under consideration, interested Japanese companies, working with the government, prepared to invest there by appointing several top South American economists to university positions in Tokyo. The information these economists provided helped the Japanese determine the most promising industries, products, and trade strategies to invest in and pursue, given Brazil's structure, resources, and other overall economic factors affecting the future. In this way, the Japanese could target prime investment areas and develop ways to manage investments most profitably from an *overall economic theory perspective.*

In *The Competitive Advantage of Nations,* Michael Porter describes new forces affecting international trading strength, including the ability to support innovation, economies of scale, and rapid change (Porter 1990). Large companies (such as steel and automobile firms) often use overall economic studies, because these companies deal in major segments of an economy and so may be directly affected by broader movements. These overall economic factors are less important to many companies, however, since most companies devote their energies to responding to, and managing, a wide range of industry and competitive market factors.

### Exchange Rates and Controls

As inflation fluctuates, so do exchange rates. This can cause considerable variations in reported income for companies that report their income in the United States based on current exchange rates. In many instances, it can also lead to extraordinary income gains and losses. For example, in mid-1996, Japan's automakers were expected to gain considerable sales price advantages in the U.S. market as the value of the U.S. dollar increased by 39 percent in relation to the Japanese yen. Countries noted for widely fluctuating exchange rates, such as Brazil, pay particular attention to formulating strategies and tactics—such as dealing in currency futures—that are designed to minimize losses incurred from such fluctuations.

### Legal Systems

Since most business activity involves explicit or implied contracts, understanding different legal systems is critical in multinational business. Most countries base their laws on *civil law* (an explicit codified system), as opposed to *common law,* which is based on tradition, precedent, custom and usage, and interpretation by the courts. In some countries, for instance, whomever *registers* a brand name first (civil law) is more important under the law than who *uses* the name first (common law). The U.S. legal system combines aspects of civil and common law.

A third type of legal code is based on religion. Islamic law, for example, is based on the Koran, the Sunnah, the writings of Islamic scholars, and the consensus of the Muslim countries' legal communities. Such laws can affect the way in which interest is paid. Under Islamic law, for instance, interest cannot be charged. Consequently, it must be collected or paid indirectly through, for example, profit sharing—as is done with mutually-owned savings banks in other countries.

Labor laws are also a key planning factor. Many countries have strict laws governing such matters as the hiring and firing of workers, which severely limits management flexibility.

Law enforcement is lax and misused in many countries. For example, over the years, a rash of successful lawsuits against U.S. firms have terminated distribution agreements/contracts with Ecuadorian firms and discouraged investment there. In China, contracts are often broken (Rosenthal 2000). Many former USSR countries have little experience with Western contracts and also often break them. Ex-Soviet firms are often controlled by organized crime groups and corrupt government officials, making contract enforcement and free market operation difficult and dangerous. At the same time, the Internet's twenty-four-hour availability of discounts and special offers has led to changes in retail laws in countries such as Germany, which in turn has affected company strategies and strategic management (Atkins 2000).

Bribery and government corruption can be problems for firms operating overseas (Pope 2000; Reed and Portanger 1999). This is slowly changing, however, as many countries have begun to act against corruption in multinational business.

The key international business management issues affected by laws are: trade and investment regulation; intellectual property protection; regulation of financial flows; taxation; reporting requirements; ownership regulation; contractual relationships; international treaties; and dispute resolution.

### National Economy of Foreign Countries

Major differences exist among controlled (that is, public ownership of property and controlled resource allocation) and market-driven (that is, private ownership and a much lesser degree of control) economies. In a market-driven economy, wages and prices are generally set by market forces; labor and product availability are dictated, and resources are allocated by supply and demand. Consumer sovereignty and freedom to operate are key aspects of a market-driven economy. In controlled economies, such as those in the former USSR and China, the opposite is true. In most instances, the type of economic system is closely allied with the type of political system in place.

In practice, most economies are hybrid mixes of the two extremes, developed over the years to meet changing needs. In the United States, a major free-market economy, the government runs some utilities and, until recently, the postal service. In China and Russia, substantial entrepreneurial business activity exists even though neither country has moved fully away from being a controlled economy. In late 1999, for example, during its celebration of fifty years of communism, China made it clear that the government would continue to exercise tight control of businesses there ("The

Fireworks to Come" 1999). An uneven application of control in emerging economies was blamed in part for the crises in Asia and Russia during 1997 and 1998. Such crises are an ever-present danger when doing business multinationally.

Many economic factors impact on business activities whether countries have controlled, mixed, or free-market economies, and whether they are developed or emerging/developing countries. These include: convertibility of currency, unemployment, environmental protection, government spending and debt (external and internal), level of inflation, gross national product growth, privatization (degree and level of activity), existing infrastructures (for example, transportation, telecommunications, schools), balance of payments, disposable income, etc.

Countries with low per-capita income (so-called emerging or third-world countries), such as Brazil and China, present higher percentage growth opportunities than countries such as Germany where income levels are similar to or higher than those in the United States (so-called developed, industrial, or first world countries) but growth rates are lower. The inflation rate also affects how money is invested in a country. Local borrowing and low cash investment are preferred as a hedge against inflation when expanding into areas of high inflation, such as in Brazil in 1991 when the inflation rate exceeded 1,200 percent.

### Availability of Capital and Danger of Deflation

More recently, the abundance of capital has led to an increase in competitive market turbulence (Colvin 1999). For example, auto firms have rushed into China in anticipation of growth there—to a point where it is estimated that it will be ten years before the market will be able to absorb existing plant capacity. McDonald's will have doubled its locations worldwide from 1999-2002 (it took thirty years to build its present outlet base), another example of how available capital enables rapid growth today. Yet McDonald's same store sales in countries such as Argentina have fallen on a year-to-year basis due to intense local competition. Business's ability to increase production apparently far exceeds the market's ability to consume. As supply continues to exceed demand, deflation can result, creating pressures on profits, as in China in 1999, when the government restricted new factory building to stem deflation (Faison 1999b).

### Cultural Factors

Cultural factors—customs, values, beliefs, and behavior—are discussed in Chapter 10. Such factors can affect a wide range of business decisions, for example, colors used in advertising, product design and features, distribution systems used, the way employees are compensated, and how business negotiations and meetings are conducted. Culturally-based protocols can affect positioning at conference tables, the way people are addressed, and the order of introducing people. In the Muslim world, and specifically the Arabian Peninsula, women have not yet fully achieved a recognized place in business. For this reason, many Saudi Arabian merchants may be unwilling to deal with a female representative from an overseas exporter.

Several years ago, Coca-Cola adapted its logo "Enjoy Coke," to different cultures. In Russia, the word "enjoy" was changed to "drink," because "enjoy" had a more sensual connotation there. In China, Coca-Cola settled on a combination of Chinese characters meaning, "A thirst quencher that makes you happy." As a bonus, those characters are pronounced much like "Coca-Cola."

What a culture "believes" may outweigh facts. Monsanto Company, a U.S. crop-biotechnolgy firm, faced a major problem in Europe in 1999. Food grown from its bioengineered seeds was criticized as dangerous, even though U.S. and European regulators said that the food was safe and farmers loved the seeds which made crops easier to grow. Negative public attitudes, however, substantially hurt sales, and such reactions were spread to Japan, India, and Australia (Kilman and Cooper 1999; Stipp 2000). Some attributed the problem to cultural differences: Americans generally do not object to tampering with nature; European and other cultures do. In France, where McDonald's franchises are French-owned and sell mostly French-grown food, protesters seriously vandalized a McDonald's store to protest the "McDonaldization" or "Americanization" of France (Daley 2000).

### *Education and Skill of the Labor Force and Labor Costs*

Workers' education and skill levels can range from superior (in Japan) to very low (in developing countries like Bangladesh). The strategic choice of a country in which to locate facilities is dictated in large measure by the education, skill, and cost levels of the workforce. For example, this factor is especially important in industries where skilled employees are needed, such as the manufacture of computers. When market entry involves the manufacture or delivery of noncomplex products and services, such as McDonald's hamburgers or 3M's "Soft Scour" cleaning sponges, less skilled labor is needed, so this factor is much less critical.

Porter's 1990 study concluded that the skill level of a country's workforce is critical to a country's ability to gain and maintain a competitive advantage through innovation and change (Porter 1990). For example, workers in Japan are known for their capabilities in applied research. This has led some firms to set up joint research projects with Japanese groups, because of the Japanese capacity to apply basic research to producing marketable products and services. Costa Rica's 95 percent literacy rate, nurtured by its extensive educational system, was a key factor in Intel's decision to build three microchip plants there, whose production accounts for close to 30 percent of Costa Rica's export trade (Mockler 2000).

Labor costs also affect planning. For example, in the early 1990s, German labor costs were the highest worldwide. This led to high unemployment and the exporting of jobs to other countries. These problems were compounded by extensive government red tape, and regulations and rules that discouraged investment and caused the German economy to stagnate in the mid-1990s. One reason Compaq Computers opened a plant in Scotland in 1987 was due to the high unemployment rate which made labor more plentiful and less costly.

### Raw Material, Suppliers, and Physical Resource Infrastructure Capabilities

Physical resources include the abundance, accessibility, quality, and cost of a country's land, water, mineral, or timber deposits, hydroelectric power sources, and fishing grounds, as well as other physical characteristics. For example, time zone and geographic location may be relevant. London's geographic location is an advantage in financial service industries because London-based firms can do business with both Japan and the United States during a normal working day. Istanbul's strategic location (Turkey) has for centuries made it a focal point for firms doing business between Asia and Europe.

Infrastructure factors that affect competition include the type, quality, and cost of transportation systems, communications systems, mail and parcel delivery, payments and funds transfer, health care, and so on. Infrastructure also includes the housing stock and cultural institutions—factors that affect the quality of life and the attractiveness of a country as a place to live and work. Related infrastructure factors include the availability of supplier networks in industries related to the company under study, as well as the availability of capital resources and relevant raw materials locally.

Northern Britain has become a popular location for foreign investors, for example. The number of foreign projects in Northern Britain more than doubled, from 183 in 1980 to 434 in 1995, while jobs that those projects created or kept from moving to other countries rose to 88,000 (from 14,000). However, in the late 1990s several of these projects were abandoned (Rose 1998). Major reasons for the Northern British boom included relatively low wage rates, supporting supply and parts infrastructure, a highly skilled labor force, and Britain's membership in the EU.

### Technological Trends

The impact of new technology on future opportunities and threats, as discussed in Chapter 7, is evident in many industries. The introduction of the

World Wide Web has stimulated wide use of the Internet. The impact of the Internet and Web page, as well as of other computer technologies, has been far-reaching. For example, not only has the Internet enabled better coordination, improved efficiency, and speedier communications, it has also created strategic opportunities (e.g., Amazon.com and others discussed in Chapter 2), as well as opportunities for strategic operational improvements in organization, marketing, production, and management, improvements which are described in the chapters in Parts II and III (Downes and Mui 1998).

Developments in telecommunications are also expected to produce major changes. For example, in the mid-1990s, almost three dozen satellite development projects, totaling more than 1,500 satellites and costing an estimated $43 billion, were announced (Schine and Elstrom 1997). Alcatel Cable SA of France and the AT&T Corporation agreed to cooperate to design, manufacture, supply, and install an underseas cable system which would encircle Africa by the early twenty-first century; its estimated cost was $2.6 billion. Developments such as these are expected to give new areas instant access to major information sources worldwide and in this way influence the way people view and respond to the world.

Genetic engineering advances are also creating new opportunities, as are developments in medicine, transportation, fiber optics, marine biology, solar energy, micromachines, superconductors, and metallurgy (Coates 1996).

Technological developments can also threaten existing products. For example, RCA Corporation—a name once synonymous with music—continued to produce vinyl albums while Sony Corporation began producing compact discs. General Electric has since acquired RCA and sold its record business unit. More recently, the Internet has had a destabilizing strategic impact by changing buying habits and creating new strategic competitive threats. For example, newspapers are losing classified advertising to new e-commerce ventures.

In addition to creating new product opportunities and threats to existing products, technological developments can affect how business is done. In the banking business, development of advanced computer systems has led to twenty-four-hour banking through automated teller machines. First Bank, a telephone-only bank in Leeds, England—with half a million accounts and not a single branch—is a dramatic example of the power of telecommunications when linked with computer information systems. Likewise, the development of cellular phones has allowed people to communicate while driving or walking and has led to the creation of a billion-dollar industry (Baker and Capell 2000; Shillingford 2000).

## CRITICAL FACTORS AFFECTING INDUSTRY
## AND COMPETITIVE MARKET ENVIRONMENT

As outlined in Figure 1.2 (p. 7), a structured situation analysis takes into account specific external industry and market forces. These include: overall industry/competitive market attractiveness, target market, industry/competitive market structure, competitive market environment (included in Porter's Five Forces), competitive market opportunities, competitive market keys to success, and anticipated and existing competition.

### Overall Industry and Competitive Market Attractiveness

The following industry and market analysis examines areas discussed in the first half of this chapter. These include: the economic, industry, and business factors both worldwide and in the geographic areas being studied; technological trends; political, social, and legal factors; market structure; and customer segments and trends.

In addition, both threats and opportunities in the market under study are examined (as described in Chapter 3) in the discussions of the Asian, South American, Western European, African, Indian, Central European, and North American markets.

An analysis of industry/market attractiveness also includes other areas such as: overall competitive market opportunities; overall competitive market environment (included in Porter's Five Forces); industry or market structure; specific target market; competitive market keys to success (of value drivers which create value for a firm when met) in specific opportunity areas (profit zones); anticipated and existing competitors and their strengths and weaknesses in key-to-success areas.

The evaluation of the industry and market can have a major impact on both *when* and *how* a company exploits that market.

### Competitive Market Opportunities

The study of industry/market attractiveness identifies profiles of opportunities in different types of industries:

- Emerging industries: early entrant opportunities
- Mature industries: product refinement, service and process innovation
- Declining industries: leadership, niche, harvest, and divestment
- Fragmented industries: consolidation

Neutralizing and overcoming identified general threats from competitive market forces can also provide other opportunities. For example, market threats have led many firms to enter joint ventures with suppliers and customers. Polish banks did this in 1996 by buying equity in their customers.

Ideas about opportunities come from various sources. For example, ideas about opportunities for new products and services can be stimulated by:

- Raw data (baby boom demographic projections, for example)
- Market niche analysis (ethnic trends and groups, for example)
- Ecological and social needs (low-fat health concerns, for example)
- Technological trends (Internet and the World Wide Web, for example)
- Changing lifestyles (two working parents, for example)
- Analysis of new growing/developing international regional markets

Ideas are stimulated in other ways, such as by reconceiving a situation, as shown in Figure 4.1. For example, busy lifestyles and a lack of free time, combined with a need for some vacation or "feel good" relief have created many new business opportunities. These include inexpensive airline "long weekend" travel packages, services that give people more discretionary time (cleaning, dog walkers, party planners), and a shift from giving packaged goods to giving "feel good" presents, such as theater tickets. Ideas can also be stimulated by juxtapositioning and reconceiving data, as can be done when creatively comparing consumer goods' characteristics to consumer buying habits reconceived in a similar way, as in Chapter 5 in Figures 5.2, 5.3, and 5.4.

These are only a few of the hundreds of ways available to stimulate creative thinking and find new opportunities. For example, it helps to analyze customer profitability by customer groups. This has been done in the banking and credit card industries. Firms such as Citibank have observed that groups of customers selectively use services in a way that is unprofitable. To correct this, many firms now reduce services and add charges in areas where customers are not profitable (Clemons 1999).

This "kind of" or conceptual analytical process—grouping, analyzing, and interpreting and responding to underlying market trends—can be pursued in many areas at operating, strategic business unit, and enterprise-wide levels. In addition to customer patterns, companies have found new winning strategy opportunities through studying channel, product, value chain, organizational, knowledge, and technology patterns. For example, anticipatory trend patterns may also be observed when analyzing product areas. Competitors may be developing strong links to customers, a compression of the value chain, as Intel did in helping customers design products with Intel chips, indicating that customer perceptions of service/product were changing. Or, the importance of brand names may be increasing to offset decreasing product differentiation among customers. Adrian Slywotzky and David Morrison conducted an extensive study on how to search for patterns within

FIGURE 4.1. Reconceptualization and Inferential Reasoning Worksheet Segment: Identifying Opportunities and Keys to Success

| Object | Attributes | Values | Controlling Concept | Implications | Implied Keys to Success of Opportunities |
|---|---|---|---|---|---|
| Customer | Age | Infant<br>Teen<br>Young Adult<br>Middle-Age<br>Older | Experimental Growing, etc. | Fashion-conscious, Frequent brand changes etc. | Provide current, even faddish products |
| | Income | Under $12,000<br>$12,000-$24,000<br>$24,000-$48,000<br>etc. | High Disposable | Higher living standard High discretionary income | High-quality product needed Price not a barrier |
| | Education | High School College Graduate | Well-Educated | Perception of being informed, more sophisticated but sometimes naïve | Provide new technology or image of new technology and value |
| | Sex<br>Location<br>Other Demographic information | M/F | | | |

Confirmations and Combinations } Provide a product which appears to be high-tech, state-of-the-art, and in vogue or soon to be in vogue changing markets and exploring how such pattern studies can stimulate thinking about future business trends and ways to exploit them (1999).

A planner might also search for changing patterns in the industry value chain that may lead to anticipating changing keys to success and new opportunities in the marketplace. Are companies that controlled the value chain beginning to outsource less profitable segments, such as was done with chip manufacturing by some microchip design companies? Are segments being filled with focused specialists, such as Internet trading companies? Or, are some companies, such as retailer Marks and Spencers (UK), developing new integrated strategic models which link in specific appropriate ways to Internet selling with a firm's existing retail outlets? (Voyle 2000).

This pattern approach is only one way to learn to "listen" systematically to what the market is telling us. There are many ways to do this "listening" creatively. For example, brainstorming sessions—noncritical generation of new ideas by groups or individuals—are another way (Clark 1989; Michalko 1998). Scenario writing—developing a series of stories of possible future events and their impacts on businesses—is also frequently used (Coy 1999; Schwartz and Ringland 1998). Such studies often also involve examining the future using such techniques as trend extrapolation, regression analysis, and the delphi method (Scott 1998; Slywotzky and Morrison 1997). All of this creative idea stimulation and exploration is an extension of the traditional structured analysis shown in Figure 1.2 (p. 7).

As seen from this discussion, conceptualization skills are useful in analyzing a situation in a way that stimulates thinking about future trends in the marketplace. Such conceptualization studies are continuous. They help to "hear" what the market is saying about the future, as well as to stimulate ideas of specific strategic approaches to that market for the firm under study. As is also seen from these discussions, it is important to identify the keys to succeeding in opportunity areas and how these success factors relate to competitors' positions and to a firm's own competencies (strengths) in a way that enables a firm to take advantage of these opportunities in some differentiated way.

### *General Competitive Market Environment: Porter's Five Forces*

In *Competitive Strategy* (1980), Michael Porter identifies several specific competitive forces that can influence future competitiveness or rivalry in an industry in many strategy formulation situations. Analyzing these factors and their impact can help a firm anticipate the kind of and amount of future competition to expect, and at times can provide a useful method for spotting threats and less-obvious opportunities.

*Barriers to entry of new competitors.* Realistically, the harder it is to enter a market, the less likely there are to be new competitors. Several factors influence market entry:

- *Customer brand loyalty and preferences* usually occur when products are differentiated sufficiently to create customer attachment to existing brands. In situations in which considerable brand loyalty exists, a new entrant may have to spend considerable money and time to overcome this loyalty—through lowering prices, increasing service and quality, and more aggressively advertising and promoting.
- *Economies of scale* can create barriers to entry, because they may raise initial costs, reduce profits, and generally lead to overcapacity in the market. Economies of scale can involve not only production, but also advertising, distribution, marketing, purchasing, and financing.
- *Limited access to marketing channels* can also create barriers by increasing costs or slowing growth for a new entrant.
- *Large capital requirements* may limit entrants into a market. Large companies with large amounts of available capital can usually overcome these restraints when major opportunities exist.
- *Experience advantages of existing firms may* discourage potential competitors. The accumulated know-how of existing firms may give them significant cost and position advantages.
- *Cost advantages held by existing firms* can create barriers to new entrants. These advantages may include access to lower-cost raw materials, favorable locations, patent protection, and technological advantages.
- *Government regulations* can create barriers by limiting or barring competition; this is especially true in developing countries.
- *Anticipated reactions of existing firms* may limit new entrants. Existing firms may have financial resources to cut prices and create buying incentives. They may defend their market in other ways—by increasing advertising, limiting access to supplies and marketing channels, and taking other steps to hurt new entrant chances of success. This is especially true when it is costly for existing competitors to abandon a market.

In Porter's (1980) view, the higher the barriers, the lower the likelihood of competitive pressures from outside the industry.

*Rivalry among competing firms.* Porter (1980) identifies several conditions that can increase the potential of intense competitive rivalry in a market:

- It costs more to get out of a business than to stay in it.
- Customer switching costs are low.
- The number of competitors is increasing, and they are becoming more equal in size and strength.
- It is possible to increase unit volume by cutting prices or using other competitive strategies.

- The competitors are diverse.
- Product demand is growing slowly.

*The threat of competitive products from other industries.* Porter considers substitute products from other industries to be potential competition. For example, all beverages can, to some degree, satisfy the same customer needs, therefore, fruit juices, sodas, bottled water, and other beverages can be considered competitive products. Customer switching costs are low, so competing products from different areas (the beer, soda, or bottled water industries, for example) are considered part of the competitive environment for any beverage and can affect future competition.

*The bargaining power of suppliers and of customers.* As with the other three forces, the impact of these two factors on success in the market under study is examined, and their impact on future competitive conditions is assessed. For instance, when the products are relatively undifferentiated and many suppliers exist, supplier bargaining power is unlikely to be strong. At other times, suppliers can be a new source of competition. Intel Corporation, once just a supplier of computer chips to other manufacturers, began making computers in the late 1980s and competing with its customers. By 1990, Intel's computer sales accounted for over 30 percent of total company revenues.

These five competitive forces—barriers to entry, rivalry, possible substitute products, power of suppliers, and power of customers—provide a structured way to view the competitive environment and the forces at work in it. Estimating the kinds and degree of competition to be expected is valuable in identifying available opportunities for new and existing firms.

However, Porter's is only one analytical tool useful in studying market competition. Other factors affect competition and related threats and opportunities which can be expected in the future. For example, the availability of Internet Web sites has disrupted the traditional value chain in many industries, as producers bypass intermediaries, new competitors enter markets easily, and existing market relationships change—all major strategic management considerations (Downes and Mui 1998). Other forces, such as increased deregulation, globalization, and new knowledge growth, also impact on multinational markets.

### Industry/Market Structure

The market study covers industry/market components that are part of the industry value chain, such as: distribution and sales channels; customer characteristics; advertising and promotion media; existing manufacturing facilities; suppliers and supplies, including parts and raw materials; and competitors and competing products. Such studies yield information about opportunities, as well as keys to success, at the threshold level (low prices are needed to compete in the discount brokerage field, for example), and in the intermediate and long-term differentiation levels (going beyond providing customers with quality products by providing solutions to customer problems, for example, as Intel did). Distribution channel access is often severely restricted in Japan, a problem Chrysler resolved partially by buying controlling interest in a dealership chain. Coca-Cola bought partnership interests in bottler/distributors both to gain rapid access to foreign markets (a key to success) and to earn substantial returns on those investments.

The industry/market description, which might be only a few paragraphs in summary and backed up by several volumes of detail, covers such information as:

1. A summary description of the industry, including an outline of it.
2. Major industry trends, forces, and events that are expected to have a major impact on strategic management, as well as the underlying factor analysis and reasoning which led to naming these trends. Particular attention needs to be paid to the impact of digital technologies (such as the Internet), deregulation and resulting privatization, new competitors, new relationships among value chain components, globalization, and new knowledge.
3. Each industry/competitive market component, including characteristics of each component (from material source to customer starting from either end of the value chain) and their interrelationships, past and future trends affecting opportunities (often called profit zones) and keys to success (often called value drivers) in each component and in the industry/market in general, and some indication of future characteristics and the factors upon which future expectations are based.
4. Market factors such as the buyers (kind and numbers), products and their differences, market structure, the competitive market environment (Porter's Five Forces), competitive market opportunities, present and future factors affecting success, cost structures, industry pricing practices, available equipment and technology, and supporting services, such as electricity, gas, transportation, communications, and housing.
5. Existing and anticipated major competitors, including relative size and importance, number, pricing patterns, products, research and development, advertising, investment in plants and equipment, possible neglected opportunity niches, strengths and weaknesses in opportunity/key-to-success areas, and some indication of the reasoning behind the evaluations.
6. Major sources useful in obtaining information about the business under study.

Such structured studies often uncover and highlight relationships among components that yield insights into current and future threats and opportunities.

### Specific Target Market Analysis

The target market analysis includes not only the total number of actual and potential customers. It also identifies customer characteristics (cultural and other) and tastes (buying habits and motivation), amount and kinds of purchases expected, present market penetration, purchasing patterns, income elasticity, legal requirements regarding product composition, comparative pricing and price regulations, anticipated technological advances, market gaps, geographic location, climate, and other factors. These factors affect product design, market selection, entry method, packaging and other marketing programs, type and location of facilities, and other enterprise-wide, business unit, and operating level decisions and actions (Hiebeler, Kelly, and Ketteman 1998).

During the 1990s, stimulated in part by the 1992 opening of Euro Disneyland near Paris, the theme park idea spread throughout Europe, where in 1995 over 60 million people visited theme parks. These theme parks often use American theme park consultants and Disney ideas. For example, after the French theme park Parc Asterix (based on Gallic chieftain and antihero Asterix) opened in 1989, it was transformed from a passive format, almost like a public park, to a participatory one, like U.S. theme parks. In early 1997, half a dozen theme parks were under construction in Argentina and Brazil (Friedland 1997). The theme park idea was not universally accepted, however. In China, over 2,000 theme parks were built in the 1990s; 80 percent of them reportedly lost money, and several hundred went out of business (Faison 1999a).

As in other multinational management areas, these theme parks balance universal approaches with local country cultures and customer requirements. For example, the two biggest complexes in Europe—Blackpool Pleasure Beach in England, with 7 million visitors a year, and Tivoli Gardens in Copenhagan, Denmark, with 3.8 million visitors a year, *have retained their original character* while adding rides and other features (Tagliabue 1995).

Target markets in many areas appear to be attractive. For example, in 1996, the Italian firm STET bid for a cellular phone license in Poland, calculating that the market there was ripe for this new technology. In the mid-1990s, the U.S. firm, Philip Morris, purchased a majority stake in Poland's biggest cigarette firm for $372 million in a move to position itself in a market where cigarette consumption was strong, in contrast to the U.S. market, where cigarette consumption has fallen.

## Competitive Market Keys to Success (Value Drivers) in Opportunity Areas (Profit Zones)

The analysis of keys to success in opportunity areas attempts to determine which competencies are needed to succeed, both at the threshold or survival/entry level and at the competitive differentiation winning level in a market. A segment of such an analysis is given in Figure 4.2. This analysis identifies the areas in which a company has or can develop core competencies that are valuable in entering and competing in a market and in providing something distinctive that customers value. It is the basis of the strategic framework development discussed in Chapter 2.

### Existing and Anticipated Competition and Competitors

In addition to studying the general competitive market, as described previously, both competitor groups and specific major competitors need to be examined. Aspects of competitors' competencies to be studied can include: market position; strategic profile; management's actions and thinking patterns (someone in a firm should be assigned to think like a competitor); all aspects of their customer/market value-added chain; operations/production; information systems; stakeholder relations; and finances (Fahey 1999).

Worldwide competition is increasing in both developing and developed countries. For example, Chinese computer makers with advanced systems that are as sophisticated but lower-priced than IBM and Compaq models are major competitors in China (Roberts 1997). Argentina's Disco SA, the supermarket unit of the largest retailer in South America, offers distinct competitive advantages including child care for customers, telephone ordering, home delivery, management efficiency, marketing savvy, and convenient locations with its more than seventy-nine stores in Buenos Aires. The unit's $1.8 billion annual sales in Argentina, Paraguay, Chile, Peru, and Ecuador, make it a formidable competitor to any entrant into the Latin American retail market (Friedland 1997). In Brazil, in 1999, there were three fiercely competitive local news magazines fighting for market share, leaving little room for new competitors (Rohter 1999). In early 2000, China's leading computer company, Legend (which the author has worked with), introduced Internet stock trading using television, a significant new strategic business model (Kynge 2000a).

Local competitors almost always have some advantages over worldwide competitors. These can include familiarity with the market and government support in protecting local business, for example, with protectionist trade measures. These factors can create major market-entry barriers and often lead an entering company to seek a local joint venture partner. This analysis might also include studying the five marketplace forces identified by Michael Porter (1980), as well as new marketplace trends that tend to predict

FIGURE 4.2. Medium-Sized Baked Goods Company: Keys to Success in Major Opportunity Areas

**Products:**

*Standardized.* The keys to success are:

1. Substantial capital resources to maintain competitive manufacturing advantage (automation) and to be price competitive.
2. Wide (mass) distribution and strong point-of-sale presence.
3. Wide advertising to insure brand identificaton and continuing reputation of good quality at a standard price.
4. Maintain present quality.

*Specialty.* The keys to success are:

1. Strong new product development capability, to be able to develop continuing flow of new products.
2. Good market intelligence, to be able to find out about and quickly copy new products as competitors bring them out.
3. Flexible production processes and organizational flexibility to make quick decisions and to get the products to market quickly.
4. Target market access and point-of-sales visibility, since the products tend to be more impulse items at first.
5. Brand recognition, for producing a high enough quality product to justify a premium product.

**Outlets:**

*Chains.* The keys to success are:

1. Strong relationships with individual store managers, through having a strong company-controlled sales force, to obtain shelf space and position (for exposure—many of the products are impulse items), and to maintain freshness of products sold.
2. Strong relationships with chain buyers.
3. Wide line of products.
4. Continuing flow of incentives, point-of-sale promotions, specials and advertising.

*Independents.* The keys to success are:

1. Keeping distribution costs per unit in line, either through volume or unit pricing.
2. Strong relationships with individual store managers, through having a strong sales force, to obtain shelf space and positions (for exposure—many of the products are impulse items).
3. An appropriate product line for market.
4. Continuing flow of incentives, point-of-sales promotions and specials.

future competition (Downes and Mui 1998; Porter 1980). Finally, it is not always easy to anticipate competitors' moves. For example, in Europe in 1999, UPS was experiencing major competition from soon-to-be-privatized national postal systems such as Deutsche Post (Germany), which had huge capital resources and very little debt and so were able to build modern servicing systems and offer lower prices (Blackmon 1999).

Space permits illustrating only one key competition analytical and evaluation tool, the comparative competitive position evaluation. This comparison is built on a study of competitors' strengths and weaknesses in key-to-success/opportunity areas. Table 2.2 (p. 58) shows a sample developed after a similar comparative study was done of a company's strengths and weaknesses in the same key-to-success/opportunity areas. Additional analytical tools are discussed in Chapter 2.

## CRITICAL FACTORS AFFECTING THE INTERNAL COMPANY ENVIRONMENT

As seen in Figure 1.2 (p. 7), an indispensable component of the situation analysis is a study of the company involved—its resources, competencies, and limitations—because this is the basis and perspective which controls multinational strategy formulation and implementation. During this phase, a manager intuitively begins formulating preliminary ideas of possible alternative strategic directions for the company under study. Nine of the factors listed in Figure 1.2 are discussed here.

### Company Strategies and Policies

Existing company strategies affecting a firm's multinational operations should be studied when making multinational management decisions. For example, a firm such as Borden may have a policy of owning subsidiaries 100 percent. However, changing circumstances can dictate that a joint venture is preferable. General Motors' initial policy of 100 percent ownership was later abandoned in favor of a wide range of joint ventures (Del Garda 2000). The impact of such strategies at all levels—enterprise-wide, business unit and operational—are covered in the remaining chapters of this book.

### Marketing

Marketing factors such as existing customers, products, sales, service, and distribution in a company's home country, as well as in its present overseas operations, are studied. The experiences of major automakers, airlines, consumer product firms, mail-order marketers, and pharmaceutical firms described throughout this book provide examples of analyses of marketing and product factors in multinational strategic management situations. It is especially important to identify core competencies upon which competitive advantages can be built, sustained, or extended. For example, company/product brand strength has been effectively exploited by Coca-Cola, has been extended by Gillette to a family of personal-care products and by Nestlé and Groupe Danone to a family of food products, and has been used by McDonald's in the retail franchise area to gain worldwide competitive advantages.

### Production/Operations

Production/operations capabilities include factors such as facilities, workforce, quality, flexibility, research and development, and inventory management—all possible sources of core competencies that can provide major competitive advantages. For example, the Southern Company, a U.S. electric utility company, determined that its core competency in effectively producing and delivering low-cost electricity services was a major competitive advantage. It exploited that advantage by buying electric utilities in other countries.

As shown in Gillette's decision about where and how to manufacture and supply its Atra shaver (described in Chapter 1), product availability, transportation costs, raw material costs, foreign-exchange risk, duties, tariffs, and production economies of scale, can vary over time and by country. This information affects decisions about where to purchase raw materials, where to manufacture or purchase components and parts, where to assemble or manufacture products, how to provide services, and how to determine the appropriate mix of production/operations functions. Solutions often involve combining internal company facilities and supply sources with external facilities and sources.

### Information Systems

Information systems are included in most companies' internal analyses because of their importance to both surviving and developing winning competitive edges. Telecommunications and related computer information systems are important due to the problems involved in managing geographically dispersed and diversified organizations, rapidly transferring information among divisions, reconciling differences and serving local needs, and achieving global efficiencies, as noted throughout this book.

### Financial and Accounting Resources

In analyzing a company's financial situation, the obvious and necessary factors examined are the income statement, balance sheet, and cash flow. These analyses—which make use of computer simulations of projected scenarios, financial ratios, and other analytical tools—provide a basis for estimating the financial resources available for overseas operations—overall, country-by-country, or target market-by-target market.

Going beyond ratios and tools can uncover hidden resources and opportunities. Imaginative financing arrangements, preferably involving local money sources, are especially important in countries with high inflation. The applicability of existing company accounting systems and practices in each overseas market, as well as identifying and developing the new kinds of systems and practices needed, are factors considered during this phase.

### Management, Leadership, and Other Human Resources

The availability of personnel experienced in multinational operations is critical to success, since international operations are different from domestic operations. Knowledge and experience are needed to deal with the many local factors affecting success, including political, legal, custom, cultural, personal, and attitude factors. Knowledge and experience are also needed to establish necessary contacts to open up and exploit opportunities in target markets. Gillette's group of more than 300 expatriate managers is one example of human resources as a core competency that gives a company a major competitive advantage.

Former GE CEO Jack Welch, a dynamic leader who built an adaptive corporate culture at GE, was a competitive advantage and—along with his other managers—a company core competency. Leadership skills are more relevant to success in today's entrepreneurial-oriented, rapidly changing market environment. The organizational and human resources aspects of multinational strategic management are discussed in Chapters 10 through 12.

### Stockholders, Owner/Managers, and Other Company Stakeholders

Interest groups that impact on multinational strategic management include: owners (stockholders), customers, suppliers, creditors and lending institutions, unions, franchise holders, government agencies, society (local or in general), company managers, professional staff, and hourly workers. Interest groups can impact on company strategy, as was shown by the number of companies that sold their South African operations during the 1970s and 1980s as a result of shareholder pressure. Unions can also have a major impact on company decisions, as shown by the widespread labor unrest in Europe in 1997 and 1998.

Studies of stakeholder relations also can lead to finding new opportunities for partnerships and alliances (Mockler 1999).

### Core Competencies Valued in the Marketplace: Comparative Strengths and Weaknesses Relative to Competitors

Although a firm's strengths and weaknesses can be identified, to be useful these strengths or competencies must have perceived and actual value in the marketplace, as well as have economic value to the firm. In addition, these core competencies are often not sustainable without renewal. For example, Gillette's brand image is constantly reinforced and renewed through product promotion, deeper market penetration, continually improved service, and a continual flow of new or improved products. As a market develops, new competencies are developed to replace or supplement existing ones and to meet, overtake, or surpass the competition.

How a firm's core competencies compare to the competition's now and in the intermediate and longer-term future affects a firm's ability to win against the competition in the targeted market. Are they that different from or superior to the competitors'? Are they easily imitable? For example, one problem in the technology area is that products often are quickly imitated and rendered obsolete. This was the problem faced by Motorola's cellular phone business in 1996 and 1997, as competitors imitated and improved on its products.

Such a comparison is shown in Table 2.2 (p. 58). The actual values given are not important. They are devices for stimulating and guiding thinking, not strict indicators of decisions to be made. What is important is (1) defining more precisely those factors influencing success and their relative interrelationship in a competitive environment, and (2) formulating and evaluating alternatives in light of these success factors and opportunities.

Such a study attempts to identify and then strategically exploit, or acquire and exploit, core competencies in light of company and market factors, and the competition and its core competencies. Chapter 5 describes how Mitsubishi Motors Corporation did such a comparative analysis and built a strategy around its potential strengths in new markets, while at the same time assessing its comparative weaknesses in its home country market, Japan.

Competitive market success requires differentiation, that is, doing something different from, and hopefully better than, the competition. Therefore, comparative knowledge is needed of the core competencies that a company and its competitors have now or can develop. This information is needed to enable focusing on the most critical (potentially high-profit impact) areas of the value chain market, the areas in which specific winning strategies are formulated over the short, intermediate, and longer-term future.

## SUMMARY

Multinational management is affected by many situational factors. This chapter gives an overview of the context analysis involved in acquiring and restructuring knowledge needed for multinational management decision making and action. Within such a structured context analysis, a considerable amount of unstructured entrepreneurial and innovative thinking and action is needed to gain the insights needed to win against the competition in the short, intermediate, and long term. The time and effort required for a context analysis depends on the manager involved. The situation analysis begins with the external environment.

Studying the situation goes further than what is presently being done, however. Colman Mockler, former CEO of Gillette, noted that

> building effective enterprise-wide strategies involves *learning to listen systematically to what the marketplace is telling us,* as was done in the Tashkent cellular phone venture in Chapter 3, about:
>
> - what is happening now and its impact over the near-term future,
> - what is anticipated to be likely to happen over the intermediate-term future, and
> - what can be made to happen in the long-term future.

Exploring how a competitive situation works now and might possibly work in the future provides a necessary knowledge base for developing threshold survival near-term strategies and action plans and for implementing them. It is also a systematic *indispensable* basis upon which innovative visions and strategies, appropriate enabling systems and plans, and effective leadership and management of human resources and operations are built over the intermediate and longer-term.

In recognizing the work required to do creative analyses and evaluations, Unilever took the dramatic step of setting up a formal structured enabling mechanism, as described in Chapter 2.

As a situation study progresses, therefore, relationship evaluations can lead to exploring ways that new forces and trends can be exploited. This can be done at the enterprise-wide (Amazon.com, for example), or strategic business unit level (Coca-Cola, for example), or operationally (compressing the value chain, dramatically lowering transaction costs, and increasing customer service, for example, through the use of electronic media such as the Internet).

This is part of the opportunity search, within the perspective of the specific firm and market under study. During this phase, preliminary ideas about possible alternative strategies and strategic plans are formulated, using one's own and others' business experiences and one's own thinking about the situation (Slywotzky and Morrison 1997). These syntheses are initially treated as hypotheses to be studied later. The following chapters continue the discussion of these activities begun in Chapters 2 and 3.

## REVIEW QUESTIONS

1. Discuss the relative importance of careful and thorough situation analysis to effective strategic leadership and management. Cite specific examples that illustrate your points.
2. Describe the ways in which the political climate can affect market entry and the way a multinational company does business in a particular overseas country. Discuss experiences that support your points.
3. List some of the selective nontariff barriers used to restrain trade and describe why governments might impose such barriers. Give examples of the ways they can be harmful to specific companies and ways they might benefit multinational companies.
4. Explain the differences between a controlled economy and a market-driven economy. Give examples of how each can affect, and have affected multinational companies.
5. What strategic situation factors are considered when considering the attractiveness of a country? Give an example of favorable country conditions and describe how multinational companies benefit from such conditions.
6. Describe cross-national agreements, such as the European Union. How do they affect a multinational business in particular and the economic business world in general? Name and discuss examples that support your points.
7. Compare China and Russia in terms of overall industry and competitive market attractiveness. Give examples to support your answers.
8. Ultimately, success comes from outperforming the competition. Describe ways in which information about competitors is developed and used in multinational strategy formulation.
9. Discuss the impact that new technology can have on multinational corporations. Give examples to support your answer.
10. Describe some of the ways in which carefully investigating industry/market structures in overseas markets can lead to more effective multinational strategic management decision making.
11. List some of the information that would be covered in a definition of the industry/market structure.
12. Describe the significance of identifying and nurturing core competencies to success in rapidly changing, highly-competitive multinational competitive markets.
13. Discuss the usefulness of Porter's five competitive forces in understanding and succeeding in multinational markets.

## *EXERCISES*

1. Read recent periodicals of your choice and select two companies that have entered or tried to enter an overseas market. Discuss their successes and failures and focus on the steps they took to improve their chances of succeeding in light of specific situation conditions in the country they were entering.
2. Select a company and a country that you would consider recommending that a company enter or expand company operations in. Develop a strategic plan for your selected company including plans for: 1) entering a new overseas market, and 2) expanding in an existing overseas market. Be sure to write a detailed report of how the relevant factors discussed in this chapter—both external and internal—affected your decisions.

# PART II:
# MAKING STRATEGIES WORK—
# BUSINESS PROCESS ENABLERS

# Chapter 5

# Enabling Multinational Marketing Processes

Chapters 5 and 6 concern two familiar critical enabling processes, marketing and production/operations. These two business processes often can be viewed as a seamless network of integrated activities rather than as separate functions. Electronic links using the Internet and computer information systems make this a widespread reality today.

Benetton, an Italian retailer, for example, links many of its in-store registers worldwide to its information systems base in Italy. Product sales and inventory stocking needs for each outlet can be tracked daily to generate production schedules and supply chain orders, in essence creating a seamless marketing/production cycle. These types of innovative approaches have led to more effective and efficient cycle time management in industries such as banking where it is now possible for customers to do their banking wherever, whenever, and in the way they want through online (Internet-based) banking systems, such as Citibank (described in Chapter 2).

As described in Chapters 2 and 3, marketing and production/operations functions are managed within the context of enterprise-wide and strategic business unit frameworks. They are major enablers in implementing these frameworks in today's rapidly changing markets. This chapter discusses the marketing function.

In a multicultural, multinational environment, marketing strategy situations can vary from time to time, country to country, and firm to firm, even for global products. For example, in 1987, the Eastman Kodak Company agreed to observe apartheid sanctions and left South Africa. At the time, it had a 60 percent share of the market; when it returned in 1994, it had only 4 percent. By 1996, of the firms that did not leave the market in 1987, the Fuji Photo Film Company had 52 percent of the market, and Agfa and Konica combined for 37 percent, compared to Kodak's 10 percent (McNeil 1996).

Faced with the same situation, other companies chose a *balanced strategy*. For example, Goodyear Tire & Rubber Company maintained its presence in South Africa through a technology and licensing pact, after selling its tire operations in 1989 to a local company. In response to the sanctions, Coca-Cola moved its operations to Swaziland, a small independent nation surrounded by South Africa, and distributed its products through South African Breweries.

As with Kodak, PepsiCo also left South Africa. Both firms had to regain market share and overcome the continuing resentment of the South African white population, which saw the moves as a betrayal. PepsiCo closed its South African operations in 1977. Many problems such as these have discouraged some companies from returning to South Africa (Thurow 2000).

Chapters 5 and 6 describe multinational management marketing and production/operations tasks within the strategic context framework discussed in Chapter 2. Specific strategies, plans, and programs are continually integratively implemented, refined, and revised, as shown in Figure 1.4 (p. 11). Making strategies work can require considerable entrepreneurial management, the basic strategic management skill outlined in Figure 1.1 (p. 5) and discussed throughout this book. Both Chapters 5 and 6 include self-learning, step-by-step, decision-making exercises.

## MULTINATIONAL MARKETING

Marketing refers to all business tasks involved in getting a product or service from producer to consumer. These include selecting a product (or service) and customer/market, as well as decisions concerning warehousing, distributing, pricing, selling, advertising, promoting, and servicing. The marketing planning process shown in Figure 5.1, and the kinds of strategies formulated and implemented in each task area, are discussed below.

### Strategic Framework

The relationship of the factors discussed in Chapter 4—such as target market, competition, and other industry/market and internal factors—to the formulation of strategies was discussed in Chapter 2. Chapter 2 and Chapter 3 discussed defining basic marketing strategies, such as the decision to go international, selecting markets and products/services, and choosing the method of entry and operation—key aspects of strategic frameworks. These are refined as strategies, plans, and programs and are developed in six critical marketing areas: target markets, products and services, distribution, pricing, promotion, and entry/operating method.

### Specific Target Markets

Target markets are defined more specifically as plans are developed and implemented. For example, as Citibank refocused on the consumer banking market worldwide, it studied each country's market and targeted upwardly mobile and higher income segments. When entering China, Gillette focused on more densely populated urban centers which could be reached efficiently through mass distribution and media. The cellular phone entrepreneurs described in Chapter 4 targeted Tashkent, a city with poor phone service.

FIGURE 5.1. Developing Enabling Marketing Plans

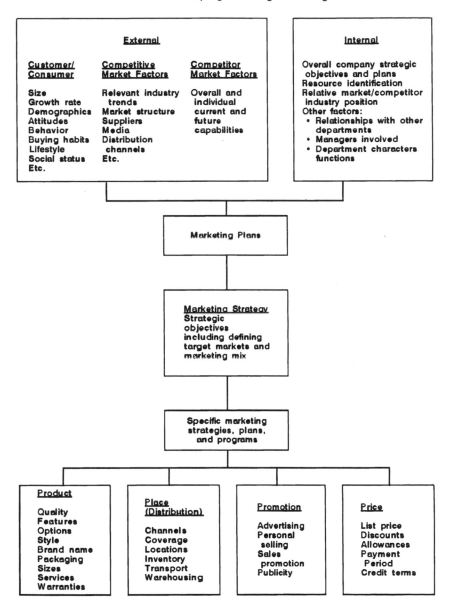

Existing and potential target consumer markets for products and services can be defined according to: size and growth rate; demographic profiles (age, sex, family size, income, occupation, education, religion, race, nationality); psychographic profiles (social class, lifestyle, personality); behavioral profiles (attitudes, benefits sought, readiness stage, perceived risks, innovativeness, loyalty status, usage rate, user status); and geographic location (region, city, county, state, international and national segments, population density, climate).

When industrial buyer markets are involved, a planner identifies existing and potential customer factors such as: overall size; growth rate; size of individual companies; average size of purchases; usage rates; product applications; types of business; source loyalty; locations; purchase status (how long and how frequent); and performance (reliability, price, durability, etc.).

A key decision involves identifying those factors which affect decisions about what products to sell and how best to serve the market. For example, market planning decisions about which target markets best suit existing products, or about which products to sell to selected target markets can be made using tools, such as the product and customer profiles shown in Figures 5.2 and 5.3 and in the discussion of Figure 4.2 in Chapter 4. Nestlé discovered a major market through creative market analysis. In India, the water in small towns is so bad that even though monthly salaries are as low as 1,500 rupees, local residents would willingly spend 18 rupees a bottle for Nestlé's bottled water (Beck 1999).

Target market opportunities, threats, and keys to success can be identified at both the overall industry and competitive market levels, as described in Chapters 3 and 4. Target market analyses, however, can be difficult to interpret. For example, in Great Britain, experts said that the multiplex cinema concept would not work—they were declining in popularity in the United States. AMC Entertainment read the market differently and opened a ten-screen theater there in the 1980s. Its success led to eighty multiplexes in Great Britain by the mid-1990s. A total of $1 billion was expected to be spent on multiplex development in Western and Central Europe, including Russia, some with 30 screens and 6,500 seats (Guthrie 2000; Tagliabue 2000). The concept has also spread to Mexico, Southeast Asia, China, India, and the Ivory Coast in Africa. Although the food served varies, as do the films, the concept is global.

### Products or Services

Strategy decisions in the product or service area include defining the following: the type of product or service; the special distinguishing or differentiating features of the product; the breadth of the product or service line; the degree of customizing; the relationships with global clients; brand

FIGURE 5.2. Selected Database—Consumer Goods

| Type of Product: Convenience Goods | Type of Product: Specialty Goods |
|---|---|
| Brief Description: Nondurable, quickly used and frequently purchased | Brief Description: Goods for which a customer is willing to make a special purchasing effort |
| Examples: Cigarettes, candy, magazines | Examples: Gourmet foods, Rolls-Royce |
| **Product Characteristics:** | **Product Characteristics:** |
| Brand Loyalty: Brand loyalty is high | Brand Loyalty: Brand loyalty is high |
| Product Info: Goods bought with a minimum amount of shopping effort, low information search | Product Info: Product information required is high but customers do not generally compare brands |
| Distribution: Wide geographic distribution/Mass merchandisers | Distribution: High-Image retail outlets/Specialty stores |
| Performance Risk: Low | Performance Risk: High |
| Price: Generally low-priced items | Price: High priced but customer is usually relatively disinterested in price |
| **Implications:** | **Implications:** |
| Involvement=Low involvement product | Involvement=High involvement product |
| Benefit sought=Convenience | Benefit Sought=Prestige/Fashion Homogenous goods |
| Product Info Required=Low | Product Info Required=High |
| Advertising Requirements=Promotion is aimed at brand identification; packaging is important to differentiate product through advertising. Short duration messages, focusing on a few key points. | Advertising Requirements=Selling image and prestige to market, reinforcing brand name. May need national campaign to reinforce brand name, but use local advertising to inform the the public where products can be purchased. |
| Media Implications=Convenience stores require massive selling and large volumes. | Editorial content geared toward an upscale market would be good place to advertise |
| Target Market=Broad/General | |

## FIGURE 5.2. *(continued)*

| Type of Product: **Impulse Goods** | Type of Product: **Shopping Goods** |
|---|---|
| Brief Description: Goods bought without planning | Brief Description: Items which are subject to price and style comparisons |
| Examples: Toys, inexpensive clothing and food | Examples: Fashion clothes, television sets |
| | Two types of Shopping Goods: |
| | Heterogenous — Customers compare style and quality for suitability with price relatively unimportant. Example: high-priced clothes |
| | Homogenous — Customer comparisons of competing merchandise is limited to price. Example: television set |
| **Product Characteristics:** | **Product Characteristics:** |
| Brand Loyalty: Brand loyalty is low | Brand Loyalty: Brand loyalty is low |
| Product Info: Low information | Product Info: Requires as much shopping time and information search |
| Distribution: Wide geographic distribution/ Mass merchandisers | Distribution: Specialty/Mass Merchandisers |
| Performance Risk: Low | Performance Risk: High/Medium |
| Price: Generally low-priced items | Price: Medium/High-priced items |
| **Implications:** | **Implications:** |
| Involvement=Low involvement product | Involvement=High involvement product |
| Benefit Sought=Convenience | Benefit Sought= a) Fashion/Style & Prestige/ Status=Heterogenous goods b) Economy or Fashion/ Style=Homogenous goods |
| Product Info Required=Low info search | Product Info Required=High |
| Advertising Requirements=Short duration messages, emphasizing a few key points, visual & sound components are important | Creative Requirements=Media to be used as a shopping medium to compare prices and product offerings |
| Media Implications=Requires massive advertising, large media budget | |
| Target Market=General | Target Market=Selective/General |

## FIGURE 5.3. Selected Customer Database

| | | |
|---|---|---|
| **Customer Category** | **Customer Category** | **Customer Category** |
| Family Life Cycle= | Family Life Cycle= | Family Life Cycle= |
| teenager/young adult | young/single | married no children |
| | | |
| **Fact/Demographics** | **Fact/Demographics** | **Fact/Demographics** |
| Age: 12-17 | Age: 25-34 | Age: 25-34 |
| Income: | Income: $21,000 - $49,000 | Income: $50,000 or more |
| Education: high school | Education: college grad | Education: college or higher |
| Sex: M/F | Sex: M/F | Sex: M/F (household) |
| Social Status: | Social Status: upper middle | Social Status: upper middle |
| | | |
| **Implied Customer Characteristics** | **Implied Customer Characteristics** | **Implied Customer Characteristics** |
| flexible to change | socially oriented | affluent (dual income) |
| brand switchers | fashion opinion leaders | high purchase rate of durables |
| generally buy impulsively | well-educated | fashion/style-conscious |
| shop in mass merchandisers | appreciate product quality | well-educated |
| | seek product information/evaluate brands | career-oriented |
| | shop in specialty/department stores | |
| media habits=radio, magazine | media habits=read magazines more than watch television | media habits=read magazines more than watch television |
| innovators | innovators | innovators |
| other-directed | inner-directed | inner-directed |
| degree of brand loyalty=low | brand loyalty=medium/low | brand loyalty=medium |
| impulsive buying habits | planned buying habits | planned buying habits |
| dist. outlets frequently used= mass merchandisers | dist. outlets frequently used=dept/ specialty stores | dist. outlets frequently used=dept/ specialty stores |
| benefit sought=fashion/style | benefit sought=fashion/style | benefit sought=status/prestige |
| buyer=irrational buyer | buyer=rational | buyer=rational |
| **Customer Category** | **Customer Category** | |
| Family Life Cycle= | Family Life Cycle= | |
| married/with children | elderly | |
| | | |
| **Fact/Demographics** | **Fact/Demographics** | |
| Age: 35-44 | Age: over 65 | |
| Income: $20,000 or less | Income: $20,000 or less | |
| Education: high school grad | Education: high school grad | |
| Sex: M/F (household) | Sex: M/F (household) | |
| Social Status: upper lower class | Social Status: lower middle | |
| | | |
| **Implied Customer Characteristics** | **Implied Customer Characteristics** | |
| working class/wage earners | group will pay higher prices to receive service | |
| generally do not search for product information | seek product information | |
| buy standard well-known products | tend to shop in specialty stores | |
| tend to buy lower quality products | flexibility to change is low | |
| media habits=television is an important medium for this group | media habits=television is important | |
| late adopters | late adopters | |
| other-directed | other-directed | |
| brand loyalty=high | tend to be brand loyal | |
| impulsive buying habits | information search is high/low** (**high/services, low/products) | |
| | dist. outlets frequently used=specialty stores | |
| disc. outlets frequently used=discount stores or mass/merch. | buyer=rational | |
| buyer=irrational | | |

name emphasis and positioning; what services to offer with products; and the frequency of product change.

Having a globally recognized brand image can be important to world-wide firms (Tomkins 1999a). The strategies used in achieving such an image vary from using a single global approach worldwide, to modifying that approach as required by each locality, to modifying and extending different existing brands in a coordinated way (Kapferer 1998). Many brands transcend the actual product; for example, Virgin is a name found on everything from an airline, to vodka, to railroads (Tomkins 1999b). Pepsi's Funyuns (an onion-flavored snack) prospers ($43 million in 1998 sales) with no brand manager, advertising, or marketing support (Egan 1999).

Brand was not important to Shiseido, Japan's leading cosmetics company, however, as it began mass marketing a line of low-priced cosmetics through 1,200 outlets in China under a new brand name (Robinson 1997). Global brands, such as Levi's, can fade, and so must be reinvigorated. Many local country cultural perspectives can create negative reactions to global brands, such as Gillette, Coca-Cola, and McDonald's (Tomkins 2000). Many traditional firms, so-called "old economy" companies, have found that they have had to move into online Internet ventures, so-called "new economy" ventures, to refurbish their image and avoid being labeled out-of-date (Iskandar 2000). In late 1999, Unilever announced that within five years it would cut marketing support for, or eliminate, more than 1,000 brands in order to focus on its 400 major brands, cut costs, and simplify its supply chain worldwide (Cowell 2000).

A Russian company was able to create an instant brand, using millions of dollars of competitor advertising, when it named its washing powder "Ordinary Powder" and set its price at less than half that of competing products. Procter & Gamble, one of the competitors, advertised the virtues of its Ariel detergent with "ordinary powder," and gave the new product instant recognition ("Spin Style" 1999).

Creating innovative products rapidly can be important. For example, when faced with intensifying competition, Japanese automakers unveiled sixty-four new models in fiscal 1998-1999, double the previous year's number. Citibank emphasized high quality and fast, convenient service as part of its new marketing strategy targeting high-income consumers in Asia, while BankBoston broadened its product line in Latin America in response to increasing affluence there.

Adapting products and brands to local needs is often required. For example, Pillsbury, a U.S. food giant, found that there was a market for packaged flour in India, a product no longer popular in the United States. In India, in smaller villages, women normally took raw wheat to be ground at local mills. Pillsbury saw this marginal product as a way to build a brand image, useful over the longer-term in selling higher-margined food products. Pillsbury even made over their "Doughboy" in advertisements in India, having him press his palms together and bow in the traditional Indian greeting, and speak one of six regional languages (Jordan 1999). In Thailand, the small U.S. fast-food chain, Big Boy, had to adapt its menu to include Thai food (for locals) and European food (for German tourists especially), train local food suppliers to meet new specifications, and even change worker eating habits (Frank 2000).

A major product/service support strategy is helping companies better serve their own customers. As noted in Chapter 2, this was a strategy Intel used to win against its competition.

Customer Relationship Management (CRM) refers to many activities involved in acquiring and retaining customers: (1) the collection, storage, and analysis of customer data; (2) the matching of products and services to specific customers and customer groups; (3) the services provided customers; and (4) the cohesive single view of customers whether they interact in person, by mail, Internet, or telephone ("Understanding CRM" 2000). The Internet is also becoming an effective strategic tool for studying customers—their tastes, buying habits, motivation—and ways to win them over, studies that are important to providing a basis for creating strategic plans (Hamm and Hof 2000).

The decision-learning exercise to follow gives a detailed example of an overseas product decision.

### *Sales and Distribution*

Strategies are also formulated for sales and distribution of products or services. A major strategic decision in this area involves the outlet or channel used and includes direct to consumers, through owned or exclusive dealerships, through wholesalers, direct to retailers, or some combination of these.

Whirlpool followed others in agreeing to sell its appliances through national retail chains in Japan in 1996. In China during 1996, in contrast, Gillette was working to bypass national distributors and deal directly with local and regional ones. Gillette's distribution strategy was combined with other marketing strategies, such as increased personal selling, new product introductions, and pricing (Mockler 1996-1999). Other foreign firms were still facing similar distribution problems (Kynge 2000). In Russia, Coca-Cola grew rapidly by using privately owned channels, and in China, it developed a network of over 400 warehouses (Smith 1999a). Direct selling and distribution, for example, selling Avon products through field salespeople, has become popular in Latin America and Europe. Dell Computers uses direct selling in China and Europe (Ascarelli 1997; Chowdhury 1999).

One of the keys to success for the Unilever Group (United Kingdom) in India has been its distribution, which extends into villages where 70 percent of India's population lives. Unilever has accomplished this through a variety of marketing tools, such as stalls at village markets, sales from minivans that visit villages with TV entertainment during evenings, salesmen on motorcycles, smaller size packages for poorer villagers, and aggressive advertising. Kehi Dadeseth, former chairman of India's $2.9 billion Hindustan Lever Ltd., whose profits doubled from 1996 to 1998, attributes his success overall to Lever's "global base and local roots" (Kripalani 1999, p. 114).

The Internet has led to major strategic changes in the sales process by enabling more effective and efficient selling directly to consumers. This process of bypassing intermediaries not only in selling, but also in distributing information content, has continued in newspapers. This process is called "disintermediation," and it has created a variety of new e-commerce strategic business models. The experiences of brokerage firms, such as Schwab, and banks, such as Citibank, in using the Internet in this way were described in Chapter 2.

A critical task often neglected in planning in the e-commerce area, a major marketing channel, especially when dealing in business to consumers (Maloney 1999) such as at eToys, is the amount of manual labor needed to support e-commerce operations, including: warehousing, picking, packaging, and shipping (Quick 1999).

### Pricing

Pricing decisions (including discounts, allowances, markups, and terms of sale and service) depend on such factors as market practices, production costs, anticipated competitor responses, the product demand, and marketing objectives. Pricing decisions have a significant impact on volume, market penetration, and profits—all strategic concerns. Strategic pricing choices include: above-market pricing; market leader, which is pricing below the competition; temporary price reduction; pricing to meet competition; and pricing for different classes of customers and services.

Jollibee Foods Corporation, a Philippines fast-food chain, used below-market pricing strategies in combination with quality and service advantages, as part of its strategy to compete successfully with McDonald's and dominate the market. This approach helped the firm continue to grow during the Asian financial crisis in 1997-1998 (Marozzi 1998). In 1996, Unilever Group had profitability problems when Procter & Gamble Co. introduced its U.S. "everyday low pricing" strategy across Europe. As part of this strategy of slashing prices, P&G eliminated promotional offers and discounts (Parker-Pope 1996).

### Promotion

Decisions about *promotion*—the effective communication of product messages (benefits) to the target market—include personal solicitation, advertising, sales promotion, and publicity. Almost every company now makes some use of the Internet to promote their products/services, brand, and image.

Bertelsmann, the German media giant, used personal solicitation in China to sign up 640,000 members for its book club in 1996 and 1997 (Knecht 1998). Major worldwide brands use global events to promote, as Gillette did with championship broadcasts of World Cup Soccer, which reached some 3.5 billion people. Continually reinforcing a brand image is critical, and this approach accounted for the major investment ($250 million) Coca-Cola made in advertising in the 1996 Summer Olympics. For Coca-Cola and Gillette, these events were part of an integrated program of sales promotion, advertising, personal selling, and publicity. Such global approaches are not always effective, however, as Nike, Inc. found when its iconoclastic worldwide advertising approach was unsuccessful in Russia and had to be modified to suit the local culture (Fuerbringer 2000).

Competition today is becoming so intense that giveaways are becoming more widespread. For example, when introducing its new 140-channel digital pay-TV service, British Sky Broadcasting, the pay-TV group, gave away the set-top boxes needed to receive the services, in much the same way that some manufacturers offer free Internet access to sell more machines, and some Internet service providers, such as British Telephone, give away computers to entice customers to sign up for online services (Lewis 1999; Newman 1999; Taylor 1999). In Cambodia, distributors use uniformed "Beer Girls" to promote a company's beer at local bars (Marshall and Stecklow 2000).

## Integrated Marketing Mix:
### Finding an Effective Global/Local Balance

In the previous examples, the individual strategic moves were often part of an integrative *marketing mix* strategy of coordinated, balanced, and integrated plans and programs. When Frito-Lay, for example, moved to create markets overseas for its products, product taste testing determined that adapting flavors to local tastes was not always a good idea. In Thailand, for instance, prawn-flavored potato chips did not sell well even though prawn is a favorite flavor there. Familiar flavors, such as barbecue, sold well instead. In 1995, Frito-Lay blitzed the Thai market by buying out its Thai joint venture partner, taking over a production plant, hiring 1,500 farmers to grow potatoes meeting its standards, and unleashing a marketing campaign featuring TV ads and a brigade of "promoter girls" to greet shoppers in stores. Frito-Lay's sales tripled in Thailand in the twelve months after the takeover (Zachary 1996).

In late 1997, Wal-Mart was still developing an effective global/local mix for its South American operations. Many compromises were needed (Friedland

and Lee 1997). By comparing local tastes in São Paulo, Brazil, with those in Peoria, Illinois, Wal-Mart discovered, for example, that in Brazil, sushi was favored over live trout, soccer balls were substituted for American footballs, and "knockoffs" priced at $9.99 replaced American-style jeans priced at $19.99.

In addition to the comparatively easy adjustments of products offered according to local tastes, the company faced much tougher obstacles during its expansion into Brazil and Argentina, which led to losses. These problems included fierce competition, the inability to achieve economies of scale due to unfavorable market conditions, and some mistakes such as insisting on doing things the "Wal-Mart way," which led to alienating employees and some local suppliers.

In addition to adjusting to local product tastes and pricing competition, distribution was a major problem. Because Wal-Mart did not have its own local distribution system there as in the United States, delivery was dependent on local suppliers and contract shippers, forcing it to handle as many as 300 deliveries a day instead of the seven commonly handled at U.S. locations. Easy-to-handle packaging and quality control were difficult to obtain locally, forcing reliance on imports, which raised costs. Local suppliers resisted discounted pricing. Other problems included the nonadaptability of U.S. accounting systems to local tax systems; different credit practices (such as accepting postdated checks from customers); equipment adaptability problems (U.S. forklift trucks built for different pallet sizes); inability to use sophisticated, integrated, computerized inventory-management systems; and Wal-Mart's policy of stocking a broad range of products (58,000 in its La Plata, Argentina store, for instance) when the competition stocked only 22,000, therefore operating more efficiently with less cost. It has taken Wal-Mart many years to adapt to doing business in South America. One effective method that was used was to hire and train managers who were capable of dealing with local cultures and meshing local practices with the "Wal-Mart way." Such an approach is time-consuming and costly, however. Wal-Mart avoided many of these problems when it entered South America through the acquisiton of existing firms.

Marketing's mixed decisions involve studying present and future competitor factors, as well as individual competitor strengths and weaknesses in critical, opportunity, and key-to-success areas, as outlined in Figure 5.1. Figure 5.4 illustrates the amount of detail involved in such competitor-by-competitor studies.

Existing and potential company resources should be examined to define a company's strengths and weaknesses in identified opportunity areas, and these resources should then be compared to those of competitors. Wal-Mart did this when major mergers and acquisitions worldwide positioned a worldwide French retailer as a major competitor with operations in twenty-five countries

FIGURE 5.4. Outline of Competitor Profile

**BACKGROUND:**

- company identification
- location
- description
- brief history
- state of incorporation
- affiliates
- how is the company organized
- how often has it altered its structure?
- number of shares outstanding
- ownership (insiders, institutions, major shareholders)

**FINANCE:**

- statistics and performance analyses (revenue, earnings, growth)
- sales by division
- profitability by business unit/product line
- banks/investment banking firms used
- stock market data
- current market value
- rations and industry comparisons
- do they track, lead or lag the industry?
- cash flow analysis
- assets and return on assets
- capitalization
- working capital
- internal rate of return on investment

**PRODUCTS:**

- description of products and services offered (product mix - depth and breadth of product line) and market position by product
- product strengths and weaknesses (individually and the line as a whole)
- how committed is the firm to a particular product line?
- analysis of new product introductions
- R&D expenditures and apparent interests of technical personnel
- an analysis of the company's design and development process
- patents held/pending
- product standards (specs), quality and technical analysis
- pricing policies (Who decides flexibility in pricing levels?)
- note special selling arrangements (Are they competing for your customers?)
- licensing and joint venture agreements

FIGURE 5.4 *(continued)*

**MARKETS:**

- market segmentation and customer analysis
- customer base (markets targeted, regional sales analysis, penetration, importance to the firm, dominance of market)
- profiles of markets/customers (including product mix and sales data by product line)
- market growth and potential for future growth
- market share by product line
- how does the company view the direction of the industry?
- market and geographic area targeted for expansion
- marketing tactics
- distribution network/channels of distribution
- advertising/marketing/sales efforts including budgets and firms used
- foreign trade analysis
- recent orders
- government contracts
- analysis of sales force (experience, compensation)

**FACILITIES:**

- location
- size
- domestic vs. foreign
- capacity
- capacity utilization
- announced capacity expansions
- product mix by plant
- shipments and profitability data
- unit cost/price
- capital investments
- equipment purchases
- key suppliers
- number of production lines and shifts
- regulatory issues

**PERSONNEL:**

- employees - total, management, R&D staffing, engineers - number, education, training, experience
- biographies of senior management including employment contracts, incentive (bonus) programs and golden parachute agreements
- description of the members of the board of directors
- consultants used by the firm
- labor union information (relations with management, results of recent negotiations with other firms in the industry, date of next contract renegotiation)

FIGURE 5.4 *(continued)*

- detailed corporate structure
- who has profit and loss responsibility?
- safety information (accidents) and government/industry regulations violations
- management style and flexibility
- fringe benefits and compensation practices
- track managerial changes for indications of disputes in upper management (turnover of personnel)

**APPARENT STRATEGIC (LONG-RANGE PLANS):**

- detail of acquisition and divestiture strategy
- new products on the horizon (Does it indicate a new direction for the firm?)
- statements of plans to enter new markets or improve their market position (increase their share of market)
- apparent strategic objectives
- corporate/divisional/subsidiary company priorities
- business units/segment goals
- basic business philosophy/targets
- analysis of company's decision-making process
- overall corporate image and reputation
- assess company's ability to adapt/change
- how will the company look/perform in the future?
- anti-takeover measures instituted
- shareholder actions
- lawsuits pending
- what are the firm's key successes and failures?
- why have they been successful?
- overall corporate strengths and weaknesses
- attitudes toward risk

Adapted from Barbie E. Keiser, "Practical Competitor Intelligence," *Planning Review,* September/October 1987, pp. 18-19.

(Matlack, Resch, and Zellner 1999). Competition can come in many different forms, as was seen with Procter & Gamble's experience in Russia with detergents. In Krasnoyarsk, Russia (Siberia), an imitation cola named Crazy Cola had 48 percent of the cola market against Coke and Pepsi (McKay 1999).

As discussed in Chapter 4, company resource areas to be studied include financial, production, marketing, manpower, information systems and related internet services, telecommunications, and image. Because marketing strategy formulation is done within the context of enterprise-wide strategies, these worldwide strategies and related plans should be scrutinized. For example, the development of global automobile platforms (or frames) resulted in an economically feasible way to create global products adaptable to different country needs in the auto industry. Other companies in other industries also consider adaptation costs when developing products to be marketed in many countries (Sahay 1998). Marketing strategies, plans, and programs should be developed or evolve within the context of these national and global critical situation factors.

Almost every major multinational company has had to adapt to and make use of the Internet as part of its enterprise-wide marketing strategy. The strategic impact has already been felt in the retail book industry. Amazon.com made major inroads into Barnes & Noble's business and forced that traditional company to open its own Internet book-selling operations. Companies in the travel, banking, insurance, mail-order marketing, retailing, newspaper, broadcasting, and book publishing are among the many companies in many industries that have felt the strategic impact of the Internet and have had to introduce and integrate the Internet into their strategic and operating plans to remain competitive.

## EXERCISE: IDENTIFYING PRODUCTS OR SERVICES TO BE OFFERED: A SHORT-TERM PERSPECTIVE

The following section describes how a local foreign affiliate of an international health care products company evaluates new-product proposals generated by the international company headquarters. Seven alternative strategies (grouped in three categories) are considered:

- Introduce the product (without change to the formula) as a new brand, as a line extension to an existing brand, or as a replacement of an existing brand.
- Change one or more elements of the proposed product and introduce it as a new brand, as a line extension to an existing brand, or as a replacement of an existing brand.
- Reject the proposed product.

In this study, corporate management had already developed the product formula and recommended overall marketing strategies. These strategies were based on preliminary research in other countries where the product has demonstrated significant international sales potential. Headquarters has requested input from the local affiliate manager as to the feasibility and strategic "fit" of the new product in the local manager's country.

In this case, a new product proposal received from international headquarters would normally include:

- Complete information about the product—its formula and manufacturing (or other important) specifications
- Full details (and necessary supporting documentation) of its medicinal purpose—that is, what it is designed to do
- The basic costs of raw materials and manufacturing or of importing the product
- The product's proposed consumer promise, brand name, and suggested promotional strategy (for local adaptation); an identification of the suggested target market segment(s) for which the product was designed; and the product's recommended positioning versus competitive products
- Summaries of experiences (both positive and negative) to date in other international markets, including: consumers, competitors, and trade reactions; initial levels of product sampling and purchase; likelihood of "me too" copies or generic competition; and regulatory barriers.
- Other information pertinent to local product decisions, such as the strategic importance to the parent company of introducing the product in as many countries and as soon as possible in order to preempt competition

### *Examining Critical Factors Affecting the Decision*

The proposal is evaluated in light of the key customer, market, competitor, and company factors, shown in Figure 5.5—a situation-specific application of the analyses described in Chapters 2 and 4.

#### *Customer Factors*

In the local country, it is first determined whether there is a sufficiently large, definable, and potentially viable market—or market segment—to which the product can be sold. This involves comparing the target market as defined in the proposal with local demographics and conditions. In evaluating the *viability of a target customer market segment,* such factors as appropriateness and potential receptivity of the product are considered, as are *market size* and per capita income.

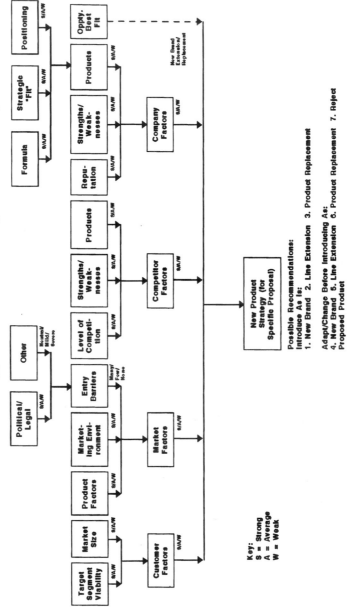

# New Product Strategy for Local Country Product Proposal

*Market Factors*

Market factors involve conditions faced in marketing products in a specific country and can be grouped into three categories. *Product factors* require judgments, based on market research, of such factors as product awareness, usage, brand loyalty, purchase frequency, and overall consumer involvement levels. Evaluating the *marketing environment* involves determining the strengths and weaknesses of the existing marketing structure in the local country. Key considerations are the availability of distribution channels and advertising media. *Entry barriers* may include:

- *Product* regulations, which can hinder a company's ability to register or distribute a product or formula.
- *Price* regulations, in the form of either price freezes or direct profit constraints on manufacturers or retailers.
- *Promotion and advertising regulations,* which can hinder a firm's ability to communicate new product information to a specific target population.
- *Place/distribution* regulations, such as those restricting nonprescription drug sales to pharmacies.
- *Foreign exchange controls,* which can hinder the efficient purchase of raw materials or finished products from international sources.
- *Cultural factors,* such as those in Middle Eastern countries concerning women's dress and behavior, that could prohibit the introduction of products such as personal-care products.
- *Inflation,* which in some Latin American markets can exceed 1,000 percent a year.
- *Market saturation levels,* which could indicate diminishing returns for investments in new products.

*Competitor Factors*

Analyzing competitor factors involves examining the level of competition, the strengths and weakness of specific competitors in the industry, and competing products. *Level of competition* measures the number, size, and effectiveness of competitors. *Competitors' strengths and weaknesses* are measured to assess the overall strength of competitors' financial, pricing, distribution, manufacturing, promotional, and other resources. *Competing products* are examined for their similarity to the product under consideration, their market position and brand strength, and the likelihood of "me-too" products (Fahey 1999).

*Company Factors*

A firm's reputation or standing in a country is considered, along with its operating strengths and weaknesses. The evaluation also weighs the specific attributes of the proposed product and the product's relation to the firm's existing product line. *Reputation* is measured by examining the firm's relations with three key groups (industry trade groups, the medical community, and consumers), and by assessing the strength of its sales force. The *company's strengths and weaknesses* include the firm's distribution, manufacturing, and promotion capabilities, its pricing flexibility, and the resources available to support a new product introduction. A firm's strengths and weaknesses are then compared with those of competitors.

*Product evaluation* involves examining the proposed product's formula and positioning as described in the new product proposal, and weighing its strategic "fit" in terms of both the local company and its international parent. In evaluating the product, the degree to which the proposed *formula* conforms to locally accepted medical practice is determined, as well as whether some aspect of the formula (for example, an ingredient) needs to be changed before the product is introduced. The need for change can arise from regulations, accepted local norms for self-medication treatment, availability of raw materials, and other factors. Whether the product can be made in the country or must be imported is also studied. Formula considerations include estimates of the new product's value to the market: Is it unique? Does it present a significant improvement over existing products in the market? The absence of any such advantages would mean that the product is a "me-too" product—usually in a weak competitive position.

Judging *strategic fit* requires evaluating how well a proposed product would blend with, or improve, a firm's existing product mix. It also involves studying a firm's worldwide enterprise strategy to determine if this introduction is consistent with the firm's broader market penetration or positioning strategy. Three separate, though related, evaluations are made of a proposed *product's positioning*. These determine whether the positioning, or consumer promise, is *clear and understandable* to the consumers in a local country, *relevant* to their wants, needs, and lifestyles, and *believable* to potential product customers.

*Opportunity: Best Fit*

A number of other strategic factors, classified under the heading "Opportunity: Best Fit," are considered. For example, if a firm has no existing brand in the proposed product category, the product would be introduced as a new brand, provided that other factors are favorable. If the firm already has a strong brand in the category, it is often advisable to incorporate the new product into the existing line as a line extension rather than introducing a new brand. An example of this was Sterling Drug's Midol 200, a pain-killing product introduced as a line extension to the existing Midol line, rather than as a new brand. This was a sound move because the firm lacked the resources to compete head-on with similar products such as Johnson & Johnson's Tylenol and Medipren. When a firm has a strong existing brand in the new product's category, but that brand is declining, it is often advisable to introduce the product into the market as a new, improved (replacement) version of the existing brand, rather than as an entirely new brand. When existing brands are weak and declining, introduction as a new brand is preferable, as long as other factors are favorable.

### Possible Recommendations and How They Are Made in Light of the Identified Critical Factors

After evaluating the impact of these major factors, the possible strategic recommendations listed on pages 131 and 132 should be examined as possible responses a new product proposal.

In an ideal situation, customer, market, and company factors would all strongly favor the company, and competitor factors would be weak. In this situation, the final strategy choice is made by combining the appropriate "best-opportunity-fit" values—new brand, line extension, or replacement—with information as to whether changes are needed. For example, if the best-opportunity-fit analysis concludes that the proposed product should be introduced as a new brand, and that changes in the product are not needed, then the recommendation would be to *introduce the proposed product, as is, as a new brand.* If changes in the formula are needed, the recommendation would be to adapt/change the proposed product before introducing it as a new brand. If the best-opportunity-fit analysis indicates the product would be best as a *line extension,* this would be the recommended strategy, depending on whether changes were needed.

However, more complex judgments are required in most situations since conditions are rarely totally favorable. For example, when customer and market factors are either average or strong (indicating that the market could support a new product), but competitor position factors are stronger than company position factors, a new brand introduction would not be recommended under any circumstances. Instead, assuming that the firm has a strong existing brand in the category, the recommendation would be to introduce the product as a *line extension or replacement.* This strategy relies on the company's existing brands' strengths when all other factors are weak. If a strong existing company brand does not exist and there are no other special strategic corporate considerations, the proposed product should be rejected.

If competitor factors are strong, and customer, market, and company factors are weak, the recommendation would be *not to introduce the proposed product*—at least until conditions changed. Other factors that would trigger a rejection include severe political/legal or other entry barriers, a combination of weak formula and positioning, and weak customer and marketing factors.

Figure 5.6 outlines a prototype knowledge-based system based on this type of structured situation analysis. The outline, called a dependency diagram, indicates the reasoning rules (or heuristics) used in the system, as well as the other information contained in the situation diagram shown in Figure 5.5. The system is described in detail in *Knowledge-Based Systems for Management Decisions* (Mockler 1989), which contains a disk file (AIMS. REV) that can be used by readers to practice making decisions in this area and to study in detail the specific reasoning steps involved in making these decisions.

## IDENTIFYING PRODUCTS OR SERVICES TO BE OFFERED: A LONGER-TERM PERSPECTIVE

As short-term decisions are made and marketing strategies, plans, and programs are developed and implemented, intermediate and longer-term product and marketing strategic frameworks can be studied. These include:

- Intermediate-term decisions, such as those faced by Volkswagen (its Beetle automobile) and by Ford Motor Company and its competitors (their global car initiatives)
- Long-term, enterprise-wide decisions, such as those made at Microsoft, Hewlett-Packard, IBM, and the Oracle Corporation

### Anticipating and Exploiting Global Market Trends Over the Intermediate-Term Future

Many decisions and actions in the product area involve the intermediate-term future. Motorola, Inc. attempted to overcome major losses by revamping its product focus to concentrate on software rather than technology hardware, for example, by equipping all of its cellular phones with an Internet browser (Barboza 1999).

For years Volkswagen had produced limited numbers of its old "Beetle" auto (called the "Bug") at its plant in Mexico. The car was sold mainly in Mexico as well as in limited export markets. In 1995, because of demand for the Beetle worldwide, especially in the United States, Volkswagen announced that in four years it would begin producing a new model of the Beetle at its Mexican plant, which made the old-style Beetle, where exchange rates and manufacturing costs were favorable. Its major target market outside of Mexico was the United States, a receptive nearby market. In keeping with modern marketing

FIGURE 5.6. Dependency Diagram: New Product Strategy Selection for Local Country Product Proposal (Initial Prototype)

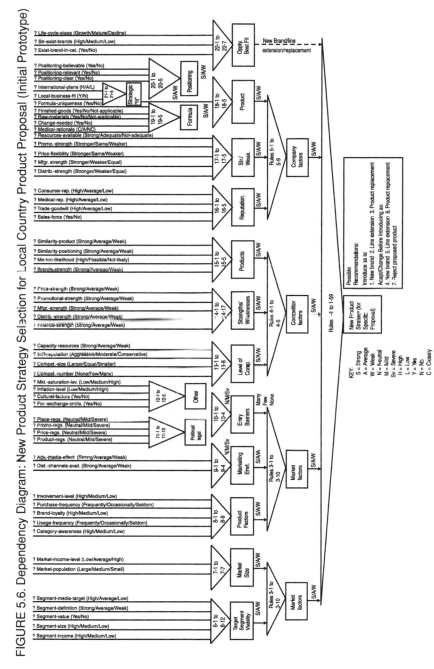

139

practices, the firm announced that it would retain the essentials of the original model but would adapt its design to the tastes of modern-day customers (Stodghill 1998). The new Beetle's introduction in 1998 was a success.

In the mid-1990s, Ford Motor Company's former Chairman, Alex Trotman, launched a much bolder move—to build a global car and consolidate its worldwide product design and development facilities. Other auto firms were pursuing different strategies. Fiat designed a small, inexpensive car—the Palio—for developing countries, where such basic autos are preferred. General Motors' strategy was to create a basic engine which could be used worldwide while modifying its four basic models for international markets rather than creating unique models for each market. Using another strategy, Mercedes-Benz, Germany's luxury carmaker, entered into a joint venture with Switzerland's SMH watchmaker (Swatch watches) to build a two-seater minicar and then used that as a base to create a second (A-Class) model to compete in the lower-end car market. However, major design problems caused its other small A-Class car to roll over during test turns, leading Mercedes to suspend A-Class car production, as well as production of its two-seater minicar (Bowley 1997; Simonian 1997). However, by 1999, after design and marketing changes, the two-seat minicar (called the "smart" car) was selling well (Miller 2000). Building on its global reputation in the low-price auto market, VW announced in 1999 that it would be building a newly designed low-priced car for the China market, the first such venture in China by an overseas company (Smith 1999b). As discussed in Chapter 2, Toyota used yet another mixed strategy.

Many firms pursue mixed intermediate-term global strategies. For example, Interbrew SA (Belgium) pursued a global strategy (its Labatt label) at the same time that it used its local distribution networks to distribute its many smaller beer labels (Stella Artois, Hoegaarden). For example, when it bought into a Hungarian brewer, Borsodi, it continued to promote that brewer's local brand, Borsodi Vilagos, while using the Hungarian distribution system to promote Interbrew premium brands which were popular in other countries (Voyle and Pretzik 2000).

Competitor moves can stimulate strategic rethinking. For example, Wal-Mart's move into Germany forced musty retailers there to grudgingly shake off some century-old business habits involving pricing, purchasing, computerized inventory control, store hours, store layouts and size, and especially customer service and formulate a new strategic and operating approach (Lewis, Voyle, and Revlon 2000).

### Creating Future Markets: Long-Term Marketing Planning Decisions

In the mid-1990s, a major move to control the future was made by Microsoft, the world's largest software firm (in 1995, nearly half of the world's PC software revenue went directly to it) (Banks 1999; Edstron and Eller 1998; Moeller and Himelstein 1999; Wallace 1997). Among other products, the firm was developing "wallet computers" that carry digital signatures, money, and theater or airplane tickets; new generations of fax machines, telephones with screens, and car navigation systems; Microsoft-run interactive TV boxes; and office and wireless networks. Microsoft was also seeking a controlling role in the Internet itself as described in Chapter 14, for example, by focusing on electronic financial-transaction processing. By making connections among all of these areas of modern computing and controlling the architectures governing those connections through its PC operating systems, Microsoft was trying to transform the structure of the world's computer businesses, to the point of being criticized for trying to control the Internet revolution, a major enterprise-wide strategic management move. In addition, Microsoft was forming overseas partnerships in sixty countries to develop local software firms, who, in turn, would promote and develop its products.

Although Intel's microprocessor industry was changing rapidly, due to competitive actions, microprocessing technology did not seem in danger of being replaced in the foreseeable future. This made the future to some degree controllable, as demonstrated by Intel's evolving strategic actions. Microsoft's software industry was experiencing different kinds of changes, such as the introduction and explosive growth of the Internet. This created a highly uncertain environment, much different from that in the microprocessor industry. The situation was especially uncertain for Microsoft. In 1998 it was being sued by the United States Justice Department over its alleged monopoly position.

Microsoft's position was unique in many ways. First, its Window's operating system was the *industry standard,* since it was used in 90 percent of personal computers (PCs) sold. This gave it a major degree of control over the use of competing PC software. In addition, it had a very large cash flow that enabled it to experiment in an almost unlimited way with innovative product and marketing ideas. Because of these unique internal and external situation circumstances, in 1999 Microsoft remained flexible as to which strategic direction to pursue, beyond maintaining its dominant operating system position and moving quickly into all related software areas. It was also able to pursue a much less systematic (unstructured) market and customer-based strategy formulation process, because of its substantial resources.

Unlike Coca-Cola and Intel, Microsoft's strategy has been described as unpredictable, unstructured, inefficient, proactive, continuous, and diverse—*an opportunistic approach* appropriate for a highly uncertain volatile high-tech industry (Foley 1999). For example, its first approach to the Internet was to attack America Online (AOL) directly; it then shifted, using Sun

Microsystems' Java technology, buying Internet firms, and partnering with AOL, an *unpredictable* approach to strategy formulation. Much of Microsoft's Internet strategy came from lower-level managers as researchers pressed Bill Gates to fully embrace and innovate in the Internet area, an unstructured strategy formulation approach. Microsoft was also in some ways *inefficient* in 1999 in often pursuing internal development of products that were eventually bought from other firms or abandoned, in order to move quickly into potential growth areas.

Microsoft's strategy in the entertainment field was *proactive* during the period when computer software applications were starting to expand in the late 1990s, as Bill Gates bought rights to use many works of art in his electronic media. Microsoft's strategy was *continuous,* as it moved quickly into every possible related growth area to position Microsoft in growth areas early. By moving into every related area, its strategy was also *diverse,* making use of a variety of alliances where the need dictated it. For example, during 1999, Microsoft spent more than $7 billion to buy stakes in everything from tiny Web startups to mighty AT&T and undertook new Internet initiatives (Markoff 1999; Moeller and Himelstein 1999).

Microsoft is an example of a large, cash-rich, leading-edge firm (whose major product was an industry standard) in a rapidly changing, uncertain, high-tech industry that used an unstructured approach to strategy formulation, an approach appropriate for the industry and firm involved. It is an example of how successful strategies and strategy formulation are dictated by specific situation factors and of how strategy formulation and strategies can vary from situation to situation and year to year (Lohr 2000).

Hewlett-Packard, the Oracle Corporation, and IBM, as described in Chapter 1, provide additional examples of how a company can look ahead and strive to create markets and initiate changes that have a long-term impact on a market.

## ENTRY/OPERATING METHOD

Another critical enterprise-wide, business unit, and functional planning decision involves the choice of how to enter into and operate within a market. In keeping with the integrative nature of multinational management, method of entry/operation situations can involve marketing and production/operations tasks.

A wide range of situation factors should be examined when making market entry/operating decisions. As shown in Figure 5.7, this context factor analysis can be broken down into two segments:

*External factors:*
Target country market factors

Target country general environmental factors
Target country production factors
Home country factors

*Internal factors:*
Company product factors
Company resources/commitment factors

The following section briefly introduces how these situation factors shown in Figure 5.7 are studied and used to formulate an initial market entry/operating strategy concept. For this introductory discussion, the possible strategies have been limited to three commonly used alternatives: a wholly-owned subsidiary; joint venture/contractual partnership agreement; and exporting.

To successfully pursue a *wholly-owned subsidiary* strategy, either by starting one's own subsidiary or by buying an existing firm, a firm must have adequate financial resources. Regardless of other factors—for example, strong sales potential, a low level of political risk, the availability of technically skilled workers, or even favorable responses by the foreign government—a lack of adequate financial resources will limit use of this strategy. In 1995, Siemens of Germany used this strategy to locate a new $1.8 billion semiconductor plant in Northern England. Favorable factors included Siemens' financial resources, the area's low labor costs and high unemployment rates, political stability, availability of skilled labor, and an infrastructure of technical schools and electronics capabilities which could support computer firms (Stevenson 1995). Global competitive pressures, however, eventually led Siemens to close the plant; several other overseas firms were forced to do the same for similar reasons (Rose 1998). General Electric built a polycarbonate plant in Spain based on the incentives provided (the Spanish government paid 60 percent of the fixed investment), availability of land and labor, and the nearby port through which 90 percent of the factory output could be exported (Burns 1999).

Available finances do not, however, always mean that a wholly-owned subsidiary is recommended. For example, the market infrastructure may be difficult to penetrate, legal restraints may be hard to overcome, or wholly-owned investments may not be allowed. In such situations, if it is clearly desirable for other reasons that a firm enter this market, the strategy considered might involve a *shared-ownership joint venture.* This was the approach used by the Daewoo Group when it made a massive investment in Central Europe to take advantage of the market's potential for auto sales. Joint ventures involving two or more firms can be structured in many ways, from setting up a new joint venture combining existing assets to creating new facilities.

FIGURE 5.7. Decision Situation Diagram: Entry/Operating Strategy—International Market Overview Diagram

144

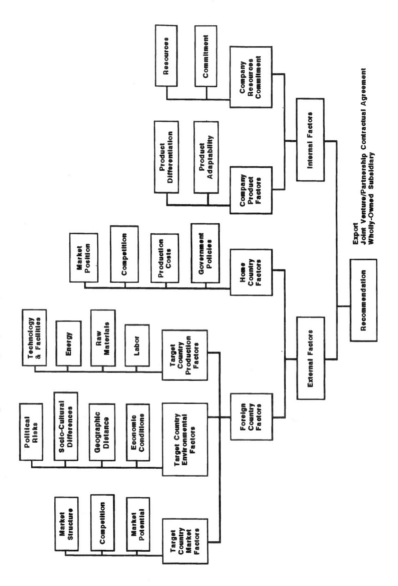

Extensive studies show that there is significant multinational activity in this area and that strategic alliances increase profitability in major ways (Harbison and Pekar 1997a,b,c).

Problems can occur with such strategies, however, as PepsiCo found out in Central Europe when it failed to maintain adequate control of its joint ventures. PepsiCo also failed to keep pace with the massive investment Coca-Cola made in its joint ventures—which enabled Coke to overtake Pepsi in a five-year period. Even though it entered the market much later than Pepsi, by 1997, Coca-Cola was outselling PepsiCo two-to-one in Central Europe. Furthermore, in Venezuela in 1996, Coke announced that it had entered into a joint venture with Pepsi's present distributor there, in effect gaining instant access to 85 percent of the market and reducing Pepsi's share to less than 25 percent (Collins 1996).

*Contractual (such as licensing) partnership agreements* are considered a viable alternative, if management is unsure as to the sales potential of the target market, product adaptation is high, political conditions are unstable, and/or a firm's level of international expertise is limited. Joint venture/contractual partnership agreements are often used to limit a company's exposure to risk when entering a new and unfamiliar market. Many of the companies which began to move overseas in the 1980s, such as Motorola in China, cited some of these reasons for initially choosing contractual arrangements. Partnerships are especially popular among airlines, where they enable partners to function as a single carrier while remaining separate companies.

An *exporting* strategy is considered a minimum-risk approach. In a joint-venture partnership agreement, a firm may have to fund part of the project and/or relinquish a substantial portion of the venture's ownership. An export strategy eliminates these costs and associated risks. If the sales potential for the target market is high, the estimated production and distribution costs are lower at home than in the foreign location, product adaptability requirements are low, import and export restrictions are favorable, raw materials are relatively more expensive abroad, the political climate abroad is unstable, and the firm has limited financial resources, then exporting is a recommended strategy.

U.S. mail-order firms have used exporting to penetrate the Japanese market. They have been successful because they know the mail-order business, it is the easiest and cheapest way to penetrate the market, distribution costs through mail-order are much cheaper than through normal retail channels in Japan, and Japanese tastes and buying habits are similar to those of Americans. In 1994, L.L. Bean's mail-order sales in Japan reached $100 million, up 66 percent from the prior year. Total U.S. mail-order sales to Japan were about $750 million in 1995—approximately 2 to 3 percent of total retail sales in Japan. In response to complaints about size and fabric differences, several companies, including Eddie Bauer and L.L. Bean, opened retail stores in Japan. Customers can examine and try on products at these outlets before ordering them by mail—creating in effect a mixed strategy appropriate for their specific businesses.

In practice, decisions such as these are more complex than the discussion of basic contingency processes at work indicates. In addition, the process outlined in Figure 5.7 is not the only way to reconceive or model the cognitive processes involved in strategic management or in multinational market entry/operating situations. Readers of this book are encouraged to formulate their own cognitive conceptual approaches, as suggested in Figure 1.1 (p. 5). In the words of one executive seminar participant, the process in Figure 1.1 is the way "to be the boss" in any situation one encounters.

A small, knowledge-based prototype system based on this decision process outline, developed to guide users through basic decisions in this area, is described in detail in *Strategic Management* (Mockler 1993, Chapter 13), which contains a disk file (INT-ENT.STG) that can be used by readers to practice making decisions in this area and to study in detail the specific reasoning steps involved in making these decisions.

### *SUMMARY*

This chapter has identified and discussed the marketing activities involved in strategic leadership and management: strategic framework formulation within the enterprise-wide strategic framework, target market definition, and formulation of strategies and action plans within products and services, sales and distribution, pricing, and promotion areas.

As in other areas, this also involves integrating these area activities into a balanced marketing mix. The experiences of companies such as Wal-Mart in integrating marketing activities while trying to penetrate an overseas market in South America gave a detailed description of the problems and how they can be overcome in a fairly typical situation.

The chapter also discussed a specific marketing strategic decision in the product area. This experience included a detailed description of the factor analysis and of how those factors are used to make decisions. The discussion gave the actual decision rules at work in a manager's approach to making the decision.

Company experiences in longer-term multinational marketing strategic decision making were also discussed. These discussions again made the point that while there are general decision models for strategic marketing management, success depends as much on the ability to handle the implementation activities within an ever changing multinational competitive market.

The chapter concluded with a detailed description of how market entry and operating decisions are made. This is a major area of multinational marketing strategic management and provides further strategic models to guide strategic decision making and help to learn strategic decision making.

## REVIEW QUESTIONS

1. Explain the concept of marketing and its role as an enabler in multinational strategic leadership and management.
2. Describe the major decisions made when formulating a strategic marketing plan and use examples of actual company experiences to support your answer.
3. Discuss product and service strategy decisions. Describe company experiences which show successes and failures in identifying and attempting to serve multinational target markets in light of competitive pressures. Explain the importance of superior core competencies to success in these experiences.
4. Discuss the critical factors affecting strategic product and service decisions by examining and explaining the impact of different factors on the decisions, as illustrated in Figure 5.6.
5. Describe situations in which pricing was of strategic importance. What factors does a manager focus on in these situations and what are the choices a manager generally has in pricing strategy decisions?
6. Discuss the long-term marketing plans that Hewlett-Packard and Microsoft were implementing in 1996 to gain and maintain a competitive edge in highly competitive computer markets.
7. Identify three commonly used methods of entry/operating in multinational expansion situations; explain in what situations each is useful. Use company examples to illustrate your points.

## EXERCISES

1. Review current periodicals to determine how well Hewlett-Packard and Microsoft succeeded in implementing their strategies since 1996. Be sure to discuss the impact of critical situation factors on the outcomes you describe.
2. Research Sony's venture in multiplex cinemas in the United States and compare their success and/or failures with AMC Entertainment's venture in Great Britain.
3. Select two examples of a firm's entry/operating decisions in an international market. Describe their approaches, compare them, and evaluate their relative success or failure.

4. Based on your research, select a company whose recent international product initiatives have created problems for its competitor(s). Evaluate the move, discuss ways in which it might have been anticipated and handled by one of the competitors, and suggest possible actions which might now be taken by the selected competitor to catch up.

Chapter 6

# Enabling Multinational
# Production/Operations Processes

New developments occur rapidly in the multinational production/operations area. For example, under the leadership of former General Motors executive, Jose Ignacio Lopez de Arriortua, Volkswagen constructed a state-of-the-art factory in Brazil in 1996. The new truck plant in Brazil was designed with work space assigned to major suppliers who supply their own workers to assemble and add components to trucks rolling down the assembly line. Volkswagen employees supervise the work and inspect finished trucks; suppliers are paid only when trucks pass inspection (Schemo 1996). The Mercedes-Benz and SMH alliance's micro compact (Smart) minicar production plant in Brazil uses a similar approach (Simonian 1998), as will other auto plants planned for Brazil (Romero 1999).

Volkswagen anticipated that the new production system would reduce the number of defective parts, improve efficiency, and cut labor costs. However, many problems were encountered, and in late 1998 potential savings and efficiencies had to be realized ("The Modular T" 1998).

Different production/operations situations dictate different solutions, as in other multinational areas. For example, Nissan and Honda operate "lean" auto production facilities by performing many subassembly tasks themselves, using proprietary technology, and outsourcing only selectively (Gibson 1998; Thornton and Kerwin 1999).

## MULTINATIONAL PRODUCTION/OPERATIONS

The production/operations process involves rendering or producing a firm's services or goods. As shown in Figure 6.1, this process consists of converting *inputs* (personnel, materials, components, facilities, equipment, information, and capital) into outputs (goods and services) through a *transformation process. External environmental factors,* such as customer needs and government regulations, can affect the transformation process. The *overall control* function involves measuring results, comparing them with desired results, and deciding if changes are needed. *Feedback* is an essential

FIGURE 6.1. Production/Operation: The Transformation Process

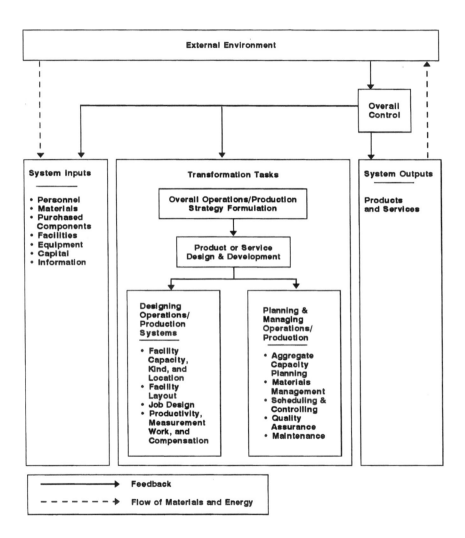

part of control. The production/operations transformation process shown in Figure 6.1 involves four areas:

- Developing general planning directions: *formulating overall production/operations strategies*
- Creating the product or service: *formulating product and service design and development overall strategies*
- Developing facilities to produce the product or render the service: *designing production/operations systems*
- Producing the product or rendering the service: *planning and managing the production/operations function*

The transformation process varies by situation. Producing products, such as television sets, light bulbs, or refrigerators, can involve a continuous production line, where a product's parts and materials move through different assembly stations and processes. When a product is too large or fragile to move along a production line—such as a large aircraft—the labor, materials, components, and equipment are moved to the product work site. In contrast, chemicals may have common processing, but segregated facilities may be needed where contamination might occur.

The transformation processes for rendering a service have differing characteristics. For example, offices handling large volumes of paperwork, such as insurance claims, may be arranged to move documents through computer-related facilities. In contrast, a cafeteria customer may pass from operation to operation—from silverware to salad to entree to dessert to beverages to cashier. An air transport operation uses computer systems and, increasingly, Internet-based technologies to handle customer queries, ticket purchases, etc, and human service systems to handle customer flow, equipment servicing, and the aircraft themselves. People who repair furnaces, handle medical and police emergencies, paint bridges, or deliver flowers must go to a location to perform the desired services.

## *OVERALL PRODUCTION/OPERATIONS STRATEGIES*

This section and the following section examine common production/operations strategies, as shown in Figure 6.2.

One key strategic production/operations strategy decision is whether to *make or buy* the product or service being sold. For example, in 1999 Airbus reorganized to be more competitive with Boeing; a key element of its new strategy was to buy parts from outside suppliers and let price and quality dictate supplier choice (Zuckerman 1999a).

FIGURE 6.2. Developing Enabling Production/Operations Plans

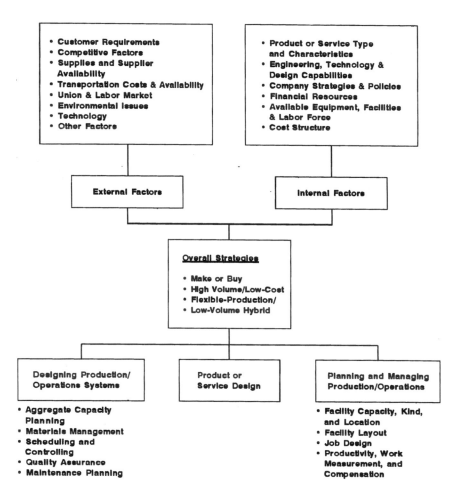

*Outsourcing* (using outside firms to perform functions formerly done within a firm) is a major tool used by multinational firms (Cordon, Vollman, and Heikkila 1998; Willcocks 1998). The Body Shop (United Kingdom) sold two cosmetics manufacturing plants in 1999 in an effort to focus on its core strengths, retailing worldwide and product innovation (Sharpe 1999). New Internet companies often call on outside suppliers (called Application Service Providers—ASP) to provide quick access to needed technology (Moran 2000). Gillette, in contrast, continued to make its Sensor razors at its own plants, especially when involved in joint ventures overseas, to protect its technology.

Mainly through joint ventures, Mexico has become a major low-cost manufacturing base for U.S. appliance and auto firms, because of its cheap labor pool and zero tariffs on exports to the United States (Miller 1999). This strategy, at times called *contract manufacturing,* is growing. More and more companies are specializing in producing such products as electronic components in low-cost, low-tariff, geographically closer areas such as Mexico (which services the U.S. market) (Friedland 1999).

A *high-volume/low-cost* strategy focuses on cost efficiency to obtain a strategic advantage. In the retailing industry, this strategy has been a key element of Wal-Mart's overseas expansion into Canada, Mexico, Brazil, Argentina, China, South Korea, and Germany (Hollinger 1999; Kahn 1999; Robinson, Wighton, and Edgecliffe-Johnson 1999; Tomkins 1999). In general, lowering operating costs is an implied strategic goal of most manufacturing operations. This goal is specifically promoted periodically through special programs, such as Vauxhall's (a UK auto subsidiary of General Motors) "lean" cost-cutting program in late 1999 in response to UK government probes of allegedly high auto prices there (Burt 1999).

A *flexible production/low-volume* strategy emphasizes flexible production and service processes. For example, steel *minimills* grew out of the need for economic production facilities designed to meet rapidly changing customer needs in different geographic areas (Wagstyl 1997). In 1998, Toyota announced that it would revamp its factories worldwide so that it could quickly switch to making exportable autos—if local markets weakened (Schuckman 1998); in 1999, it announced that it had developed a way to make a car within five days of a custom order (Simison 1999). Honda Motor Company revamped its factories in the late 1990s to make them modular and able to produce any model in Honda's line (Shirouzu 1999). American companies have become more flexible than many Japanese companies, however, especially in areas such as computer disk making (Bylinsky 2000).

Production/operations strategies built on *quality* can provide competitive advantages (George 1997). For a time, Airbus was able to charge a premium price because of its planes' fuel efficiency and other superior operating cost-saving features. Toyota has consistently devoted more time and money to insuring quality than have American car firms (Matta 1999). In contrast, in 1996, Whirlpool experienced problems due to a lack of quality in its Chinese operation, as was the case for the Korean auto manufacturer Daewoo Group as it attempted to expand rapidly in Central Europe.

Many companies employ a *high-tech leading-edge* strategy: the degree and kind of modernization strategy is dictated by situation circumstances. For example, Caterpillar, a U.S. earth-moving equipment firm with nearly half of its sales outside the United States, drastically modernized its plants. At one plant, it formerly took 6,000 workers twenty-five days to get one big back-loader through the plant. Today 3,000 workers can process it in six days. "Just-in-time" techniques have been used to eliminate piles of metal parts, cut inventories by 60 percent, and clear floors. Some parts are carried silently overhead on conveyor belts, and heavier subassemblies are moved about in self-guided vehicles. These vehicles are summoned by an operator at a computer who notes that a given chunk of metal has been drilled, milled, ground, or bored and is ready to move on to another workstation where one of forty-seven robots will weld it to another part. The vehicle navigates with the assistance of laser beams and bar codes at every junction on the production lines. No longer is welding a messy, dirty job; today, the welding hall is completely clear and the giant slabs of thick sheet steel are quietly cut into shape by high-voltage plasma guns which produce a much more precise cut and no smoke ("Manufacturing Survey" 1998).

The concept of the *digital factory* goes even further. Computer and Internet technologies can be used to create an enterprise-wide computer solution that enables manufacturers to plan, simulate, and optimize a complete factory, its production lines, and its processes at every level of detail, supporting the development of a product from conception throughout production (Beit-On 1999). Such computer solutions are often part of a broader *enterprise resource planning* system, which are integrated business software and Internet telecommunications systems that power a corporate information structure, thus helping companies to plan and control their inventory, purchasing, manufacturing, finance, marketing, and personnel operations multinationally (Taylor 1999).

In 1999, Honda Motor Company, which has what has been referred to as "state-of-the-art" production facilities, was developing new manufacturing methods designed to cut the cost of making a car in half (Thornton and Kerwin 1999), even though in a 1999 study, Honda's labor cost per vehicle was half that of GM (Ball 1999). Labor costs per vehicle at Nissan Motor Company's North American operations ($1,058) were close to half those of GM ($1,979) (Lundegaard 2000).

Some firms use *hybrid* strategies which combine two or more of the previous strategies. Nissan Motor Company installed a new *flexible* manufacturing system for its *high-volume* auto body assembly line in its Smyrna, Tennessee, plant in 1991. The system, which uses sophisticated computers, was already installed in Nissan's Japanese plants. Nissan claimed that the system decreased the time needed for costly model changeovers from nine to twelve months to two to three months.

*Mass customization* is a hybrid strategy that enables creation of individualized products—for example, shoes, autos, clothing, toys—to satisfy individual customer needs, and yet achieves the advantages of mass production, a feat requiring extensive use of computer technology.

Another hybrid production/operations strategy, sometimes referred to as *lean production* (Womack and Jones 1996), is found at the Toyota Motor Corporation auto plant in Georgetown, Kentucky. This strategy combines a high-tech approach with other approaches based on elaborate programs designed to teach workers and supervisors to perform multiple tasks and to identify problems and provide instant feedback on how to correct them. For example, workers set up and operate machines, inspect for quality, perform minor maintenance, clean up, and offer improvement suggestions. They pull accessible cords (about 3,500 times per day) when problems arise. Suppliers are generally located nearby to cut costs and enable just-in-time delivery of supplies and parts, the inventory reduction method pioneered by the Japanese in the 1970s, which, in the late 1990s, was a key to the increased efficiency of European manufacturing operations (Marsh 1999a). Workers are urged to study routines and make changes to increase efficiency. This has led to many low-tech improvements—from visual markings and cartoon sketches posted everywhere to prevent factory floor foul-ups, to calculating the seconds required for each workers' tasks and making changes to eliminate wasted motion. In a new plant in Alabama, Mercedes-Benz used a similar strategy (Vlasic 1997).

In its new factory in Brazil, Volkswagen has created a plant in which 800 of its 1,000 workers are contract workers, employed and paid by VW's suppliers. It has been referred to as a *modular consortium*—an assembly plant run mostly by suppliers who assemble subproducts manufactured elsewhere and subassemblies assembled in locations adjacent to the main assembly line. The plant is managed by 200 VW employees responsible for overall quality control, marketing, and research and design. Developing such a factory seems easier to do from scratch, judging by VW's problems in converting its older Sao Paulo plant to the new design (Barham 1999).

Manufacturing must often be viewed from a broader strategic viewpoint, for example, from a viewpoint of the value chain starting with the customer, that is, as an *integrated facility*. Economies made through changing distribution patterns, for example, can at times justify some higher expenses in the production operation ("Manufacturing Survey" 1998). Production/operations strategy may also be designed to support aspects of the value or supply chain within the manufacturing facility. For example, one supplier (Ingram Micro, the world's largest wholesale computer distributor) assembles computers for different firms, such as IBM, Compaq, Digital, and Apple. On its three-quarter mile assembly line Ingram also performs such former retail tasks as installing software and packing and shipping the computer directly to the customer in a carton marked with the local dealer's name (Hansell 1998).

This situation is an example of the blurring of lines among manufacturers, distributors, and retailers that is occurring in industries ranging from energy to medicine. Many firms now merely design products and advertise their brands, assigning the assembly to others. The dominant theory in some industries is moving beyond "just-in-time" to "on someone else's time," where inventory is foisted on another player in the chain.

## OVERALL STRATEGIES FOR PRODUCT
## OR SERVICE DESIGN AND DEVELOPMENT

Product or service design involves designing or redesigning a product or service, as well as developing new product or service specifications within the context of overall company and production/operations strategies. Several basic corporate strategies in this area are discussed in this section.

Companies can choose to be *followers* or *leaders* in product development and design. For example, companies such as Oracle and Toyota choose a leader strategy because their strategy (based on their market analysis) stresses innovation and they have adequate financial resources, as well as engineering and technical expertise, to generate more new products and services faster (Bremner et al. 1997; Griffiths 1997; Raymo and Jackson 1997).

Product development and design, like production, can be done *in-house* or by an *outside* company. Large firms, such as Gillette and Sony, design and develop products in-house. However, because of cost, time, technology, or the special expertise required, many firms use alternative methods: paying someone else to perform the task; purchasing licenses and patents; buying an existing design; using suppliers or the government for product development; and designing and/or developing products through joint ventures (World Wire 1997). As seen in the auto industry, design can be crucial. For example, Asian cars need much different specifications from cars made for Western countries such as: road clearance; design; engine computer position; engine size; suspension; and turning radius (Pollack 1996b).

A *basic research* strategy involves investigating an area or phenomenon without being sure how new knowledge will be used. For example, in 1982, the Dow Chemical Company allocated $500,000 to basic research on ceramic compounds—compounds as strong as steel that weigh half as much. Only years later did the firm find uses for that research in such areas as armor for military equipment (Woodruff 1989). In the mid-1990s, U.S. firms were substantially reducing their investment in basic research (Uchitelle

1996). *Applied research* involves choosing a potential application area based on a factor such as a customer need, and devising ways to meet that need.

Braun AG, a Gillette kitchen appliances and personal-care products German subsidiary, increased sales from $69 million in 1967—the year Gillette purchased it—to $1.2 billion in 1991 by emphasizing technological innovations, superior design and user functionality, and superior quality—all applied research areas. In a similar way, a 1999 *Financial Times* survey of 20 European manufacturing firms identified their key success characteristics: an innovative approach to new product development; a global focus—less than 18 percent of those firms' sales came from the countries in which they were based; and continual interaction with customers (Marsh 1999b). In the late 1990s, many firms, such as the Ford Motor Company, began to use the Internet to speed up and facilitate the design process, as described in Chapters 2 and 9.

## DESIGNING PRODUCTION/OPERATIONS SYSTEMS

As seen in Figures 6.1 and 6.3, designing production/operations systems involves decisions in four task areas: facility type, capacity, and location; facility layout; job design; and productivity, work measurement, and compensation.

### Facility Type, Capacity, and Location

Overall facilities decisions are dictated by the nature of the business. Restaurants, auto manufactures, and clothing retailers, for example, have their own general facility type and location requirements. In many situations, facility decisions can affect a company's long-term success. For example, Blockbuster Video set an industry trend with its successful strategy of opening large video stores, a *type* of store that was not common at the time. By 1999, the "hyperstore" or "megastore" concept had spread to products such as toys, home improvement items, office supplies, groceries, general merchandise, and even books in many countries (Chang 1999; Pereira 1997; Woodruff 1999). At the same time, retail chains such as Staples, a U.S. office supply firm, were testing very small stores in selected appropriate areas (Forest 1999), while Wal-Mart was opening "Neighborhood" markets to fill a market gap between its superstores and small convenience stores (Nelson 1999). Many companies were experimenting with kiosks for Internet ordering that were located within shopping malls or in existing stores.

When faced with the need to increase *capacity,* a firm has several strategic options. *Expanding existing facilities* can be an easy solution in many

FIGURE 6.3. Tasks and Planning Decisions Involved in Designing Operations/Production Systems

| Facility Type, Capacity, and Location | Facility Layout | Job Design | Productivity, Work Measurement, and Compensation |
|---|---|---|---|
| • Determining Capacity Needed, Based on Long-Range Demand Forecasts<br>• Evaluating Market Factors, and Tangible and Intangible Cost Factors<br>• Determining Whether New Facilities Should Be Built or Purchased, or Existing Facilities Expanded<br>• Selecting Region, Community, and Site | • Selecting a Materials Handling Methods and Support Service<br>• Choosing a Layout<br>• Evaluating Costs of Construction | • Specifying Jobs In the Context of Technical, Economic, and Social Feasibility<br>• Deciding When to Use Machine and/or Human Labor<br>• Managing Machine-Worker Interaction<br>• Motivating Employees<br>• Developing and Improving Work Methods | • Measuring Work<br>• Setting Standards<br>• Selecting and Implementing Compensation Plans |

158

situations. Often, however, factors such as availability of space, raw materials, labor, other support facilities, and customer demand create problems that prevent using this approach. An alternative is to *buy or lease an existing plant or service facility* from another producer, or, as an alternative, form a joint venture with an existing company. Problems encountered with this option are that partner's existing plants may not have the facilities needed in the future, or its facility may be in an undesirable area from a supplier, labor, or customer viewpoint. A third option would be to *build a new facility.* A major obstacle in pursuing this strategy can be finances, since major capital outlays may be involved, a problem sometimes resolved through joint ventures. The choice of any of these strategies will also depend on the urgency and duration of the increased capacity requirements and on enterprise-wide strategies and requirements.

Another strategic facility decision might involve whether to centralize or decentralize locations. For example, a firm can have one central plant or warehouse that produces or stores all of the products in its product line. Olivetti did this with its PC division in Italy in an effort to revive the business (Kline 1996). The advantages of this approach include economies of scale, reduced operating costs per unit, higher equipment utilization rates, faster order processing, and reduced fixed costs per unit. Problems associated with this strategy are potentially higher distribution costs and the risks inherent in having only one plant when power failures, strikes, and natural disasters disrupt production.

Another alternative is to have several smaller plants with each either specializing in one product in the product line or producing the entire line. This brings production closer to customers and reduces the risks of a disaster disrupting company production. However, lower volume may increase unit costs. A third strategy is to have each smaller plant specialize in a particular component or components of the product line. This can reduce production costs by increasing economies of scale, but, at the same time, will increase transportation costs.

External economic factors also affect facility location decisions. For example, the Aiwa Company, a Japanese electronics maker, announced in 1996 that it was moving part of its production from other Asian countries back to Japan partially because of the weakening yen—in spite of generally higher labor costs in Japan. This affected products that were mostly sold in Japan or used in components made in Japan (Pollack 1996a). A study of the European market indicates that a "local presence" of manufacturing facilities can have a major impact on success (Steinmetz and Chipello 1998).

The point is that production is now viewed as part of a supply chain, from raw materials to the customer. The low cost of manufacturing the actual product is only one consideration. The ability to serve the customer quickly, to integrate with suppliers and distributors to reduce total costs, not just manufacturing costs, and to adapt to customers' changing needs are also factors affecting facility location ("Manufacturing Survey" 1998). The ability to do all of this has been helped considerably by the introduction of the Internet. Ford's experiences in this area, for example, are described in many places in this book.

Facility location decisions, and the factors affecting them, are discussed later in this chapter in relation to the learning exercise and accompanying expert system description.

### Facility Layout

Layout—the physical arrangement of the various departments, support functions, and equipment within a production or service facility—improves communication, enables the smooth flow of materials or customers from one area to another within a facility, eliminates bottlenecks, and reduces excess inventory, customer backlogs, and handling costs. Five commonly used strategic approaches to layouts are: flow-line layouts; process layouts; fixed-position layouts; manufacturing cells; and hybrid layouts.

### Job Design, Productivity, Work Measurement, and Compensation

The tasks in each of these areas are shown in Figure 6.3. The importance of these and other production/operations tasks to the success of overall manufacturing, business unit, and enterprise-wide strategies was illustrated in 1996 by the experiences of Great Britain's Ispat International N.V., which had become one of the world's ten biggest steelmakers by buying and turning around state-owned steel mills. Various "never dreamed about" production/operations problems requiring considerable entrepreneurial skills prevented, however, the turnaround of its Karmet steel plant in Termitau City, Kazakhstan (Pope 1996). The problems in this plant were many: hundreds of employees came to work drunk; its major customer was broke; and Chechen gunmen and KGB agents prowled the plant's perimeter, threatening suppliers, and asking customers for bribes. However, Ispat's buy-turn-around strategy (including slashing costs and installing new technology) was successful in Mexico, Indonesia, Ireland, Germany, and Trinidad and Tobago; it just did not transfer to the unique conditions in Russia at that time.

Productivity is a constant competitive concern. For example, one of the major problems faced by U.S. automakers is the high productivity of Japanese manufacturing facilities. For example, a Daewoo facility in Korea produced 165 cars per employee, while a General Motors facility in Doraville, Georgia, produced 51 cars per employee in 1998 (Griffiths 1999).

## PLANNING AND MANAGING PRODUCTION/OPERATIONS

As shown in Figures 6.1 and 6.4, planning and managing the production/operations function involves tasks dealing with aggregate capacity planning, materials management, scheduling and controlling, quality assurance, and maintenance. The use of computers in these areas was illustrated by Gillette's decision-making experiences involving the manufacture of its Atra razor in the Pacific Rim for Australia, a situation discussed in Chapter 1. Two key multinational operations planning and managing activities, logistics and sourcing, are described in the learning exercises and accompanying expert system discussion which follows.

## ANALYZING SITUATION FACTORS

Based on the company experiences discussed previously, many factors can be identified which affect strategy formulation and implementation in production/operations, as shown in Figure 6.2.

### *External Factors*

Various external factors affect production/operations strategy formulation and implementation. Analyzing *customer requirements* involves considering customer demand, as well as the types of products and services needed by customers, customer location, when customers need the products or services, the quality desired by customers, customer negotiating power, seasonality of demand, and a variety of other special requirements. *Competitive factors* have an impact on such decisions as the type and kind of products and services offered, where and how they are made and rendered, and the overall production strategy used. This was the case when Airbus began its 1997 reorganization; of Sony as it developed products which linked consumer electronics and computers; and of Jollibee (Philippines) as it replicated services provided by McDonald's—all experiences described in earlier chapters.

*Transportation cost and availability* can affect facilities location decisions. Location choices are often dictated by the availability of transportation methods that make it possible to meet customer demands in a cost-effective manner. In a similar way, *the cost and availability of supplies and suppliers* significantly affect sourcing decisions. *Unions and labor market* factors also influence production/operations decisions, especially those dealing with plant location, as was shown from the success of Northern England in attracting multinational plants. Firms considering plant location decisions also evaluate wage rates, worker availability and qualifications, and

FIGURE 6.4. Tasks Involved in Planning and Managing Operations

| Aggregate Capacity Planning | Materials Management | Scheduling and Controlling | Quality Assurance | Maintenance |
|---|---|---|---|---|
| • Forecasting<br>• Balancing Capacity and Demand<br>• Materials and Labor Requirements Planning<br>• Other Resource Requirements Planning<br>• Selecting an Aggregate Planning Time Horizon<br>• Allocating Insufficient Capacity Among Competing Uses<br>• Determining Technical Upgrading Required to Remain Competitive | • Managing Independent Demand Inventory<br>• Managing Dependent Demand Inventory<br>• Purchasing, Traffic Control and Receiving<br>• Production Control<br>• Materials Handling<br>• Packaging<br>• Logistics Management Including Management of Shipping and Warehousing | • Developing and Assigning Specific Dates for the Start and Completion of Tasks<br>• Monitoring Work in Progress<br>• Collecting and Analyzing Data Needed to Measure the Actual Progress of Jobs<br>• Comparing Actual Progress of Jobs<br>• Comparing Actual Progress to Plan and Taking Corrective Action | • Ensuring Reliability<br>• Ensuring Product Value<br>• Evaluating Usability<br>• Process Control<br>• Product Screening<br>• Service Assurance<br>• Taking Action to Correct Problems<br>• Deciding Where and When to Inspect | • Procuring Tools and Equipment<br>• Establishing Priorities<br>• Maintaining a Parts Inventory<br>• Forecasting Malfunctions<br>• Scheduling Routine Repairs & Handling Emergency Repairs<br>• Preserving a Company's Investment in Assets & Prolonging the Life of Assets<br>• Minimizing Loss of Productive Time and Cost Due to Malfunctioning Equipment |

competition in areas close to the site of a proposed plant, as well as the existence and nature of unions.

*Environmental issues* can affect the way products are made and delivered. These factors are likely to have a continuing impact on production/operations management, as environmental concerns grow globally. The availability and cost of *technology* can influence the design of manufacturing facilities and the ability to deliver services in more innovative and customer-effective ways. This has been shown in the many service innovations based on computer information systems technology and the Internet by banks (such as Citibank) and airlines (such as British Airways). *Other external factors* affecting production/operations decision making may include exchange rates, availability of outside financing, cultural climate and educational facilities of communities being considered for new plant locations, and proposed and existing government regulations.

### Internal Factors

As shown in Figure 6.2, many internal company factors affect production/operations planning decisions. A company's *product and service type and characteristics* affect decisions ranging from overall strategy formulation, to facility design, location, and layout, to quality, maintenance, and materials. *Engineering, technology, and design capabilities* affect such decisions as whether a firm designs products in-house or externally, and whether a firm should make or buy a product. When faced with the need for a new microfilmer, Kodak decided to produce it because it had the required engineering capabilities and a policy of controlling price, quality, and delivery through in-house manufacturing.

*Company strategies and policies* influence production/operations decision making in many ways. For example, a firm may have a policy of innovation, as Intel did to be a leader in making new generations of computer chips. Overall policies governing quality can influence such decisions as whether to make or buy a product, since it is easier to control quality when products are produced in house. The availability of *financial resources* affects production/operations planning, just as it influences other decision areas. For example, depending on the availability of money, a firm may decide to lease rather than buy new facilities, have products designed externally as opposed to in-house, or decide to pursue a strategy of not owning facilities and outsourcing production. *Available equipment, facilities, and labor force* and *company cost structure* are important to production/operations strategy decision making. For example, when a firm's existing facilities or labor force do not permit expansion but the firm needs to increase capacity, then the firm may have to satisfy demand by leasing a facility or building a new one.

Within the context analysis framework and strategic framework described here and in Chapters 2 and 4, strategies are formulated and tasks are performed in the four production/operations areas shown in Figure 6.1.

## EXERCISES:
## SELECTED PRODUCTION/OPERATIONS SITUATIONS

This section reviews several production/operations contingency decision situations using fictitious companies. The objective of these exercises is to help readers review the contingency processes involved in different task areas (by printing out and examining the reasoning processes), practice using key factors to guide decision making, and even to make some preliminary decisions.

### Location and Type of Facility

The following introductory learning exercise uses structured outlines of contingency decision processes in another multinational task area, determining facility location and type—one of the tasks involved in designing production/operations systems. The decision process is outlined in Figure 6.5; the knowledge-based system replicating that process is given in Figure 6.6.

The Plastixx Corporation (a fictitious company), a multinational manufacturer of plastic goods, has built two new plants, one in South Korea and one in Malaysia, in addition to the two it has in Japan and the plants it has in Hong Kong and in Singapore. The company is considering setting up a regional Plastixx warehouse to reduce shipping costs for Plastixx goods being shipped from the Pacific Rim to Europe and the United States. The goods are plastic containers and plastic seals, packaged in lots of 1,000 onto standard packing crates. The items do not need special storage conditions. After initially surveying available sites, the vice president in charge of international operations has narrowed the list to four locations. The choices are: a shore-side lot in Seoul, South Korea; a downtown lot in Taipei, Taiwan; a warehouse just outside Kowloon, Hong Kong; and a lot in an industrial park in Manila, in the Philippines.

The vice president starts the evaluation by examining requirements the new warehouse must meet. For each country, he determines whether U.S. laws govern the relationship between the U.S. and the country. In a similar manner, he checks Plastixx's corporate policies and finds no obstacles to operating in any of the countries considered. Since each of the sites has already been found, he does not exclude any of the alternative countries due to a lack of available land. Next, he checks to make sure that the plastic products to be stored meet health and environmental standards applicable at each location. Because Plastixx will take delivery of the goods, the terms of trade will not be a factor with this warehouse, nor will inventory policy, since the need for the warehouse has already been established. The final consideration is culture and language. Because a warehouse is needed in the Orient, and the company has set no particular requirements as to language and culture, none of the four alternate locations are excluded after analyzing the prerequisites.

The vice president then evaluates other factors at each location. He observes that the United States has trade agreements with several Pacific Rim countries, but determines that none of the agreements pertain to the storing or moving of plastic containers. He then checks to see whether any of the governments have policies favorable to a company such as Plastixx; he finds that none do.

He then does a financial analysis. First, in each country he calculates transportation costs from production sites to potential warehouse locations,

FIGURE 6.5. Factors Affecting an International Warehousing Decision

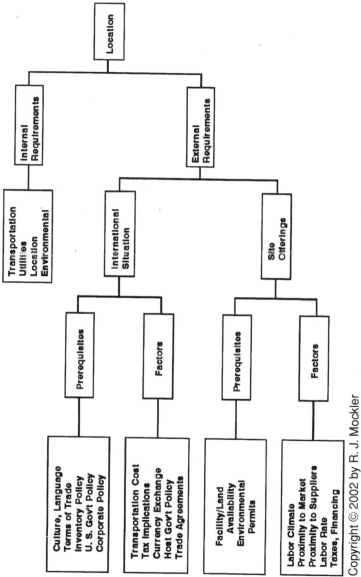

FIGURE 6.6. Dependency Diagram: Warehouse Location Decision

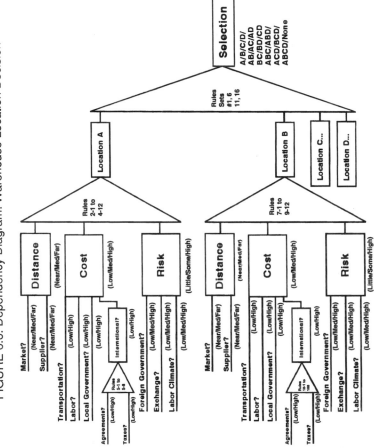

166

and then on to the United States and Europe. He calculates labor costs and evaluates the overall labor environment in each country. The taxes and financing costs at each location are studied, as are their effects on Plastixx's U.S. tax obligations. The effects of currency-exchange problems and the costs of currency transactions in each location are also factored into the analysis. Because all of the nonfinancial factors at all of the locations are favorable, the vice president chooses the site that is most favorable to Plastixx based on the financial analysis.

The system replicating this type of decision is given on the computer disk accompanying *Strategic Management* (Mockler 1993), in a file named LOCATION. The system can be run by following the instructions accompanying the disk and used to practice making decisions in this area. The reader can also print out the contingency rules leading to the decision to study, in very specific detail, the contingency reasoning involved.

### Supply Chain Management

Supply chain management, an important part of planning and managing the production/operations function, involves the sources and methods used to obtain and move material, products, and services required in a firm's business operations. A sophisticated example of using computers to make this type of decision is given in Chapter 1 in which the sourcing and logistics decisions implemented for Gillette's Atra razor cartridge was described.

Sourcing and logistics management is increasingly computer driven and dependent on the Internet, as more suppliers and distributors worldwide— the so-called global partners in the supply chain of many multinational firms—are linked by electronic data interchange (EDI) systems through the Internet. Such systems allow companies to carry less inventory, meet production parts needs at less cost and on a more timely basis, and even design products (Newing 1999). Many business-to-business supply systems have been developed using the Internet, an explosive trend, which has, for all practical purposes, eliminated the formal purchasing function in many firms—a major strategic management change for companies operating in any industry (Deutsch 2000).

The degree of integration of computer systems with delivery and production scheduling, transportation, and warehousing has led to the development of worldwide logistics service firms, such as FedEx's and UPS's new logistics services (Brooks 2000a,b). An increasing number of independent internet auction services also exist, often called business-to-business (B2B) cybermarkets, companies through which manufactures in many industries, such as chemicals, automobile parts, and electronics, can buy from suppliers who bid for their business. FreeMarkets was one of the first such companies. Such seamless network supply-chain thinking has led to more effective cycle time management, which focuses on purchasing and delivering products and services more quickly and cheaply (Hult, Frolick, and Nichols 1995; Stein and Sweat 1998).

The following is an example of how a sourcing situation was handled in an actual situation in Asia. The process described here is outlined in Figure 6.7; the knowledge-based system, given on the disk accompanying *Strategic Management* (Mockler 1993), is outlined in Figure 6.8.

The RXC Company in Malaysia sends a sourcing request to its headquarters for a pharmaceutical product: Feldene 25 milligrams (mg) in bottles of fifty capsules, packaged in boxes of 100 bottles per box. RXC needs 100 boxes per month for six months. Following the steps given in Figure 6.7, the materials analyst first determines Malaysia's closest supply area to be Asia, specifically Hong Kong. The analyst determines from computer reports that Feldene 25 mg in bottles of fifty capsules is not in inventory at present in Hong Kong and that no shipment of the product to Hong Kong is forecasted.

The analyst next determines that two manufacturers are producing Feldene 25 mg in bottles of fifty capsules in Australia and the Philippines. Computer reports indicate that Australia has a capacity problem and is currently manufacturing Feldene 25 mg for domestic consumption only, so this source is ruled out. The product is available in the Philippines and the financial factors studied show that the product cost is average, product markup is low, and the percentage of profits that can be sent back to the parent company in the United States is high. Therefore, financial factors are favorable. Philippine manufacturing factors show that actual product cost is average, product quality is high, and plant capacity is ample. Materials availability and transportation costs are also favorable. Overall, then, manufacturing factors are also favorable. In the Gillette computer sourcing and logistics system discussed in Chapter 1, most of these analyses were done by computer using online computer connections with manufacturing and warehouse units.

An analysis of legal factors reveals that import laws are flexible (low), the need to export is high, and ownership status is high (wholly-owned investments are allowed). Overall, legal factors are favorable. Political factors show that the government is not stable (low), relations with the United States are good (high), and the economic situation is weak. In this case, overall political factors are average. A recommendation is made, based on this analysis, to use the Philippines to supply Malaysia with Feldene 25 mg in bottles of fifty capsules. This decision is taken to the Pricing/Cost Department, which, after a review of the relevant factors, agrees to use the Philippines.

In this situation, an Asian manufacturer was found. There are, however, situations in which a viable sourcing candidate is not available in Asia. The analyst would then check European plants, beginning with Germany due to favorable export laws. If the search for a European source fails, Brazil would be considered because it has excess capacity, followed by Canada,

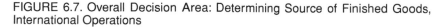

FIGURE 6.7. Overall Decision Area: Determining Source of Finished Goods, International Operations

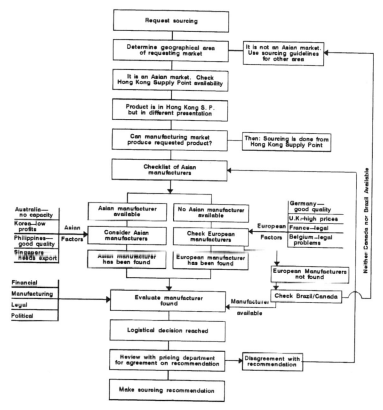

due to its high quality and reasonable prices. Once a country outside Asia is found, the choice is reviewed in light of the financial, legal, manufacturing, and political factors analyzed and described.

This exercise and the prototype knowledge-based system (KBS) given on the disk accompanying *Strategic Management* (Mockler 1993) (file name: SOURCING) replicates the sourcing/logistics decisions that are made to determine a suitable finished goods source for nonmanufacturing countries. The reader can run this system to practice making decisions and to print the contingency rules leading to the decision to study in detail the contingency reasoning involved.

FIGURE 6.8. Dependency Diagram for Logistics Planning: Determining Source of Finished Goods—(Initial Prototype)

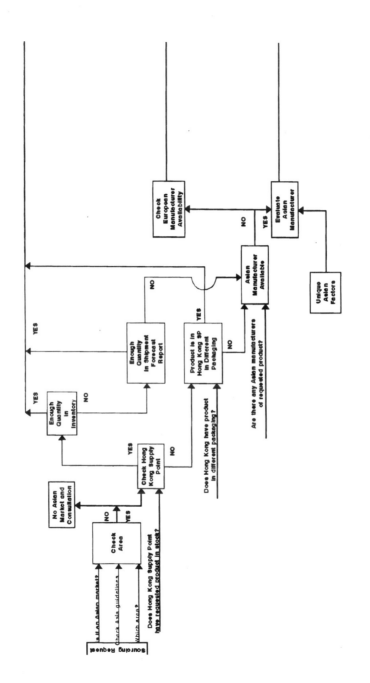

FIGURE 6.8 *(continued)*

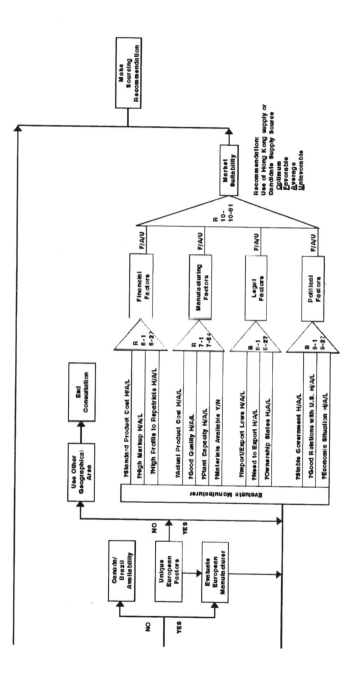

171

## *INTEGRATING FUNCTIONAL STRATEGIES, PLANS, PROGRAMS, AND BUDGETS*

Functional strategic management involves developing and integrating strategies, plans, programs, budgets and controls.

- The first level of integration of functional areas is through enterprise-wide and business unit strategies and plans. Functional management is best done within the perspective of overall strategic management frameworks.
- A second requirement is to coordinate functions, as programs are developed. Later chapters discuss the many techniques used today to integrate operations through team efforts and other integrating human processes and information systems, such as the Internet.
- The third strategic integrative focus is the external environment. Functional areas must have an external focus that enables anticipating and meeting the challenges of the marketplace (marketing management) and advanced technologies (product development and production/operations management). Exploiting these new directions requires strong internal enabling systems that encourage interaction among functional areas and organizational learning. These systems are nurtured by entrepreneurial organization and leadership, as described in Chapters 9 through 14.
- A fourth key requirement is control mechanisms, including budgets. These are discussed in Chapter 8. They include control systems that function to stimulate innovative entrepreneurial thinking as well as those designed to control outcomes. Both kinds are needed.

Strategic management involves more than planning and decision making, however. It also involves doing what is necessary to get the job done within well-defined, general moral, legal, ethical, and policy strategic guidelines, as an enterprise carries out its strategic framework. An essential part of this process is the emerging formulation of specific strategies and plans at all levels. This chapter discussed this phase and provided specific exercises in learning how to study a competitive market in a structured way to develop strategies, plans, and actions.

This implementation process, along with the enterprise-wide and business unit strategies and strategic plans, strives to integrate company operations with each other, as well as with the different contexts in which a firm operates. The cultural contexts affecting interpersonal relationships are also important in multinational strategic management, as discussed in Chapter 10.

## SUMMARY

Although the focus of this chapter and Chapter 5 was on the functional areas of marketing and production/operations, the tasks involve decision making at all levels—enterprise-wide, business unit, and functional—because functional decisions are made within the context of broader strategic planning frameworks. In addition, the situations discussed in Chapters 5 and 6 included reacting to immediate market needs, meeting anticipated changes, and responding to, and creating, new long-term markets. Such situations require balancing global efficiencies with local responsiveness and the rapid transfer of new knowledge in changing global markets. These situations also require balancing and integrating diverse, and often conflicting, forces, as in other multinational management task areas.

Most of the examples discussed in this chapter and Chapter 5 were, however, designed as examples of basic multinational decision making to provide introductory learning experiences. For this reason, they are somewhat simplistic and so do not necessarily fully replicate the synergistic complexities of actual situations. For example, although it is useful to segregate task areas for discussion and learning purposes, and while many functional decisions are task-specific, decisions in each area are often interrelated. Mitsubishi's decisions concerning method of entry/operations, market selection, and product offered, were part of a strategic decision involving all three task areas.

In addition, like an actor or a skier training to learn his or her chosen field, mastering techniques, such as those given in Chapters 5 and 6, is only a first step. Using techniques creatively and integratively is the key to finding good solutions and getting the job done. Learning to synergistically and effectively put to work the different aspects of a discipline, such as multinational strategic management, to make things happen in real life goes beyond book learning—it requires experience in actually doing it.

The Boeing Company, in response to a soft world jetliner market, turned to China, a fast-growing jetliner market where it had already sold 100 planes valued at $4.5 billion by 1995. In exchange, Boeing gave China (the world's biggest jetliner market) parts-making contracts, manufacturing expertise, and assistance with safety problems. For example, a state-owned Chinese factory was making as many as 1,500 tail assemblies for Seattle-based Boeing operations. Such exchanges are needed because China is a very competitive market, and to compete with Airbus Industrie of Europe, Boeing has had to make concessions.

Although such a move furthered Boeing's intermediate-term prosperity, it created local labor problems that had to be balanced with its longer-term strategic moves. Boeing's cutbacks had reduced its workforce by 30,000 since 1989. In October 1995, Boeing's 33,000-member machinists' union went on strike to demand that Boeing cease or reduce subcontracting. The union was also pressing the U.S. government and President Clinton to halt exportation of jetliner production and technology to China, which was trying to build its own airliner industry. The press has called Boeing's position a high-wire balancing act. The problem is that Boeing is competing against foreign firms with lower costs in worldwide markets that are growing faster than the U.S. jetliner market. Without effective cost control and new joint manufacturing/marketing ventures, the firm's long-term future was cloudy. The problems increased during the Asian financial crisis, and in late 1998 Boeing announced layoffs of an additional 40,000 workers (Parkes 1998; Zuckerman 1999b).

The paradox at Boeing to be resolved affected the unions, the company, and the U.S. government. Unions wanted Boeing to compete globally because, without foreign sales, employment would drop substantially—over 70 percent of Boeing's sales were overseas. Boeing had to subcontract production overseas to get sales and compete with competitors with lower labor costs. In addition, foreign nations that agree to buy planes from Boeing often require some of the work be done in their countries. In late 1996, Boeing was also going through a major internal reengineering and a proposed merger with McDonnell Douglas to achieve the strategic advantages needed to compete in the future with a much stronger Airbus.

In early 1997, Guess? Inc., an apparel firm, was criticized for having reduced the percentage of garments made in Los Angeles from 75 percent to 35 percent over a five-month period, through moving much of its production to Mexico. According to the company, this resulted from the impact of the North American Free Trade Agreement (NAFTA) and the General Agreement of Tariff and Trade (GATT), two trade agreements alleged to have led to the loss of over 100,000 textile jobs (out of a total of 1.6 million) in the United States. The company reported that the move to cheaper foreign plants was necessary to maintain competitive costs and prices (Hornblower 1997; Rundle 1997). The unions responded with lawsuits and a push for government investigations, creating major problems for Guess?.

A problem faced in manufacturing management is the continuing pressure to reduce prices, a growing worldwide deflationary trend (Jackson 1998). Increasing operating efficiency is a primary manufacturing task; the Internet has provided a major enabler for doing this. Adding value to increase profit margins is also an important task. GE, for example, has increased margins by selling all kinds of services to buyers of its aero engines, turbines, and medical scanners. Increasingly, GE has made its money from related services, not from manufacturing.

The situations faced by Boeing, Guess Inc., and GE, as with the problems faced by Anheuser-Busch over the use of the Budweiser brand name in Czechoslovakia (described in Chapter 1), are encountered worldwide. Such situations illustrate how multinational situations can, in practice, be much more complex than the examples described in this chapter. Many of these complexities are explored further in the following chapters.

## *REVIEW QUESTIONS*

1. Explain the concept of marketing and its role as an enabler in multinational strategic leadership and management.
2. Describe the major decisions made when formulating a strategic marketing plan and use examples of actual company experiences to support your answer.
3. Discuss product and service strategy decisions. Describe company experiences that show successes and failures in identifying and attempting to serve multinational target markets in light of competitive pressures. What is the importance of superior core competencies to success in these experiences?
4. Discuss the critical factors affecting strategic product and service decisions by examining and explaining the impact of different factors on the decisions, as illustrated in Figure 6.7.
5. Describe situations in which pricing was of strategic importance. What factors does a manager focus on in these situations and what are the choices a manager generally has in pricing strategy decisions?
6. Discuss the long-term marketing plans that Hewlett-Packard and Microsoft were implementing in 1996 to gain and maintain a competitive edge in the highly competitive computer market.
7. Identify three commonly used methods of entry/operating in multinational expansion situations. Focus especially on the many kinds of joint ventures used. Use company examples to illustrate your points.
8. Describe in detail the production/operations functions outlined in Figure 6.1, including their interrelationships. Give specific company examples in international markets.
9. Describe the major external and internal situation factors that affect strategy formulation and implementation for production/operations. Give examples of their impact on decisions and actions in multinational companies.
10. Describe in detail some of the overall production/operations strategies commonly used by multinational companies. Identify the situations in which they can be effective. Use company studies to illustrate your answers.

11. Describe the ways in which several of the production/operations tasks covered in the chapter function as enablers of enterprise-wide strategic plans.
12. Discuss some of the complexities involved in integrating planning and action in the functional areas when working to carry out enterprise-wide strategic plans.

## EXERCISES

1. Review current periodicals to determine how well Hewlett-Packard and Microsoft succeeded in implementing their strategies. Be sure to discuss the impact of critical situation factors on the outcomes you describe.
2. Research Sony's venture in multiplex cinemas in the United States and compare their success and/or failures with AMC Entertainment's venture in Britain.
3. Based on your research, select two examples of a company entering or operating in a new international market. Describe their approaches, compare them, and evaluate their relative success or failure.
4. Based on your research, select a company whose recent international product initiatives have created problems for its competitor(s). Evaluate the move, discuss ways in which it might have been anticipated and handled, and suggest possible alternative actions which competitors might take to catch up.

# Chapter 7

# Enabling Advanced Technologies: Telecommunications and Computer Information Systems

Technological advances are having a substantial impact on multinational strategic management. For example, development of new energy forms—solar energy, fuel cells, and other alternative fuels and energy sources, such as windpower—could reduce pollution and increase efficiency of energy production and use. British Petroleum projected that its annual sales of solar energy equipment would increase to $1 billion in the early 2000s. New energy forms have nurtured the development of new kinds of auto engines, some using combined energy sources ("Cleaner Cars" 2000a; Port 2000).

New developments in genetics, another advanced technology area, promise to produce new forms of plants and foods, new cures for diseases, and even suggest the possibility of human reengineering (Golden and Lemonick 2000; Hall 2000; Lemonick 2000). Brain studies are helping to discover new ways to train people and help them learn more efficiently and effectively. Increased knowledge of the ways the brain appears capable of renewing itself over a lifetime, and the way it may or may not affect child development, could lead to discoveries in behavior and personality modification (Johnson 1999).

In the computer area, since 1971, microprocessors have increased in power from 2,300 transistors processing 60 million instructions per second (MIPS) to 5.5 million transistors processing 400 MIPS. By 2011, microprocessors are expected to contain a billion transistors processing 100,000 MIPS, or even considerably more if molecule-size switches built with chemical processes are perfected (Markoff 1999), which will revolutionize computers and related fields.

The Internet is among the most widely recognized technologies affecting businesses and their strategic management. By enabling people to shop at home and businesses to deal with suppliers electronically, the Internet is changing the way many businesses operate. Having direct access to consumers, for example, allows businesses to bypass traditional sales, distribution, and retail channels. Internet capabilities in this way significantly affect business strategy. For instance, the Internet has become an efficient media for classified advertising, a lucrative income source for newspapers, and threatens to provide a convenient alternative media to newspapers at lower costs. In this sense, the Internet has been called a "disenabler," because it enables easy market entry of new competitors. It is also an "enabler," because in many situations it provides a means of reducing selling and servicing costs or of communicating changes in strategy rapidly across all company divisions worldwide. In changing the ways people and businesses work, then, new technologies create business opportunities *and* threats.

Telecommunications is defined as any transmission, emission, or reception of signs, signals, writing, images or sound, and intelligence of any nature by wire, radio, optical, or other electrical or electromagnetic systems (Akwule 1992). Telecommunications and information systems are among the advanced technology areas which, especially through the Internet, are having a major impact on business (Schlender 1999). Telecommunications and the *computer information systems* that use them have had a substantial effect on business. For example, these technologies are expected to be a major contributor to the creation of a truly "global village," as rapid expansion of satellite programming worldwide accelerates global communications and the way people think, live, and work.

A wide range of business computer information systems use worldwide telecommunications. Many are proprietary and/or Internet-linked company *(intracompany)* information systems, such as the globally linked production/operations computer systems at Gillette (described in Chapter 1) that determined the locations in which the Atra razor could be most economically manufactured.

*Business-to-business* systems include the Electronic Data Interchange (EDI) systems linking companies and their suppliers. Such systems allow, for example, hand-held computers in a retail store to generate information that can be used to check inventory, order replacement goods from warehouses, or generate orders to suppliers for replacement goods—all without human intervention. An example of a *business-to-individual customer* system would be Federal Express links with the Internet which allow customers to check on the status of their package by computer.

This chapter discusses both telecommunications and computer information systems and their impact on multinational strategic management. It also discusses problems encountered in diffusing these technologies worldwide, especially in developing countries.

## TELECOMMUNICATIONS

Telecommunications systems provide the access and speed needed for global information systems to function effectively. In theory, over the next decade, through advances in telecommunications, it will be possible to link every home (and so every person) in the world through any one of a number of telephone, video, radio, computer, or facsimile devices. The implications of this (total and instant communication among all people worldwide) for business is vast.

## Transmission Systems

Telecommunications systems use electrical or electromagnetic energy to transmit information, in the form of sound, light, or mechanical energy, between two or more points. The information is first converted into energy and transmitted over wires or radiated through space to a receiver, where it is then reconverted into its original form or another form understandable to a person or machine (Akwule 1992). The signals can be either *analog* (electronic frequency sound or acoustical waves) or *digital* (a series of electronic signals representing discrete numeric values, represented by the binary numbers (0 or 1) that are used by a computer) (McDaniel 1994). Digital signals are more commonly used since they are more efficient for business purposes.

Telecommunication transmission systems can be either wireline or wireless (or some combination of the two).

### Wireline Transmission Systems

Three wireline systems are commonly used. *Copper wire* is used for basic telephone systems. *Optical fiber,* which transmits light waves and so permits much faster communication (186,000 miles per second) and which enables more conversations to be carried over a narrower cable (making it cheaper), is replacing copper wire as an essential component of telephone transmission systems. Another advantage of optical fibers is that they can carry video in addition to voice and data. *Coaxial cable* uses two conductors: a hollow metal tube about the diameter of a pencil, and wires wrapped in insulation inside the metal tube. It is used especially for long-distance communication since it can carry more channels than copper wire.

### Wireless Transmission Systems

Current global wireless communication networks are made possible by the use of two abstract properties of nature: electromagnetic energy and orbital space. Long-distance wireless communication systems—telephone systems, television networks (Cable News Networks, for example) and computer networks (the Internet, for example)—function by converting information into energy that is then radiated through space. The electromagnetic spectrum—the range of available natural energy resources that make transmission of telecommunications signals possible—and the orbital space available for satellites are limited natural resources. As these resources are increasingly used for a rapidly growing number of functions, problems are expected to arise involving their allocation (Akwule 1992). The following paragraphs discuss several familiar wireless transmission systems.

*Mobile radio communication* networks are widely available, due largely to developments in cellular radio and related personal communications services (PCS), which make the limited number of frequencies available to many more users. Cellular radios function by dividing an area geographically into cells with each cell having its own base station; each mobile terminal communicates with a base station (cell site) using specially allocated ultra high frequency (UHF) channels. Advances in integrating cellular technology with satellites and computer-assisted technology create endless possibilities for individual subscribers on the move. Modern cellular networks, introduced in 1981 in Scandinavia, in 1984 in the United States, and in 1986 in the United Kingdom, were growing rapidly worldwide during the late 1990s. So great were the hopes for cellular phone growth that major firms in Europe (such as Vodafone Air Touch and Mannesmann) were bidding extraordinarily high prices (thirteen times revenue) for available cellular phone companies (Cane 2000).

*Microwaves* use a frequency band (3,000 to 12,000 megahertz (MHz)) for line-of-sight microwave relay links in which signals are transmitted from antennas mounted on tall towers. Repeater stations, which pick up, amplify, and transmit signals, are also towerlike structures placed at twenty-five- to thirty-mile intervals, usually on hilltops. The microwaves connect large population centers and can carry thousands of telephone channels on a single microwave carrier.

*Satellites,* giant microwave relays in a geostationary earth orbit (a nearly circular orbit 22,300 miles over the equator), operate in the microwave band. A satellite can, at any one point, view 40 percent of the earth's surface. Its antennas can be designed to send a weak signal to this entire area or to concentrate stronger signals from an earth station in one country to several different stations located in the same, or different, continents or countries. This technology enables close to 4 billion television viewers to watch a World Cup soccer match, more than thirty times the number of people that watch a U.S. Superbowl football game.

Satellites have to be separated to avoid radio interference, so only a limited number of orbital positions in geosynchronous orbit can be used for communication. In spite of this, satellite transmission capabilities are developing quickly. For example, in early 2000, Hughes Electronics launched three satellites to supply digital "Direct TV" for the home. Direct TV antennas are becoming the fastest-selling consumer electronics product in history and are becoming available well ahead of cable companies' efforts to use digital processing to create hundreds of television channels, and of broadcasters' and TV and computer manufacturers' efforts to create digital

TV systems. A major advantage of "Direct" television installations is their size—they are only 18 inches in circumference and are easily attached to the side of a house, which enhances their portability and ease of installation.

The most popular transmission systems will likely integrate optical fiber, coaxial cable, mobile communications, and satellite systems where cost effective technology enables such integration. Some argue that mobile telecommunications will spur and lead the next major technology revolution as new wireless technology enables mobile phones to more fully conform to developing "wireless application protocol" (WAP) standards and interact more effectively with Web sites (McCartney 2000; Shillingford 2000). Others argue that opportunities in the mobile area are often oversold since mobile is not always the most cost effective telecommunications media. In addition, the time needed for mobile technology to be developed for profitable mass marketing may be much longer (up to ten years) than now anticipated (Hamilton 2000).

## Types of Telecommunication Transmissions and Connecting Devices

The most commonly used types of telecommunication transmissions are voice, data, and video.

*Voice.* Voice transmission is accomplished using different kinds of equipment. The *basic telephone* uses a microphone to convert speech or sound into electric signals transmitted over various wireline and wireless systems. *Cellular phones,* which are now small enough to fit into a pocket, use wireless systems.

*Data.* The first transoceanic cables were laid in 1858 for *telegraph* data communications. The *facsimile or "fax" machine,* a popular form of data transmission, can transmit still pictures and printed matter by telephone, radio, or telegraph, for reproduction by another fax machine. *Computers* are another popular means of communicating data, which can be stored in memory, processed by components, and sent and received through input/output devices. Communication systems such as the Internet and the development of network computers (NC) has increased the capability of computers to link information systems globally. Modern computers also have video capabilities.

*Video. Videophones,* introduced twenty-five years ago by AT&T, were initially not successful because of the fuzzy picture and the fact that while people like to see others while phoning, they do not like to be seen. New versions, however, have recently been introduced for use in health-care services and a wide range of businesses. In the future, *Videodialtone* will allow a dialtone to be activated directly through a television set, thus enabling and enhancing video-on-demand services and other interactive online services. *Videoconferencing* uses video cameras to capture activities of groups at different locations, with each group having the ability to view the other on a television monitor. Each location has a similar setup. Many firms now use such conferencing worldwide: one division of General Electric uses video-conferencing as many as 1,000 times a year. *Desktop videoconferencing,* another emerging technology, enables adding Internet-based videoconferencing capabilities to a computer at a cost of less than $1,000.

### Expected Future Telecommunications Technological Developments

A number of new developments promise to make telecommunications even more effective and efficient for multinational management. The integrated services digital network (ISDN) provides a means of combining high-quality voice and high-speed data transmission in a single economical line. ISDN can improve any communication that requires voice, data, image, or video, whether separately or together. Efforts are being made to combine ISDN, voice mail, and long-distance telephone services. Ansynchrous Transfer Mode (ATM) is a new technology capable of offering users high bandwidth for sending and receiving mixed video, data, and voice transmissions.

Telecommunications technology trends are affecting competitive positions in the telecommunications industry and stimulating international expansion, mergers, and partnerships (Waters 1999b). Many cable and telephone firms are forming joint ventures and merging. For example, in 1998, AT&T, the largest long-distance telephone carrier in the United States, acquired Tele-Communications Inc., the number two cable television company in the United States, for $31.8 billion, and MediaOne Group for $57 billion in 1999 to become the largest cable company in the United States (Blumstein and Cauley 1999). In addition, in 1998, AT&T bought Teleport Communications for $11.3 billion and formed a $10 billion joint venture with British Telecommunications PLC (Schiesel 1999). AT&T's strategy was to be able to deliver voice, data, and video from and to cellular and wireline phones, TVs, and computers ("Now for the Hard Part" 1999). Other firms, such as the French-based Vivendi, Vodafone Air Touch, Deutsche Telekom, and Telefonica Terra Networks (Spain) are working—often through mergers, acquisitions, and alliances—on developing similar integrated systems that enable linking TVs, phones (cellular and wireline), and computers to the Internet and all forms of communication media, a fully integrated global telecommunications dream (Baker 2000a,b; Greenwald 2000; Maitland and Bianco 2000). This is an integrated industry trend often called "convergence" which, because of technical limitations, will take several years to fully realize (Schiesel 2000a,b).

As part of this integration trend, telecommunications firms are merging with media and entertainment firms. Time Warner now has cable programming and cable operating systems, as well as music, publishing, and TV production units, and Vivendi has allied with Seagrams and Vodafone to create competitive advantages arising from its communications links combined with programming capabilities, including movie and music units (Boudette and Delaney 2000). In general, international telecoms, such as British Telecommunications and Telefonica de Espana SA (the largest communications provider in Latin America), have been seeking mergers to become more competitive worldwide (Rich 2000; Edmondson and Malkin 2000).

In 1999, plans were announced for thirty-six satellite development projects, involving more than 1,700 satellites, at an estimated cost of $50 billion, a trend that threatened to saturate the market (Pollack 1999; Shillingford 1999). In 1995, France's Alcatel Cable SA and AT&T joined to design, manufacture, and install an underseas cable system to encircle Africa by the year 2002, at an estimated cost of $2.6 billion. Underwater fiber cable capacity will double by 2002, as the market for data and voice communications grows an expected $350 billion per year in Europe and North America.

## WORLDWIDE INFORMATION SYSTEMS

Information systems are the organized transmission and dissemination of information in accordance with defined procedures, whether automated or manual. Worldwide computer and other information systems use and are enabled by telecommunications frameworks. Everywhere in the world, business is being challenged and changed by the explosive growth of computer information technology in what is now termed the "wired world."

There are many ways to create and use information systems. Prior to Johannes Gutenberg's invention of the movable-type printing press, people relied on town criers, Irish monks who copied books by hand, smoke signals, carrier pigeons, strolling troubadours, and others for the latest news and information. As time passed, electronic media were introduced. In 1893 in Budapest, Hungary, the *Budapest Messenger,* a local newspaper, offered the first electronic news service—a five-inch telephone speaker connected to two receivers, one for each listener (Ferrarini 1985). It has taken more than 100 years and many technological advances to reach the computer information age, which gives people an overabundance of information through a wide range of media. For example, today, a weekday edition of *The New York Times* contains more information than the average person was likely to come across in a lifetime in seventeenth-century England. Technology advances, the proliferation of media, the increase in the number of people and companies involved in data production and processing, and the low cost of collecting data have contributed to the explosion of information.

## Worldwide Computer Information Networks: Information Superhighways

Telecommunications systems provide the superstructure along which information superhighways may be built and information systems may flow. In this sense, telecommunications systems are only one aspect of that superstructure. They are the electronic or electromagnetic wireline and wireless rails or roadbeds along which the information systems trains may ride or superhighways may be constructed.

Many of the connecting links that enable people to use the telecommunications systems superstructure have already been discussed: computers and their software and processors, telephones and cellular phones, telegraph and telefax machines, facsimile machines, video cameras and videophones, satellite dishes, and other sending and receiving devices, all of which are only another part of a much larger information superstructure.

The most dramatic telecommunications superhighway developed has been the Internet, which functions as the world's largest computer network. The Internet is a network of procedures, protocols, and other computer-based software mechanisms that enables instantaneous, worldwide information transmission. It is a wide area network that connects thousands of disparate networks in industry, education, government, and research.

The forerunner of the Internet was ARPANET (Advanced Research Projects Agency Network), which was created by the U.S. Department of Defense (DOD) in 1969, both as an experiment in reliable networking and to link the DOD to military contractors. It grew quickly, and eventually split into a military and nonmilitary network. These two networks were connected through International Protocol (IP), a system of internationally accepted transmission protocols. All networks in the Internet are connected by IP, which enables traffic to be routed from one network to another (McDaniel 1994). Additional government (the National Science Foundation, for example) and commercial (IBM and Sprint, for example) networks have been created.

During 1990-1991, Tim Berners-Lee wrote the Web multimedia software and put it on the Internet without charge. A major technological breakthrough, the World Wide Web enables anyone to use the Internet to access and establish a home page, on which an individual or company can advertise, sell products, publish notices, and generally communicate throughout the world. Berners-Lee has refused to license the software to any commercial interest, since he believes that it should be available to everyone, which essentially means that the Internet now has a major strategic and operational impact on every business in every industry (Berners-Lee and Fischetti 1999). Today, anyone can create a Web page or site and many have: professors (for their students), businesses (to advertise and sell products), news media (for readers to locate information), and individuals (with special interests, for example). Care must be taken, however, to adapt the page to the cultural differences of those using it.

The introduction of the World Wide Web and graphical interface software, such as Mosaic and, later, Netscape, has led to an explosion in Internet usage. Between 1999 and 2000, Internet usage as a whole doubled in size; it appears that in the future, growth could be even faster. The Internet (and the World Wide Web) will in all likelihood forever change the way business and research is done worldwide, clearly a major strategic impact.

The Internet also promises to yield major cost savings by reducing substantially fax and phone transmissions for example (Romero 2000). The Internet's open accessibility has also led to major changes at firms such as Microsoft, which can no longer control markets with such products as their DOS operating software. The 500 biggest business information technology users were expected to spend more than $20 billion on Internet and other new media initiatives in 2000. Although the following pages describe many success stories, there have been major failures: more than 40 percent of large information systems projects have reportedly failed.

The Internet is only one of many ways to use telecommunications superstructures. The following sections discuss computer information systems developed and used by firms to communicate information globally in three categories: *intrabusiness, business-to-business,* and *business-to-customer.* Some of these systems use the Internet; others existed long before the Internet and e-commerce revolution. Many firms are, however, switching to the Internet to save money and development time, especially when security is not a concern. For example, in 2000, General Electric used the World Wide Web throughout its dealings with suppliers and customers to drive costs down and improve efficiencies.

### *Intrabusiness*

Many firms have developed their own global information systems. For example, in 1999, Tricon Global Restaurants Inc., with 30,000 Taco Bell, Pizza Hut, and Kentucky Fried Chicken locations worldwide, was only one of dozens of firms establishing or expanding internal global computer systems. Once installed, for instance, store locations with EDI access would be able to order supplies from one global clearinghouse (Dalton 1999).

Festo, a medium-sized company headquartered in Esslingen, Germany, with 3,500 employees worldwide and branches in 187 countries, is a world market leader in pneumatics and device control. One of its four major product groups is Festo Pneumatic, which manufactures valves and cylinders and provides complete solutions for device control, offering 35,000 components and 4,000 products by catalogue. All products are manufactured in Germany, and 55 percent of products are exported through one of the company's thirty-five subsidiaries and more than 100 branches. Festo's computerized information and integrated worldwide order processing system are linked to manufacturing and warehouse management systems.

At Festo, between 200 and 300 orders with an average of four items each are received daily from each of the major subsidiaries. Customer orders come into a branch office by fax or phone and are sent by computer to the appropriate subsidiary. If a component is unavailable in that subsidiary's warehouse, the order is sent by computer to the German headquarters where the central computer checks inventories and production schedules, confirms the order, and sends a delivery date to the subsidiary. The computer system then issues either warehouse or production instructions.

Europcar, a rental-car firm headquartered in Paris, created a new information system to match a company reorganization in the early 1990s. The new system replaced fifty-five different systems that were used in nine European countries. It integrated reservations, fleet management, billing, cost control, and corporate finance across all rental car stations and administrative offices.

Westinghouse has developed the Westinghouse Information Network to link more than 600 locations in Europe, Asia, and the Americas. This network is used daily by more than 90,000 people. In the manufacturing area, parts for circuit breakers can be made in the Dominican Republic and fitted neatly into finished products in North Carolina. Orders are placed, parts configured, and shipments confirmed, all machine-to-machine over the network. From a monitoring point in Orlando, Florida, technicians use the network to keep tabs on the performance of Westinghouse turbine generators in the United States and several foreign countries, as well as to spot small glitches before they become big ones.

Westinghouse's network also helps the sales process with such innovations as its "EDGE" advanced negotiations system, which automates pricing and order engineering. Complex negotiations involve far more than face-to-face interchanges; they also involve the people who sell a product, as well as those who price, make, and deliver it. EDGE creates a database of product information that all these groups can access, ensuring that coordinated information flows quickly and smoothly to the people in the negotiation.

Westinghouse's network includes an internal e-mail system which makes virtually every employee worldwide instantly reachable. If desired, employees can even connect their home phones into the network. Managers on the road can tap into the network from laptop computers, and a global voice-mail system helps travelers keep track of messages. Advanced digital technology carries massive amounts of data, including technical drawings. A videoconferencing system enables low-cost, face-to-face meetings globally. These interactive decision-support systems in the network are in addition to normal finance, accounting, and control systems. The Westinghouse Information Network also has links with business customers.

Many problems involving local differences can arise in developing global informations systems, often making it difficult to transfer systems from one country to another. Esprit de Corp, a clothing manufacturer in California attempted to use a manufacturing system developed at an Asian affiliate. The Asian computer system tracked where an item of clothing was manufactured, sewn, pressed, finished, and washed. Unfortunately, the methods used to complete these tasks differed around the world. For instance, in Asia, the shop doing the sewing customarily handled pressing and washing; in the United States these tasks were contracted out. Such differences prevented the transfer of the software, so the company elected to develop new software rather than to redesign the Asian software.

Federal Express had to redesign its billing system for Great Britain and Japan because local customers used different invoicing procedures. Europcar encountered substantial problems in adjusting for foreign currency fluctuations and the different languages in each foreign location.

Worldwide information systems within multinational firms are made up of a variety of systems—from highly integrated global corporate systems and industry networks to individual systems for accounting and finance, manufacturing planning and control, sales support and marketing management, information exchanges through the Internet, e-mail, videoconferencing, voice mail, human resources management, and group/team work.

The most significant stimulator of intracompany worldwide information systems in the coming decade will be the Internet. Weyerhaeuser Co.'s former door division, Marshfield, Wisconsin, attributed its turnaround (return on net assets growth 1995-1998 from 2 percent to 27 percent, market share growth from 12 percent to 26 percent) to its new *intranet,* which is linked to its business to business intranet (Stepanek 1999). British Telecommunications (BT) recovered its intranet investment more than ten times over in the first year when it put the internal paper telephone directories sent to 45,000 staff members on its intranet. Financial services firm Merrill Lynch put its research online to 15,000 consultants and cut paper use by 90 percent.

In general, where huge paperless intranet communications systems are capable of linking to the Internet, outsiders cannot link to the internal intranet without having a password. In many companies, these Internet-based company systems are replacing older proprietary computer information systems. These systems are also the building blocks on which electronic commerce systems linking customers, suppliers, and the company are being built using the Internet. Over 50 percent of large- and medium-size firms in the United States have or will be deploying some sort of intranet by the year 2000.

### Business-to-Business

Electronic Data Interchange (EDI)—the computer-to-computer exchange of business documents and data such as that needed for invoices, purchase orders, letters of credit, solicitations, and proposals—is a widely used form of business-to-business information system. EDI links a business's internal computer systems with those of other businesses. The volume of transactions processed by these systems dwarfs retail sales over the Internet today, and in the future, is expected to grow much faster than Internet retail sales ("A Survey of Business and the Internet" 1999; Tedeschi 1999). The function of EDI is to use electronic transactions to replace the manual flow of paper, faxes, and verbal communications involved in processing orders. For example, EGL (Eagle Global Logistics), an international freight-shipping company, uses EDI technology to support its deliveries worldwide. EGL has an EDI link with 500 of its larger business customers, including Honda Motor Company of Japan. Honda ships more than 300,000 cars and trucks to the United States each year, and EGL handles all the required arrangements including those involving U.S. Customs.

To initiate the shipping process, Honda sends its commercial invoices electronically from Japan to the U.S. Honda office in Los Angeles. The information—details of the cars and parts being shipped, tariff numbers, and the value of each item—is then transferred electronically to EGL's mainframe computer in San Francisco where EGL supplements this data with antidumping (below cost pricing) information, visas for floor mats and other textiles used in the car, and the freight carrier's name. The complete order file—consisting of up to 100 pages—is transferred electronically to U.S. Customs several days before the ship docks in the U.S. port. Customs calculates and sends to EGL the amount of payments due on each shipment and Honda's duty payments are then transferred electronically from a bank designated by EGL's mainframe to Customs. Finally, EGL bills Honda electronically for its services and is paid via electronic transfer of funds.

In 1996, the Campbell Soup Company spent $30 million to redesign its order-processing system around EDI. Called Compass, the new system made 80 percent of orders received paperless, whether they were received from a salesperson's laptop computer or from automatic supplier purchasing systems. The system saved Campbell about $18 million per year by processing orders in eighteen hours, instead of the forty-eight hours formerly required, and by reducing mistakes and the time spent correcting them.

Business experts are predicting incredible growth in online purchasing through the Internet (e-commerce) in the coming years as firms such as General Electric adapt purchasing practices developed through EDI software to the Internet (Waters 1999a), and as firms worldwide rapidly expand their business-to-business Internet systems (Kahoe 2000). For example, Ford, General Motors, and DaimlerChrysler joined together in 2000 to create the world's largest electronic marketplace to fulfill their procurement needs, a marketplace involving tens of thousands of suppliers and over $200 billion in purchases a year (Tait and Kehoe 2000).

Business-to-business Internet systems are also found in the media industry. In the past, many creators and users of photographs, such as news agencies (e.g., United Press International (UPI)), newspaper and magazine publishers, and stock photo houses, did not have automated access to photos nor the means to distribute them electronically. A new Internet software application developed by Phrasea has made this possible. Like World Wide Web sites, Phrasea's archiving or authoring software can be set up on one workstation. Clients seeking photos can then dial in and browse through the available photos, select, and instantly download the high-resolution (digital) photos they have chosen. Prior to this, UPI and other companies had to do a daily analogue broadcast of 400 to 600 faxlike quality news photos. Business clients would select the photos they wanted, and the originals would be couriered to them or delivered via satellite.

Internet developments in the late 1990s were enabling even small companies to automate their EDI. Studies indicate that business-to-business Internet transactions could approach $1 trillion by 2003, over six times business-to-consumer internet sales (Cohn, Brady, and Welch 2000).

### Business-to-Individual Customer (Consumer)

By early 2000, many companies had developed computer links with their customers. Dell Computer, an outstanding example of e-commerce success, was selling more than $2 billion online, more than 16 percent of its total revenues and 50 percent of its revenue was expected to eventually come from Internet-based sales.

During the mid-1990s, Citibank's Hong Kong branches offered automated teller machines (ATMs) and accounts in ten different currencies, enabling customers to exchange currencies instantly. Citibank has used automated business-to-customer information systems extensively in Asia to expand rapidly there. In 1999, Citibank launched e-Citi (at a cost of $200 million) to provide Internet-based services tailored to its retail bank, brokerage, and credit-card businesses worldwide. In April 2000, even GE announced that it too was starting an online bank, joining the rapidly growing online banking industry (Beckett 1999; Deutsch 2000; Harris 2000).

First Direct, a telephone-only bank in Leeds, England, has 500,000 accounts without having a single branch. Telephone banking, sometimes using voice recognition systems, has grown in popularity worldwide. The ability to deal directly with customers has grown rapidly with the expansion of the Internet and the growth in the number and sophistication of Web pages. In Sweden, SE Banken's Internet banking service was handling

42,000 transactions a day in the late 1990s. The Internet has fostered a rapid expansion of financial service offerings by other financial and nonfinancial institutions, as well as by newly formed online banking ventures (Fairlamb 1999). A U.S. discount brokerage firm, Charles Schwab, was doing more than $2 billion in stock trades weekly in 2000, and 20 percent of Nasdaq International's (an over-the-counter U.S. stock exchange) business was being done over the Internet.

Electronically gathered and analyzed data on store shoppers and their buying habits is also widely used by retailers to determine customer buying patterns and adjust stocking accordingly, and to target promotions to specific customers and customer groups. One problem this has led to is many complaints of invasion of privacy on the Internet (Petersen 2000).

Federal Express has a Web site server on the Internet that allows both business and home customers to enter their waybill number when inquiring about the status of a package. FedEx's Web server then sends a query to the FedEx shipment tracking system and the answer is then automatically returned to the customer.

By 2000, many Internet services for small businesses were introduced. Many small companies now use the Internet to serve and enter new markets. For example, Hot Hot Hot, a small store in Pasadena, California, was able to sell its homemade sauces in many countries using a Web site ultimately becoming a pure online business, closing the store. Similarly, a toy firm, lacking Mattel's power to make expensive sales calls, used an inexpensive Web advertising service to advertise its wares around the world for $10 an ad. As part of its expansion into logistics services, in 2000, FedEx began allowing small- and medium-size business to use FedEx's site to set up an online store (Brooks 2000).

Even though business-to-consumer Internet commerce was still in its infancy in early 2000, the promise of e-commerce technologies appeared to be great, though not as great as some were predicting. Late 1999 figures indicated that the Internet could well be just an alternate shopping channel, not an endlessly growing retail leviathan (Koretz 2000). Direct consumer sales through the Internet were expected to rise to $184 billion by 2004, up from $20 billion in 1999 ("E-Commerce: Survey" 2000). In addition to financial services and computer sales, strong Internet sales groups have included travel; books and music; games and toys; gifts/flowers/greetings; jewelry; apparel and footwear; sporting goods; and food and beverages—both domestically and internationally. In 2000, there were estimated to be "thousands" of retail online ventures worldwide.

Weaknesses in Internet commerce include payments security, customer unfamiliarity, the lack of human interaction with customers, privacy, and the fact that businesses are still creating more effective ways to sell on the Internet, (Gomes and Weber 2000; Green et al. 2000; Hamilton and Cloud

2000; Luh 2000; Sager et al., 2000). Still, considerable potential exists for Internet selling as these problems are solved, and as major firms such as Wal-Mart and Marks and Spencer initiate multichannel Internet selling in response to new smaller online competitors (Voyle 2000; Zimmerman 2000), and as European, South American, and Asian countries catch the Internet fever (Cowell 2000; Harding 2000; Nusbaum et al. 2000; "Japanese Internet Tsunami" 2000; Vogel and Druckerman 2000; Wagstyl 2000).

## A Growing Phenomenon with Many Problems to Overcome

Although there are many exciting developments in the computer information systems area (such as the IBM computer's defeat of master chess champion Garry Kasparov in 1997), and many systems now in existence are truly global, many companies, even in industrialized countries, do not yet have such systems in place. For example, Nestlé's policy of decentralizing authority has resulted in different company information systems around the world. Only in the mid-1990s did Nestlé begin to develop global standards for its information systems, as well as other aspects of its business. However, the size and diversity of the subsidiaries worldwide and the differences in the systems then in place made integration expensive and slow, especially given Nestlé's policy of allowing the subsidiaries considerable autonomy (Parsons 1996).

The problems that Europcar, Esprit de Corp, and Federal Express encountered and overcame in order to develop coordinated global information systems included language, foreign exchange, and business practice differences. Differences in organization cultures and local customs have also created resistance to change. Obstacles to diffusing technology and creating integrated global systems using state-of-the-art computer information systems and telecommunications technology are greater when developing or emerging countries are involved, but significant barriers also exist in many developed countries. Overcoming these problems in diffusing information technology requires balancing flexibility and adaptability in local markets and the economies and other benefits provided by standardization processes and systems.

## DIFFUSION OF TECHNOLOGY IN DEVELOPING COUNTRIES

Creating integrated information systems in developing countries is difficult for several reasons:

- Lack of advanced telecommunication systems infrastructures
- Lower level of technical skills
- Lower education levels, making training more difficult

- Lack of substantial financial resources
- Lack of technology, technology infrastructures, and related equipment in place
- Lack of business support services

In developing countries, infrastructures for gathering and disseminating news are needed. For example, within Africa, news does not flow quickly and smoothly among its fifty-four separate countries or to the outside world. Although local publications may fill basic information needs, news of epidemics, floods, or other events is often supplied by the leaders of one government to the leaders of other governments. The general public and outside world often find out about a situation only weeks or months after it occurs.

Telecommunications are a major problem in Africa. The entire continent has fewer telephones than New York City's Manhattan borough, and, in the early 1990s, the waiting list for phone service was 3.6 million customers long; in sub-Saharan regions the wait was nine years. In the mid-1990s, only twelve of Africa's fifty-four countries were linked to the Internet. Recently, South Africa has taken major steps to improve phone service. In addition, AT&T's and Alcatel's fiber-optic underseas cable project encircling Africa will be a major enabler for improving telecommunications.

The education levels of Africans are low by international standards, due to political, economic, and cultural reasons. This makes it difficult for any large number of people to be trained for jobs requiring basic skills such as math, writing, or complicated thinking processes—jobs such as those involved in developing and operating telecommunications and computer information systems.

The Pan-African News Agency (PANA), funded by the United Nations and the government of Senegal, was launched in 1979 and published its first report in 1983. PANA's objective was to gather information about and around the African continent and then distribute it to all African countries as well as others who wanted it. Financial and political control problems arose during PANA's early years and it was reorganized in 1991 with three objectives: develop state-of-the-art global telecommunications, privatization, and independence. In the mid-1990s, most internal communications in Africa were still done by radio or telephone. Although faster than mail, it still took several hours to get to a radio or telephone when a newsworthy event occurred, in rural locations it could take days or weeks.

In an attempt to bring it up to international standards, PANA was connected to the Internet in 1994 through a satellite system called VSAT (Very-Small Aperture Satellite Terminal) at its main office in Senegal (Greenwald 1994). Problems at the home office in introducing the new Internet/satellite systems were typical of those encountered in technology diffusion situations. A VSAT representative and a United Nations Educational, Scientific, and Cultural Organization (UNESCO) representative spent several days installing the system. PANA lacked the funds to hire an expert to operate and maintain the system and no staff members had the needed expertise. As a result, a two-week intensive training program with periodic refresher courses was needed. Many staff members resisted learning how to use the new equipment or were unable to adapt to or learn the new system. Many new people were hired; some left very quickly due to the work load or personality conflicts. Others left during the year for better-paying jobs after they had learned to operate the new equipment. The need for parts and repairs also caused problems, since repair persons were hard to find in Africa.

Gradually, the problems were solved, and by early 1996 the headquarter's international communication system was functioning. PANA now had the capability to send, receive, and search for information worldwide. The next equally difficult phase planned was to upgrade all major local news bureaus throughout Africa.

In another situation, in 1994, Deutsche Telekom reported that it had developed "Infobahn" software that could be used with videoconferencing by operating room surgeons to get an instant second opinion from colleagues thousands of miles away. Through the system, doctors could exchange data with laboratories, general practitioners could communicate with hospitals by online video, and scientific research could be disseminated worldwide for others to use immediately. Such systems proved extremely useful during the war in Bosnia in the mid-1990s. A much more limited satellite system, called HealthNet, is now in operation worldwide. It allows written requests for help to be made and diagnostic replies to be returned by satellite fourteen times a day.

Rapid diffusion of computer information systems technology is an exception in emerging countries, however. In Africa, for example, even though wireless communications, computers, and the Internet were widely accessible in major cities in 1998, their high costs hindered their widespread use throughout Africa (French 1998).

Even in emerging countries that have already made considerable progress in developing market economies, the development of computer information systems does not come easily. For example, a 1996 field study (begun in 1994) of a wide range of firms in China illustrates the continuum of problems and painfully slow progress in diffusing computer information systems (CIS) technology in emerging countries. At one end of the continuum (shown in Figure 7.1) privately-held, wholly-owned, or joint-venture companies in high-tech fields in a highly competitive environment were moving quickly in 1997 to adopt new computer technology. A fiber optics joint venture (FO), a software development firm (FS), which was a partnership of young Chinese computer experts, and a chemical company joint venture (Zenith) were all well-advanced in adopting new computer infor-

FIGURE 7.1. Diffusion of Technology: Continuum of Receptivity

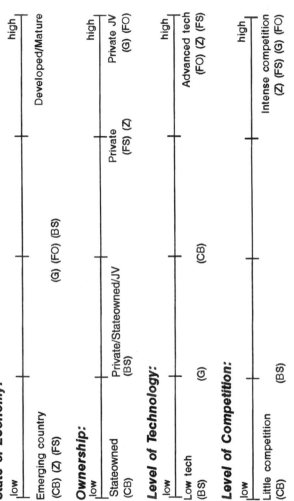

*State of Economy:*

low ├────────────┼────────────┼────────────┤ high

Emerging country          (G) (FO) (BS)          Developed/Mature
(CB) (Z) (FS)

*Ownership:*

low ├────────────┼────────────┼────────────┤ high

Stateowned     Private/Stateowned/JV     Private          Private JV
(CB)           (BS)                      (FS) (Z)         (G) (FO)

*Level of Technology:*

low ├────────────┼────────────┼────────────┤ high

Low tech       (G)            (CB)                        Advanced tech
(BS)                                                      (FO) (Z) (FS)

*Level of Competition:*

low ├────────────┼────────────┼────────────┤ high

Little competition     (BS)                              Intense competition
(CB)                                                     (Z) (FS) (G) (FO)

| G = Gillette | FS = Fourth Shift | BS = Briggs & Stratton |
| FO = Fiber Optic | Z = Zenith | CB = China Bank |

mation technology. These firms needed to use new technologies to support their businesses in general, and had access to the technologies either through their overseas joint venture partners or through training and education.

In the middle of the continuum, several other privately-owned joint ventures in low-tech fields, such as consumer personal-care products (Gillette), and gasoline motors (BS), were moderately successful in introducing basic CIS technology.

At the other end of the continuum, state-owned banks (China Bank) and other companies (Briggs & Stratton, Zenith, Fourth Shift) were very slow in adopting even basic computer information technology. In China in 1997, banks were still protected from privately-owned banking competitors. In the past, these firms had little incentive to upgrade their computer information systems because competition was nonexistent, access to the technology was limited, the basic business was low-tech, and the mindset of managers was to discourage new thinking. The situation was considerably helped by the introduction of development zones that encouraged the formation of software development firms to provide access to and rapidly diffuse computer information systems technology.

These field studies suggested that four factors influenced the rapidity of diffusion of technology: political and economic environment; ownership (private versus state-owned); the level of technology required by the business; and the competition.

## SUMMARY

The creation of the systems described in this chapter at whatever level—enterprise-wide, business unit, or functional/operating—regardless of the company, country, or competitive market, starts with a situation analysis. This basic contingency process approach outlined in Figure 1.1 (p. 5) is discussed in Chapter 1.

Such a contingency process is involved in developing computer information systems. The systems analysis, design, and development approach recommended and used by systems developers is grounded in a thorough identification of the situation requirements. Systems must be built to meet situation, especially user, requirements. Figure 7.2 shows one such systems development process. As in other strategic leadership and management situations, the analysis phase focuses on strategic market and company factors with which computer information systems need to be aligned.

This chapter discussed the difficulties of meeting conflicting situation requirements and reconciling them when developing informations systems in both developing and developed countries. Different languages, accounting procedures, customs and currencies; employee resistance; technological de-

FIGURE 7.2. Systems Analysis Design and Development Process

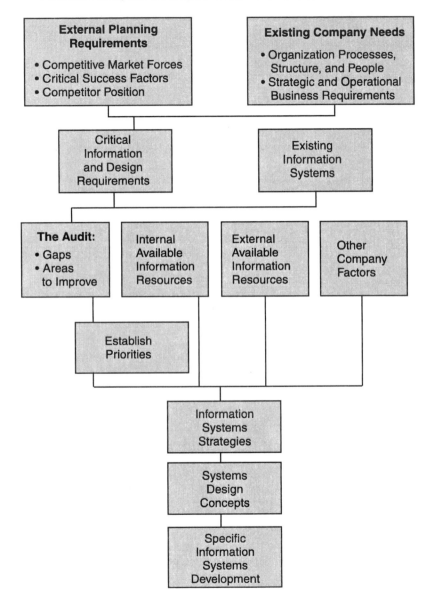

velopments; limited funds; established working procedures; cultural barriers; government regulations; geographical distances; available human resources; and workforce skills and education levels—all multinational factors—can impact systems development and so must be taken into account. Europcar, Federal Express, Esprit de Corps, and the African news service, PANA, are firms that developed advanced information systems which reconciled these local differences.

For many businesses, telecommunications and computer information systems are critical enablers—that is, they are necessary to be competitive. For example, in early 2000, airlines reported the many ways they had developed computer systems to improve operating efficiency—in seat distribution, staffing, services such as meals, ticket selling, dealing with travel agents, etc. (McCartney 2000). Although a well-developed global telecom infrastructure is in place, technologically advanced access to and use of it is still developing. As ways to use existing and anticipated telecommunications infrastructures and technologies are developed, multinational enterprises will be required, as in many other task areas, to manage the elusive balance between global efficiencies and local responsiveness. Many examples of how this balance has been achieved were described in this chapter. The precise solution will be contingent on specific situation requirements, as it is in other multinational task areas.

Given the advances expected in these technologies, a manager can expect the pressures for change and adaptation to continue in what is rapidly becoming an increasingly competitive global market.

## REVIEW QUESTIONS

1. Assess the impact of advances in telecommunication on worldwide businesses. Cite examples to support your answer.
2. Explain how telecommunication systems transmit information. Describe the two types of telecommunication transmission systems and the most commonly used types of telecommunication transmissions.
3. Discuss some of the expected future telecommunications technological developments and how companies plan to take advantage of anticipated breakthroughs. Cite specific company examples.
4. Discuss the importance of worldwide computer information systems networks to a multinational company, as well as some of the problems that may be encountered in developing worldwide information systems. Cite specific company examples.
5. Describe some examples of individual company *(intrabusiness)* computer information systems.

6. What is one widely used form of business-to-business information systems? Explain how specific companies have utilized this method of transmitting information electronically to their advantage.
7. Describe computer information systems that involve businesses dealing with individual customers. Cite specific company examples.
8. Discuss the impact of the Internet on developing intrabusiness, business-to-business, and business-to-individual customer computer information systems.
9. Describe the impact the World Wide Web has had on the Internet's growing popularity.
10. Describe the special problems encountered in creating computer information systems in developing countries.

## *EXERCISES*

1. From recent periodicals, select two companies that have developed worldwide computer information systems. Describe their objectives, how they developed these systems, the problems they encountered, and the benefits achieved through the systems.
2. From your reading of recent articles on the Internet's impact on different business areas, discuss the steps you would recommend that a firm in one of these areas might take both to protect and enhance their present business and to create new business opportunities.
3. Find articles on a new company that uses the Internet and on an existing company that has significantly expanded its business through the Internet. Evaluate the Internet's impact on both companies' futures.

# Chapter 8

# Finance, Accounting, Taxation, and Control Enablers

Rupert Murdoch's News Corporation, an Australian-based multinational company, reportedly makes very effective use of tax regulations when structuring joint ventures. Overall, the company pays about 7 percent in taxes on sales of $10 billion. For instance, a company official acknowledged that almost no taxes have been paid on U. S. businesses, though they account for 70 percent of the company's operating profit. To accomplish this, for example, when News Corporation acquired Ziff-Davis travel publications for $350 million in 1985, it was purchased by a News Corporation subsidiary in the Netherlands Antilles, a country with virtually no income taxes. That subsidiary also legally published the company's other U.S. magazines. To avoid U.S. taxes, a high portion of the profits from U.S. publishing ventures were paid to the Netherlands Antilles company in the form of a royalty—for instance in 1989 around $100 million—in this way reducing U.S. taxable income substantially. Other transactions were also conducted through the Netherlands subsidiary. For example, when Ziff-Davis magazines were sold for $325 million profit, News Corporation avoided most U.S. capital gains taxes by having the profits go to the Netherlands subsidiary (Fabrikant 1996).

Such maneuvering, which is legal and profitable, makes it hard to analyze and evaluate a multinational firm's investment value.

Adapting to and succeeding in the international financial area can be a risky transition for a nationally based financial institution. For example, Deutsche Bank made a high stakes plunge into British/American-style global finance (investment banking), a business fundamentally different from the traditional commercial banking business practiced by German banks. Such a strategy, of course, entailed considerable risks, especially because the bank, for all of its immense size and historic clout on the European continent, was rushing headlong into a number of investment banking fields where it was still a novice. Moreover, Deutsche Bank was faced with the challenge of reconciling enormous cultural divisions, such as the gap between the bank's German management with its vast ranks of managers who had been bred to be solid and dependable corporate lenders and the British/ American deal-oriented investment banks which have made their mark dreaming up and marketing novel financial moves.

As a result, Deutsche Bank encountered many problems, such as when one of the star fund managers at its recently acquired Morgan Grenfell asset management division improperly established big stakes in several dubious companies. The bank fired the fund manager and had to spend close to $300 million in a bid to restore confidence and cover potential customer losses. In spite of such difficulties, Deutsche Bank planned to continue its move toward globalization through expansion in investment banking (Rhoads, Fuhrmans, and Raghavan 2000).

This chapter discusses basic finance, accounting, taxation, and control enablers used by multinational companies. First, finance and accounting are defined, as are their relationships and the related management tasks and processes involved in multinational business situations. Finally, this chapter discusses their combined integrative role in enabling an enterprise to effectively realize its strategic vision by directing and stimulating innovation and by controlling performance.

## FINANCE, ACCOUNTING, AND TAXATION

Finance is the means and methods by which funds are obtained, managed, allocated, and used. Accounting is defined by the American Accounting Association as the process of identifying, measuring, and communicating economic information to permit informed judgments and decisions by users of that information. Tax authorities are a major user of this information. In essence, accounting *measures* financial transactions, while finance *manages* financial transactions and the firm's underlying financial position.

Although accounting and finance are distinct functions, the two are closely related. For example, a U.S. company deciding whether to invest in a joint venture with a Chinese company would examine accounting reports on the financial condition of the potential partner—reports prepared according to different standards and which may be unreliable. Investors in Russia also face obstacles in obtaining accurate information on potential investments. This is not only because financial statements may be unreliable, but also because Russian business managers face many political and criminal pressures which can influence the disposition and reporting of a company's funds. Such difficulties were highlighted in 1999 when Bank of New York was accused of being used by Russian companies to launder money allegedly done to evade taxes and/or other government regulations (O'Brien 1999).

## FINANCE: MANAGEMENT TASKS AND PROCESSES

Multinational financial management presents many challenges because it requires balancing many factors worldwide. Each country has its own reporting requirements. For example, in the securities area, inadequate financial reporting laws often make it difficult to evaluate equity investments in newly privatized Russian and Chinese firms. Inflation rates vary by country and over time: in the 1990s, several South American countries had annual inflation rates over 1,000 percent. Exchange rates can vary from hour to hour, as during Mexico's 1994 peso crisis. Political instability can also create problems, as in India during 1995 when a Kentucky Fried Chicken outlet was temporarily closed and Enron's power plant project was temporarily stopped.

At the same time, many developments in the finance area have made the management of this function more challenging and more efficient. For example, in the late 1990s, worldwide financial institutions were rushing to offer customers electronic access to products and services. In 1997, Citigroup (U.S.) formed e-Citi, creating from scratch an online bank which would eventually provide all the services that Citibank does (Violino 1999). In 1999, Barclays had 400,000 retail banking customers for its Internet banking services and was signing 10,000 more every week (Portanger 1999). American Express (U.S.) started its own online bank in 1999 (Beckett 1999). Even retailing chains in such countries as Japan have started online banking operations, a major strategic change (Tett 2000). The financial services industry as a whole, as well as competitive forces in the industry, have been changing rapidly as electronic, computer, and telecommunications links among institutions worldwide enable faster, easier, cheaper, and more efficient global financial services.

If financial services firms continue to take the steps needed to keep up with and use new technologies, the resulting active markets will enable greater global liquidity of capital, which is good. However, the greater activity also makes capital markets more volatile as traders react to government and economic actions and events. This can make it difficult to effectively time investment decisions.

Developments in the financial area are helping to reconcile cultural and national differences and enable a more global approach. These include:

- the rapid development of global computer networks for information transfer, and the resulting ability to transfer and exchange money, information, and other banking services online through global networks using the Internet and Web sites (Siwolop 1997)
- the increasingly wider range of financial instruments available for investment and borrowing as new kinds of "derivatives" are developed

and computer networks developed for trading them ("Derivatives" 2000)

- the continuing mergers of major banks in different countries and the privatization of banks in many developing and mature countries (Andrews 2000; Betts 1999; Cowell 1999; Raghavan 2000; Wagstyl and Bobinski 2000)—making competitive, diverse, international financial services more readily available worldwide
- the transfer of modern computerized branch banking technology and techniques across borders to nurture global approaches at the local banking level (Remenzi and Cinnamond 1996)
- the automation of stock and futures exchanges and their consolidation across borders in Europe, a process enabled in large part by the Internet (Boland 2000; Ewing and Ascarelli 2000; van Duyn, Rahman, and Labate 2000; Wendlandt 2000).
- the introduction of a new European-wide currency, the euro (Euro) in 1998 ("Survey: Birth of the Euro" 1998)

The tasks involved in managing a multinational company's finances are discussed in the following sections. They include: obtaining the funds (from external and internal sources) needed to start and run a multinational enterprise; determining capital structure; managing global working capital; managing financial risks; financial management of business transactions; making capital budgeting and foreign investment decisions; and the expanding concepts of financial and risk management.

### Obtaining Funds from Global Sources

International operations can be financed from external sources, such as local or international borrowing and equity financing, or from internal sources, such as funds generated by the parent company, or by local or other subsidiary operations.

### External

The external sources of funds in the international area include the following:

*Local capital markets.* When borrowing money (short- or long-term) in the home, host, or another country, many avenues can be explored to obtain the best interest rates. A firm may decide, as did LSI Logic Corporation, that a joint venture (in which LSI retained a majority interest) yields several benefits. First, a firm gains access to local marketing expertise. Second, by setting up a local company, a firm gains easier access to local financing—both long-term bonds and equity and short-term lines of credit—when raising capital for expansion. Local capital sources include commercial banks, investment banks, securities firms, pension institutions, insurance firms, savings banks, equity (stock) markets, and large individual investors. Borrowing locally can help protect the home-country multinational corporation, as it did the Walt Disney Company when its 49 percent-owned Euro Disney operation—which had borrowed heavily from local French banks—ran into financial problems between 1992 and 1994. The local banking situation in developing countries is often unstable, as in Russia and the Czech Republic where the uncontrolled expansion of banks after the 1991 end of Soviet rule eventually led to severe loan problems, many bank closures, and stricter government regulation (Jack 1999). In addition, local banking regulations can change, as in late 1999 in the United States when banking legislation was passed allowing all kinds of financial industries/institutions to sell a wide range of financial products, which can have a major impact on dealing with capital sources (Labaton 1999).

*International capital markets.* Money can be borrowed through several types of international bonds using intermediaries who now operate around the clock. *Foreign bonds* are sold outside the borrower's (issuer's) country. Argentina, for example, has issued bonds in eight different countries (Friedland 1997), and in early 1997 Siemens launched simultaneous issues in deutsche marks, French francs, and guilders with the same coupon and maturity (Gewitz 1997). Trading in emerging-country debt has increased sevenfold since 1992, fueled in large part by the introduction of electronic trading in foreign debt (Lapper and Luce 1997). *Eurobonds* are normally taken to market by a syndicate of banks from different countries: they are borrowed by a company in one country in that country's currency (for example, Italy and lira), and sold in countries other than the one in whose currency the bond is denominated. Eurobonds are the most widely used type of international bonds. In 1996, for instance, Russia sold $1 billion in Eurobonds in its first offering since the Soviet Union breakup, an offering which was oversubscribed. A *global bond,* which combines domestic and Eurobond configurations, is registered and issued in different markets (usually Europe, Asia, and North America).

A variety of underwriting arrangements have been, and are being, developed by investment banks (for instance, Goldman Sachs) and securities firms (for example, Nomura Securities). A company may issue a dual-currency bond, through which one pays interest in one currency and repays principal in a second currency. Bond swaps are sometimes used by a firm to balance its obligations (both principal and interest) in different currencies, as company and market requirements change (a company, for example, may want to reduce risks by spreading its obligations over many currencies, for example). In one instance, the Walt Disney Company borrowed $400 million on which the minimum guaranteed interest rate was 3 percent—interest which could rise to 13.5 percent depending on the success of a package of thirteen Disney movies. Comparable rates at the time were around 8 percent.

Major international banks, such as the Bank of China, Bank of Tokyo-Mitsubishi, Deutsche Bank, National Westminster Bank, Credit Lyonnais, and Citibank, are also a source of funds. These banks provide worldwide commercial banking services (for example, short-term trade financing, currency exchange, and funds transfer) and outside-the-United States investment banking services (for example, packaging long-term debt, mergers and acquisitions arrangements, and equity funding). Because of government regulations, investment banking services in the United States are supplied by securities firms.

*Equity capital markets.* The equity capital market is another major source of funds for multinational companies. To make it easier to raise money this way, many companies list their stock on several different stock exchanges, even though it is expensive to do. In Asia, even major cities in China list their stock on the Hong Kong Exchange (Ridding 1997). In addition to the three major exchanges—the New York Stock Exchange (NYSE), the Tokyo Stock Exchange, and the London Stock Exchange (LSE)—several other developed countries have established exchanges (Canada, Switzerland, the Netherlands, Germany, France, Belgium, South Africa, and Hong Kong). Markets are emerging in many developing countries: Russia, Mexico, Brazil, Argentina, Singapore, Chile, Malaysia, Korea, Taiwan, India, Thailand, and several Central European countries. Many differences exist in how exchanges operate, the hours of operation, settlement times (in Russia an average of two weeks, in the United States three days), to transaction execution (in Russia all executions are made in person by hand; in the United States they are made electronically or over the phone). This is changing rapidly with automation and consolidation of exchanges and the introduction of financial reforms worldwide. Local stock markets are also gradually becoming more attractive as entrepreneurs learn how to overcome problems such as a lack of adequate company financial information, local market and economy information, and adequate trading volumes (Thornhill 1998).

*Eurocurrencies.* Eurocurrencies are any currency on deposit outside the country of origin or issue. They may involve the euro, Euro Yen, Eurosterling, Euromarks, Asiadollars, and other currencies. The deposits are made by governments, individual multinational corporations, and/or banks that have excess cash or wish to maintain local currency deposits outside their home country. Internationally, over $6 trillion is available through Eurocurrencies. Eurocurrencies are a very inexpensive way to borrow and the risks are lower (large transactions by credit-worthy borrowers, fewer government regulations. Most transactions are interbank, but over $1 billion involves multinational corporations. Changes have occurred in this area, however, with the introduction of a common European currency (EU) in the late 1990s and the many problems it has created ("A Survey of International Banking" 1999).

*Offshore financial centers.* Offshore financial centers are located on island states such as the Cayman Islands, Bermuda, the Bahamas, Bahrain, and the Netherlands Antilles, and in countries/major cities such as Switzerland, London, New York, Hong Kong, Singapore, and Luxembourg. These centers offer banking and financial services to nonresidents and are often used by multinational corporations to obtain Eurocurrency loans. The larger centers perform a wide range of banking activities; the smaller ones function mainly as booking centers where transactions are recorded to take advantage of secrecy and low (or no) taxes. Such centers are often part of the global private banking industry which competes for the estimated $15 trillion in investable assets controlled by private individuals, and are often challenged as being a means of laundering illegally earned money.

Even with the wide range of available global sources of funds, questions are often raised as to the availability of capital to meet growing industry needs. For example, telecommunications company expansions in Europe reportedly required in excess of $150 billion in bank loans in 2000, an amount which many considered dangerous to the stability of the European banking system (Sesit 2001).

*Internal*

One source of funds is internal company cash flows generated from operations. The complexities of moving funds among subsidiaries depends on the number of subsidiaries, the needs of the host and home country enterprises, legal regulations, exchange rates, inflation rates, and ownership status. For example, if a foreign country subsidiary is only partially owned, then partner or other shareholder interests and restrictions on the movement of money may have an impact. The amount of cash (cash flow) available and needed is also related to the capital structure of each enterprise; these topics are discussed in the following sections.

Excess funds available in either the host or home country company can be put to work in many ways. For example, money can be transferred by equity investments or loans, dividends can be distributed, or licensing fees can be imposed. In 1993, U.S. companies received more than $20 billion in licensing fees and royalties from their foreign subsidiaries. Another way to meet working capital needs is to adjust the transfer price between units, though this must be done in such a way as to avoid tax and performance evaluation problems.

### Determining Capital Structure

Financial, and other company, political, and competitive market factors affect decisions about capital structures of operations in other countries. For example, in 1990, Rally Dawson Sports (fictitious name) ($29 million in sales) was considering opening a plant in Pakistan and marketing its products (tennis, cricket, soccer, baseball, skiing, football, badminton, and field hockey equipment) in that part of the world. Labor and material costs were low there and the Pakistani government encouraged foreign investments. At first, Rally wanted to create a wholly-owned subsidiary, as it had done in other countries. In the end, Rally decided to find a partner to overcome local political, supply, distribution, and marketing problems.

Rally obtained its potential joint venture partner, Hamid Sports (fictitious name) of Pakistan, through the Pakistani Trade Office in Washington, DC. As negotiations progressed, it was decided that Rally would own 60 percent of the $4 million joint venture (called Ampak International, Ltd., fictitious name), purchasing its interest with machinery and cash borrowed in the United States. The reason Rally did not use Pakistani sources to finance the purchase was that the Pakistani government did not want to dip into foreign exchange reserves. Instead, local banks were to be used for working capital borrowing. The government limited the profits which could be taken out of the country to the amount originally invested ($2.4 million), plus half of all cumulative profits. Detailed financial forecasts of profits, costs, return on investment, and cash flows were then prepared (Fatehi 1996; Springate 1990). As in other multinational management situations, decisions in the finance area are not isolated. Many situation factors have to balanced with financial considerations in making final decisions about financial structure.

Generally, it is better to finance through debt than equity in countries that limit profit repatriation and dividends, but not loan repayments. In countries with high inflation, equity investment of cash should be limited, local borrowing used as much as possible, technology or know-how investment substituted where possible for cash equity investment, and licensing and management fees explored.

In general, the overall financial structure of the parent multinational should be considered when creating subsidiary capital structures, with the objective of minimizing costs worldwide. For example, LSI Logic Corporation needed capital from as many sources as possible, and so local capital was an important source. In contrast, Rally Dawson Sports had cheaper financing sources outside Pakistan, so in that case local financing was used mainly for short-term operating needs. Whether a multinational parent firm invests through equity, debt, or machinery/services may depend as much on other situation factors as on finance factors. Furthermore, the parent can at times leverage its worldwide strengths in unusual ways. As seen from these experiences, what is "best" depends on many factors and must be balanced with what is feasible when making the final capital structure decision.

### Managing Global Working Capital

Three objectives guide managing the flow of capital within and among units of a multinational company: minimizing working capital balances, currency conversion costs, and foreign-exchange risks. Achieving these objectives is affected by local and corporate cash needs and the way in which cash is transferred. A fourth objective is to earn as much as possible on cash held, which depends on the amount, its location, and how long it is available.

Cash budgets and forecasts are used to estimate the minimum level of cash or liquid assets needed, such as instantly marketable securities. Once the need level is determined, decisions can be made concerning whether to invest the cash locally or centrally, and, if centrally, how to transmit it.

Dividends are the most direct way to transfer (or repatriate) cash from a subsidiary or partially-owned overseas unit. However, such transfers are often limited by law or taxed heavily by the host country to control its balance of payments (inflow and outflow of cash). Repayment of loans, management fees, and payment for technology transfer are other useful, but limited, ways to repatriate funds. Licensing fees and royalties are also used extensively to transfer cash. However, fixed import prices can be used when this is not possible. Gillette used this method in Russia. Funds repatriation was accomplished largely through sales of imported Gillette personal-care products and appliances, while all the profits from the sale of razor blades manufactured at a jointly-owned plant in Russia were kept for reinvestment there.

A finance center (regional or international) is one way to balance cash needs with the need to invest excess cash. These centers determine varying cash needs in different locations and the best means of transferring cash to each location daily from central reserves built up with cash inflows from units with excess cash. Internet technology has helped considerably in increasing the efficiency of this strategic activity.

When there are transfers among divisions of parts, supplies, and other services, such as at the Ford Motor Company, *multilateral* or *bilateral netting* is used to minimize currency conversion costs. Netting involves recording all transactions at a finance center. The monies owed among the different units are then, where possible, netted and settled by book transfers instead of by actual multiple payments for each transaction. For example, if a parts exchange occurred between a French and a Spanish unit of a multinational firm (a bilateral netting situation), the two transactions would be netted and only the difference actually paid. When three units or more are involved (a multilateral netting situation), payments among all units during a specified time period would be netted and only the remaining differences actually transferred. Companies, such as the Dutch airline KLM, deal in as many as 180 different currencies, therefore, complex computer decision support systems and the Internet are normally used to coordinate transactions. In making these transactions, an effort is also made to minimize foreign-exchange risks.

### Managing Financial Risks

Foreign-exchange risks involve transaction, translation, and economic (including inflation) exposure (Logue 1998).

*Transaction exposure* arises when the receivables or payables of a multinational firm change in value as exchange rates change. For example, if a German firm is due to pay $1 million for imports in three months at a fixed U.S. dollar price and it expects the German mark to weaken relative to the dollar, it has several options:

- Purchase an option to buy U.S. dollars three months from now at today's exchange rate to protect itself if a drop occurs. If the mark gains in value, the firm can allow the option to lapse and pay for the imports with cheaper dollars.
- Buy U.S. dollars on a forward contract, collect the dollars in three months, and pay the bill with them. If the dollar weakens in relation to the mark, the manufacturer has lost an opportunity to profit from the exchange fluctuation and paid a contract fee as the price of protection.
- Buy an offsetting asset (such as a three-month U.S. treasury note), earn interest on the note, and pay the bill with the proceeds of the note.
- Do nothing and bear the risk.

Each alternative has a cost and a risk contingent on the specific situation factors—these are weighed when making the final decision.

*Translation exposure* occurs when subsidiary balance sheets are translated into the home-country's currency when accounting records are consolidated. For example, Gillette's annual income and balance sheet statements must be translated from foreign currencies into U.S. dollars. Fluctuating exchange rates will impact favorably or unfavorably on consolidated statements. Balance sheet hedges can be used, as when a non-U.S. firm with $50 million at the year's fiscal closing (an asset) borrows Eurodollars to build facilities outside the United States during the coming year (a liability) as a way to protect itself against possible unfavorable exchange fluctuations.

*Economic exposure* arises from possible exchange fluctuations that could affect pricing, which in turn might affect sales. For example, such an economic impact led German and Japanese automakers in the 1990s to build plants in the United States to protect their sales positions there when the value of the Japanese yen and German mark substantially rose in relation to the dollar. The move was also stimulated by a desire to avoid government import regulations and consumer resistance to "foreign-made" products. Since exchange rates generally follow inflation rates, estimates of inflation affect the amount of risk expected from exchange fluctuations and the steps taken to reduce or avoid risks—each of which has a price.

This is only a brief introduction to financial risk management. With the introduction of a variety of new financial instruments, many ways now exist to hedge risks. As mentioned earlier, the Walt Disney Company bonds that were tied to future revenues from thirteen movies is one example of an imaginative financial hedging strategy.

## Financial Management of Business Transactions

When buying and selling in the international market, several financial management decisions may arise:

1. Which currency should be used for the transaction?
2. When and how should credit be checked?
3. Which form of payments should be used?
4. How can financing be arranged?

### Currency Choice

Both parties prefer to be paid in their home currency to avoid risks. When two weak currencies are involved, a compromise is to have payment made in a stable currency, such as the euro. Each country and many industries have their own customs; ultimately the choice of currency is a negotiated item.

### Credit Checking

Checking on a purchaser's creditworthiness is necessary, though sometimes difficult when doing business in a developing country. Simple and inexpensive mechanisms for checking credit are available in many countries; these are similar to the Dun & Bradstreet credit checking service in the United States. International banks are a good source for locating these public and private services, as are country desk officers of embassies and consulates.

### Methods of Payment

Methods of payment include:

- Payment in advance (a rare but negotiable method)
- Open account (best limited to well-established, long-term customers with very good credit ratings)

- Documentary collection (commercial banks handle the paperwork and facilitate payment using such documents as bills of exchange and bills of lading, along with acceptances with and without recourse)
- Letter of credit (a document issued by a bank that promises to pay an exporter upon receipt of proof of fulfillment of the obligation from the exporter), in this area, as in other financial areas, Internet applications are being developed
- Credit cards
- Countertrade (including barter, counterpurchase, buy-back, and offset purchase)

*Financing Trade*

For large contracts, exporters from industrialized countries should develop global financing sources for low-cost loans to support their exports because financing from local sources may be expensive and difficult to obtain. In many countries, government agencies (such as the Export-Import Bank of the United States) will help guarantee contract payment in instances where the exporter finances the purchase in some way.

## Making Capital Budgeting and Foreign Investment Decisions

International finance management involves several areas: funds acquisition from global sources; capital structures; cash flow and working capital; foreign currency transactions; and business transactions. Managing these areas requires making decisions on how funds should be allocated, budgeted, and/or invested.

For example, in the Rally Dawson/Ampak situation discussed earlier, financial management assisted in making the investment decision by preparing estimates of costs, profits and losses, cash flows, and return on investment. These decisions involve *determining the value of an investment* to an international company. This value was studied from the enterprise-wide perspective of the parent (Rally Dawson) and from the viewpoint of the subsidiary business unit (Ampak) as an independent venture.

Decisions were also needed on the *financial structure* of the subsidiary. This was determined by the needs of the local subsidiary (Ampak) and its local competitive environment, by the financial resources and structure of the two joint venture partners, and by the availability of funds worldwide. In the Ampak situation, an *allocation* problem also arose when Rally's subsidiary in Spain needed additional capital investment. This forced the company to secure an external source of financing—the Export-Import Bank—and to structure the joint venture in a way that kept cash investment low in order to have funds available for Spain.

Business investment decisions such as Ampak's, then, involve many *planning and budgeting* steps. First, they involve screening and selecting projects based on financial forecasts and analysis. As seen from the experiences described earlier, many factors affect this decision. Furthermore, budgeting requires that the future flow of funds be projected and decisions be made about how to maximize and use funds generated. These decisions help determine an investment's payback period. Once the situation is structured, funds allocated for the project must be obtained from various sources.

Throughout the budgeting process, attention is paid to potential risks arising from: changes in government regulations, policies, and parties; changes in competitive market conditions; fluctuations in foreign currency rates; local and global factors affecting all areas of costs; and other aspects that require assumptions to be made about what is likely to happen in the future.

The Ampak study is a small, integrated example of the complexities of financial management at work in just one area—capital budgeting for investments in foreign subsidiaries. The decisions and actions in this area involve balancing many business factors to reach the best decision in light of assumptions about the future and of financial options available internationally.

### Expanding Concepts of Financial and Risk Management

The concept of financial management has expanded beyond just managing firm finances (Iversen 1998). First, there is more emphasis on value-added activities through focusing more on financial consulting and business partnering when dealing with domestic and overseas operating unit managers. For example, financial managers are becoming more involved in helping develop organization-wide performance measurements and reward systems that assist operating managers in developing strategies and making decisions that align with long-term strategies, some of which are discussed later in this chapter. Second, nonfinancial and financial risk management has become a major part of the financial management job.

Risk management attempts to balance risks overall and to balance risks against opportunities, something which becomes more difficult in rapidly changing, nontraditional multinational environments (Schneier and Miccolis 1998). *Risk* is the possibility that something will go wrong to prevent—directly or indirectly—the achievement of specific business objectives. *Risk factors,* contingent conditions which give rise to risk, can be managed. Financial risk reduction through currency hedges was discussed earlier. Operations risk factors (more predictable and quantifiable risks) can involve a single new product failure within a broad line, inconsistent systems and systems crashes, loss of key people, lack of management depth, rushing new products to markets, reducing advertising expenditures, plant maintenance, customer service, relocating major facilities, etc. Past experience with similar situations provides guidance for managing these risks.

Enterprise-wide risk management involves many nonfinancial strategic risk factors, such as natural disasters, political changes, competitors' moves, assimilating newly acquired companies, managing alliances, and entering new overseas markets. Scenario development is useful in reducing these identifiable risks through quantifying the impact of their risks and then developing contingency plans for handling them (risk mitigation). The failure of many Internet ventures in 2000 and 2001 was attributed to a lack of attention to the risk management activities discussed here.

## ACCOUNTING AND TAXATION: MANAGEMENT TASKS AND PROCESSES

Accounting is the process of collecting, identifying, measuring and communicating economic information—primarily financial in nature—about economic entities (in this case, international businesses). The accounting process involves observing or being informed of some economic event (for example, a sale or purchase of a product or service) and determining if the event needs an accounting entry. If it does, the accounting system measures the economic changes that took place and records them in an accounting entry which is used to update financial records. This information is then reported in forms needed by different users, for example: tax forms, income statements, balance sheets, cash-flow statements, and management control and decision support reports.

Accounting processes and the reports produced vary depending on the intended uses of the financial statements and on accounting standards. Accounting information is used for different purposes by many people: managers and owners of businesses; creditors, suppliers, customers, and lending institutions; government bodies; employees; financial analysts, potential investors, stockholders, and investment advisers; and reporting agencies.

Business managers use accounting information as a *diagnostic* tool to determine how different operations are performing. Both financial and management accounting reports can be used to spot problems and opportunities so that corrective action *(control)* can be taken or new initiatives *planned.* Management accounting reports, such as *forecasts,* are needed for planning. For example, Rally Dawson used detailed forecasts of costs, return on investment, profits, and cash flows in making its decision to enter a joint venture in Pakistan (Fatehi 1996; Springate 1990). *Budgets* of sales, costs, production, and other performance outcomes are also produced and then used as standards against which to measure performance in management accounting reports so that corrective action can be taken.

Creditors, suppliers, customers, lending institutions, and other external users examine a firm's financial accounting statements (annual balance sheets and income statements, for example) before lending money, negotiating payment for supplies, making large purchases, or extending credit on purchases.

Government agencies use financial accounting information for tax purposes. Because of the importance of government control of taxation, company accounting records and reports in Germany are created and used as a basis for tax reporting and auditing. In the United States, in contrast, two sets of accounting books may be kept—one for tax purposes and one for reporting company financial information to external users in compliance with Securities and Exchange Commission (SEC) regulations, Generally Accepted Accounting Principles (GAAP), and the U.S. Financial Accounting Standards Board (FASB). Financial advisors use accounting information to make investment decisions for their clients, as do individual investors.

The reporting required by these external users can be classified as management accounting, financial accounting, and tax accounting.

### Management Accounting

Management accounting is the process of identifying, measuring, accumulating, analyzing, preparing, interpreting, and communicating financial information which is *used by management to plan, evaluate, and control activities within the organization.* Because this information and related diagnostic, forecasting, and budget reports are used internally by business managers, management accounting—unlike financial accounting—is not required to follow generally accepted accounting standards.

Cost accounting, a systematic set of procedures for recording and reporting measurements of the cost of manufacturing goods and performing services in the aggregate and in detail, is one type of management accounting. Cost accounting includes methods for recognizing, classifying, allocating, aggregating, and reporting such costs and comparing them with standard costs. The major purpose of cost accounting is to accumulate data for inventory valuation done for internal management purposes (Shim and Siegel 1989, 1990).

### Financial Accounting

Financial accounting is the gathering and reporting of historical financial information to groups interested in a firm's financial position—especially profits, losses, cash liquidity, debt and assets. These reports, which generally concern overall business operations, are used by suppliers, stockholders, customers, creditors, financial analysts, potential investors, and government regulatory bodies, as well as by business managers. Electronic reporting, especially for governments, is becoming more widespread as Internet use spreads.

Financial accounting supplies information to people who are generally not interested in the day-to-day operations of the company—the external users of accounting information and reports. To keep financial statements uniform and to prevent the statements from being misleading, financial accounting in industrialized countries is governed by accounting standards. In the United States these standards are referred to as Generally Accepted Accounting Principles (GAAP). The fact that different countries have different accounting standards and practices can create problems.

### Different Financial Accounting Standards and Practices: A Multinational Perspective

Differences in the way financial accounting reports are prepared from country to country can create huge differences in the assumed profitability of an operation overseas. For example, using U.S. accounting principles, France Telecom, a state-owned company, incurred a net loss of about $5.82 billion (33.9 billion French francs) in 1996; under French accounting rules the company reported a net profit of 9.2 billion francs (Owen 1997).

Lack of strong enforcement permits firms outside of North America to be less forthright about financial disclosures. Only firms in the United States and Canada, for example, issue quarterly profit reports; Germany does not require financial data from majority-owned subsidiaries to be consolidated. In countries where stock exchanges are relatively small, such as in Holland, Spain, and France, government regulation and oversight of company disclosures are often weak. Insider trading overseas, for instance, is often ignored by government regulators. Because of such differences, the German automaker, Daimler-Benz, best known for its Mercedes-Benz car, was initially not permitted to list its stock on U.S. exchanges, because the New York Stock Exchange (NYSE) and the SEC did not have the appropriate accounting information (according to GAAP) to properly monitor the business for regulatory compliance. Many less-developed countries, such as Russia and Rumania, have not yet developed such accounting standards. Lack of adequate financial statements can create problems. For example, in a 1999 privatization situation, the main reason bidders were reluctant to bid on Nicaragua's state-owned telephone company was the lack of reliable financial statements (Druckerman 1999).

Financial accounting standards and practices differ for many reasons. First, the basis of law in countries differ. Accounting standards in the United States, Canada, and the United Kingdom, for example, are common-law based, that is, they evolved from decisions and practice. Ireland, New Zealand, and Australia share this base. In contrast, countries relying on code law, such as France and Germany, codify their national accounting procedures and standards. In these countries, accounting practices are determined by law, not by the collective wisdom of professional accounting groups. Enforcement also is influenced by legal origins, with private enforcement through lawsuits more common in the United States and public oversight more common in France and Germany. The U.S. Securities and Exchange Commission adds a legal dimension to government enforcement in the United States.

Second, cultural differences exist, with countries such as France being more statist and so inclined to favor state intervention. France also requires social balance sheets, which detail the treatment and composition of workforces. Australia, on the other hand, with its more frontier, individualistic culture does not have nearly as much government intervention in setting accounting standards and practices.

Third, economic differences exist. In countries with high inflation, such as those in South America, financial accounting statements are adjusted for inflation. Financial accounting in most other countries, at least in part, is based on the historical cost principle, that is, values are entered at the cost price and are not adjusted subsequently for inflation or are assigned unrealistically long life expectancies to reduce annual depreciation charges and so inflate earnings.

These are only a few of the differences which have to be considered when comparing, judging, planning, and controlling subsidiary performance in different countries or when consolidating financial statements. Other differences include (Mueller, Gernon, and Meek 1994):

- *Pensions.* Along procedural lines, the United States is the only country that requires an annual revaluation of all pension plan obligations. Revaluations every three years are the international norm. Moreover, U.S. pension accruals are high by international comparisons, which means that comparative net earnings reported by U.S. firms are relatively lower. For example, a Morgan Stanley Dean Witter study of fifteen auto firms showed that many overseas companies would have shown losses if they had used U.S. accounting standards (MacDonald 1999).
- *Goodwill.* A firm that acquires a second firm often pays more than the book value of the acquired firm's stock. The excess payment is called *goodwill*. In the Netherlands, firms typically amortize goodwill over a five-year period, although they may write it off instantaneously or over a period of up to ten years. French firms may amortize goodwill over five to twenty years. Japan, however, severely limits the ability of firms to write off goodwill.
- *Capitalization of financial leases.* United States, British, and Swedish firms must capitalize financial leases, while French and Swiss firms may, but are not required, to do so.
- *Capitalization of R&D expenses.* Most countries permit firms to capitalize R&D expenses, but this practice is forbidden in the United States except in limited circumstances.

The differences among accounting systems, practices, principles, and reports in different countries create both financial and management accounting problems. For example, comparative financial analysis across borders is very difficult and time-consuming, because adjustments have to made for the different factors, unless financial statements have been converted to a single currency and accounting system. Management accounting also requires reconciling different viewpoints in order to compare results, evaluate and measure performance, and adjust and plan operations based on these analyses.

### Reconciling Differences: Global Efforts

Steps are being and have been taken to make accounting systems more global and so easier to use across national boundaries and cultures. An International Accounting Standards Committee (IASC) was created in 1973, and today has over 100 members from professional societies in over eighty countries. One of its goals is to make it easier to compare financial statements in different countries by establishing standards for inventory valuation, deferred income taxes, depreciation, improved disclosure, etc. Since 1998, the committee continuously has had an impact.

The United Nations (UN) has issued some guidelines, but, because of the composition of the UN and pressures from Third World countries—social, as well as financial—performance is a major reporting consideration. The Organisation for Economic Cooperation and Development (OECD), an organization of twenty-four governments representing nearly all industrialized countries, has issued guidelines for voluntary disclosure of financial information. More recently, it has been studying accounting principles in different countries with a view toward encouraging greater harmonization and comparability of accounting and financial reporting.

The European Union (EU) also has taken steps to standardize its member states' accounting systems. Other regional organizations interested in harmonizing accounting practices are the African Accounting Council, the Confederation of Asian and Pacific Accountants, the Association of Southeast Asian Nations (ASEAN), International Federation of Accountants, and the Federation of European Accountants. However, competition for international business among accounting firms in different countries makes it appear unlikely that global standards for accounting will be adopted.

A computer software package developed by a German company, SAP, coordinates information reporting across borders. Although its main function is to link different departments within a company—for example, sales, manufacturing, warehousing, and accounting—it also has the capacity to automatically calculate exchange rates and translate foreign languages. SAP has encountered major strategic management problems in adapting its systems to the Internet, which is being used in almost every accounting and finance area both within and outside individual companies, all of which have to be integrated with SAP systems.

Other forces creating pressure for change include: global integration of capital markets, which increases the need for comparable statements; expansion of major Western accounting firms into developing countries; and regional and political forces, such as China's efforts to adopt U.S. accounting standards to facilitate trade and investment between the two countries. Although progress is being made, serious obstacles to global accounting standards remain.

### Reconciling Differences: A Management Perspective on Financial Reporting

Until international accounting standards are created, multinational managers must deal with differences when meeting their own reporting and management needs.

#### Overall Approach

When faced with reconciliation problems, a multinational company has several choices (Mueller, Gernon, and Meek 1994):

- *Do nothing.* This is the best choice if a multinational company is not listed on worldwide stock exchanges, uses a language and currency that are widely known and understood, and raises little capital outside its home country, since the cost of the other alternatives can be very high.
- *Prepare convenience translations and statements.* Convenience translations are financial statements that are translated into English but use the home country's accounting standards. Convenience statements translate the monetary amount into the reader's currency. They are a low-cost alternative to doing nothing.
- *Restate the information to a limited extent.* These statements usually contain footnotes which reconcile the net income amounts and shareholders' equity from the home country to the reader's country's accounting standards.
- *Prepare secondary financial statements.* This is a complete restatement of financial statements in the reader's language, currency, and accounting principles. This can be very expensive and so is done only when the investment and investor needs justify the cost.

Other problems that a multinational manager might have to consider include: disclosure and foreign currency translation.

## Disclosure

Disclosure is the information in an annual report that supplements the financial statements. Disclosures can cover financial and nonfinancial information and, depending on local laws, may be mandatory, suggested, or voluntary. Samples of disclosures might include information on breakdowns of sales by geographic area or product line, share and shareholder distribution, social benefits and contributions of the company, employee data (age and seniority, training, fringe benefits, and absenteeism), and environmental aspects of a company's operations worldwide.

## Foreign Currency: Accounting for Transactions and Translation of Statements

Accounting for transactions in different foreign currencies and reporting on operating results of foreign subsidiaries in consolidated parent company financial statements are two additional problems which managers much resolve.

One problem that arises concerning *transactions in foreign currencies* is that one exchange rate may be in effect on the date a sale is made and recorded, and another rate may be in effect on the day the payment is received. For example, according to FASB statement No. 52, on the day a sale of $1,600 is made the accounting entry would be:

| | |
|---|---|
| Accounts receivable | $1,600 |
| Sales | $1,600 |

The day the account is paid, the exchange rate is taken into account. For instance, if the sale was made by a U.S. firm to an English firm that paid in English pounds (£ 1,000) and the exchange rate dropped from $1.60 per pound to $1.50 per pound between the day the purchase was made and the bill was paid, the American manufacturer would lose $100. The entry would be:

| | |
|---|---|
| Cash | $1,500 |
| Foreign exchange loss | $100 |
| Accounts receivable | $1,600 |

The American firm's income statement would show the cumulative profit and loss from foreign exchange as a separate item. If the firm had anticipated such a loss, it would have considered some of the protective steps discussed earlier in the chapter, such as buying currency options or using forward contracts.

*Foreign currency translation,* another multinational financial accounting management decision, involves the process of restating foreign currency statements in the currency of the parent's home country. Translation is needed to create consolidated multinational company statements. In the United States, three translation methods are allowed under FASB statement No. 52: the amount can be shown as cost (if less than 10 percent ownership stake), as equity (if 10-to-50-percent ownership stake), or consolidated (if over 50 percent ownership stake). Under the cost method, the historical exchange rate is used to enter the cost in accounting records, while the current rate is used to enter current earnings. Under the equity method, the initial cost accounting entry is at the historical exchange rate, and this figure is adjusted for dividends each reporting period at current exchange rates. Profits and losses are recorded at the current exchange rate.

For U.S. firms, consolidation requires restating a subsidiary's financial statements using U.S. GAAP. The subsidiary's functional currency—that of the subsidiary's primary economic environment—is first determined. If most of a French subsidiary's business is done using French francs, then the franc is its functional language; if the subsidiary supplies a global market through the parent company and does most of its transactions in U.S. dollars, then its functional currency is dollars.

Three methods are allowed for translation. The *current-rate method,* is used when the functional currency is the host country's currency, and requires that all assets and liabilities be translated at the spot exchange rate on the date shown on the balance sheet. All income items can be translated at the *weighted-average exchange rate* for the period or the exchange rate on the day each transaction took place. The owner's equity is translated at the rate in effect when capital stock was issued and retained earnings were accumulated. If the functional currency is the parent's currency, the *temporal method* is used. The temporal method requires monetary assets and liabilities to be translated at the current exchange rate; inventory and property, plant, and equipment, in contrast, must be translated at the rate in effect when the assets were acquired. In general, net income is translated at the *average exchange rate,* but the cost of goods sold and depreciation are translated at the appropriate historical exchange rate.

An accumulated translation adjustment is made for foreign exchange losses and gains. Under the temporal method the gain or loss is taken directly to the income statement; under the current-rate method, the gain or loss is taken directly to the balance sheet as a separate line item.

### Tax Accounting

Tax accounting deals with the processes, records, and reports needed to determine the taxable income to be reported to tax authorities. This type of accounting is primarily governed by laws or regulations of accepted tax authorities in the countries in which a multinational enterprise operates. These authorities are the primary users of this information.

Because this type of accounting is normally governed by local regulations, major differences exist across national boundaries and an expert is needed to deal with tax planning. Many multinational management decisions are affected by tax considerations, including:

- *Market selection.* Tax rates and tax concessions can impact on the choice of market. For example, a U.S. breast implant firm moved its headquarters to Switzerland largely because of the tax incentives that nation offered the company.
- *Method of entry.* The method used and the structure of the venture can change the tax costs considerably. For example, during the early 1990s, China had a policy that gave tax concessions to foreign investors, if they had a Chinese joint venture partner. These concessions were related to both import taxes and taxes on income.
- *Method of financing.* In some situations, it is desirable to finance a new overseas venture with high debt. This enables repatriating the investment without paying taxes on repatriated profits, though the parent would then be liable for taxes on the interest earned.
- *Transfer pricing.* Taxes have a major impact in this area as seen in the section on transfer pricing.


Tax planning can impact both profits and cash flow. For example, a parent firm can choose to set up a foreign operation as a branch or a subsidiary. If losses are expected in the early years and those losses are deducted by the parent, a branch often may be better off during those years. However, there are exceptions to this, as seen in the Rally Dawson experiences described earlier, since factors besides taxes can be important in making these decisions.

Loans might be used instead of equity to make it easier to repatriate capital, as at Rally Dawson. Interest on loans is generally deductible by the subsidiary but taxable to the parent company; dividends are not a deductible expense by the subsidiary, but they are taxable to the parent.

Tax havens may be considered when appropriate to the situation. However, as in other tax-planning areas, careful situation analysis is required to balance all relevant factors. The News Corporation's experiences in the area of taxation and the tax savings resulting from the enlightened use of tax laws were described at the beginning of this chapter. Such maneuvering is legal and profitable, but at the same time can make it very difficult to comparatively analyze and evaluate a multinational firm's investment value.

## STIMULATING INNOVATION
## AND CONTROLLING PERFORMANCE

Managing a multinational enterprise requires balancing diverse control objectives:

- stimulating the innovations needed to realize an enterprise's strategic vision, while
- meeting the strategic challenges of making timely changes and continually reducing costs and simultaneously improving quality, delivery time, and customer service.

Achieving this balance requires management guidance and control systems, which are the formal, information-based routines, systems, and guidelines managers use to maintain or alter patterns in organizational activities (Mockler 1973; Simons 1995). A balance of planning and control systems is needed to manage the complexity, contradictions, and rapid change in today's business environments. The paradoxical forces that need balancing include motivation and coercion, reward and punishment, guidance and proscription, control and stimulation, self-interest and the desire to contribute, and intended and emergent strategies. The three guidance and control systems discussed in the following sections—strategic belief and boundary, diagnostic guidance and control, and interactive planning and control—are used to create a dynamic tension between specific goal achievement and creative innovation (Simons 1995).

### *Strategic Belief and Boundary Systems*

Strategic belief and boundary, when given in strategic frameworks such as those discussed in Chapter 2, provide organizational definitions that senior managers can formally communicate and systematically reinforce to provide core values, shared purpose, and direction to subordinates. These systems are used to inspire and focus the search for new opportunities.

These systems also provide policy and other guidelines used to set limits—based on defined business risks—for organization participants on opportunity-seeking behavior designed to achieve the enterprise's shared vision. Belief and boundary systems transform unbounded opportunity space into a focused domain that organization participants can be encouraged to exploit. In the sense that they provide direction *and* necessary benchmarks or standards against which performance can be measured, they serve as planning and control systems. Formal belief and boundary systems are communicated through such documents as the strategic frameworks given in Figures 2.1 and 2.2 in Chapter 2. They are generally nonquantitative.

### Diagnostic Guidance and Control Systems

Diagnostic control *reporting systems,* as well as other kinds of diagnostic control *systematic processes,* are used by multinational managers. It is important to distinguish between actual control systems, that is, *systems* that *compare performance to standards and report on deviations* (such as the cost accounting reports described earlier and the sales reports shown in Figure 8.1), and the wide range of systems that *only report information* and *are used by managers as part of planning and control management processes.*

#### Diagnostic Control Reporting Systems

Diagnostic control systems are comparative performance feedback reporting systems. Designed to ensure goal achievement, they are the backbone of traditional management control. These systems, some of which were described in the accounting section, are the formal information systems used to motivate employees, to monitor outcomes, to correct deviations from standards, and to reward achievements.

Three features distinguish diagnostic control systems: (1) the ability to measure outputs of a process; (2) the existence of predetermined standards against which actual results can be compared; and (3) the ability to correct deviations from standards.

The standards, which are the key element of control systems, may include: budgets, performance benchmarks from industry competitors, adjusted historical figures, spending limits, financial ratios, agreed-upon objectives, and even financial forecasts. Cost accounting reports are an example of control reporting systems, since they report on cost results and compare them to established standard costs. The simplest form of control report is a comparative sales report, such as the one shown in Figure 8.1.

Because standards need to be appropriate for the specific situations being controlled and variations (in labor costs, materials costs, transportation times, and exchange rates) occur from country to country, international control systems are difficult to establish. For example, in Figure 8.1, if the sales results were translated into dollars for consolidation purposes, both the budget and the results would have to be converted at the same rate when evaluating the subsidiary's performance to make the comparison meaningful. In addition, if the performance of this subsidiary is compared with a similar one in another country, then local circumstances—such as whether a recession or labor problems exist, new competitors have entered the market, or other circumstances or events have affected the results—would have to be noted and factored into the evaluation.

Because of differences from country to country, comparative statements across borders have to be constructed to meet individual situation requirements. Transfer pricing provides a typical example (Mueller, Gernon, and

FIGURE 8.1. Comparative Sales Control Report, United Kingdom Subsidiary (in English Pounds)

|  | Actual Unit Sales | Budget | Deviation |
| --- | --- | --- | --- |
| Product A | 14,000 | 15,000 | −1,000 |
| Product B | 8,000 | 8,500 | + 500 |

Meek 1994). The need for determining a transfer price arises when goods or services are exchanged between international subsidiaries. When goods are transferred, the price set is not a market price. Although the current market price may influence it, the transfer price is determined by many other situation restraints: minimizing taxes and worldwide import duties; winning host government approval; taking into account financial and other government restrictions and regulations; covering product costs; meeting competitive market conditions; enabling profit evaluations of subsidiaries; and managing currency fluctuations.

Some ground rules have been developed for subsidiaries in light of these restrictions. If a country has a low tariff on imports, a higher transfer price is recommended. If a country has a high corporate tax rate, then a high export transfer price is recommended to minimize profits and thus taxes on profits. If expatriation of profits is restricted, a high export transfer price is one way to take profits out of a country. If devaluation is continual, a high export transfer price is one way to minimize currency losses. If a subsidiary needs to boost profits or sales by lowering its costs and selling prices, on the other hand, a low import transfer price is one way to do this. If a government prefers either a cost-based or market-based price or strictly controls transfer prices, then these limits would be taken into consideration. All these conditions are rarely met in a specific situation, so the decision should strive to balance factors to achieve the best overall solution. Computer-analysis systems, which are making more and more use of the Internet, are useful in moving control reporting online in all types of situations. An example of this is given in Chapter 2, in which the experiences of Cisco Systems in speeding up control reporting are described.

A manager exercising control over transfer pricing transactions must also weigh the impact of these prices on profitability performance of the business units involved. Transfer adjustments may be best overall for the multinational parent company, but the impact of such nonperformance factors must be considered when evaluating the performance of a unit and its managers. A business unit should not be penalized for generating improved overall company profits at the expense of lowering its own reported profits.

Comparative control systems cover many areas in addition to finance and accounting: quality, productivity, sales (dollars and units), costs, unit output, inventory turnover (days or weeks), debt-to-equity ratios, customer satisfaction (monthly comparisons of customer complaints, for example), on-time performance (airlines, for example), employee turnover, compliance with government regulations (racial mix of the workforce, for example), supplier performance (meeting just-in-time schedules, for example), manager performance, and compliance with policies (limits on speculative currency trading, for example).

## Diagnostic Guidance and Control Processes

Many management information systems do not contain standards or generate comparisons to standard measures; instead, they provide information that can be *used for* planning and control decision making. For example, financial accounting statements provide historical information that is useful in planning stock investment decisions. In the broadest sense, any operating report that analyzes or decomposes operating aggregates can be considered a management guidance and control system. For instance, the cost breakdowns by category of expense on profit-and-loss statements contained in a company's annual report are analytical tools that can help an investor *diagnose* how healthy a company is. In an international situation, such analyses are much more difficult if a company chooses not to translate its annual reports into the language or accounting standards familiar to the user. For this reason, an expert is often needed to interpret them.

In an operational situation, reports on competitors' sales, for example, can be sufficient to trigger action by executives. At PepsiCo, top managers carried charts in their wallets with the latest Nielsen industry sales figures by product to stimulate their drive to top Coca-Cola in all products and all markets (Simons 1995). The weekly conferences described in the next section are another example of effective control processes.

### Interactive Planning and Control Systems

Managing and balancing the tension between stimulating creative innovation and controlling predictable goal achievement is the essence of management control. Diagnostic control systems can constrain innovation and opportunity seeking by trying to ensure that outcomes are kept in line with intended strategies. Interactive control systems are designed to produce the opposite effect. They stimulate research and learning, allowing new strategies to emerge as participants throughout an organization respond to perceived opportunities and threats.

An interactive control system is *not* a unique type of control system. Many types of control systems that are generally referred to as decision support systems can be used interactively. For example, a computer-based spreadsheet that allows a manager to enter different price assumptions and then calculates the effect on profits of each assumed price change is a basic interactive planning and forecasting tool. Such systems enable a manager to make different sets of assumptions about future circumstances, for example, assumptions about the future market in a given country, and then recommend appropriate strategies based on his or her assumptions. Mathematically based forecasting software packages that permit a manager to forecast economic environments, for example, gross national product, under different sets of assumptions are another example of interactive systems, as is the system that Gillette used to determine the best way to manufacture and supply its Atra razor (described in Chapter 1) given the many facility locations involved.

Interactive and diagnostic systems can be any kind of systematic use of information to stimulate thinking about new directions (planning) or correcting problems (control). The weekly phone meetings and videoconferences used at many multinational firms are good examples of systematic interactive and diagnostic exchanges of information. In the development area, brainstorming sessions can be used to stimulate free-flowing idea generation. Such group-based interactive structures are described in Chapters 9 (organization) and 11 (leading and managing teams).

Multinational management control and planning systems are not limited to the finance and accounting areas. Human resources and their management, described in Chapters 10 through 12, also enable planning and control systems, as do the organization structures, cultures, and processes discussed in Chapter 9.

## SUMMARY

This chapter discussed four enablers used by multinational companies: finance, accounting, taxation, and control enablers.

Finance, accounting, and tax accounting systems are extremely important enablers in multinational strategic management, as are management control and planning systems. Management control and planning systems are not limited to those found in the financial and accounting areas and discussed in this chapter. Further discussions of multinational strategic management organization and leadership will be discussed in the following chapters.

## REVIEW QUESTIONS

1. What is the difference between finance and accounting?
2. Describe the impact of technology on multinational business. Give specific examples of different technologies being put to work in different areas of multinational finance.

3. Discuss the ways in which technological and other developments in the multinational financial area are enabling greater reconciliation of cultural and national differences.
4. Identify the tasks involved in managing a multinational company's finances.
5. Identify the key factors which affected the decision on capital structure in the Rally Dawson Sports company case study. Cite examples of each and discuss their specific impact.
6. Describe the ways foreign-exchange risks are generally categorized. Cite examples of each.
7. Discuss the impact of financial considerations on buying and selling decisions in the international market. Give specific examples of these impacts.
8. Describe the ways in which differences in financial accounting standards and practices have developed throughout the world.
9. Describe some of the steps being taken to globalize accounting systems and practices.
10. Identify and discuss key multinational management decisions that are influenced by tax considerations.
11. Describe ways in which the strategic frameworks discussed in Chapter 2 can serve as guidance and control systems used to provide direction and necessary benchmarks or standards against which performance can be measured.
12. Describe in detail the two key types of diagnostic guidance and control systems. Identify the distinguishing characteristics of each.
13. Describe the importance of interactive planning and control systems and the impact they have on management control. Give specific business examples.

## *EXERCISES*

1. Through reading and research, select a firm that might benefit from expanding into a country where it does not yet operate. Describe the tasks involved in making an entry decision and discuss in detail the financial aspects of that decision, including how the funds needed can be obtained in the most effective and efficient way.
2. In mid-1997, currency crises arose in a number of countries in Southeast Asia. Select one of these countries and describe how these problems arose, the steps taken to resolve them, and their impact on local businesses as well as on the investment decisions of foreign multinationals considering investing there. Describe some of the steps a mul-

tinational operating in that country might take to neutralize or exploit the currency problems.

3. After researching the subject, describe the differences between the major financial factors affecting entry decisions in China and Russia at the time you are reading this book. Chose any size industry and firm of interest to you as a focal point for the decision situation.

# Chapter 9

# Enabling Multinational Organizations: The New Equation

In 1992, the well-ordered world of British Petroleum (BP), a stodgy oil giant, collapsed, as heavy losses forced it to halve its dividend and fire employees. Seven years later, after an aggressive cost-cutting and restructuring plan, BP was growing strong—in revenues, pretax profits, and stock market share price (Guyon 1999).

To achieve such a turnaround, the entire organization's culture was revamped. First, a reorganization shifted authority to local levels, where middle managers were held accountable for, and given a financial stake, in their own results. These managers were expected to solve their own problems and create their own opportunities, an effective way to take advantage of diversity and to adapt quickly to local requirements (Rasmusson 1999). Traditional management rituals such as meetings and memos were replaced by a livelier, confrontational communications style. This meant freer communications among all levels and divisions.

Lofty job titles and confining job descriptions gave way to looser roles where initiative, not conformity, was prized. Peers and subordinates, as well as supervisors, did performance evaluations. The underlying management structure was reordered through the development of networks or groups of employees performing similar work but located countries apart. This move severed the chain of command that had stifled BP's ability to respond rapidly to changing markets. The reorganization helped solve day-to-day problems quickly, and also laid the groundwork for a European joint venture with competitor Mobil Oil and an eventual merger of the two firms, which was followed by another major restructuring (Marsh, Barker, and Durgin 1999).

As seen from the experiences of BP and other firms, organization is a key enabler in multinational management. Three aspects of organization are discussed in this chapter: structure, processes (business and human), and culture.

## ORGANIZATION: STRUCTURE, PROCESSES, AND CULTURE

When asked about Gillette's worldwide organization, former CEO Al Zeien gave this equivocal answer:

> My answer to the question 'How do you organize our type of company?' is that if you look at our company there is no fully definable pattern. Gillette has at least six different kinds of organization structures. People ask me why we organize the blade business one way, the Braun appliance business another way, and the Oral-B business a third way.
>
> The answer to that is simple. There is no ideal way to structure, because with time, things change, and because different products, countries, and companies have different needs. But, at the same time, one thing is consistent. Throughout all those structures, all those organizations, they are matrixed in three ways: by function, by product, and by job. It's often just a question of reporting relationships varying.
>
> People ask: How can you operate with a three-way matrix? Who's responsible? Who makes decisions when you have a three-way matrix? Who has the authority? The answer is that the first rule you learn in business school—responsibility should equal authority—is wrong. The answer "everybody's responsibility" is far greater than the authority they can exercise. So, you have in effect, overlapping responsibilities. But, who makes decisions when you have this three-way matrix? Who has the authority to make decisions? The answer is: usually the person who best did his or her homework most often tends to have their way. (Zeien 1995)

This somewhat paradoxical view of organization structure—that the formal structure is and is not important—is only one of many multinational strategic management paradoxes. However, the paradox exists only if one insists on too formal a solution. When viewed from a contingency perspective, the solution to organization, as in other task areas, is that the preferred form is a basic structure (for example, a three-way matrix organization) flexible enough to be tailored to each business unit's needs, as at Gillette. This perspective enables developing an organization that balances situation factors: the firm's core competencies, the local country, the global scope of operations, the changing competitive market, the business processes, the people, the communications systems, and other relevant situation factors. One result of this is that organizations often change over time as situation factors change. AT&T, for example, originally built an integrated telecommunications firm only to find that customers didn't seek integrated services. This led AT&T in late 2000 to propose a split into four major segments.

In addition, while organization *structure* provides an important enabling environment, as seen at Gillette and British Petroleum, the *processes*—the way the organization works—can be more important. These processes include business and administrative processes, cooperative activities, interpersonal relationships, and frequency and quality of the communications. These human and business processes, the essence of an organization, are supported by an enabling corporate *culture,* the lubricant that helps make the processes work. What happens within the structure is often more important than the structure itself in enabling a firm to prosper in a rapidly changing, intensely competitive market.

Over the next decades, successful multinational companies will be those that take advantage of global economies of scale by selling similar products worldwide and by offering the same services in dozens of countries. However, they also must blend their operations locally to gain market acceptance, as well as to find out what their customers want, and to gain access to new ideas, tactics, and technologies. Information sharing and innovation must be encouraged throughout a company to make sure that it is not bypassed by competitors responding more quickly to changing competitive markets. The task of creating a flexible, opportunistic organization appropriate for the countries, product, competition, and company involved is difficult. All organization structural forms—centralized, decentralized, collaborative, hierarchical, and matrix—can work in some combination, *depending on the situation.*

The concept of organizations has changed substantially, as companies have come to emphasize flexible, collaborative structures. Perceptions about how organizations actually work have also changed, as managers have realized that organizations at work do not always conform with organization charts. This contingency perspective, the new equation, was confirmed in a research study of twenty multinational corporations (Bartlett and Ghoshal 1991), in field studies done by the author, and in contingency theory research (Donaldson 1995, 1996). These studies concluded that successfully creating and changing organizations resulted from the following:

- First, the companies did not necessarily use a zero-based approach, that is, starting from scratch. Rather, they built on what they had, defended and reinforced their existing capabilities, resources, and competencies, and supported new ones *where appropriate to the situation.*
- Second, in creating new capabilities or overcoming existing problems, the companies did not try to imitate competitors' physical organization structures, but looked for ways to compensate for their deficiencies or approximate a competitor's source of advantage—*in a form appropriate for their own operations and company situation.*

- Third, these companies treated organizations as adaptive environments, able to respond to and be restructured and reprocessed as situation requirements changed.

## STRUCTURE: THE NECESSARY EVIL

Some type of organization structure appropriate for the specific company and competitive market involved is obviously needed. Just as obviously, the best kinds of structures are those that can adapt to and respond to change quickly. Within these guidelines, companies with highly centralized structures and those with highly decentralized multinational structures can prosper. The key to success, then, is not solely the structure. Within the structure, hybrid organization processes (human and business) are needed to enable a balanced approach to, and capacity for, change.

For example, rapidly changing competitive markets in the early 1990s forced Alcatel Alsthom, a giant French telecommunications equipment manufacturer, to change its organization structure (Landler 1995). The firm encountered problems after prices plummeted for its wide range of products—network switches, fiber-optic lines, and wireless communications devices. As a result, it lost $250 million in the first half of 1995. In the past, Alcatel had prospered by designing, manufacturing, and selling a full line of communications products for each of its major clients, including France Telecom and Belgacom (the Belgian phone-service provider). That market changed, however, as telecommunication equipment was increasingly designed according to uniform standards worldwide. In late 1995, Alcatel announced a reorganization by product lines rather than by geographic area served.

The former organization structure had made sense when the bulk of Alcatel's business came from European state-owned firms, such as France Telecom. However, as the European phone monopolies were privatized and challenged by new competitors, they began demanding lower prices and competitive bidding. The new structure was designed to enable Alcatel to compete in Western Europe against aggressive, streamlined competitors such as AT&T, Siemens, and Northern Telecom.

Under the new structure the company standardized its product development process across product markets (around which the new organization was structured) to meet competitive needs. This new structure was also expected to lead to a change in corporate culture, which in the past had been based on tightly controlled national fiefdoms that communicated very little with each other. Moreover, the move was expected to reduce the company's workforce by around 30,000, sharply reducing costs.

In 1996, under its new CEO, Roger A. Enrico, PepsiCo reorganized internationally by product strategic business units, instead of by region (domestic and international) as follows: Frito-Lay Company, a newly formed unit that included all of PepsiCo's domestic and international packaged-goods businesses; Pepsi-Cola Company, a newly formed unit that included all of PepsiCo's domestic and international beverage business; and the existing worldwide restaurant business, which was eventually spun off. In 1998, Pepsi announced plans to also spin off its bottling operations, as Coca-Cola had done.

A British company, Cunard, one of the largest cruise ship lines in the world, fared poorly in the early 1990s as profits fell from over $60 million in 1991 to a loss of more than $20 million in 1995 (McDowell 1996). As part of its new strategy to target the luxury end of the market—affluent, aging, baby boomers (so-called "ancient mariners")—a major reorganization was initiated. The new organization relied on consensus among semiautonomous business units, a process similar to that found at Rolls-Royce (the luxury British automaker) where Cunard's new president had previously worked. Under the new structure, each ship was run as a separate business with its own chief executive and management team. Each team was accountable for that ship's performance and profitability. There was one exception: purchasing and logistics were done from the home office, because in the past, Cunard's ships had paid excessive prices when buying independently at 360 ports of call worldwide.

As part of the new strategy, an effort was made to create an ambience or culture similar to that of Rolls-Royce—an ambiance of opulent luxury, attentive service, and a generally pampered experience. Cunard's new organization combined changes in structure, processes, and culture, and was crafted in an adaptive way suited to competitive market and company requirements.

The Internet and digital technology explosion has also led to organization changes. For example, in an effort to realize the Internet's digital technology potential, Philips, the Dutch electronics giant, reorganized its core electronics division into five businesses, each of which would be freer to think more entrepreneurially about new markets (Cramb 2000). In an effort to exploit the Internet, in 2000, the Ford Motor Company was again reorganizing every aspect of its organization and business processes—including the way it bought parts, made cars, linked with customers, and sold cars (Kerwin, Stepaniek, and Welch 2000). German banks, in reaction to major losses in retail banking operations, were also considering major reorganizations (Fairlamb 2000), and Unilever completely reorganized its brand of marketing structure in response to rapidly changing consumer trends (Cowell 2000).

Airbus Industrie, founded in 1969 and backed by a consortium of the governments of Britain, France, Germany, and Spain, had been primarily a marketing company that sold planes manufactured jointly by its four partners: Aerospatiale Matra (France, 37.9 percent, state-owned, manufactured cockpits and parts of fuselages and assembled finished planes); Daimler-Benz Aerospace (Germany, 37.9 percent, privately-owned, manufactured portions of fuselages and assembled some planes); BEA Systems (United Kingdom, 20 percent, privately-owned, manufactured most of the wings and some small fuselage parts); and Construcciones Aeronauticas (Spain, 4.2 percent, state-owned, manufactured horizontal tail stabilizers). Heavy competitive pressures from Boeing, which had introduced new models, cut lead times, and pared prices, as well as the merger of McDonnell Douglas Corporation and Boeing, forced Airbus to make major enterprise-wide strategic changes.

In addition to Boeing's increasing competitiveness, Airbus's problems included: tightening government budgets; a cumbersome company structure leading to noncompetitive, long lead times; higher production costs than competitors' which led to noncompetitive pricing; an inability to raise the huge sums of money needed to develop new models; and heavy losses at Aerospatiale Matra and Dailmer-Benz. Airbus' competitive advantage was that its planes were more fuel efficient and had lower operating costs than Boeing's.

To overcome these problems and carry out the strategies that would alleviate production cost and lead time problems, Airbus CEO Jean Pierson proposed an enterprise-wide reorganization. This proposal, formalized in 1997, would unify functions such as design (done at four locations), eliminate white-collar bureaucracies such as market forecasting, and assign work on a competitive-bid basis, even to the point of using lower-cost, outside contractors (Zuckerman 1999). The expectation was that the strategic model of enterprise-wide organization for both Boeing and Airbus would have centralized management for designing and marketing aircraft and a centralized production operation composed of its own units with a changing cast of low-bidding contractors.

Under the restructuring, Airbus would be a stand-alone firm with the four partners having equity positions: BEA Systems 20 percent; European Aeronautics Defence and Space Company (a merger of the other three existing Airbus partners) 80 percent (Andrews 2000a). The new firm would hold its own assets (now held by the partners), raise its own financing, and be responsible for its own debts. As expected, negotiating and finalizing the restructuring was a difficult process (Michaels 2000; Rossant 2000). During this period, because of problems at Boeing, Airbus increased its dollar market share from 40.2 percent in 1996 to more than 50 percent in 1999 (Michaels and Cole 2000). In 2000, Airbus again moved ahead of Boeing by announcing it would develop a two-story super jumbo jet to carry 550 passengers.

## CREATING A BALANCED ORGANIZATION

Al Zeien, former CEO of Gillette, believed that organization structure must be flexible and capable of change, as well as appropriate for the business involved. In his view, people make structures work, and this happens only with cultural imbedding, leadership, and training and selection processes create internal administrative processes and an entrepreneurial spirit. Gillette's greatest core competency, according to Zeien, has been its 350-plus expatriate managers, who have been at Gillette an average of twenty years. These managers know Gillette's core global culture and how to manage different country operations within that global culture. Gillette's approach to creating this culture is described in Chapters 11 and 12.

This entrepreneurial approach is consistent with the management philosophy of Gillette's former president, Colman Mockler, who defined strategy implementation as doing whatever is necessary to get a job done, within well-defined legal, moral, ethical, and policy restraints. According to Mockler, success depends on having managers throughout the company who know Gillette's core culture—managers who talk freely with other Gillette managers and who have the entrepreneurial instincts to respond creatively to local conditions within a general company enterprise-wide strategic framework.

Organization change is not easy for existing companies that are considering going, or have already gone, multinational. The way in which change is managed does not follow some universal theoretical formula, only general contingency guidelines that are situation-based. For example, not all companies have the luxury of creating adaptive organizations over an extended period of time, as Gillette did. Alcatel had to move quickly to create a new structure to suit its specific needs and overcome its specific problems.

Ford Motor Company attempted a daring change (Treece, Kerwin, and Dawley 1995) when former CEO Alex Trotman introduced a new globally centralized organization structure in January 1995. With independent auto subsidiaries designing and selling their own vehicles on each side of the Atlantic, high costs associated with duplicated effort and waste in product development had cut Ford's profits substantially. Top-heavy and bureaucratic, Ford spent too much time and money designing new cars. By combining the North American and European units into a unified company, Trotman hoped to transform Ford into a more nimble, efficient competitor.

Within the new structure, a newly reorganized, centralized product design/development unit with global product teams designed cars to be sold worldwide. Ford had to make such a move because competitors were more efficient in getting new car models to market faster. Ford's Taurus, for example, took five years to redesign, while Japanese competitors redesigned competing models in under two years, and Chrysler developed its Neon subcompact in thirty-one months. Toyota also led in productivity—30.38 labor hours per vehicle, versus 34.79 for Ford, and 45.60 for General Motors (Ball 1999), as well as in its ability to fill custom auto orders in five days (Simison 1999)—a strategic goal which GM was striving to match in 2000, in part through greater use of the Internet (Simison 2000).

It was uncertain whether Ford could respond locally within the new global structural framework. For example, under the new product development organization, design engineers were asked to consider the needs of diverse markets, which could slow new-car development rather than speed it up. Moreover, cars designed to satisfy drivers around the world might end up pleasing no one. Ford's first venture into a global car, the Mondeo, sold well in Europe but not in the United States. Design variations for Europe (for example, small back seats and powerful motors) either were not popular in the United States or led to prices higher than those of competitors.

The product development function was organized in centers by vehicle type (for example, the Taurus), not by function (for example, structural design engineers) as before. Hundreds of workers were transferred around the world to the new centers. To facilitate this transition, managers went through nine months of reengineering sessions to help ease the cultural disputes and integration problems. Still, very many employees found themselves in new jobs with new bosses, creating management and morale problems.

Many parts specifications differences needed to be reconciled while drawing upon and integrating the best worldwide manufacturing and tooling procedures. The most efficient ways to adapt different car components and models to local needs, for example, adding heaters in Scandinavian cars and air conditioners in Singapore models also had to be considered. In theory, the savings could be enormous, provided that the newly integrated product design units could capture global efficiencies while allowing for responsiveness to local market conditions. Ford estimated that the reorganization would save the company $1 billion annually.

Toyota had also reorganized, centralizing product design and development in Toyota City in Japan, while using design teams at its manufacturing hubs in Asia, North America, and Europe which used local suppliers and tailored vehicles to local tastes.

What made the Ford strategy even more daring was that General Motors was using the opposite approach, with decentralized regional units developing distinctly different autos for their own markets. GM's strategy was to subsequently examine crossover potential among countries and make minor design adjustments as required. GM claimed that such ad hoc efforts were cheaper, more effective, and more flexible. GM did, however, pursue developing an engine which could be modified and used worldwide.

Ford was continuing to fine-tune its organization in 1999, as it made other strategic changes (Kerwin and Ewing 1999; Kerwin and Naughton 1999). Under the leadership of Jacques Nasser who become CEO of Ford in 1998, the centralization strategy was maintained, especially for design and production. Within that structure, however, more flexibility was being introduced to focus on major market and brand needs. In that sense, Nasser wanted his managers to be more entrepreneurial, thus creating a balanced structured and entrepreneurial organizational mix. It was anticipated that further decentralization of brand management functions would continue into 2000 and that substantial additional changes would be made to adapt organization structures and processes to the Internet (Kerwin, Stepanek, and Welch 2000).

Hewlett-Packard's success with ink-jet printers is an example of how a balanced organization approach and the ability to adapt and change quickly benefits a firm (Gillooly 1995). In 1984, HP did not make printers; more than a decade later, its annual printer sales were more than $8 billion, even in the face of major competition, especially from the Japanese. In 1994, HP held 55 percent of the world ink-jet printer market, and its success in printers (both laser and ink-jet) had made HP one of the two fastest-growing U.S. multinationals.

Richard Hackborn, the former HP executive who led the successful effort to make and sell printers, believed in the balance of entrepreneurship and central control in order to leverage US culture to compete around the globe. According to Hackborn, a good mix of rough individualism and central direction must be achieved so as not to forfeit the advantages of local innovation and accountability. Although HP headquarters became increasingly more bureaucratic in the 1980s, its individual business units functioned as fiefs, with each having great autonomy. Each unit had the resources of a large company, but was separate and so able to make decisions rapidly. For example, the printer business teams were in outposts such as Boise, Idaho—far from HP's bureaucratic Palo Alto, California, headquarters—where they were permitted, though sometimes reluctantly, to go their own way.

During the early 1980s, HP developed its ink-jet technology, which was cheaper and better than that of its Japanese competitors, such as Epson's dot-matrix printers. HP took out a blizzard of patents on its new ink-jet technology and developed a family of products. In 1989, HP reexamined its target market strategy—it had initially positioned its ink-jet printer as a low-cost alternative to HP's own high-quality commercial laser printer—and decided instead to focus on the consumer dot-matrix printer market, a market dominated by the Japanese. The decision was made in Autumn 1989, and *within weeks* HP, with its nimble entrepreneurial organization, had made major moves at all levels to target primarily Epson products and customers. It used every available mass-marketing technique, including price adjustments, store positioning, and cost cutting. HP even adopted a Japanese strategy of rapid product variations.

In these situations, the key to successful structuring was implementing a flexible, adaptive organization appropriate for the situations. *Flattened hierarchies*—an organization tool used to encourage the development and use of collaborative infrastructures, promote individual effort, more effectively put to work precious knowledge assets, and help create a learning organization—are structures with many segments reporting to one person, as shown in Figure 9.1. Within such structures, survival depends on increased delegation and entrepreneurial initiative, not on hierarchical organization channels such as those shown in Figure 9.2, to overcome the boundaries among different functions. In other words, success depends on developing interactive collaborative business and human processes within the organization structure (Iverson 1998). This collaborative process has been enabled considerably by the use of the Internet to quickly transmit and exchange knowledge.

Many companies have gone further in restructuring their organizations to encourage more entrepreneurial interaction and initiative to enable moving quickly to meet rapidly changing market conditions. For example, a multinational computer company in China revised its flattened structure into a more circular one, as shown in Figure 9.3. A Chinese multinational chemical firm eliminated the hierarchy entirely, making the manager only one member of the business processes, as shown in Figure 9.4. This approach has been called the "centerless" corporation (Pasternack and Viscio 1998) or a "networked" organization (Fukuyama 1999). These structures reflect the actual processes at work—processes instituted and imbedded in the culture by the managers involved. The structure diagrams are used mainly to reinforce the working processes (business and human) and culture changes brought about by the leadership of the managers involved.

## THE HUMAN AND BUSINESS SYSTEMS: COLLABORATIVE INFRASTRUCTURES

An organization can be viewed from two perspectives: as a structure of tasks, functions, and reporting relationships; and as a set of day-to-day working processes, which include both integrated *business* work-flow processes as well as *human* activities, such as communications practices, working relationships, coordination, and teamwork. Focusing these business and human processes on market and business needs compensates for many of the deficiencies, imbalances, and limitations inherent in any organization structure. The company experiences described in this book make the point that human and business systems and processes can be as critical to success as formal administrative processes and organization structures.

FIGURE 9.1. Flatter Network Organizations

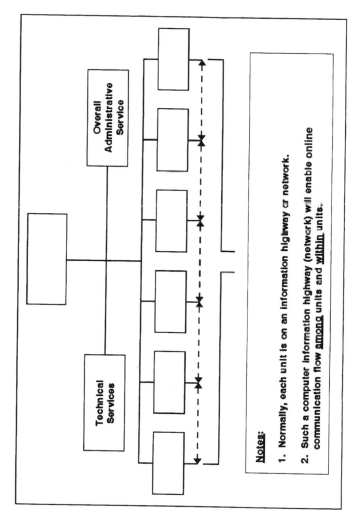

Overall Administrative Service

Technical Services

Notes:

1. Normally, each unit is on an information highway or network.

2. Such a computer information highway (network) will enable online communication flow <u>among</u> units and <u>within</u> units.

*239*

FIGURE 9.2. Traditional Hierarchical Organization

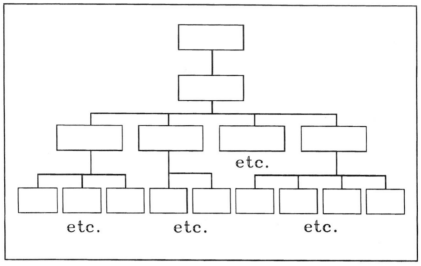

FIGURE 9.3. Interactive Flat Organization (A Software Development Company)

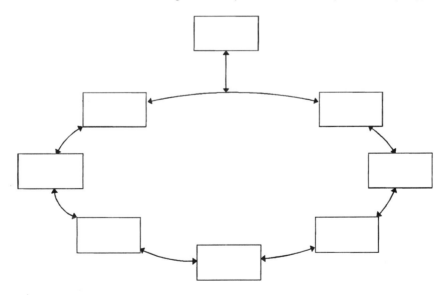

FIGURE 9.4. Integrative Organization Structure (A Multinational Chemical Company)

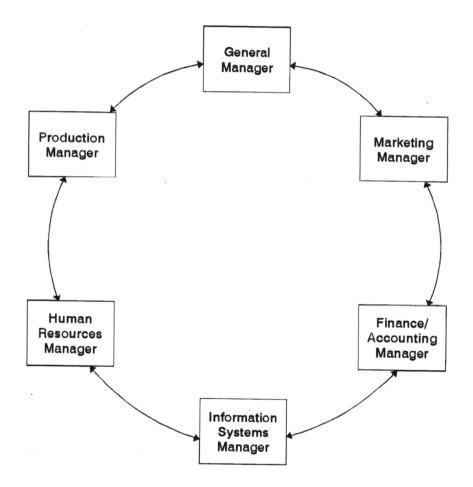

Human processes are sometimes referred to as the "human system." The time and effort required to realign these systems to meet competitive market needs is one reason why Philips needed fifteen years to reorganize and Gillette needed twenty years to create its core of expatriate managers. For this reason, new companies sometimes find this easier to do since they are starting from scratch.

Initiating and maintaining these systems within the overall organization structure to achieve global and local balance is done in many ways. Collaborative team structures, especially those supported by electronic communications systems using the Internet, are one way to achieve and maintain this balance in certain types of situations. These structures can range from formal (initiated from the top) to those that form in response to daily working needs.

Special company SWAT teams are an example of a more formal task team structure at the multinational parent organization level. Many multinational companies have developed SWAT teams to actively promote integrative action, respond to local needs, and rapidly transfer technology across cultural boundaries. For instance, in 1994, Texas Instruments had 200 professionals—dubbed the "Nomads"—who had set up chip fabricating plants in Italy, Taiwan, Japan, and Singapore in the past four years. U.S. West's former CEO Richard Callahan boasted that he could "put a team into South Africa by Friday" to begin setting up a cellular phone system. "We're faster than any telephone company in the world," he added (Dwyer et al., p. 84). Similarly, when opening up and expanding operations in China, along with hiring experienced local Chinese professionals, Unilever dispatched a team of Chinese-speaking troubleshooters from the company's 100-country operation. They helped build detergent plants, market shampoo and other personal-care products, and sell Lipton Tea to the world's largest tea-drinking population (Dwyer et al. 1994).

Because of its specific situation requirements, General Electric used a very different approach at its lightbulb factory in Budapest, Hungary—"action workout"—sessions similar to those used in its U.S. plants. These "workouts" involved teams of workers tackling specific problems; they reflected GE's belief in a "borderless" organization culture in which employees remove obstacles in order to work more efficiently. These and other worker/management changes were used to change work habits left over from the communist era (Perlez 1994).

Teams are not a cure-all or universal solution, since the usefulness of teams is contingent on situation circumstances (Griffith 1997). The problems faced in introducing self-managed teams into Mexico, for example, have been studied. Nonetheless, teams have proved effective at many companies. For example, Gordon Bethune, CEO of Continental Airlines, a U.S. airline serving over 200 destinations worldwide, attributes his firm's success to its ability to work integratively, as a team, across all company functions (Puffer 1999).

Many other approaches are available for creating and sustaining linkages within an organization. Many metaphors exist for describing and initiating an infrastructure of different relationships within a formal organization structure. A relatively new metaphor called the "Web," an obvious play on the World Wide Web, is described in *The Web of Inclusion: A New Architecture for Building a Great Organization* (Helgesen 1995). Webs of inclusion are flexible units that can adapt, contract, or expand according to situation needs. They are not necessarily as stringently configured as the corporate SWAT teams described earlier, and people's responsibilities in Webs can alter over time since Webs evolve through a process of trial and error. They are not always conceived of as a formal strategy, but often arise out of learning during tactical implementation. They are examples of the human processes that can develop within a learning organization in response to business process needs.

Webs function as open channels across divisions and within organizations. People who work side-by-side often share expertise and knowledge or afford each other access to certain resources. In many situations, these interactions ("Webs") cross organizational boundaries and so subvert the organization hierarchies of which they are a part. Webs are permeable around the edges, which makes them open to the world outside the organization. They are not necessarily internally focused, which makes them particularly useful in forging strategic alliances and joint ventures with other firms.

Although Webs are task focused, they do not completely dissolve once a task is completed. They can affect the entire organization by creating new networks that may redistribute power and resources throughout the organization. In Webs, the people who make and implement decisions are often the same. In contrast, in other infrastructures decisions are conceived and initiated at the top, where the mission is firmly set, and then task forces (such as the corporate SWAT teams described earlier) are called in to execute.

"Partnerships" is another working metaphor for cross-functional infrastructures within formal organization structures. In one firm, the strategic plan was summarized on small cards that employees carried in their pockets. The plan pointed out that the firm's strategy was built on partnerships between employees and their customers, employees and their suppliers, and the firm and its financial backers, as well as among employees in different divisions. The employees' mission was to work together efficiently and effectively to satisfy all partners. This partnering strategy worked, but an active CEO had to translate these concepts into working guidelines on a day-by-day basis. Today's successful multinational companies, such as Nestlé, tend to think of national subsidiaries as strategic partners whose knowledge and local entrepreneurial capabilities are vital to the multinational firm's ability to maintain a long-term global competitive advantage.

Furthermore, firms are emphasizing the creation of an environment in which individuals can learn, grow, compete and cooperate, and contribute (Robbins and Finley 1998). GE went through such a revitalization, led by former CEO Jack Welch, who continually communicated the need to take responsibility, initiate, question, and challenge.

As suggested in this chapter, a multinational firm can use multiple organizational and leadership linkages to maintain global efficiencies, respond to local needs, and transfer knowledge rapidly. These linkages are especially important to helping new product developers understand local market needs and obtain commitment from those responsible for introducing new products.

In 1995, the Ford Motor Company was attempting to solve this linkage problem by using cross-training assignments, permanent transfers of international researchers to new locations, dual assignments, Internet-based electronic communication links, and product-oriented teams. Gillette also used various formal and informal linkages, including frequent assignment changes, computer-aided decision making, a loosely defined three-way matrix organization, distributed decision-making power, and multifaceted cross-functional, cross-national training programs.

Several formal organization tools that stimulate collaborative linkages— flattened hierarchies and circular organizations—were discussed earlier. Open office layouts is another tool that encourages the development of collaborative human and administrative systems. This type of layout, which has no walls or separate offices and links all workers by computers, has been used at many firms.

Each of these working metaphors (and organization techniques such as learning organizations, rejuvenation through individualized corporations, flexible or collaborative workplaces, collaborative team organizations, strategic alliances, and organizational transformation), the concepts underlying them, and the formal structures devised to support them, can be used to inspire, initiate, and guide the development of informal, linking organization infrastructures. These infrastructures can be useful within any type of formal structure (hierarchical or flat, centralized or decentralized, matrix, or structures based on product, division, geographic region, or function) to enable learning, adaptability, cooperation, and balancing diverse organization elements.

The key to success is to develop an organization concept, and a metaphor to describe it, that works within a company. For example, organizational learning may involve transferring precise knowledge on "how to" manufacture effectively from one location to another, as Intel did. Or, it may involve learning how to diagnose problems, improve customer relations, and respond quickly to change, something which GE and other firms have learned to do well. It is usually unwise to adapt another company's metaphor and organization design concept completely; rather, a company should find an organizational tool that exactly matches its own situation requirements.

As noted in this chapter and Chapter 13, human, administrative, and business processes need leadership to ensure that they are translated into working guidelines and that the company culture which emerges is sustained and supports this infrastructure.

## CREATING AN ENABLING, SUPPORTING, ENTERPRISE-WIDE CORPORATE CULTURE

National cultures must be bridged when doing business internationally. Internal company cultures (religious, ethnic, and professional) must also be integrated, as well as enterprise-wide corporate culture, which needs to be formed and sustained as a company grows and changes. For example, Deutsche Bank of Germany encountered many of these problems as it attempted to find a new place in the global investing banking field through its purchase of Morgan Grenfell (Sesit and Reghavan 1998). As described in Chapter 8, its traditional bank managers and the deal-oriented British-American managers, many of whom were newly hired and highly paid, clashed. Old line German bankers criticized the erosion of firm loyalty as the bank downsized, and they were inevitably envious of the highly-paid new hotshots. To avoid these problems when it took over Banker's Trust in a $10 billion deal, the largest takeover of a U.S. bank by a foreign bank, Deutsche Bank announced that it would allow Banker's "no autonomy" (Rhoads 1998b). In a similar way, cultural clashes created major problems at both the insurance company Travelers Group (United States) and Nikko Securities (Japan) when they formed a joint venture, as the hard charging ethos of Wall Streeters had to be meshed with Nikko's notion of a genteel investment banker (Spindle 1999). Parmacia AB (Sweden) and the Upjohn Company (United States) had to overcome many cultural problems when the Europeans chafed under U.S. management rules (Barrett 1999). Even when merging firms within one culture, for example, when Norwest and Wells Fargo banks (both United States) merged, there can be problems, which in this case were resolved only through skillful management that focused on building employee and customer trust and loyalty (Rasmusson 1999). Cultural gaps between older and younger workers can also cause problems, as recent studies have shown (Aeppel 2000).

Cultural changes from a different perspective were important to BP's revival during the early 1990s—the situation described at the outset of this chapter.

In 1992, John Mumford was sent to Bangkok to head the BP Thailand operation and 2,000 Thai employees. He faced language and cultural barriers and his management style was one of "lord of the manor" (giving orders to follow). In 1994, BP announced that it would cut its workforce basically in half and Asia was hit as hard as any other area despite its growth.

Mumford began to participate in conferences and teach-ins organized by Pamela Mounter. As a BP Oil communcations advisor, she was in charge of changing the company's information flow. The result was that Mumford launched a newsletter in Thai and began monthly lunch get-togethers with staff. These moves clashed with the existing, rigid, almost complicated organizational hierarchy in Thailand. One of the rules is that one should not treat a subordinate as a peer—that will lead to much confusion. He arranged for birthday lunches, thereby getting different workers from different organizational levels together to initiate communication and dialogue as well as to hear about problems he would otherwise not know about. The result of bringing different cultures together was a doubling in profits and strong support from staff.

In today's rapidly changing multinational markets, a corporate culture needs to be a special kind of entrepreneurial one that encourages individual initiative that meets local requirements and leads to innovations useful both at the local and global level. At the same time, however, individual entrepreneurial initiative must take into account the limits, interconnections, and global perspectives of the international company environment within which it works. Above all, it should be a culture dedicated to *purposeful* change.

The approach to strategy implementation discussed in Chapter 1 encouraged people "to do whatever is necessary to get a job done, within well-defined legal, moral, ethical and policy restraints," a guiding principle set forth at Gillette by Colman Mockler during his seventeen years as CEO. Obviously, there are risks to such a loosely defined entrepreneurial working environment. Leadership, therefore, first requires creating a culture that accepts failure. More than that, however, it requires defining these general guidelines (or boundaries) through daily leadership actions, such as those of Jack Welch at General Electric and Al Zeien at Gillette.

The *organizational* enabling environment that is required for fostering such a controlled entrepreneurial culture has been covered in this chapter. Chapters 11 through 14 discuss the *human resource* enablers—both the *leadership* aspects and the *staffing and training* tools—that are useful in creating an organization culture/environment that balances global efficiency, local responsiveness, and adaptability.

### The Strategic Impact of Intranets

Company intranets—essentially internal company Web sites—have had a major impact on internal company communications. At IBM, for example, employees rated the intranet as one of the two most important sources of information about the company. Research firms report that nearly 90 percent of large organizations have some type of intranet. These organizations report that their intranets are becoming essential for improving productivity, reducing the cost of tasks such as publishing staff directories, and giving employees more autonomy and flexibility in how they do their work.

The impact of an intranet can be strategic. For example, Ford Motor Company, which has more than 350,000 employees, estimates that it has accrued more than $1 billion in value from a portion of its intranet devoted to so-called best practices. The site enables employees to post information about "anything that works well," such as the way to improve the process in one of Ford's paint shops. Overall, Ford estimates that its intranet is saving up to $2 million a year just by automating many paper-shuffling tasks.

At Charles Schwab, close to all of its 25,000 employees make use of the intranet each week. The intranet is especially useful to customer service employees, since internal investment information is available to answer customer inquiries online quickly. In a survey conducted by the company, 52 percent of Schwab employees said the intranet was the first place they looked for answers.

It would appear that through intranets, Internet technologies are having a major strategic impact on the way organizations function.

### *Multinational Megamergers*

Another major multinational trend is megamergers. In late 1998, Deutsche Bank finalized its acquisition of Banker's Trust (U.S.), which created the largest bank in the world. A few days later, Deutsche Bank announced its purchase of the Belgium business Credit Lyonnais (Rhoads 1998a). In 2000, Deutsche Bank explored merging with Dresdner Bank to form a bank with more than $1 trillion in assets (Andrews 2000b; "Banking in Europe" 2000).

During the late 1990s, Total Fina SA, France's second largest oil group, announced its takeover of PetroFina, the Belgian oil group, to form a $52 billion company (Buckley, Owen, and Corzine 1998); and Daimler-Benz concluded its takeover of Chrysler to form DaimlerChrysler, the world's fourth biggest auto group (Ibrahim 1999). DaimlerChrysler Aerospace (DASA) of Germany and Aerospatiale Matra of France merged in 2000 to become the world's third largest aerospace and defense firm (Major and Nicoll 1999).

In early 2000, the British drugmaker, Glaxo Wellcome, agreed to buy one of its chief rivals, SmithKline Beecham, for $78 billion to form the world's largest pharmaceutical company (Sorkin and Petersen 2000). During the same period, Vodafone AirTouch announced a planned $189 billion takeover of Mannesmann (Germany), which would have been the largest takeover of all time, ranking above AOL's earlier deal with Time Warner in the United States (Atkins and Lewis 2000).

Global merger and acquisition activity was expected to set a record in 1999 (Harris 1999) in spite of the apparent mixed record of this activity. For example, a 1999 study by the accounting firm, KPMG, of 107 cross-border mergers revealed that 53 percent destroyed shareholder value while another 30 percent produced no discernable difference in shareholder value (Cohen 1999). By mid-2000, global megamerger activity had dropped substantially (Pretzick 2000).

This is only a sample of the activity which has led some to predict that trillion-dollar worldwide megacorporations will one day control major industries such as banking—through mergers, acquisitions, and strategic alliances (Friedheim 1998). Such megaorganizations can be a force for good, if they increase productivity, expand markets into new locations, accelerate the development of new technologies, increase consumer choice, reduce prices and regulations, and create new markets that create new jobs. If, on the other hand, the megamultinational firm becomes a modern version of monopolistic cartels, inhibits competitive forces, corrupts governments, bullies competitors and suppliers, lowers productivity, restrains trade, circumvents laws, and slows the development of new technologies, new markets, and new jobs, then the concept can do great harm.

This organizational trend, which is likely to continue (Zachary 1999), presents major challenges to governments in all legislative, regulatory, and policy areas, and could lead to the formation of regional and local city-states to counterbalance the megacorporations' influence and protect individual rights. It will also require new leadership, organization, and management skills in an environment which is both cooperative and competitive, involving complex, diverse relationship links among individuals, operating units, and enterprises, both within and outside the firm (Robbins and Finley 1998).

### *Simultaneous Movement Toward Smaller Organizations*

Simultaneous with the megamerger trend, is a movement toward smaller organizations. For example, many smaller firms have been successful at using the Internet to target specific markets more economically than larger firms (Maitland 2000; Meredith 2000). Specialized firms are also being formed and used for outsourcing by larger firms to reduce costs and increase efficiencies in select areas. As large oil and other firms merge, they sometimes sell off operations to smaller independent firms for strategic, legal, and financial reasons (Liesman, Tajada, and Cooper 1999). In the organization area, as in other enabling strategic management areas, then, diverse and often seemingly conflicting trends are becoming more pronounced, requiring management to tailor solutions precisely to situation needs and balance conflicting forces in new and often nontraditional ways.

### Integrative Strategic Management at Renault

The experiences of Renault, the giant French automaker company, under the leadership of Louis Schweitzer, illustrate the many ways in which the different approaches described in this and earlier chapters can be integrative in formulating and carrying out strategic frameworks (Tagilabue 2000).

Renault believed that one day the auto industry would be dominated by a half-dozen giant companies, and its strategic focus was to be one of them. When Schweitzer joined Renault in the late 1980s, it was struggling with bad quality, a narrow product line, and overreliance on the French market. After Schweitzer's arrival, Renault had problems with its American Motors division and a failed merger with Volvo (Sweden). One major strategic move was to focus Renault's production solely on cars, and to spin off and dispose of the firm's foundry, bus-making divisions, and Renault Automation, which made auto factory equipment, to Fiat. The industrial vehicles division was sold to Volvo, with a 20 percent stake in that firm.

Schweitzer convinced the French government to slash its stake in Renault to 44 percent—its majority ownership had killed the Volvo deal earlier. He expanded globally in a variety of ways: building a $1 billion factory in Brazil; paying $40 million for 51 percent of the Romanian carmaker Dacia to gain a stepping-stone into Eastern Europe; arranging to manufacture Renaults in an idle factory near Moscow; buying a controlling stake in Samsung, the bankrupt South Korean carmaker; and paying $5.4 billion to acquire a controlling stake in the Nissan Motor Company in Japan. The risks, were, of course, enormous in 2000: economic progress in Romania had been dismal; Samsung had yet to reorganize; and Nissan was a stumbling, debt-ridden company.

By 2000, considerable progress had been made, and Renault's profit in 1999 before absorbing Nissan's losses was $1.4 billion. Renault's quality problems have been solved and its autos and minivans are among Europe's most reliable. In 1996, Schweitzer hired an experienced cost-cutter from Michelin, Carlos Ghosn, who cut the number of suppliers to reduce administrative costs, created teams to develop new products, reduced the number of models per plant, and negotiated more flexible shifts, all of which saved $2.8 billion annually. He also increased manufacturing capacity usage to 90 percent. Ghosn was assigned to Nissan after its purchase to turn it around.

Renault also challenged the French unions for the first time by successfully closing its first plant, in Vilvorde, Belgium, and stopped being a "social laboratory" where politicians tested labor reforms before introducing them nationwide. Schweitzer's background in government and business enabled him to manage both the politics and the business aspects of the turn-around.

A third key to success was the hiring of a new chief designer, Patrick Le Quement, who had earned a reputation at Ford and Volkswagen for daring, innovative car design. His designs at Renault resulted in a series of hot-selling new autos. He also reorganized the design center by centralizing it in a new Technocentre, which opened in 1998. The technocentre brought to-gether experts from design and research, vehicle engineering, purchasing, and product cost analysis—once scattered over fifty sites—who worked together to bring down costs and new model development time (from forty to twenty months).

Other steps taken by Schweitzer included: reorganizing Renault's sales and distribution system; making more cars to order; reducing customer de-livery time (fourteen days in some instances); cutting purchasing costs fur-ther by joining an online marketplace; targeting different Renault brands in different markets; and to developing 10 common platforms or underbodies which reduced costs and enabled the production of a wider range of models at individual plants.

All of these steps, which have been discussed throughout this book, were part of the strategic framework and implementation steps designed to carry out Renault's new enterprise-wide strategy.

## SUMMARY

Organization is another key enabler in multinational strategic manage-ment. Three aspects of organization were covered in this chapter: structure, process (business and human), and culture. The discussion focused on the underlying perspective of this and other chapters—the basic contingency process and its usefulness in helping to understand and structure organiza-tion processes at work in a multinational environment.

The key to success here is not solely the structure, but within the struc-ture, the hybrid organization processes are required to enable a balanced ap-proach to, and capacity for, change.

This chapter explored the impact of organization culture on successful multinational strategic management. Additional aspects of how culture in general can contribute to success are discussed in Chapter 10.

## REVIEW QUESTIONS

1. Describe and define the three key aspects of organization discussed in this chapter.

2. Identify the key situation factors that affect organization development and management.
3. Discuss the basic function and limitations of organization structure. Give specific examples.
4. Describe the role of business and human processes in organization development and functioning. Give specific examples.
5. In what ways does today's approach to organization require an adaptive entrepreneurial perspective? Identify the advantages and limitations of this approach and the ways in which organization approach and effectiveness are contingent on situation circumstances.
6. Describe the organization experiences of Hewlett-Packard. Discuss other situations in which the approach used by HP may and may not work effectively.
7. Define the concept of flattened hierarchies and their advantages and limitations. Cite specific examples.
8. Discuss the functioning of human and business processes within an organization and ways in which they can be managed to enable effective strategy implementation. Give specific examples.
9. Identify key approaches to encouraging collaborative linkages within an organization and discuss the situations in which each may or may not be effective.
10. Discuss the strengths and weaknesses of using teams in different situations.
11. What is the role of corporate culture in enabling strategy implementation? Describe different ways to cultivate an enabling organization culture. Give specific examples.
12. In what ways does organization integrate with and relate to the other enablers discussed so far in this text?

## *EXERCISES*

1. Based on your own research, select a company that has recently reorganized and discuss the process they employed in doing the reorganization and the organization approach they used. Carefully trace the relation of situation factors to the process employed and the approach developed.
2. Find some examples of corporate culture clashes which created major problems during mergers and acquisitions. Analyze the causes of the problems, the appropriate solutions developed, and the lessons learned about how to manage organizations more effectively.

3. Based on your own research, select a company in which both collaborative and individual entrepreneurial approaches were used. Describe the circumstances which led to this and evaluate the effectiveness of the balanced approach used.

# PART III:
# ENABLING HUMAN RESOURCES

# Chapter 10

# Managing Multicultural Diversity: Interpersonal Interaction

*The Wall Street Journal* describes McDonald's experiences in balancing global business perspectives and local cultural differences.

When McDonald's expanded into India, the company had to drastically adjust to local needs and demands. "In coming to this Hindu nation, where cows are sacred and most people don't eat beef, McDonald's Corp. ditched the Big Mac for an Indian stand-in, the Maharaja Mac" (Biers and Jordan, 1996, p. A14). This Indian outlet serves various types of sandwiches and other offerings, all of which are beefless. Instead, the customer can order Vegetable McNuggets and Vegetable McBurgers.

McDonald's used a common framework, the golden arches, and their name, adapted to local tastes and customs—a global-multilocal or "glocal" approach. In Serbia, McDonald's promoted a domestic pork burger, included Serbian cultural symbols in its ads, and even let Serbians use the basement of one of its restaurants as a bomb shelter during the war (Block 1999). This balanced approach has enabled McDonald's and other firms to blend more easily with local cultures while avoiding the resentment which can be created when an "American" approach is imposed. In France, however, McDonald's has run into problems even though the franchises are owned by the French and almost exclusively sell food grown in France. In late 1999, French protestors bulldozed a McDonald's construction site causing $120,000 in damage (Daley 2000).

In China, such "Americanization" fears led to major reworking of the U.S. children's program, *Sesame Street*. New characters were created, Chinese educational themes such as the importance of beauty and poetry were emphasized, only culturally appropriate segments of the U.S. shows were used, the traditional Sesame Street characters spoke Chinese, and the show was structured to appeal to both the rural and urban Chinese family markets—a good example of a "glocal" approach. In 1999, *Sesame Street* developed a program aimed at ten-year-olds that was designed to bridge the ethnic divide in Macedonia and Albania and so prevent conflict by showing how Christian and Muslim families in a community bridge ethnic gaps (Cook 1999).

Using common frameworks, as McDonald's did, to bridge cultural gaps and reconcile cultural diversity when *formulating enterprise-wide, business unit, and functional strategies and plans,* and when *putting enabling environments in place* can take a lot of hard work and luck to adapt them in a way that enables them to work.

This chapter and those following focus on the enabling phases of strategic management that involve human resources, especially leadership, management, staffing, and interpersonal interaction. These activities are listed in the lower half of Figure 1.3 (p. 9), which gives an overview of the strategic management job. These phases begin with a context analysis, such as that described in Chapter 4 and shown in Figure 1.2 (p. 7). Human resources—the people working in an enterprise and their interpersonal interactions—are a key strategic driver profoundly affecting a multinational enterprise's success.

Several aspects of the relevance of human resources to strategy formulation and implementation in multinational business situations are examined in this chapter. First, the nature of cultural differences and their diverse impact are discussed from six perspectives. These perspectives provide a framework for exploring ways to understand, adapt to, and effectively manage cultural differences. Within these perspectives are cutural differences which must be recognized within each country, as well as changes occurring with the rapid spread of the Internet and computer-based telecommunications media. Ideally, this review process helps produce synergies by enabling managers to creatively build on the strengths of each culture involved in a situation.

The chapter concludes with a discussion of other less systematic and disciplined ways to manage multinational interpersonal interaction. In many situations, creative, innovative, resourceful, entrepreneurial, ad hoc management solutions that break the mold and go beyond any framework are needed to succeed.

## CULTURAL FACTORS

*Culture* refers to shared values, beliefs, expectations, attitudes, and norms found within countries, regions, social groups, businesses, and even departments and work groups within a business. Over 160 definitions of culture can be identified (Ferraro 1998). A widely accepted definition of culture is "that complex whole which includes knowledge, beliefs, art, morals, customs, and any other capabilities and habits acquired by man as a member of society" (Herskovits 1952, p. 17). Culture is a distinctive way of life of a group of people—its complete design for living (Kluckholn 1951); it is "the behavioral norms that a group of people, at a certain time and place, have agreed upon to survive and coexist" (p. 86).

Culture is acquired. Rather than inheriting culture at birth, individuals learn a set of rules and behavior patterns. These norms and behavioral responses develop into cultural patterns passed down through generations, with continual embellishment and adaptation.

Most individuals are largely unaware of their cultural conditioning. The process of inculcating culture over time through example, and by reward and punishment, is generally more powerful than direct instruction, and individuals tend to unwittingly adopt cultural norms. *Acculturation,* the process of learning cultural patterns, conditions individuals so that large portions of their behavior fits their culture's patterns and are determined below the level of conscious thought (Herskovits 1963). The depth and length of the acculturation process explains in part why it is so difficult to break cultural patterns.

Many dimensions of culture can be identified. The first experience of a new culture is often through the more concrete aspects, the *explicit culture.* Explicit culture refers to aspects such as observed communication styles and language, time and space orientation, work habits and practices, all forms of interpersonal and social relationships, types of food and eating habits, dress and appearance, fashions, art, public buildings, houses, monuments, agriculture, shrines, and markets (Trompenaars 1994).

Explicit culture can change over time. For example, even in Paris, which has long been considered a smoker's haven, antismoking lawsuits have arisen and cigarette sales have declined. In London, traditional British merchant bankers have been gradually replaced by more aggressive European- and American-style bankers; French and other foreign firms are also increasingly adopting American business practices (Miller 1999). Corporate cultures in Japan are also changing, as total devotion to employers, consensus thinking, and jobs for life are being replaced by Western-type models of successful employees—entrepreneurial people concerned with personal development. The Internet is providing women with a way to combine both work and family, as in Western cultures, therefore bucking the Japanese tradition that women who have babies should quit their jobs (Guth 2000). The Internet has led to other changes in Japan. It has enabled businesses to prosper by bypassing controlled distribution channels, changed the way people apply for jobs and schools, and changed the way employees are assigned and promoted at some firms (Strom 2000).

Shopping malls and MTV have transformed India's retail culture (Guha 1999; Jordan 1999). Changing cultural values among the under-twenty generation has led to new advertising approaches and new distribution channels (Kripalani 1999). Attitudes toward capitalism and women in the workforce are also moving closer to Western norms. At the same time, negative European attitudes against genetically modified food products (GM) were beginning to enter the American culture in late 1999 (Dunne 1999).

Although these and other changes are evident, significant, explicit cultural differences persist. Explicit cultural differences are often symbols of a deeper level of culture that involves norms and values, beliefs and attitudes, and mental processes. *Norms,* a group's collective sense of what is right or wrong, can develop on a formal level as written laws or on an informal level as social control. Norms are sometimes referred to as character traits in educational programs. *Values,* on the other hand, define good and bad and are therefore closely related to the beliefs and attitudes shared by group members. To understand basic differences in values, beliefs, and attitudes, and the mental processes that reflect them, the history of a group and its struggles for survival need to be examined. Labeled *implicit culture* factors, these basic assumptions are *imbedded* in a culture (Trompenaars 1994).

Deeply imbedded cultural differences can significantly affect society. For example, cultural differences in Czechoslovakia led to its division into two sections, the Czech Republic, and Slovakia, after the 1991 USSR breakup. This occurred in spite of the country's small population (10,298,731) and size (30,442 square miles—smaller than the state of Maine) and the fact that the division created major economic hardships for Slovakia. The fighting among Russians in Chechnya and among the Serbs, Croats, and Muslims in the Croatia/Bosnia/Yugoslavia area of the Balkans arose in part from deeply imbedded cultural differences. In 1995, such differences led the Quebec province in Canada to almost vote (only 50.6 to 49.4 percent against it) to form a new nation and secede from Canada. Deep cultural distrust of capitalism in France has led to protests against such French firms as Michelin (tires), Axa (insurance), and Total Fina (oil) (Graham 2000), as well as U.S. firms such as McDonald's (Daley 2000), indicating that global firms must continually think locally to accommodate local cultural perspectives.

Developed over hundreds of years in isolation from the rest of the world, Japanese culture in the twentieth century evolved into a closed society, suspicious of the rest of the world. These deep cultural biases have been cited as a major cause of the World War II Japanese aggression (Chua-Eaon 1995, p. 43): "Hiroshima was simply the end of a ferocious clash of cultures, fueled by intense hatreds and a history of humiliation." Even today, considerable distrust, and even hatred, persists among some sectors of the Chinese, U.S., and Japanese people—a basic cultural barrier to be considered in business and political dealings among the countries (Kristof 1997).

The Chinese culture has been influenced significantly by Confucian philosophy. For example, China's tradition of family-based business draws on Confucian philosophy. The international impact of this tightly controlled, family-based approach has been enormous. For instance, in Malaysia in the early 1990s, the Chinese comprised only 28 percent of the population yet controlled over 50 percent of the wealth (Dologite and Mockler 1993). The Chinese tradition of international trade extends back thousands of years to its ancient "silk road" which served as a trading link westward to Europe. This tradition encourages international exchanges and suggests that China is primed to eventually become a major force in international trade.

At the same time, Chinese schools teach younger people to remember how historically, foreigners (the British, American, and Japanese especially) tried to suppress China. This has led the Chinese to be suspicious of foreigners and provides a cultural explanation of the intensity of negative reactions to the 1999 UN bombing of their embassy in Belgrade which killed three Chinese (Chang 1999).

Cultural differences can affect many business areas. U.S. agricultural exports worth billions of dollars were threatened in 1999 because of European fears of genetically altered (GA) crops (mostly U.S.), a cultural belief labelled the fear of "Frankenfood" (Magnusson, Palmer, and Capell 1999). The *Metro* in Moscow refused to run an Ikea furniture ad with the headline "Every 10th European was made in one of our beds" declaring it in bad taste (Fuerbringer 2000).

Failure to recognize and effectively manage cultural differences accounts for many of the blunders committed daily by multinational managers worldwide.

## UNDERSTANDING AND MANAGING CULTURAL AND PERSONAL BIASES AND MENTAL SETS

Developing an understanding of, and acquiring a facility in managing cultural differences begins with understanding one's own cultural and personal biases. Because this book is written by an American, that stereotype is used as a reference point in the discussions. It would be just as useful to use any (preferably the reader's own) national culture as the reference point. This perspective, therefore, should not be taken as a recommendation to "think American" in all multinational interpersonal situations.

Not *all* Americans, nor all people of any nationality, are like those described in the following examples. Therefore, it is helpful to review the following general guidelines before going on:

- Although it is useful to explore generalities and their implications, individuals do not always conform to cultural stereotypes. Not all Japanese, for example, are "typical" Japanese, and "typical" Japanese may vary by age, sex, and other demographic categories. For instance, young women in all countries now share many common values, as was demonstrated in the August 1995 United Nations Fourth World Conference on Women in Beijing. Significant differences are apparent in Japan between the values of younger and older groups of women. The

Internet, with its worldwide communications links, has stimulated considerable changes in value systems within and among cultures, especially among the younger age groups.

- Differences are not always culturally based. Some arise from individual personality differences and some from personal, institutional, or business factors. This is true in any country. In addition, any given action may be stimulated by a variety of cultural biases that reinforce each other, not just by one bias.

- Something that works in one culture will not necessarily work in another. Communality sometimes exists across cultural boundaries, as in the common frameworks described earlier, and there are increasing trends toward more global products, services, and communications, especially through Internet links. This is especially true among younger generations in all countries. However, differences will always exist, even among teenagers, in different countries which share many common values (Warner 1996).

- Understanding one's own culture creates an awareness of one's own biases or mental set, and provides a benchmark against which to study other cultures.

- Studying cultural diversity within one's own country yields clues to cultural differences and assists in understanding how to handle diversity.

- The following discussion focuses on continuums, that is, on sets of two extremes between which there can be many varied gradations. Thinking in terms of extreme black-and-white stereotypes should be avoided.

- Ultimately, cultural and personal sensitivities *specific to the situation* must be recognized. This applies to any situation involving other human beings.

- The same words often have different connotations in different cultures: for example, the French sense of "individualistic" is very different from a North American's sense of "individualism." Both definitions differ from a Latin American's understanding of the words.

## SIX PERSPECTIVES ON MANAGING CULTURAL DIFFERENCES

The conceptual framework described in this section has proved useful in organizing, understanding, and dealing with the wide range of cultural differences that impact on multinational management. This conceptual guideline has helped many managers become sensitive to cultural differences—a critical first step in managing cultural differences. Six critical aspects of cultural diversity can be identified as reference points or perspectives for busy managers:

1. The role of personal relationships: business or people first?
2. Focus on the individual or on the group?
3. Status: is everyone created equal?
4. Language/information flow factors
5. A question of priorities: what is the value of time?
6. Other factors: corporate culture, institution, business, individual

These points are presented for discussion and understanding purposes only. In practice, actions and motivation do not always fall into such clearly defined categories.

General cultural categories are useful reference points during interpersonal interaction situations. For example, many French think Americans are naive, shallow, uninteresting, and unaware. U.S. managers at times cite such typical French traits as self-congratulation, stubbornness, arrogance, and unwillingness to compromise. Both views are imprecise, because individuals can differ from preconceived national personality profiles, depending on personality, age, and upbringing, and these differences must be taken into account when interacting with individuals.

Often, it is useful to view cultural differences as opportunities. For example, the Japanese are noted for their concern for cleanliness. This has inspired such products as: automated teller machines that iron and sanitize the dispensed bills; germ-free pens and pencils with barrels impregnated with antiseptic chemicals to kill bacteria; antibacterial stationery, origami paper, bicycle handles, and even maracas and tambourines. When managed creatively, such differences can lead to synergies that create new and better solutions.

## *The Role of Personal Relationships: Business or People First?*

Human aspects of a situation are emphasized differently in different cultures. Asians, for example, tend to strive to *develop personal relationships* with the parties involved before proceeding with business negotiations. This partially explains why family relationships are so important when doing business in China. At the other end of the continuum, as shown in Figure 10.1 (Section A), Americans are likely to rely on superficial friendly remarks to begin a conversation and prefer to get to the point of negotiations quickly. This cultural bias is reflected in such phrases as "I don't have to like someone I do business with." As with most cultural biases, this statement is true and can be useful in cultures similar to that in the United States. It can, however, create problems in other cultures.

FIGURE 10.1. Sample Continuums Representing Range of Cultural Differences

**A. Importance of Personal Relationships**

**B. Dealing With Difficult Problems**

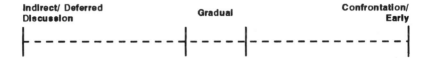

**C. Working In Teams**

**D. Importance Of Status And Position**

Two aspects of this cultural trait can affect the way cultural differences are managed: the importance of developing personal relationships, and the way people form relationships. For example, Douglas Daft, the newly elected CEO of Coca-Cola in 2000, set out to develop personal relationships with European officials after having determined that developing such relationships was a major key to solving Coke's substantial problems in Europe (McKay 2000).

In another situation, for example, a multinational company with a subsidiary in Mexico, a culture in which personal relationships are important, would carefully consider replacement choices for an American, male sales manager in Mexico City who had long-term personal relationships with Mexican customers. Choosing a "let's-get-down-to-business" female could create problems, given the machismo, "lets-get-to-know-each-other," male-centered Mexican culture. At a minimum, the transition period would have to be carefully and personally managed by both the new and former sales managers (Foster 1992).

The notion of a personal relationship in the United States can be quite different from the view in other, more "relationship-oriented" cultures. For some Americans, relationships are often casual and do not require deep commitments, especially in business. Some Americans often do not have the time nor inclination to pursue the one-on-one learning about each other needed to form deep friendships. In some cases, they are informal and friendly, and often have difficulty cultivating friends in business situations involving cultures with opposite traditions, in which deep, long-lasting relationships are required.

For example, a Chinese firm wishing to purchase paper-making machinery negotiated with two suppliers, one French and one American. The American firm had superior technology yet lost the contract, largely because of insensitivity to the importance of personal relationships in the Chinese culture. The American firm's negotiation style was perceived as disrespectful by the Chinese, and the Americans viewed the Chinese style as time-consuming, confusing, and unfocused. Such incidents suggest that both parties should communicate mutual respect, be nonjudgmental, realize that perceptions are personal, show empathy, and tolerate ambiguity during intercultural exchanges.

Business relationships are formed in different ways in different cultures. Americans often build relationships with breezy hospitality, cheeriness, informality, a playful disrespect for status and position, and an expectation that everyone will find this charming and friendly. This is friendliness—not necessarily friendship. Europeans, on the other hand, are less open, especially in England, where respect for differences and status is particularly important. In this European cultural context, the casual, informal American approach appears shallow, superficial, and insensitive. These differences often show up in how each culture makes use of e-mail communications, a media which is essentially impersonal until after the communicating parties have had a chance to get to know each other personally, face-to-face.

The French enjoy emphasizing differences as a way to define their individualistic character and to ascertain another person's true character, an approach that may seem unfriendly to people from other cultures. They are often perplexed by Americans and others who search for similarities as a way of establishing a relationship. To the French, such an approach lacks the depth that develops from getting to know another person's distinctive character. The French traits combine personal individualism and a natural suspicion of strangers. This individualism generates a resistance to adapting to others' needs and has led to a reputation for rudeness. This is especially true of salespeople in Paris, who are known for their surliness and for not smiling or being accommodating.

Cultural variations also exist in regard to display of emotions. During business negotiations, for example, at the upper management level among individuals becoming acquainted, the range of emotional expression considered acceptable is greater for Americans than for the British, and greater still for Latin Americans. In contrast, for the Japanese and most Asians, the display of emotion is more restricted than for the British. In other settings, such as social events, these relationships can change.

Along another continuum shown in Figure 10.1 (Section B), at one cultural extreme there can be a tendency to keep relations harmonious by not talking directly about problems, as in Asian and some Latin American cultures. Confrontations are avoided in cultures in which human relationships are highly valued. In contrast, other cultures, for example in the United States, can desire to confront problems quickly and directly, in spite of the fact that such an approach might embarrass someone personally and publicly.

This direct approach can create problems if not handled in a sensitive manner. For example, an Arab negotiating with an American was puzzled by the American's insistence on specific information about future delivery dates and available quantities. The Arab felt that the relationship which had developed between the parties had created enough trust to make such detail unnecessary. After discussing the matter, the solution in this instance was for the Arab to understand the American's needs and to meet them by supplying more detailed information, even though he felt that the request was unnecessary and showed a lack of trust. Such a solution is common: first understand the cultural difference and its basis, and then take the steps needed to accommodate a sensitive situation.

Before proceeding overseas to negotiate, it is important to understand that the purpose of a negotiation may vary by culture. Often, the primary purpose is *not* to accomplish a task and arrive at a deal, as in the United States. In other cultures, negotiations may be a process for getting to know the other parties and establishing a long-term personal relationship that will serve as the basis of future deals. This is one reason why so little often seems to be accomplished during the early stages of negotiations in China, Japan, and South America, and why negotiations seem to take so long.

This does not mean that uncomplicated matters cannot be handled quickly among cultures. Nor does it mean that personal relationships are the only factor affecting negotiations. It simply means that building relationships is a significant means of doing business over a long period of time among and across cultures. It should be recognized that in some instances, interpersonal electronic, phone, fax, mail, or Internet communications across cultures might be effective for simple subjects, whereas face-to-face meetings would be more effective for complex cross-cultural undertakings.

### Focus on the Individual or on the Group?

Relative to other cultures, Americans as a whole are very extreme in the value they place on individualism. U.S. history and its educational system support an individualistic culture. For example, children are taught to be self-reliant and are rewarded for individual achievement. In contrast, Japanese children may have worked in groups with the pride of achievement and reward being for the collective group output.

This trait can cause problems during negotiations. For example, Americans often expect the Japanese to make decisions at the negotiating table. In turn, the Japanese are surprised to find the Americans advancing their own ideas and opinions, and at times contradicting one another. This creates a cultural gap that must be bridged. Again, this usually requires more time than Americans originally were prepared to spend on negotiations.

An American expatriate in Malaysia reflected on his experiences there in these words:

> When I was transferred to Penang it was a cultural shock. I remember when I tried to publicly reward some people for exceptional effort, how embarrassed they were. Rewards such as free time or free lunch for the team as a whole were more appropriate. I didn't realize that teamwork is more important there than standing out as an individual. In the states we fight for recognition. (Gogan, Zuboff, and Schuck 1994, p. 5)

Another Malaysian manager described what he learned in this way: "Australians are taught to be strong and speak their minds. Italians are more emotional. I had to role-play an American. I cannot act like Americans; they are more aggressive and individualistic" (Gogan, Zuboff, and Schuck 1994, p. 6). Cultures of the United Kingdom, the Netherlands, France, and the Nordic countries also have strong individualistic tendencies. Many Asian and Latin American countries have collectivist cultures. Guatemala is considered the most group-oriented culture, due to its Mayan tribal heritage.

Cultural values are changing, however. For example, in Japan, a system of "cram" schools has been developed to train children (two years and older) to compete for positions in better grammar schools, which leads to entrance into better universities and subsequently to better jobs at graduation. This is creating a generation of "kids like in America" nurtured in more "individualistic and independent thinking" and on availability of and familiarity with the worldwide Internet communication media (French 1999). Corporate cultures in Japan are also slowly changing, as more attention is paid to nurturing individual entrepreneurial thinking and action (WuDunn 1998).

At times, collectivist cultural values do not originate from historical traditions, but rather have been acquired, for example, during communist rule. For example, when doing business in Russia or Central Europe, one often encounters situations such as:

- The inability to negotiate individually and make decisions during meetings because approval is needed from higher authorities
- Final arrangements may have to be worked out with labor groups which control decision processes
- Constituents may have to be paid off with bribes and under-the-table payments, raising serious ethical questions for U.S. executives

Although it is easier to make decisions and take action in an individualistic frame (it takes longer to reach decisions and act in collective contexts) and although Americans are noted for being action-oriented, group-oriented cultures can also be action oriented. For example, small, family-based businesses have been very successful throughout Asia, and often grow into major conglomerates.

In the United States, one hears the phrase, "A squeaky wheel gets the grease." In collectivist, group-centered cultures, the opposite may be true: outspoken individuals may be viewed as disharmonious and a danger to the group, and so be ostracized; harmony is an important goal, harmony with groups and society, and harmony with traditions that may have developed over many hundreds of years. This dictates careful judgment and restraint as to the timing of outspoken criticism and objections during business negotiations. When appropriate, the urge to get down to business and into the task of establishing bargaining positions prematurely should be resisted.

Cultures such as in China, tend to believe that "God helps those who help each other" and prefer to *work in teams and for group consensus.* As shown in Figure 10.1 (Section C), at the other extreme are cultures, such as those in America, that place a high premium on *individualism,* and so tend to believe that "God helps those who help themselves." Such people are not always inherent team players.

In light of these cultural and historical differences, one must be contingency oriented. First, the situation context, including both the individual and culture, and the tasks being dealt with should be examined. Some factors to look at and be sensitive to have been discussed. Other factors can also be relevant. Being sensitive to these differences is a major first step in adapting to, and managing, perceived differences. Above all, when in doubt, ask questions gently to determine the context.

### Status: Is Everyone Created Equal?

As shown in Figure 10.1 (Section D), at one end of the status continuum, some cultures, such as those in Asia, Northern Europe, and South America, greatly value social status. For example, this is reflected in seating arrangements in meetings and other protocols based on position. In contrast, Americans tend to emphasize competence. The United States has an egalitarian culture—all are created equal. Next to Australia, it is probably the world's most informal culture.

In many cultures, formal protocols are important. Early in business relationships, people are referred to by their formal titles—Mr., Mrs.—not by first names as in the United States. Business cards are treated seriously, from the titles printed on them (title, corporate rank, and educational degrees) to how they are exchanged (start with the highest-ranking person). Gift-giving practices also vary by culture. Gifts are commonly given in Asia, usually for a specific service, such as giving a talk. Customs in regard to dinner invitations and appropriate host/hostess gifts vary, as do the timing and length of meals. Invitations to a business associate's home are common in Australia, but rare in China or Japan. If invited to a home in France, bring flowers, but never roses. Dinners often take place at 11 p.m. in Spain; three-hour lunches are normal in Buenos Aires. It is important to learn these protocols as quickly as possible.

Embracing egalitarianism leads to a willingness to speak frankly to anyone as an equal, a very direct approach. U.S. businesspeople tend to speak frankly regardless of the listener's rank. This approach is reinforced by the growing use of impersonal communication media, such as the Internet. In contrast, in cultures where rank and position are considered more important—such as Mexico, Italy, and France—such directness can appear vulgar, harsh, and impersonal. Many other cultural values dictate ambiguity and indirectness in order to maintain harmony, respect status, elaborate points within larger contexts, and save face. Status values also dictate that it is prudent to praise contributions to increase a listener's status before offering any criticism—a good idea in any culture.

Avoiding diminishing another's status in public can lead to confusion. In Asia especially, people have difficulty saying "no" directly. Instead, they may equivocate, saying, "We must study the question further," or "We will try to solve the problem." In Asia "yes" can mean only "I heard you"; it is not an affirmative reply necessarily. In extreme cases, store clerks in China may say "no problem" when a customer has a problem, which in fact means no problem for them, but a big problem for the customer, as the customer discovers later when nothing has been done to solve the problem.

Americans have trouble dealing with bureaucracies. They prefer to find a decision maker and obtain a direct answer quickly. This is not always possible. Hierarchies, based on history or past practice, are common in many cultures. They require time to work through, are often manipulated to exploit or win concessions, and are also the source of much crime and bribery. Hierarchical religious, social, and political environments can be especially troublesome when trying to introduce change in business, such as when empowering workers to make decisions.

Americans are often unable to understand why contracts are frequently ignored, broken, or renegotiated in Asian, Latin American, Russian, and Central European countries. An egalitarian system is built on the assumption that laws and standards (ethical and moral) permit all people to be treated equally. Other countries are more pragmatic and judge each new event based on the new circumstances, as in China, for example.

American contracts tend to be very specific because the parties try to anticipate and cover all contingencies. For the Chinese, a contract is the beginning of the negotiation, not the end, because they may depend on trust and an established relationship with their partner to help resolve difficulties that arise. For this reason, it is helpful to work through family ties when doing business in China.

Although women are viewed as equal to men in some cultures, such as in Scandinavia, other cultures do not believe in such equality. In very masculine-oriented countries, such as Japan and some Arab countries, women may have trouble negotiating and interacting with businesspeople. These attitudes are changing, especially in China (WuDunn 1999). In Russia, women entrepreneurs are becoming more numerous, and countries such as Yemen are giving more political power to women in response to local women activists. But change is coming very slowly in many countries, such as Japan (French 2000).

The direct approach can also be a problem during employee performance evaluations. Although being honest, frank, and open—or working with objective standards fairly developed during management by objectives programs—is desirable in egalitarian cultures such as in the United States, this approach is not as effective in nonegalitarian societies. First, such behavior is often perceived as threatening the status of the person being evaluated and usually violates associated cultural values related to avoiding unpleasant subjects and confrontations. Second, working with a person to set work objectives, just like asking for their opinions about work practices, violates hierarchical allocations of power, because in many collectivist cultures bosses are expected to have the answers. Cultural differences also affect performance-reward systems: individual rewards for performance are inappropriate in societies where the group or collective effort is the primary driving force.

### Language/Information Flow Factors

The most immediate cultural difference is language. Obviously, in multinational management, the more languages one speaks the better. In practice, this is almost impossible for most of us. Because English is the generally accepted language of business, many international managers will speak it as their secondary, not primary, language. People may be self-conscious, uncertain, and hesitant when using a second language. They may have difficulty finding the right word. Even when English is the language used by both parties, therefore, there can be misunderstandings and problems. For example, the word "right" can mean "opposite of left," "correct," or "redo something." Colloquialisms, such as "Run that by me again," instead of "please repeat that," are easy to misconstrue. Likewise, jargon, idioms, and jokes rarely travel well across cultural borders. Also, remember that others often think Americans are arrogant because Americans expect others to speak English. Often, this resentment has to be overcome in business dealings.

Interpretations of body language or the amount of personal space desired between speakers can also vary among cultures. For example, people from more socially oriented cultures tend to stand very close while talking, while others, including Americans, prefer more space between speakers during a conversation. Eye contact also has different meanings in different cultures; not looking directly at someone might be interpreted as a sign of respect in India, whereas intensely looking someone in the eye may be a way to show personal interest in someone in other cultures. As another example, an American businessperson whose hand is suddenly taken by a Thai associate, or who is embraced by a Latin business partner, might attribute a sexual meaning where none is intended. In turn, a Thai or Latin associate, when meeting resistance to these nonverbal gestures, might attribute it to a coldness or indifference.

The way information is conveyed also varies by culture. For example, a typical Western trait, especially in Germany and the United States, is to talk about "getting straight to the point." In other cultures, both the speed and path of information flow can vary. Getting to the "point" may first involve "getting to know each other," which can take much more time. Also, more than one point (including family affairs) may be discussed along the information flow path as a means of becoming acquainted.

### A Question of Priorities: What Is the Value of Time?

Northern Europeans (strongly) and Americans (moderately) tend to favor treating events in an "orderly" fashion, one at a time. In such a monochronic perspective, time is linear: things are done separately, one after another. Time is compartmentalized, organized, controlled, and viewed as a valuable commodity due to its scarcity and usefulness in defining the context in which activities occur.

Polychronic time, on the other hand, is more circular: It is plentiful and has no beginning or end, and many activities can occur simultaneously. This cultural perspective is prevalent in Arab countries, Central and Southern Asia, and Latin America where topics involving both family and business may be discussed concurrently as part of the "getting to know each other" ritual and there is less pressure to strictly adhere to an agenda.

Monochronic cultures tend to focus on the present or immediate future and foster a belief that an individual can affect future outcomes. Polychronic cultures tend to be more futuristic and fatalistic—reflected in the phrase "whatever will be, will be." This can lead to an attitude that tomorrow cannot be controlled, so why not make the best of today. Time factors, therefore, affect approaches to dealing with people from other cultures. For instance, *in a specific situation at hand* will decisions be made and action taken quickly, or will many meetings be needed just to get to know each other? Can the task be discussed directly or will it be necessary to socialize, avoid confrontations, and talk about side issues first? Will the meetings proceed in a linear fashion, moving logically and incrementally toward a conclusion, or will a less task-focused, discursive discussion take place? Managing cultural differences requires prethinking along these contingency lines. The specific situation requirements, not theoretical universal formulas, dictate how cultural differences are managed.

Such flexibility should not surprise Americans familiar with the contrasts between rural and urban lifestyles. In the United States, managers in New York City work on tight time schedules, and hurry from one meeting or task to the next. In contrast, managers living in smaller towns might be less controlled by tight time schedules and more accustomed to dealing with people—shopkeepers, postal workers, and repair persons—whom they have gotten to know personally over the years. Managers who can imagine, or have experienced, such different settings are aware that managing styles change in different environments. The same is true among national cultures.

When conducting training or other business in France, for example, work hours should be adjusted for lunch and breaks. For the French, lunch can be a two-hour or longer event and time must be allocated to accommodate such habits. For the French, as for many business people around the world, lunch is not just a time to eat. It is also a time to conduct interpersonal business, carry out internal politicking, and clarify possible misunderstandings.

Even in societies that favor tight schedules, decisions may be made slowly. Other traditions may intervene. Traditions related to long histories which create the feeling that the near-term future is not very important and that other considerations, such as society, respect for other group members, etc, are more important and so must be given equal time. Deadlines are also affected by cross-cultural differences, since their importance can be diminished when a culture emphasizes other agendas. Although the French value efficiency, they also have great respect for quality. When problems arise, they may disregard a deadline to meet quality standards.

Cultural perspectives about time also affect training programs. Schedules have to be adjusted to allow for discussions of related contexts, contexts which may initially seem irrelevant to the task objectives. Times also must be allocated for interpersonal sessions in which individuals are given the opportunity to get to know one another. In addition, it should be recognized that the amount of time allocated for breaks and for meals may vary by culture.

Another adjustment across cultures involves the difficulty of setting agendas and of "sticking to the subject." Polychronic cultures have different agendas which allow for the simultaneous discussion of related topics. Such discussions, which may include family matters, related social and group matters, or the need for information to make broader context decisions, may annoy and frustrate someone accustomed to narrowly focused tasks/decisions, tight time schedules, and point-by-point agendas.

When doing business across borders, then, it is important to accept cultural differences and use them as a working premise when managing business activities.

### Other Factors: Corporate Culture, Institution, Business, and Individual

Individual actions are influenced by many factors, not just cultural factors.

An individual's personality may influence action. Some people are contentious by nature, a character trait that may be stimulated and conditioned by the individual's culture, but which may not be totally caused or explained by cultural influences. In other words, actions may not have a single cause or stimuli.

Institutional policies may affect behavior. In Russia, and in other controlled economies, approvals may be required by executives at different levels. In these cases, the delays may not necessarily be related to cultural perceptions of time nor to a reluctance to talk directly about controversial subjects; they may be related to institutional policies. Corporate cultures may also be the source of a behavior. In another negotiating situation, for example, a country's high inflation rate, over 100 percent per month, prevented businesses from making long-term commitments. Cultural factors created a reluctance to talk about the problems directly, but the root cause was an economic/business condition.

Often, numerous cultural or other factors generate and explain behavior. People do not always act based on one motive nor can their behavior always be traced to one cultural stimulus. The six-perspective framework developed in this chapter is, therefore, useful for discussion, understanding, and recall purposes only. Such segmentation does not necessarily replicate reality, because events can actually unfold in an integrated way.

The availability of worldwide communication media, such as the Internet, can also affect intercultural interaction, because it provides an easily accessible means of interacting in an impersonal way which can at times enable reconciling and bypassing cultural differences.

## USING CULTURAL FACTOR ANALYSIS

The cultural and historical differences encountered in multinational management make it necessary to be contingency oriented in interpersonal situations, as in other multinational task situations. This common contingency framework (discussed in Chapter 1) is the consistent underlying theme of this book.

As a first step, the situation context—both the individual and the culture involved—should be examined. Some factors to look at and be sensitive to have been discussed in this chapter. Preparing a chart similar to the one in Table 10.1 can be helpful to those involved in cross-cultural business situations. The top of the chart lists the countries involved in the situation, both home and host (Egypt, Australia, United Kingdom, Norway, and India in the figure). The left side lists characteristics appropriate for the specific situation (responsibility, participation, relationship focus, achievement, time, and change, for example). The task is described in the table's title (team management in this example).

Although useful in many situations, this is only one tool for analyzing or decomposing an interpersonal situation. Other tools are discussed in the following chapters. Being sensitive to cultural differences *in a systematic way* is a major first step in adapting to and managing perceived cultural differences.

## MANAGING CULTURAL DIFFERENCES: SITUATION-BY-SITUATION OVERVIEW

As seen from the discussions in this chapter, not all many multinational situations have to be handled situation-by-situation, on an ad hoc basis. This and the next section discuss some systematic guidelines for handling such situations.

As experience shows, reconciling and managing differences generally involves one of six approaches: adapting to a situation by modifying one's behavior; taking steps to change the situation environment; abandoning the

TABLE 10.1. Analysis of Cultural Differences: Team Management Decision

| Cultural Factors | Countries | | | | |
|---|---|---|---|---|---|
| | *Egypt* | *Australia* | *UK* | *Norway* | *India* |
| **Participation** | | | | | |
| Focus | Group | Individual | Individual | Individual | Group |
| Personal Space | Less | More | More | More | More |
| Needed | | | | | |
| | | | | | |
| **Relationship Focus** | | | | | |
| Task or Relationship | Relationship | Task | Task | Relationship | Relationship |
| | | | | | |
| **Responsibility** | | | | | |
| Authority Focus | Leader | Individual | Individual | Individual | Leader |
| Communication | Indirect | Direct | Direct | Direct | Indirect |
| | | | | | |
| **Time** | | | | | |
| Short/Long-Term Focus | Short | Long | Long | Short | Long |
| Punctuality | Less Important | Important | Important | Less Important | Important |
| | | | | | |
| **Change** | | | | | |
| Risk Taking or Avoidance | Avoid | Risk | Risk | Avoid | Avoid |
| | | | | | |
| **Achievement** | | | | | |
| Reward for Performance | Group | Individual | Individual | Individual | Group |

*Source:* Adapted from: Slyvia Odenwald, *Global Solutions for Teams,* Chicago, IL: Irwin Professional Publishing, 1996, p. 89.

situation or project; using a bicultural approach; exploiting differences wherever possible; or using any combination of the first five approaches.

## Being Sensitive to, Accepting, and Adapting to Differences

Companies often modify products, reconfigure manufacturing facilities, adapt advertising, and make other moves to accommodate local requirements. A multinational or market-by-market approach is often required by local circumstances. Accommodating local tastes was, for example, necessary for McDonald's in India and *Sesame Street* in China as noted earlier in this chapter. Many cultural differences to be recognized and adapted to have been discussed—including simple things such protocols at conferences for seating arrangements, the way to and order in which to address individuals, the time to discuss personal matters and the time to discuss business matters, what to wear on different occasions, where to go for entertainment, and what to serve for meals. Knowing and adapting to customs and habits is useful in many business and personal dealings. Many books, such as *Kiss, Bow, or Shake Hands: How to Do Business in Sixty Countries* (Morrison, Conaway, and Borden 1994), provide guidance to business managers and businesses in adapting to, surviving, and prospering in local cultures. Although adapting to local customers is at times effective, it is not always the best approach. Other approaches are discussed in the following sections.

### Modifying the Impact of Cultural Differences and Situation Circumstances

With the growing sophistication of international managers, a small but noticeable trend toward increasingly sophisticated manipulation of expectations arising from the growing awareness of cultural differences has emerged. For example, a Japanese negotiator may know that sophisticated Americans are aware that negotiations in Japan can take longer because of the cultural need to get to know each other. This cultural rationale can be exploited, if it is used simply to wear down American negotiators and create time-scheduling problems and the need for hasty, last-minute decisions.

As another example, the phrase "This is the custom (or way we do it) here in our country" may surface during legal negotiations anywhere in the world. When spoken by lawyers during business negotiations, this phrase invariably is used as a justification for persuading the other party to pay additional expenses not previously agreed upon. It is essentially a negotiating ploy used to con someone into paying for something, such as a property transfer fee, which she or he is not required to pay. Such a situation can be handled by pointing out that each negotiation is a separate event and each item is open to negotiation regardless of past practices.

Another commonly encountered exploitive scenario involves depending on a relationship of trust to avoid difficult decisions. For example, during a negotiation, one party may try to avoid committing to deadlines by saying, "You can trust me," just to find an excuse to avoid making a normal business commitment. It is not always necessary to yield or adapt in this or other situations, just because there is a possibility that the phrase is culturally based; the other party may simply be testing limits.

Often, it is possible to ignore or circumvent alleged and real local differences and customs. Many readers are familiar with the picture of President George Bush becoming ill in Asia after excessive toasting. In contrast, in more than 100 business banquets that the author attended in Asia and Central Europe, no one ever served high-alcohol-content liquor or smoked. This was because the hosts were informed that someone in the party was allergic to smoke, and that for health reasons, wine was the only alcohol desired. It was understood that the Americans realized that refusing to toast with hard liquor could be construed as being impolite, and that if served liquor they would politely raise their glasses but not actually drink. It was also understood that, if anyone smoked, the person who was allergic to smoke would have to leave the room because her eyes would water and she would begin coughing.

These requests created no problems, because courtesy and hospitality to guests are strongly rooted in Asian and Central European cultures, as they are in most countries/cultures. In addition, some cultures (such as the Muslim) do not allow the drinking of any alcohol, so countries with diverse cultures are accustomed to dealing with such differences. Sophisticated executives in many countries are thus used to accommodating justifiable requests based on cultural differences providing that they are timely and politely introduced.

The impact of differences is diminishing as multinational companies mount global mass marketing programs for products ranging from Frito-Lay potato chips, to Gillette razors, to Coke. Rapidly expanding mass media, especially satellite television, has helped reduce the impact of differences, for example, as twenty-four-hour shopping channels are started, and major distributors make billion-dollar purchases of overseas films and TV programs.

### *Abandoning or Greatly Reducing Involvement in a Project*

Sometimes cultural differences cannot be resolved and abandoning or reducing involvement in a project is necessary. Gillette threatened to do this initially when negotiating to build a plant in Russia. The firm delayed investing until regulations restricting dollar repatriation were modified and other guarantees were agreed upon. In another instance, during mid-1995, a growing backlash against foreign investments in India, fueled largely by internal political rivalries, led to the temporary halting of a multibillion-dollar electric power plant project with the Enron Corporation ("Enron . . ." 1996; "Enron Plans . . ." 1997). An attempt was also made to close a Kentucky Fried Chicken outlet and otherwise discredit its multinational parent company, PepsiCo. While many firms, such as the U.S. cereal firm Kellogg, were prospering in India, many others were adopting a wait-and-see attitude towards investing in India as a result of such incidents.

## A Bicultural Approach

An approach combining cultures is sometimes effective, but finding the exact mix is not easy. For example, teenagers especially often exhibit bicultural interests. In the United States, tests have shown that Latino youths respond to advertising in both English and Spanish, using Latino or American actors. Their music interests include both American and Latino bands and songs. At the same time, older Latinos, while strongly favoring preservation of Latino traditions, have also been found to respond to mixed cultural advertising. The mixed cultural approach also applies to the media involved. Often, a situation may require testing in the geographic area and with the specific product and target audience involved (Wartzman 1999). At times, the accommodation can be very simple, as in the Mandarin Oriental Hong Kong luxury international hotel, where, each morning, the general manager beats a large gong at the entrance when he enters and passes the gold statue of a dragon in the foyer; both actions are complex elements in the oriental practice of *feng shui* (Murray 1999).

## Exploiting Differences

AFL (American Family Corporation) of Columbus, Georgia, a leading supplier of cancer insurance, found a niche market in Japan arising from cultural differences. In the United States there is very little interest in separate policies for individual sicknesses, which accounts for the low sales of cancer insurance policies. In Japan, however, where cancer is recognized as a serious concern, and existing Japanese insurance policies pay minimal cancer benefits, the market and culture were favorable for separate cancer insurance policies. It took the company four years to meet and accommodate all of the local legal and regulatory requirements needed to obtain a license to sell insurance in Japan. However, once licensed, the company received the favorable treatment generally afforded Japanese firms but denied to most foreign competitors. In 1991, 75 percent of Aflaco's $3.5 billion in revenues came from Japan (Lohr 1992).

## SYNERGISTICALLY MANAGING CULTURAL DIFFERENCES

Almost every business management situation has differences among participating parties that must be reconciled. Taking the time to establish personal relationships to reconcile these differences has to be balanced with time limitations and situation requirements. At one extreme, General Electric took more than three years to introduce changes into its workforce in its Hungarian lightbulb plant, as it gradually introduced its corporate-wide cooperative programs. Only gradually did Hungarian workers adapt to working together in teams and to U.S. participative management styles and production efficiency methods (Perlez 1994).

Often it is necessary to accommodate differences in some ways. However, it is not necessary or even advisable, for example, to adopt Japanese or Russian ways in dealing with them (Macquin and Rouzies 1998). Rather, it is reasonable for all parties to recognize and adapt to others' customs. A mutual give-and-take process helps create a balance.

At the same time, in a rapidly changing and increasingly sophisticated global business environment, overemphasizing differences can often erect barriers to building cultural bridges, create a negative, counterproductive atmosphere, and at times leave a company vulnerable to exploitation. Differences are often overemphasized early in business situations. The unique requirements of each situation must be studied and dealt with appropriately.

Multinational management involves reconciling and balancing disparate factors in many different ways. Earlier chapters focused on balancing global and local factors when both planning and doing at the operational and enterprise-wide management level to meet present and longer-term future needs. This chapter focused on another area—balancing the cultural factors encountered during interpersonal interaction. An example would be balancing an American's desire to adhere to task-sequence agendas during a meeting with another person's culture-based desire to randomly discuss problem topics that might help develop deeper personal relationships and provide information on broader contexts.

Beyond balancing and accommodating different cultures, it is possible to synergistically combine the best of different cultures. This was reportedly the case in Hungary after the purchase of what eventually grew to be a controlling interest in Matav, Hungary's state telephone company, by Ameritech of the United States and Germany's Deutsche Telekom. After initial cultural clashes over operating details, Elek Straub, the newly hired Hungarian manager, skillfully eased tensions first with off-site leadership training sessions called "Vision and Value Training." He then tapped executive strengths by dividing up responsibilities according to corporate culture and experience: the Ameritech executive at Matav was put in charge of marketing, and the Deutsche Telekom executive was put in charge of administration and personnel, with Straub representing the Hungarian state alliance partners, as the link to Hungary and the government. According to the executives, "everyone in the troika has an equal voice and equal say" (Beck, 1996, p. A10) and are able to come up with better decisions and actions than when working alone. They still have cultural clashes, but they now have in place enabling leadership, as well as an enabling organization structure, processes, and culture, that enable synergistically going beyond just reconciling differences to creating innovative solutions (Beck 1996).

The universally successful approach to balancing cultural factors seems to be respecting all cultures while adapting interpersonal interactions to some degree (where necessary), and focusing on developing personal relationships. This includes asserting oneself where necessary, being your own person, and avoiding confrontations. The secret is not so much *what* is done, as *how* it is done. The skills come largely from personal experience and from studying the experiences of others.

Personal experiences can involve mixing with other cultures within one's own culture. Many countries, for example, have been diverse melting pots of cultures and nationalities. In a sense, then, traveling and interacting overseas can be a kind of going home for many people, returning to countries of origin—whether in Europe, Asia, South America, North America, or Africa. Examining the foreigner within ourselves and our families can be a start in developing a cross-cultural perspective. In this way, reconciling differences becomes a journey in enjoying diversity and discovering the rewards arising from integrating global and local thinking and action. Ourselves and our country can, in this sense, be viewed as a microcosm of how this can be and is being done.

## SUMMARY

This chapter and those following in Part Three focus on the enabling phases of strategic management which involve human resources, especially leadership, management, staffing, and interpersonal interaction. Human resources are a key strategic driver profoundly affecting a multinational enterprise's success.

These six perspectives of cultural differences and their diverse impact provide a framework for exploring ways to understand, adapt to, and effectively manage cultural differences. Ideally, this process produces synergies by creatively building on the strengths of each culture involved in a situation.

Not all situations can be handled within the six common framework categories described in the chapter. In many situations, creative, innovative, resourceful, entrepreneurial, ad hoc management solutions which break the mold and go beyond any framework are needed to succeed. As multinational management business experiences show, reconciling and managing differences generally seems to involve six kinds of approaches: modifying one's behavior and adapting to a situation; taking steps to change the situation environment; abandoning the situation or project; exploiting the differences wherever possible; or using any combination of the first four.

## REVIEW QUESTIONS

1. Discuss the different meanings of the concept of "culture" and the different ways it can impact on society.
2. Describe some of the problems involved in balancing global and local approaches to multinational strategic leadership and management. What is the role of common frameworks in managing this balance?
3. Discuss the ways in which cultural differences can impact on multinational business operations. Give specific examples.
4. Identify some general guidelines for understanding and managing cultural differences.
5. Discuss the role of personal relationships in different cultures and the ways in which these varying roles can affect business dealings in different countries. Give specific examples.
6. Describe the different ways in which business relationships are formed in different countries/cultures.
7. Compare and contrast America's and Australia's strong individualistic traits as opposed to Japan's collaborative tendencies. Discuss the ways in which these differing views affect different kinds of business situations.
8. Describe the impact of differing cultural attitudes toward equality on business activities in different countries/companies.
9. Describe the ways that language differences can lead to misunderstandings in business dealings.
10. Discuss the ways in which cultural values are changing in different countries and how this can affect multinational management.
11. Identify the difference between monochronic and polychronic time, and the different cultures which place different emphasis on each. Discuss the ways in which attitudes toward time in different cultures affect multinational business management.
12. In addition to cultural factors, what other factors influence individual actions in multinational management situations? Describe specific examples of how this happens.
13. Discuss the various approaches to managing cultural differences. Cite specific examples.
14. Discuss the synergistic potential that is possible when effectively managing and balancing cultural diversity. Describe the many problems arising from trying to achieve such a balance.

## *EXERCISES*

1. Based on your research, identify recent cultural changes occurring in different countries around the world. Discuss the impact of three of these on different kinds of multinational businesses.
2. Describe examples from your research of how cultural differences have affected the way advertising or product selection is being done in different countries by different companies.
3. Based on your research, describe how at least two companies not discussed in the chapter have each balanced global and local approaches in two different countries.

# Chapter 11

# Strategic Leadership and Management: Emerging New Concepts

Effective business leadership, like other aspects of multinational strategic leadership and management, has become more entrepreneurial. Chapter 2 described Jack Welch's concept of leadership for General Electric (Welch, Fresco, and Opie 1996), one of the largest publicly-held companies in the world.

During his career at GE, Welch demonstrated is that it is possible to stimulate entrepreneurial, small company thinking in any size business, and that it works—he was originally an entrepreneur himself.

The first part of this chapter describes emerging worldwide concepts of leadership and management. Three sections follow. The first describes the tasks involved in leading a multinational enterprise, as well as the values and character traits, knowledge and skills, and behavior styles of successful leaders. The second section discusses contingency frameworks and guidelines used by leaders and managers and identifies effective leadership and management behaviors. The final section explores a major integrative application area: leading and managing teams.

## *STRATEGIC LEADERSHIP AND MANAGEMENT: SOME BASIC DISTINCTIONS*

Leadership and management are related but distinct concepts. In his book *Leading Change,* John Kotter (1996) defines *leading* as establishing direction, aligning people, and motivating and inspiring, while *managing* involves planning and budgeting, organizing and staffing, and control. Blanchard and Waghorn's *Mission Possible* (1999) defines leading as looking at the longer-term and seeing the new waves of activity coming after the near-term wave of activity that is foreseeable and manageable fades.

In practice, it is often difficult to distinguish between managers and leaders. In general, managers guide, staff, and control an enterprise's operations, such as those described in Chapters 5 through 9, and in Chapters 12 and 13. That is, they manage a new or existing enterprise within a short- to medium-range perspective. Managers also plan and guide plan implementation, and so at times must inspire and energize or lead and show the way. Managers, therefore, need some leadership skills and must perform some leadership tasks. Leaders, on the other hand, create visions and inspire (show the way), lead by example (by going before), and energize a firm and its people within a longer-range perspective. They also have to do some managing (guiding and controlling), when enterprise-wide crises arise, a position that Coca-Cola Chairman Douglas Ivester found himself in when contaminated Cokes in Europe led Belgium to ban Coke products for a time (Deogun 1999).

Strategic management involves both *leadership* and *management*. This is evident from the multinational strategic management tasks and activities listed in Figure 1.3 (p. 9), and from the discussions of the multinational strategic management job in Chapter 3. The exact mix will depend on the situation and task or activity involved.

For instance, enterprise-wide corporate leaders generally are called chairman or president. In theory, these leaders deal primarily—but not exclusively—with an enterprise's longer-term strategic vision. Managers are located throughout a firm's business units and operating areas. The top manager, often called the chief executive officer (CEO), works under the president or chairman. Many corporate leaders, however, choose to be called president and CEO, blurring the line separating the two. As seen from the experiences described in this chapter, both leaders and managers perform diverse leadership and management tasks.

## *LEADERSHIP*

Rarely do leaders have all the qualifications needed to handle all complex situations. Given the contingent nature of multinational management, the choice of a leader will depend on balancing an individual's characteristics and values, knowledge and skills, and behavior styles with the requirements of the specific situation involved. Although some universal traits and skills are found in all successful leaders, there are also many conditional leadership traits and skills that contribute to success only in specific situations (Brake 1997). One highly successful CEO, Herb Kelleher, of Southwest Airlines believes "There are no magic formulas" or rules for leadership success beyond creating "a culture of caring for people in the totality of their lives" (Lancaster 1999, p. B1).

### *Leadership Tasks: An Overview*

Although good managers are usually leaders, and leaders often engage in management activities, leadership implies more than simply management. It implies the vision to lead into the future, not just manage what already exists. In multinational management situations leadership is especially important to the achievement of a working balance between global centralization and efficiencies with local responsiveness in rapidly changing competitive multinational markets (Kotter 1996). As shown in Figure 1.3 (p. 9), this is accomplished by:

- Creating an overall strategic framework, as well as a strategic vision and guidelines, as described in Chapter 2.
- Stimulating and guiding the emergent development of specific strategies and plans (enterprise-wide, business unit, and functional) over time, as described in Chapters 2 through 9.
- Activating, guiding, and energizing the enabling business processes needed for achieving success in light of changing competitive environments, (as described in Chapters 5 through 9, and Chapter 13) from six perspectives: business unit; functional (marketing and production/operations) area operations; telecommunications and information systems; accounting and finance systems; organization; and strategic alliances.
- Ensuring that a core management staff with appropriate interpersonal, communications, and management skills and potential (Chapters 10 through 12), is in place and functioning to achieve that balance.
- Communicating and constantly reinforcing the strategic framework, as well as cultural values that are needed to enable the core management staff to translate the desired balance into action. The actual processes involve leadership and integrative management appropriate for the individuals and groups involved in the situation, as well as for the specific competitive market needs (described mainly in Chapters 11, 12, and 14).
- Leaving managers relatively free to manage, and pushing decision making as close to the customer as possible, but intervening when appropriate to ensure that integrative activities are operating efficiently and effectively to achieve strategic objectives (described mainly in Chapters 11 and 12).

This chapter and Chapter 12 go beyond the discussions of these tasks and focus on the leadership and integrative management involved.

### The Story of General Electric's Jack Welch

In April 1981, Jack Welch became CEO at GE, a diversified, worldwide technology, manufacturing, and services firm committed to achieving worldwide leadership in each of its business units (Lowe 1998; Slater 1999). Through Welch's efforts, GE has become one of the most profitable, respected firms worldwide (Colvin 2000). Welch's leadership model has been widely imitated worldwide (Landers 2000).

Welch's summary of the firm's mission and how it evolved and was carried out is given in Figure 2.1 in Chapter 2 (Welch, Fresco, and Opie 1996). Welch moved decisively in a very directive and autocratic way to transform GE. In essence, he "created his own crisis by delayering the management hierarchy, reducing corporate staff, and slashing 100,000 employees to focus on what he believed to be the core elements of the business." Once this period of creative destruction had passed, "he set about to release the organization's emotional energy and creativity to capitalize on the opportunities offered by changes in GE's environment" (Hurst 1995, pp. 112-113). He was firm in his convictions but flexible in their execution, and he did not flinch at making hard decisions when necessary.

During and after this crisis phase, Welch exhibited his versatility and adaptability as a leader. Welch admitted that it was hard during this time, since he strongly disliked laying off people. However, he justified these layoffs by saying that GE needed to eliminate anything formal, slow, and constraining. He said, "You can't say to a big bloated bureaucracy, 'let's be boundaryless,' because they've already got defined slots. Unless you clear the forest, you don't see anything" (Day and LeBarre 1994, p. 14).

Welch's people-oriented approach focused on releasing the untapped energy in people, to enable them to gain greater job satisfaction.

Welch's idea of "boundarylessness" was that horizontally, between functions, people should be open to sharing, even with suppliers and customers. For example, new products were designed by multifunctional teams that included customers and suppliers. In Welch's view, an idea's quality did not depend on its altitude in the company (Day and LeBarre 1994). This was only one of the ways in which Welch energized innovative thinking in GE and changed the firm's culture.

Welch moved authority and decision making down as far as possible within the organization to eliminate the "boss" factor. Managers participated with workers and work groups in managing and leading. This was the idea behind the new organization charts shown in Chapter 9, Figures 9.3 and 9.4 (pp. 240-241), which are more circular and integrative. Welch encouraged participation by example, a necessary step in making values work and sustaining their effectiveness.

To achieve this participation, Welch defined his job in these words: "21st century leaders will forgo their old powers—to plan, organize, implement and measure—for new duties: counselling groups, providing resources for them, helping them think for themselves" (Heller 1995, p. 186). He perceived his job as supporting the participation of others in running the enterprise.

Welch "stressed the sharing of the facts and assumptions behind decisions" rather than the logic of decisions themselves (Hurst 1995, p. 113). The "workout" program he developed to increase communication, for example, helped to expose managers to the vibrations of their businesses—opinions, feelings, emotions, resentments—not abstract theories of reorganization and management (Hurst 1995). The innovative workout sessions removed barriers and helped the company respond more quickly and efficiently to market changes. Reaching and stretching without punishment was a major breakthrough for Welch.

Welch was also a risk taker in worldwide markets. For example, when he was told that entering China was risky, his reply was "we may not make it in China, but there's no alternative to being in there with both feet, participating in this huge market" (Day and LeBarre 1994, p. 15).

Welch also worked with common global frameworks adapted to local circumstances. For example, he was able to use his "workout" sessions in Hungary, but only after adapting them over three years to the cultural bias left over from the communist days, when workers did not think for themselves. GE's persistence was based on Welch's belief that on one level, people are the same worldwide: they want to be more involved, not empowered. Encouraging involvement was a key ingredient of GE's success (Day and LeBarre 1994; Perlez 1994). In Europe, for example, teams were used to bring in new ideas that other divisions could learn from, and when new technologies were involved, younger executives were encouraged to "mentor" older executives (Murray 2000).

One Welch value—loyalty—created some controversy. He believed that people have to understand that the purpose of the existence of a firm is to provide economic values for the society and the country in which it operates for the the workers employed by it. He connected loyalty to excellence: "Loyalty means giving people an opportunity. Our job is to provide an opportunity and an atmosphere where people can thrive and enjoy the fruits of winning. So the word 'loyalty' per se has an old connotation" (Day and LeBarre, 1996, p. 16). In addition, he emphasized trust between customers and businesses. Ultimately, customers are interested in fair treatment based on trust.

In many ways, Welch exhibited the leadership character traits and values, and knowledge and skills, discussed in this chapter. His effective leadership activities included: stimulating and guiding, activating and energizing, ensuring that a skilled core staff was in place, creating enabling organization mechanisms, and leaving managers relatively free to manage. Welch's view of creating a strategic framework went beyond his vision and mission statements. Clear thinking and fast decision making at GE happened in part because Welch and his colleagues focused on the answers to a handful of basic strategic queries:

- What does your global competitive environment look like?
- In the last three years, what have your competitors done?
- In the same period, what have you done to them?

- How might your competitors attack you in the future?
- How might you leapfrog them?
- What kinds of products/services will customers need in the future?
- What are you doing to meet their anticipated or perceived needs?

As this list suggests, change and renewal are continuing processes. In late 1996, Welch was in the process of remaking GE again. Because of growth limitations in many of GE's businesses, Welch was pushing for growth in related areas by becoming a service provider for firms that bought GE products or similar products of competitors. For example, GE signed a ten-year, $2.3 billion contract to service British Airways jet engines, a product GE makes and sells to airlines. GE hoped to apply its manufacturing expertise further in the service area: similar service deals were expected in the medical systems, transportation, and power generation areas in which GE made products. In the late 1990s, Welch was expected to start a new round of cost-cutting, efficiency, and restructuring moves. He was especially interested in moving the company in the strategic direction of taking maximum advantage of Internet capabilities in every phase of the company's operations (Bernstein, Jackson, and Byrne 1997; Slater 1999; Waters 1999).

### Leadership Character Traits, Values, and Attitudes

Based on the experiences of Welch and others, the following character traits (psychological, physiological, and intellectual) have been identified as affecting leadership success (CE Roundtable 2000; Snyder and Clontz 1997). No one leader needs to possess all of these traits because not all are needed for success in all situations. These traits manifest themselves in different ways in different individuals.

#### Adaptability

Leaders today need to be able to deal with continuing change. For example, both IBM's CEO Louis Gerstner and Microsoft's CEO Bill Gates were actively transforming their firms to meet the challenges of the fast-growing world of networks and the Internet in 1998 and 1999, a major strategic move described in Chapter 14. The never-ending challenge of change is a major characteristic of today's multinational markets (Garrat 1999).

#### Versatility

Leaders also need the ability to employ whatever tools and techniques are appropriate to success. Lorenzo Zambrano, chairman of the board and chief operating officer of CEMEX, a Mexican multinational cement company, in general, has run his firm using a supportive leadership style. At times, however, direct orders are required, such as when technology transfer was rapidly needed at the company's Spanish plant to respond to competitive market pressures (Zambrano 1995). The global dimensions of CEMEX enabled the firm to survive 1995's financial crisis in Mexico by drawing on its subsidiaries (in Spain, the United States, Venezuela, Panama, and the Caribbean) to support its financial needs (Crawford 1997).

## Vision: Creative and Innovative

When asked what it takes to succeed as a leader, former Dean John McArthur at the Harvard Businesss School commented that to succeed "you have to dream really big dreams" ("A Conversation. . . ." 1995, p. 43). Lewis Platt, former chairman of Hewlett-Packard, had such a visionary outlook when he described HP's new strategy involving information appliances and networks.

## Risk Taker, Anchored with Good Judgment

To realize dreams, leaders need to be risk takers, not gamblers, because planning deals with the future and the future is often uncertain. When Gillette introduced its "Sensor" razor in the late 1980s, the most successful product introduction of the decade, it risked making its then-best-selling razor obsolete; it was a prudent risk, however, because it was backed by more than $100 million in advertising. Risks are necessary to move into major international markets. Chris Gent, Chairman of Vodafone Air Touch, gambled on the future potential of being a leader in mobile phone access to the Net when he bid $163 billion, double the going rate, for Mannesmann, a German wireline Internet company. This move, along with later ones involving Seagram and Vivendi, gave him the Internet expertise to be a dominant force in a major growth area (Baker 2000a,b; Boudette and Delaney 2000). At times, leadership requires innovative thinking and action "outside the box." Pat Farrah vice president of merchandising did this at Home Depot to a point where he was lovingly referred to as "whacko" at times (Hagerty 2000).

## Intelligence

Creating long-term visions requires analytical as well as conceptual intelligence. Organizing those visions also requires structured thinking, a rigorous intellectual discipline. For example, the late Roberto Goizeuta, former CEO of Coca-Cola, allowed ample time for "thinking," which he felt was needed to make and reach long-term strategic goals. Consistent with this orientation, leadership success requires the ability to manage knowledge (Davenport and Prusak 1998).

## Practical

A realistic person is needed to turn visions into reality. This is another paradox, since effective leaders are also dreamers. However, their dreams must be achievable. Practical instincts combined with intelligence are especially useful during crises. Perrier, the bottled water company, for example, moved quickly through product recalls to limit the damage to its brand image when traces of benzene were found in some of its bottles of water in February 1990. Handling unusual situations is essential to international success, because problems continually arise around the world.

## People-Oriented

Because getting things done most often involves working through and with people, an effective leader is often a "facilitator"—someone who helps others get their jobs done (Weaver 1997). Jack Welch's experiences at GE, and others' experiences provide abundant evidence of the importance of this leadership trait. Ken Iverson, chairman of Nucor Corporation, a $3.8 billion firm he led from near oblivion to be America's third-largest steel firm, has attributed his success to his ability to relate to people, especially line workers. MBA graduates, in his view, are ill prepared to meet this human relations challenge (Iverson and Varian 1998). Building and maintaining interpersonal relationships is, for some experts, the most critical skill (Bennis 1999).

## Takes Pleasure in Seeing Others Succeed

Gil Amelio, former CEO and chairman of National Semiconductor, revitalized the firm between 1991, when it lost hundreds of millions of dollars, and 1994, when it made $264 million on $2.3 billion in sales. Transformation, in his words, "demands people who can work in combined efforts, a win-win approach" (Amelio and Simon 1996, p. 74; Fuller 1998). For this reason, he valued the worker who "helps others by contributing to their success" more than the brilliant loner.

## Performance-Driven

When describing what he liked most about his job, Al Zeien, former CEO at Gillette, commented: "things are different because I went to work today." Zeien got a "great deal of satisfaction from getting things done" (Zeien 1995)—a common trait among business leaders.

## Firm in Convictions, Flexible in Execution

Successful leaders have strong convictions, but also are adaptable and flexible. Both Coca-Cola and Gillette are firmly committed to the globalization of their brands, but their CEOs are flexible when necessary in the way that this is achieved from country to country. Helmut Maucher, former chairman and CEO of Nestlé, was extremely firm in his commitment to ethical and moral values, but at the same time was dedicated to "learning" and to having managers who were "changeable" and stimulated innovation (Maucher 1994, pp. 77-80). Commentators have suggested that the reason Telecom Italia (the world's sixth-largest telecommunications firm) failed to fend off a $63 billion bid from Olivetti SpA in the largest hostile takeover fight ever settled, was the principled resistance of its inflexible former CEO, Franco Bernabe, who refused to consult the experts and appeared to be overly confident of his own judgement (Raghavan and Naik 1999).

*Balanced Orientation*

Given the diverse requirements of business leadership, a leader often needs to balance seemingly contradictory (paradoxical) forces. Hewlett-Packard's former executive, Richard Hackborn, who was responsible for the phenomenal growth of HP's printer business, was described as having his "head in the air" and his "feet on the ground" (a practical thinker). Jack Welch "cleared the forest so the trees could grow" by eliminating thousands of jobs at GE, but he continually demonstrated concern for people, as when he introduced leading-edge compensation policies for laid-off workers.

Values are also important to successful leadership (Blanchard and O'Connor 1997). Leaders need to be moral, ethical, and honest—basic human values. Nestlé's former CEO, Helmut Maucher, for example, considered being consistently credible in word and deed a significant value, since credibility is important to generating trust among employees and customers (Maucher 1994). Many leaders, for example, Jack Welch, felt that the ability to nurture trust was essential to successful leadership (Kim and Mauborgne 1998; Zand 1997). From its founding in 1936, Hewlett-Packard has been ruled by a value that represents what is today a prevailing concept of people-oriented leadership, "the belief that men and women want to do a good job, a creative job, and that if they are provided the proper environment, they will do so" (Sherman 1995, p. 92). Strategic values and mission statements need to be continually reinforced by leadership actions to be effective.

The concept of ethics is closely related to values (honesty and truthfulness, for example). In the sense that ethical action is perceived as action in accordance with universal human moral standards, ethics is a useful leadership and management concept. Unfortunately, the word "ethics" has been misused so often as a self-serving justification for arbitrary action that it often confuses rather than clarifies positions. Because of this confusion and misuse of the word, the word "ethics," a concept which is important when defined strictly, is used sparingly in this book.

Personal principles or attitudes are closely associated with values. Stephen Covey (1991) identified seven basic principles applicable to leadership that seem to lead to success in general:

- *Be proactive*—respond in your own way.
- *Begin with the end in mind*—always keep objectives in mind.
- *Put first things first*—keep your priorities straight.
- *Think win/win*—make sure everyone wins something as you negotiate through life.
- *Seek first to understand*—learn to truly listen, put other people first.
- *Synergize*—search for ways to make two and two equal five by combining energies.
- *Seek continuous improvement*—seek self-renewal and help others seek the same.

These basic attitudes of successful leaders are also human concerns that are important to success in business and in life. They are essential ingredients of a learning organization, the lubricants that enable it to function.

This section has discussed attitudes, values, and traits common in successful leaders. Whether they have been developed during childhood or from experiences during later life, they guide actions and responses to situation needs. They are, however, only one aspect of successful leadership. No one leader needs to possess all of these traits, values, and attitudes; not all of them are needed for success in all situations, and the way they are manifested can vary considerably from individual to individual. Leadership training programs have been created to help individuals develop these characteristics (Lublin 2000). The same is true for leadership competencies, styles, and behaviors.

### Leadership Competencies: Knowledge and Skills

More than just character traits, values, principles, and attitudes are needed to lead. A leader also needs knowledge and skills developed from education, training, and experience. Success in international business requires: financial acumen, knowledge of international markets, technical knowledge (especially of the strategic implications of the Internet and global computer/telecommunication systems), knowledge of company operations, and familiarity with competitive markets. Related skills include those involving communications, people handling, decision making, trust building, and building and managing teams (Zand 1997). These capabilities are called *leader competencies.*

A successful leader constantly acquires new skills. Terence Brake classified these skills or competencies as falling into one of three main categories (Brake 1997):

- *Business acumen:* refers to the depth of professional knowledge of the business involved; general professional management and leadership expertise; entrepreneurial skills; ability to perceive changing stakeholder needs; working within the context of the entire organizational system.
- *Relationship management:* refers to the ability to function as a change agent; building a community effort in the process; managing conflict and skillful negotiation; communicating across cultures; the ability to influence others.
- *Personal effectiveness:* refers to the ability to improvise; self-knowledge and confidence needed to handle setbacks and crises; assuming accountability of outcomes; ability to learn continuously; ability to think quickly, creatively, and ingeniously (thinking agility).

Kotter (1996) and Blanchard and Waghorn (1997) add to this list the ability to strategically manage activities succinctly and compactly, as shown in Figure 1.3.

Choosing the combination of leadership competencies appropriate for a given situation is a complex, uncertain process. For example, in 1997, Cable & Wireless PLC (C&W), a conglomerate of mostly small phone firms in Great Britain, hired Richard Brown, the former CEO of H&R Block Inc. (a U.S. tax advisory firm) with no international experience. By 1999, when he left C&W, Brown had turned it into a major international phone and cable television firm through a combination of astute management and mergers/acquisitions (Guyon 1997). Depending on the situation then, company needs may dictate an unique combination of leadership skills and competencies.

### Leadership Styles

Although leadership traits, values, and competencies are important to success, the true test of leadership is in the doing. Leadership in the 1990s has been described as "helping people find their way through adaptive challenges—problems without apparent solutions" (Sherman 1995, p. 95). This modern concept of leadership is exemplified in the experiences of Jack Welch and others.

Several aspects of leadership styles and behavior observed in these experiences provide useful benchmarks. First, a major objective of leadership is to create an organization culture consistent with helping people find their way through the adaptive challenges faced in multinational business. This involves all the communication, management, organization, human systems, telecommunications and information systems, and other enablers already discussed, as well as charisma, the ability to inspire, and the tenacity to continually reinforce a firm's new culture.

Second, as needs change, so can the effectiveness of leadership styles. Many leadership styles have been identified. Rowe and Mason (1987) have identified four: analytical, conceptual, behavioral, and directive; Bourgeois and Brodwin (1984) have identified five: commander, change, cultural, collaborative, and crescive; Fiedler (1967) identified two: task-oriented, and relationship-oriented; Hofstede (1983a,b, 1984, 1992) identified five: autocratic, consultative, persuasive, participative, and democratic; House, Hanges, and Angar (1993) identified four: directive, participative, supportive, and achievement. Hofstede and others have extended this type of study to multinational situations (Segalla 1998).

Each of these researchers analyzed and categorized different kinds of group and individual situations encountered, and attempted to develop a contingency framework for selecting a leadership style appropriate for the kind of situation under study. Jack Welch used several leadership styles effectively—directive, supportive, and participative—as situation circumstances dictated. In addition, the experiences of several GE executives who took jobs elsewhere show that Welch's style needed adaptation when used in other situations (Helyar 1998). Throughout Japan, Welch is admired and imitated, but his style is adapted to that culture (Landers 2000). Al Dunlap, who revived several companies, such as the Scott Paper Company, with his rigorous, cost-cutting approach, failed when he tried to apply his approach to the Sunbeam Corporation (Byrne 1999). As one study has argued, leadership failure often can be related to one or two fatal shortcomings in areas essential to success in the situation involved, a contingency perspective (Charan and Colvin 1999).

## SITUATION APPLICATION CONTINGENCY GUIDELINES

Although leadership and management generalities are helpful, their value comes from how well they are adapted and used by individual leaders and managers in specific situations. According to Setsuo Mito, former CEO of Honda Motors, Honda's leadership is tailored to specific conditions in Europe, the United States, and Asia. For example, while the company adopted the joint boardroom concept to help executives express their differences in a constructive manner, the sessions were run differently in each country. The U.S. sessions encouraged individual contributions, while the ones in Japan focused on consensus and team effort.

Attempts have been made to develop contingency guidelines for leadership behavior style selection. For example, Hofstede (1992) used two IBM preference surveys of 116,000 employees at overseas locations, one in 1969 and one in 1972, as well as a later survey of students in twenty-three countries to identify characteristics useful in analyzing appropriate leadership and management styles. For analytical purposes, he measured each culture by five criteria:

1. *Social orientation* involves the relative importance of the interests of the individual versus the interests of the group and ranges from individualism to collectivism.
2. *Power orientation* involves the appropriateness of power/authority within organizations and ranges from marginal tolerance to a great deal of respect for power and the hierarchies possessing power.
3. *Uncertainty orientation* involves an emotional response to uncertainty/change and ranges from avoidance to acceptance of it.
4. *Goal orientation* involves what motivates people to achieve certain goals and ranges from a high goal/achievement (masculine) interest to a passive interest in goals and in quality of life, social relevance, and the welfare of others (feminine) interest.
5. *Time orientation* involves a short-term versus a long-term perspective and ranges from placing less emphasis on hard work to placing great emphasis on working hard as a means of self-fulfillment and success.

Hofstede concluded, for example, that in cultures which respect hierarchies (such as Mexico's), supportive styles that include mixing with employees at social gatherings have to be carefully structured so as not to violate the culture's sense of superior/subordinate distance/power relationships. In more autocratic societies (as in Germany), a goal-oriented style is likely to be more successful than a behavioral one emphasizing interpersonal concern. Robert House and colleagues extended this type of study to additional countries and types of companies (House, Hanges, and Angar 1993; House, Wright, and Aditya 1997).

Fred E. Fiedler's (1967) similar contingency study for leading small groups analyzed groups by three measures:

1. Leader-member relations—good to very poor
2. Task structure—high to weak
3. Power position—strong to weak

Fiedler identified two leadership styles:

1. A leader can take primary responsibility for the group; she or he can be autocratic, controlling, managing, directive, and task-oriented, or
2. A leader can share decision making; she or he can be democratic, permissive, nondirective, considerate of group members' feelings, and other therapeutic leadership.

His contingent guidelines were:

- Considerate, relationship-oriented leaders tend to perform best in situations where they have only moderate influence, either because the task is relatively unstructured or because they are not well-accepted even though they hold a high-level position.
- In situations where the leader has recognized power, informal backing among group members, and a relatively well-structured task, the group is ready to be directed and group members expect to be told what to do, thus favoring a more directive leadership style.

A more recent study of European leadership and management styles had a dual conclusion (Calori and Dufour 1995). First, it identified traits typical of European managers: a greater orientation toward people; a high level of internal negotiation; greater skill in managing international diversity; and an ability to manage extremes in a balanced way. Second, the study pointed out that:

- Leadership styles are changing and becoming less homogeneous across Europe. For instance, many differences exist among European countries (the French are quite different from the Germans in many ways).
- Even when leadership styles are ostensibly similar (people concern, for example), the manifestation is quite different (much less interpersonal caring in Germany, for example, but strong unions; strong support for women in Sweden, not so much in Germany).

These studies conclude, like others described in this book, that situation requirements can change over time and in relation to the kind of leadership and management exercised. Second, the cultural characteristics of each situation should be studied before making leadership decisions. Third, as in other multinational management task areas, common frameworks for leadership tasks can be adapted to local requirements, as was done by GE in Hungary.

Leadership pressures are substantial in today's dynamic multinational environment. Moving from analytical, rational, and conceptual planning tasks to sensitive, interpersonal, day-to-day tasks requires a difficult-to-achieve mix of task- and people-oriented leadership styles. For instance, while it is good to allow entrepreneurial autonomy, it may also be necessary to intervene to create and maintain the adaptable and flexible organization environment needed for successful multinational management. Leaders who can achieve such a balance, and who also have the charisma needed to communicate with and inspire people, are rare.

As some firms have learned, alternative approaches can be used when no one leader exhibits all the desired traits for a specific situation. When the late Roberto C. Goizueta, the introverted, intellectual, former chairman of Coca-Cola, realized that he could not rethink the firm and run a sprawling multinational operation at the same time, he picked a complementary president. Extrovert Don Keogh galvanized the operation in a way that Goizueta never could have (Heller 1995). These two leaders' combined traits, skills, knowledge, styles, and behaviors provided the needed balance. The Hungarian telephone company, Matav, used a similar approach by forming a management "troika," a three-person team which balanced the skills and personalities of three executives (Beck 1996). Shared leadership can also create problems in many situations, so it has to be carefully crafted to suit the situation and individuals involved (Maitland 1999).

A leader does what she or he has to do to make things work within legal, ethical, moral, and policy restraints. Success in this strategic management task area, as in other areas, then, depends on developing a creative solution that meets the specific situation needs. Without constant use and reinforcement by managers and leaders, strategic frameworks and foundations can lose their value.

The following section discusses team management—a major leadership/management area in multinational businesses.

## LEADING AND MANAGING TEAMS

In general, a team is a group of people with complementary skills, committed to a common purpose, performance goals, and approach for which they hold themselves mutually accountable. Teams have interdependent tasks and common goals that enable them to outperform any *random* collection of individuals (McDermott, Brawley, and Waite 1998). Teams can range from groups of two with coordinated but independent tasks to integrated organizations.

Integration with cross-cultural teams is used in multinational corporations as one effective way to bridge cultural gaps, balance global efficiencies, respond to local differences, and transfer knowledge. Teams are used at many levels within multinational enterprises. They are a useful management tool, but are not a universal cure-all for problems in all situations (Griffith 1997).

Firms often join through mergers and acquisitions and through joint ventures and strategic alliances to develop synergies that enable them to compete more effectively. The success of combinations can also, to some degree, depend on the effective blending of corporate and national cultures through team efforts.

As Jon Katzenbach (1998) points out, however, corporations are rarely run by teams. A CEO often uses working groups on an interim basis to solve specific problems. Teams are more likely to be used on a continuing basis at lower corporate levels.

Intel Corp. of Santa Clara, California, has teams for many projects. For example, teams formulate product sales strategies, develop new products, redesign microprocessor elements, and improve quality testing. Typically, Intel's teams work together across geographic and cultural boundaries. As many as six or seven of the company's locations in Ireland, Israel, England, France, and parts of Asia may come together at one time. Teams assemble quickly, do their work, and then disband and regroup to form other teams.

A group of Intel managers formed a global team to determine what made teams successful. The team concluded that having simple basic procedures and processes, clear expectations, well-defined goals, roles, responsibilities, and face-to-face meetings early in the team's development were important. Cross-cultural training also made team members more adaptive, and so helped harness the synergies possible in cross-cultural and cross-functional exchanges. These early steps facilitated long-distance communications through teleconferencing, videoconferencing, and electronic mail, in essence creating a geographically dispersed "virtual" team (Lipnack and Stamps 1999). The important step needed, it has to be emphasized, is that personal interaction during a "getting to know each other" period is essential to enabling the impersonal interaction to be effective. Clear agendas are needed for meetings, and written meeting minutes should be distributed quickly to ensure that everyone understands the tasks and decisions agreed on at the meeting. Documentation also provides a means of refreshing memories and monitoring progress.

According to the Intel study, effective global groups must have enabling support that makes it easier for people to share information, obtain feedback, and communicate. People will be discouraged by physical barriers if technologies such as groupware for sharing documents, videoconferencing, or e-mail capabilities for communicating rapidly are not in place. People with an appropriate mix of technical, interpersonal, and cultural expertise should be part of global groups (Solomon 1995).

Texas Instruments Malaysia (TIM) was opened in 1974 in Kuala Lumpur, Malaysia's capital, to serve a growing regional and global demand for integrated circuits for computers and related products. TIM management believed that team development would enable it to reduce cycle time, increase output, and improve overall quality. In the early 1980s, TIM installed quality circles and problem-solving teams at the worker/operational levels that yielded modest cost savings and productivity improvements. These efforts were not initially successful because employees perceived the groups as being temporary.

TIM persisted, however, and in the late 1980s created a pilot program of self-managed teams. This time around, more than forty hours of supervisor training were held at the outset and the teams developed specific goals. Team responsibilities fell into two categories: maintenance (equipment maintenance and daily administrative activities, such as managing costs, delivery, safety, housekeeping, equipment setup, tracking attendance, and assigning daily duties and responsibilities), and customer satisfaction. Because automatic semiconductor fabricating equipment is so complex, most team members held specific jobs for at least one year, after which job assignments were rotated within teams. This assigned responsibility gave members a sense of ownership in the job and its output, and enabled training for replacements.

Facilitators were assigned, as at GE's workout sessions, to help teams develop schedules and learn how to perform other required management and leadership functions. Appraisals included both self-assessments and peer evaluations. Rewards for goal attainment included merit increases to the group, group gift certificates, and free lunches. By 1990, TIM had more than 3,000 employees organized in different forms of self-managed work teams (Wellins, Byham, and Dixon 1994).

Motorola's experiences in Malaysia were somewhat different, not only in the way it developed team structures but also in the way the team approach was adapted to suit the Malaysian culture (Gogan, Zuboff, and Schuck 1994). The cultural mix in Malaysia is generally 50 percent Malays (generally Muslims), 35 percent Chinese, 10 percent Indian and Pakistanis, and 5 percent other; the plant reflected that mix. A number of differences arising from this cultural mix led to adaptations and adjustments. In addition, most employees were women. SK Ko, the first female managing director of Motorola-Penang (MP) in Malaysia, noted that in Malaysia there is a desire to avoid decision making (whereas the Western ideal is active decision making), so shared decision making was initially not a part of team efforts (except for efforts with high technical requirements and more highly trained personnel). As one manager noted, women in Malaysia were supposed to follow their husband's directions at home. Motorola encouraged them to speak out, but their husbands did not want them to. Therefore, a program for written recommendations ("I Recommend"—IR) was instituted with formal procedures.

Steps were also taken to stimulate group relationship building through "Dignity and Respect" program initiatives. Hierarchical structure problems occurred, since initially Malaysians were uncomfortable working on the same level as managers. Therefore, the program included a "training-the-trainers" program: engineers trained technicians, and managers trained supervisors, who in turn trained the operators (who considered themselves students). A "Critical Thinking Skills" program aimed at strengthening operators' learning capabilities was instituted. This program awarded advancements and certificates to participants. Another program, "The Speed of Execution," involved improving cycle time. In 1993, the "Orient Express Team" won the competition.

Although monthly IR awards were given to individuals, the awards arising from the "Total Customer Satisfaction" (TCS) program were team awards. Rewards and training also differed by the technical complexity of the specific process involved, with more highly skilled, better educated, and more capable workers being given more advanced training. In short, the team structures, training, and awards varied within different segments of the plants, depending on the situation. In general, the higher the operator skills and the skill requirements of the job, the more useful team approaches were.

Ko was people oriented and believed that it was important to "Treat your people with respect, as you would treat your own family; no yelling, no shouting, no finger pointing; give visible rewards for achievers; create enthusiasm; share every success story" (Gogan, Zuboff, and Schuck 1994, p. 13). This approach worked because production workers and some supervisors were women, while most managers and engineers were men, and in Malaysia gender differences were important.

At the same time, Ko had a difficult task in translating her leadership initiatives into action in her culture and her situation. She explained the vision at one meeting (p. 9):

> Today 2,820 employees produce $380 million in sales. By 2000, 1,500 employees will produce $1 billion. The factory will be highly automated. We will make state-of-the-art systems. Our work force will look completely different.

Although involving employees is key to building a learning organization, it was difficult to do at MP. Ko and her managers who had visited U.S. facilities were convinced that at this time, the use of involvement was limited. As of 1994, only one small department (six women on the pager back-end assemby line) and cross-functional teams working in limited areas, such as quality improvement and cycle time reduction, had been effective. The basic cultural orientation in Malaysia meant that self-managed or even cross-functional teams were almost impossible to implement in any great numbers and that involvement was not possible to any great degree at that time. This barrier created major obstacles to meeting the challenges of the new vision.

Ko's job was not an easy one. Over the short-term, she had to build a basis for the future by developing sophisticated training approaches and organization, such as those used at other firms (such as Intel) in situations where more sophisticated workers and tasks were involved. At the same time, she had to keep her factory running efficiently and effectively during the five-year transition period. The solution was a balanced compromise, the exact dimensions of which grew from the requirements of her particular situation.

As seen from Ko's experiences, teams do not work in all situations. Rather, they generally work only when carefully planned and managed, when the situation has tasks and people suited or trained for self-directed interpersonal work in a task-oriented work environment, or when sufficient time (as with GE in Hungary) and energy have been taken to train people in working in teams. When circumstances favor team structures, a number of common approaches can help make team management more effective. Based on the experiences described in this section and elsewhere in the book, the following appear to be useful guidelines for managing teams. They should, of course, be adapted to individual situations as required.

To be successful, teams need effective leaders (McDermott, Brawley, and Waite 1998). Leadership is needed both to initiate and to manage teams. The initial task is to define the team's general objective and guidelines for the team, as well as the initial general structures. This might include the level on which the team will function, its main task, and its general organization in the following situations:

- Merging corporate entities through a short-term, formal team of top managers made up of independent business units (Whirlpool)
- Performing operating functions (product development, marketing, and technical production) that require cross-functional expertise from different cultures operating in a self-managed environment using advanced information technologies that are formed for both short-term (new product development, marketing plans) and long-term (continuing production units) purposes (Intel)
- Performing functional tasks within different manufacturing departments in a high-tech operating environment in an Asian country, using company facilitators to ensure team functioning (TIM)
- Introducing the team concept into a low-tech environment in an Asian country, using both intradepartment and cross-functional teams as a long-term means of eventually moving to a high-tech production environment in a mixed cultural environment (MP)

Leadership tasks also include ensuring that enablers (including staffing, technology, controls, and organization) are put in place, and then communicating, motivating, energizing, and guiding.

Managing teams involves actually selecting team members. This can be done by upper management before the team forms and continued by the team members on a self-renewing basis, depending on whether the teams are self-managed and continuing. Early on, it is best to have face-to-face meetings among all team members. In one instance, such meetings were not possible, so team members initially worked on small projects over a period of time to get acquainted.

To function effectively, teams need to be guided through tasks such as defining leader/manager roles, team member responsibilities, team facilitator functions, use of technical support facilities such as the Internet, and other jobs such as recorder/secretary, monitoring, meeting scheduling, and performance benchmark identification. Working together on a day-to-day basis may also require handling interpersonal cross-cultural situations. Team meetings need to be managed, starting with planning them, establishing and following agendas as much as possible in the cultural setting involved, economy of presentation, balancing controlled and free-flowing exchanges, identifying specific action assignments and deadlines, recording the meeting, and promptly communicating minutes to all involved. Self-learning exercises in team building can be found in workbooks by George and Wilson (1997), and Gorden et al. (1997), and in books and papers by Sherriton and Stern (1997) and Forrester and Drexler (1999) can provide guidance when developing and managing teams.

The guidelines presented are based on observed experiences in a small sample of situations. As in other management areas, the guidelines will evolve and be refined as emergent behavior finds new solutions to new problems in other team management situations. The guidelines are only a baseline from which to develop one's own experienced-based rules of thumb.

## *SUMMARY*

This chapter discussed common frameworks in multinational, cross-cultural leadership and management task areas including: emerging worldwide concepts of leadership and management; tasks involved in leading a multinational enterprise; as well as the values and character traits, knowledge and skills, and behavior styles of successful leaders. Contingency frameworks and guidelines used by leaders and managers, and effective leadership and management behaviors were also discussed. A major integrative application area: leading and managing teams was also explored.

The discussion, therefore, paid particular attention to the adaptations needed to meet specific situation, global, local, and knowledge transfer requirements when leading and managing.

Special attention was also given to team management, a critical aspect of today's multinational, cross-cultural management. However, teams are useful only in selective ways in specific situations. In the mid-1990s, the use of teams had in fact dropped in popularity in U.S. firms.

At Motorola-Penang in Malaysia teams were not useful given the kind of work, the makeup of work groups, and the workers' skills. Teams functioned there mainly as a change agent to meet long-term strategic goals. At other companies, the situations were different, and various forms of teams were effective.

The same was true for leadership styles. Different styles were useful in different situations. Although some heuristic contingency guidelines exist, ultimately the individual decides what is best for his or her situation. Even when there are common frameworks, such as leadership styles and guidelines for making teams work in general, the way the frameworks are perceived, communicated, and learned can vary by culture and by company situation.

## REVIEW QUESTIONS

1. What is the difference between leadership and management? Discuss the ways in which the two concepts merge in practice.
2. Describe the major leadership tasks involved in multinational situations.
3. Identify and discuss key leadership traits. Describe the ways in which they are manifested and balanced in practice, with particular attention to how one handles the fact that not all effective leaders possess all the traits identified.
4. Identify and discuss key leadership values and attitudes and how they impact on effective leadership practices.
5. Discuss the role of knowledge, skills, and competencies in effective leadership.
6. Discuss the modern concept of leadership as evidenced in the story of Jack Welch at GE. Identify leadership guidelines you have developed from studying his experiences.
7. Discuss the applicability of Welch's approach in smaller firms.
8. Describe the ways in which leadership styles are contingent on specific situation requirements. Give specific examples to illustrate your answer.
9. Based on your reading of the chapter, summarize those behaviors which identify an effective, experienced leader in action.
10. Describe the role teams can play in effective multinational strategic management.
11. Identify the key activities involved in managing teams, as well as guidelines for effective team management.
12. Describe situations in which teams are and are not effective in multinational strategic management.

## *EXERCISES*

1. As part of the learning process underlying this book, from your research, select an effective multinational business leader, describe his or her leadership experiences, and then develop a model of what you think makes an effective leader based on that experience.

2. Select a second leader, describe his or her experiences, and revise your model of leadership. In addition, identify, compare, and contrast the different situational characteristics that enabled success in each situation. Note especially the ways in which different situations can require different leadership traits, and in the process, begin to develop contingent situational guidelines for what makes for effective leadership in different kinds of situations.

3. From your research, select two situations involving team usage in a multinational setting, one that succeeded and one that failed. Identify the factors which led to success and failure in each situation.

# Chapter 12

# Staffing, Training, and Communications

Asea Brown Boveri (ABB) AG is a major Swiss/Swedish electrical equipment and engineering firm with 5,000 profit centers in 140 countries. ABB has a group of 500 multilingual managers who relocate from operation to operation to cut costs, improve efficiency, and align local businesses with ABB's global views. In 1997, its executive committee consisted of three Swedes, two Swiss, an American, and a German, and ABB's Zurich headquarters had 171 staffers from nineteen countries. English is the firm's official language (Kets de Vries, Manfred, and Florent-Treacy 1999; Wind and Main 1998). Like ABB, many international firms have multinational staffs.

In 1999, ABB established a training center near Warsaw, Poland. ABB has used this facility to train managers (by instruction and example), build a corporate culture, and help assimilate 11 ABB-owned firms in Poland with 7,000 employees. More than 1,000 ABB employees—mainly Polish, from top executives to new managers—go through the center yearly.

The enormous need for managers in developing countries can be solved by other approaches. For example, a group of leading British firms formed a joint venture, the China European International Business School (CEIBS), in Beijing, China, to train China's new generation of middle managers; it now also has a branch in Shanghai (Pudong). Another private business school, The China Europe International Business School, has since opened in 1994 in Shanghai and it trained more than 1,200 managers from local companies in short, executive development programs; it began a full-time MBA program in 1997.

Three key multinational management enablers—staffing, training, and development, are discussed in this chapter. Because communication skills training are so important for performing these and other multinational management tasks, the final section of this chapter discusses methods of communicating across boundaries. The discussion covers media such as e-mail, videoconferencing, and groupware, and the ways in which they can and cannot provide cheap, speedy, and accessible links for multinational management.

## STAFFING MULTINATIONAL OPERATIONS

Staffing tasks can vary, depending on the situation. The staffing tasks for a new company or division will differ from those at an established company, such as Gillette, Coca-Cola, or ABB. Top-level management positions have different staffing requirements than jobs at the middle-management or operator level. Staffing needs practices also differ due to the kind of company and industry, as well as because of many other situational factors.

Some corporate leaders consider staffing the most significant enabler in multinational management. When faced with a downturn in sales after its merger, DaimlerChrysler in 1999 announced moves to replace the head of its troubled Smart car (small auto) division and simplify its management board structure (Simison and Miller 1999). It was also facing another major staffing problem. Because of the merger of the U.S. (Chrysler) and German (DaimlerBenz) firms, DaimlerChrysler was having trouble finding a sufficient number of Americans from Chrysler willing to work in Germany for extended periods of time, which was causing problems in integrating the U.S. and German operations (Ball 1999).

When Colman Mockler became CEO of Gillette in the 1970s his first and, according to him, most difficult task was to have in place a substantial number (about sixty) of middle managers capable of carrying out his vision. His requirements were that these managers be entrepreneurial thinkers and doers who could work within the Gillette culture. His new strategic vision involved focusing on what Gillette did best (personal-care products and writing instruments), and eliminating unrelated businesses (such as Welcome Wagon). The staff was the main engine he needed to drive this newly conceived Gillette. Simply put, Mockler felt he could not get the job done effectively without the right people.

Many of Gillette's existing managers had the required profile, others had potential, and still others appeared not to match the profile. Because Gillette's cultural framework was concerned with people, Mockler felt that he could not make abrupt staffing changes. Instead, it took eighteen months of rotation, training, and incentives (with no terminations directly related to the strategy change) to put in place a staff that he felt was able to do the envisioned job.

At the same time, Mockler recognized that an even longer-term staffing need existed. Gillette needed more than the products, the contacts, the operations, and a presence to succeed internationally. It needed a large group of mobile, seasoned expatriates. It built that staff over a twenty-year period. In the view of Al Zeien, its CEO in 1996, this gave Gillette a twenty-year advantage over most of its competitors—a core competency consisting of some 350 trained expatriate managers who knew Gillette and its businesses, had worked in a variety of overseas locations, had the facility to move across cultures, and could move quickly and easily to new assignments.

This same staffing and training process continues today at Gillette. It starts with hiring highly competent people who are familiar with an international area, have entrepreneurial skills, and yet are able to work within a corporate framework. These people spend eighteen months to two years at the company's Boston headquarters and at various company sites. During this time, they are exposed to core company competencies and policies and meet a wide range of people in the company with whom they will interact over the years. In addition, they are expected to move from country to country every few years, on very short notice, when required (McKibben 1998). For example, one candidate, Justyna Pisiewicz, a Polish recruit with a degree from a Beijing university who spoke English and Russian, along with Polish and Chinese, was initially assigned to the local operation in Poland. She then went to Boston for an eighteen-month stay at Gillette's headquarters, and visited London and Singapore while stationed there. In general, Gillette's program focuses on hiring people with skills in specified areas, and emphasizes continual training, development, and reinforcement.

Gillette is one of many firms that has worked diligently to create a global mind-set within the company culture, using a variety of techniques (Govindarajan and Gupta 1998). Its approach was appropriate for Gillette's needs. Other firms have been equally successful in staffing their organizations in other ways as appropriate to their requirements. The following sections review some of the tasks, decisions and actions involved in managing staffing for multinational operations in a wide range of firms. These include:

- Identifying needs
- Recruiting, screening, selecting, and development
- Compensation and performance appraisal (evaluating, promoting, transferring or dismissing, and repatriating)

### *Identifying Needs*

The need for competent international staff has grown dramatically with the rapid expansion of business internationally, especially in developing countries ("The Talent Void" 1997). In an international operation, most staffing is done at the local level. This is because citizens of the countries in which the firm operates often have knowledge about how the business can be effectively run in their region. For example, in 2000, when Coca-Cola was attempting to revive its European operations, Coke's new president replaced nine of ten European senior managers with local executives (McKay 2000).

Multinational firms, however, operate both locally and internationally. At times, therefore, *expatriates* (noncitizens) are needed to staff operations. Expatriates can be *home-country nationals* (from the country in which the firm is based) or *third-country nationals*. The need for expatriates arises when special skills and expertise are needed at a specific location, when there is a significant need for integration with the multinational company and its other global divisions, and when the needs cannot be filled locally, as for example in China, where managers with training in Western management practices are in short supply (Beard 2000). At times, such needs are not readily apparent. For example, C&W, a conglomerate consisting mostly of small phone firms in Britain, hired an American executive, Richard Brown who had no international experience. In a short time, he turned C&W into a major worldwide cable TV and phone firm through a combination of astute management and mergers/acquisitions ("Global Mobil" 1998; Guyon 1997). After twenty-seven very successful months, Brown resigned to return to the United States and a better paying position at Electronic Data Systems (Cane and Kehoe 1998).

The need for specialized skills may arise at the upper management, middle/line management, or operational level. Often, with the rapid advances in technology, such as in the Internet area, the need is a technical one. It might be a one-time need for a short period, or a continuing need to support a large and growing international presence. Staffing needs can arise quickly and so be an immediate need, or there may be a need encountered by a firm just entering an overseas market. In addition, situation requirements can change over time. Staffing changes may become necessary as a firm grows globally and has growing needs for expatriate managers, and as its product mix, internal resources, and external competitive market changes. Needs may arise from a company's deteriorating market position. This was the case with Fiat SpA in Italy, when in an effort to bring Fiat some of the magic that had led to GE's spectacular growth, they brought in an Italian-born manager who had worked with Jack Welch at GE for forty years (Tagliabue 1999). Because of the range of approaches to management staffing at international enterprises, a contingency approach is needed, as in other multinational management task areas.

### Recruitment, Screening, Selection, and Development

In many firms, recruitment starts before the immediate need arises and includes recruitment and development in *anticipation* of the job need arising on a *continuing* basis. Coca-Cola, like Gillette, has an expatriate program suited to its specific needs. Such a continuing program is to be expected at a company that in 1998 obtained 80 percent of its sales from non-U.S. operations and declared itself a "world" company. The program maintains a pool of 500 expatriates who know the company well and who are available on short notice to fill varying needs around the world (Anfuso 1994). For example, when Coca-Cola started operations in Eastern Europe, an expatriate of Polish descent from Chicago was picked to be finance manager. Of its pool of 500 expatriates, Coca-Cola regularly transfers 200 each year, both to fill local needs and to enhance the pool's international experience. The company has an international service group that supports this worldwide program. The group coordinates the transfer of employees, taking care of such aspects as assuring that compensation is equitable no matter where and how quickly the expatriate is transferred (Anfuso 1994).

Other continuing anticipatory approaches are used to fulfill short-term technical needs in foreign operations. As described in Chapter 9, many firms fill technical operating needs with expatriate SWAT teams. In 1994, Texas Instruments had some 200 professionals—dubbed "Nomads"—who set up microchip-making plants in Italy, Taiwan, Japan, and Singapore. U.S. West and Unilever also have such teams.

Molex, Inc., a fifty-six-year-old U.S. technology firm that derives more than 70 percent of its billion-dollar income from outside the United States, and has 70 percent of its employees outside the United States, has a different anticipatory program suited to its specific needs. The firm uses many techniques, including extensive recruiting, training, and *career pathing,* which is the creation of a recognizable path for advancement in the firm by working on international jobs.

Molex rarely seeks potential managers that are U.S. nationals when hiring. Instead, it looks for foreign-nationals who are studying in the United States for MBA degrees, who have engineering degrees, and who want to return to work overseas. This guarantees that potential expatriate managers have exposure to at least two cultures, are able to converse in at least two languages, and have some management and technical training. Once hired, these managers are expected to spend two to three years with the firm, principally in the United States, to learn about Molex's operations and culture before being permanently assigned overseas, often to their own countries. In contrast, Gillette's program sends these new people to a third country. In addition, Molex has formal, five-week classroom training programs. Training programs and international assignments are also offered to employees who were not initially hired specifically for the expatriate program (Solomon 1995a). Even if these employees do not eventually enter the program, such training and foreign exposure acquaint them with the international aspects of Molex's operation.

Matav, the Hungarian telephone company, used another kind of balanced approach to manage a multicultural joint venture (Beck 1996). Matav hired a Hungarian as a director who had worked for a foreign company (IBM) in Hungary. A management "troika" was subsequently established through which management and leadership were shared by the Hungarian director, the Ameritech executive, and the Deutsche Telekom representative.

In an effort to internationalize, companies sometimes appoint executives from other countries. For example, in 1996, BankBoston named the head of its Brazilian operations as president and CEO of the parent firm. In 1996, three of the six executive vice presidents at Citibank (U.S.) were born outside the United States—in Pakistan, Argentina, and India. In mid-1996, Britain's Cable & Wireless chose a U.S. citizen as CEO (Guyon 1997).

When the New York law firm Weil, Gotshal, Manges opened a London office, it staffed it with British lawyers; other American law firms in London were staffed largely with American lawyers (Barrett 1999). In addition, the firm hired an aggressive younger lawyer, who was not part of the British establishment (he showed up at the first interview in shorts with a backpack) to head the venture. He, in turn, hired other young British lawyers. This somewhat unorthodox approach to staffing seems to have worked.

In 1999, worldwide, there was a serious shortage of information technology (IT) people with experience with the Internet. This situation required unusual actions, such as hiring bonuses, finder's fees for employee recommendations, and ultimately major supplemental training programs, both in Western and in developing countries (Violino and Mateyaschuk 1999).

These are examples of only a few staffing and development actions taken and programs created by specific firms. Resources and situation requirements may dictate other solutions. For example, Tellabs Operations, Inc., a Chicago-based designer and manufacturer of telecommunications products, faced short- and long-term staffing needs in 1994 when it opened a new operation in Germany.

At the outset of international expansion, Tellabs believed that the best strategy was to staff overseas operations with locals. However, Tellabs learned, as have many firms, that hiring local managers can create problems. When it opened an Irish facility staffed with locals, Tellabs' management did not adequately communicate to the Irish staff Tellabs' corporate culture: informal, flexible, and entrepreneurial. At Tellabs, employees called each other by first names, shared information widely, and had direct access to senior management. As a result of this cultural communication gap, Tellabs found that when an American executive went to Ireland, the Irish would appear to agree with suggested changes, but would fail to act on them.

In 1993, when Tellabs acquired Martis Oy, a Finnish firm, it again wanted to maintain the entrepreneurial spirit that had made the firm successful, but it also wanted to tie employees into the parent corporation. In contrast to the Irish situation, therefore, time was allowed for cultural training and frequent exchanges of executives for short periods to help make the transition work. These steps provided both the cross-pollination of resources and the imbedding of Tellabs' corporate culture that were lacking initially at the Irish facility. The Finnish operation was very successful.

Tellabs drew on these experiences in 1994 when it sent Laura Bozich, its Central European regional director and one of the few expatriates working for the company, to Munich to start operations and to staff a German branch. Her job was to introduce Tellabs' corporate culture while interviewing and hiring—before handing the office over to host-country nationals. In a sense, she was introducing the development phase during the selection process. Bozich faced many problems in a German society where cultural values seemed completely contrary to the corporate culture that she intended to create. In addition, American companies had a reputation in Germany of having a hire-and-fire mentality.

Her approach was to search for Germans who had worked for American companies and so might understand the informal American entrepreneurial style that prevailed at Tellabs. In addition, Bozich was careful to inform those she interviewed that German nationals would be promoted to top positions—a standard strategy at all of Tellabs' overseas facilities (Solomon 1995b).

As seen from these experiences and others to follow, situational needs in the staffing area vary. Few universal formula solutions exist—only heuristic situational patterns that suggest solutions appropriate to the specific situation under study. For example, many firms do not have the foresight, needs, or resources of Gillette, Coca-Cola, or ABB to build a group of middle management and technical expatriates who can be called upon as new assignments arise. Because of the high cost (both in developing and compensating expatriates) and high failure rate of expatriates in general (especially among Americans), companies generally prefer to hire nationals. This short-term approach, used by Tellabs, clearly does not work without intensive supplemental development programs designed to create integrative global synergies.

In addition, although preferable, hiring, training, and developing locals is not always possible, since competent personnel are not always available on a timely basis. For this reason, firms unable to create a pool of expatriates to fill local needs must select and train personnel currently working for the firm or hire experienced third-country or outside managers and technical people.

When recruiting, screening, training and developing personnel for overseas operations, Gillette, Coca-Cola, and other experienced international companies expect candidates to:

1. be familiar with the company, its philosophy, people, processes, and competencies;
2. be knowledgeable about the country or countries where they are working;
3. be highly skilled at their jobs; and

4. be adaptable, mobile, innovative, and entrepreneurial within the context of company guidelines.

This profile of successful expatriate managers has been used by many firms, which have used approaches different from those of Coca-Cola and Gillette in finding and developing local and expatriate managers. For example, not all firms have large and continuing international staffing needs, and some are just starting to internationalize operations. When searching for staff in these situations, it is important to assess an individual's qualifications and likelihood of success. Personal characteristics such as adaptability, innovative and entrepreneurial instincts, and mobility (qualification number 4) are essential to success in international management. Many firms, such as AT&T, have tests to measure these capabilities.

Even after thorough testing, trial periods are important to judge a person's capabilities in the workplace over several years. Molex's approach was to carefully observe and track candidates' performances during the first years of employment. In addition, during this period, the employees could get to know the company (qualification number 1) and acquire advanced technical skills (qualification number 3). As for qualification number 2, Molex most often hired foreign-nationals, but also exposed other managers to international development opportunities by providing them with foreign assignments. Molex had a flexible multifaceted approach to building a strong staff. Although its approach was structured around a common, four-qualification framework, the specific tools used were appropriate for the needs of Molex and its competitive environment.

The problems arising from failing to pay careful attention to expatriate selection and training can be costly. For example, in 1984, when Beijing Automotive Works (BAW) and American Motors Corporation (AMC) entered into a joint venture named Beijing Jeep Corporation (BJC) to produce jeeps and other four-wheel-drive vehicles, American middle managers with advanced technical knowledge were sent to China to manage day-to-day operations. These managers were not given adequate cultural and language training, and so made many mistakes. The eventual solution was to establish a transition phase in which expatriate managers worked closely with Chinese managers to transfer technical expertise. After this transition period, the Americans returned home (Aiello 1991).

In contrast, Volkswagen (VW) entered into a joint venture with China Automotive (CA) during the same period, basing its approach on knowledge gained from prior experiences abroad. From the beginning, host and home country managers were paired and shared authority. In addition, the German expatriate managers had technical expertise, prior overseas experience, knew the language and culture of the host country, and had volunteered for the assignment (Clark 1995).

As seen in these company experiences, special technical or enterprise global business needs, costs, host country business and cultural needs, existing and anticipated competitive market requirements, candidate qualifications, the amount of training required, company resources, and the urgency of the need are among the critical situation factors affecting staffing decisions. As in every situation described in this text, the successful solutions here were tailored to specific situation needs.

The Internet and intranet have become major sources for hiring. For example, Ford and IBM use their internal Internets (intranets) for posting job listings as discussed in Chapter 2 and Chapter 9. Internal company Web sites where outsiders can check job listings at a company have also been created. In addition, there are a wide range of independent job finding and Internet search firms available to anyone with a computer.

A major problem encountered in developing multinational managers has been that many firms lack clear policies or action patterns to convey the message that overseas assignments and training are paths to advancement (Dobrzynski 1996). Such policies and practices can be a major factor in recruitment, especially from within a firm. Studies have shown that success is most likely to occur when clear career paths and models of success exist for advancing in a firm along an international track, such as those found at Molex, Gillette, and Coca-Cola. Studies suggest that these conditions help create a believable, international career path that:

- Allows each person to choose an international career path or assignment
- Offers adequate preparation and training, either through rotating assignments, training and development programs, or through orientation programs that realistically preview the assignment
- Provides, through commitments or other actions, a basis for realistic expectations about what is likely to happen after the international assignment
- Provides a clear link between the overseas assignment and the long-term career paths of the expatriate within the company (Black and Gregersen 1991a; Feldman and Thomas 1992).

Other problems may be associated with overseas assignments, in addition to the absence of a well-defined international career path. For example, educating dependent children overseas can be a problem. It also can be difficult for an employee's spouse to find comparable employment at comparative salary rates (Schellenbarger 1997). Strong career and monetary incentives, as well as extensive training and development, may be needed to help overcome such problems.

### Compensation and Performance Appraisal

Compensation differentials exist among countries and must be taken into account when assigning expatriates (Donkin 1997). For example, in the early 1990s, living costs in Japan (as measured by the cost of living index) were double those of the United States. Housing costs, income tax differences, moving and schooling costs, home leave, and at times a foreign service premium are additional costs to consider. Such costs can increase the cost to the firm of using an expatriate by fourfold. For example, someone earning $100,000 might cost the firm as much as $400,000 a year as an expatriate in Japan. Because Japan is probably the most expensive country in the world to live in, this figure probably represents a maximum. However, on average, costs will likely exceed the home country salary by two to three times. This can be another major incentive to use expatriates only when absolutely necessary.

Compensation costs are not always so high. Companies such as Coca-Cola have programs for expatriates with established policies for compensation. These programs, or those based on consultants' recommendations, provide benchmarks for an expatriate to use when deciding whether to take an overseas job and for the company to use when doing a cost-benefit analysis.

In addition, performance evaluation criteria are needed for expatriates, and these can vary considerably by situation. For example, they may involve standard Western measurements such as profits and profit margins or sales and market-share growth. They may also relate to technical projects and their successful completion. The criteria may relate to specific problems and whether they were solved. When searching for causes of, and remedies for, any below-standard performance, a situational diagnosis is needed. For example, an inappropriate employee selection process or a lack of training—management tasks—may cause performance problems. Unrealistic expectations can be another problem. These and similar problems can result in a lack of professional competence in international business areas. The manner in which the evaluation is handled and subsequent actions are taken, as well as the criteria used, will define the nature of a company's international career path, the risks involved in pursuing it, and the expectations and rewards of pursuing it.

The evaluation process can be culturally dependent, because performance is judged in different ways in different countries. For example, Table 12.1 gives the contrasting cultural biases inherent in the review processes in three cultures—American, Japanese, and Arab. Success is not always defined the same way in all cultures.

Repatriation is another staffing consideration. For example, returning expatriates may need to make adjustments in such areas as: financial (it is possible to have lived better abroad, for example, through having servants and

TABLE 12.1. Cultural Contrasts: Performance Reviews

| | American | Japanese | Arab |
|---|---|---|---|
| **Objective** | Review based on preset goals; identify personal strengths/weaknesses | Find out why performance is not in harmony with group | Set employee on track; reprimand for bad performance |
| **Structure** | Formal procedure; every 6 to 12 months in manager's office | Informal, ad-hoc with employee; frequent reporting to administration; in office, coffee shop, bar | Informal, ad-hoc; recorded in manager's office |
| **Interaction** | Two-way, both sides present openly own point of view, manager as leader/adviser; employee independent, self-motivated | Employee answers manager's concerns; manager gives advice as parent, mentor, senior employee; part of group/family; continuous feedback | One-way, manager guides subordinate; authority figure, mentor, random feedback; treated like child in family |
| **Evaluation** | Success measured by performance against stated goals | Success measured by contribution to group harmony and output | Success measured by major personal contribution |
| **Outcome** | Promotion; salary increase; bonus; commission; salary freeze; loss of title; loss of power | Mainly affects amount of semi-annual bonus; less important job; job rotation; dock bonus/salary | Bonus of 1/2-day salary; promotion; salary decrease |
| **Closing** | Openness; equality; fairness | Group achievement; relationship | Privacy; authority; parenthood |

*Source:* Adapted from Elashmawi, Fadrid, and Philip R. Harris, *Multinational Management: New Skills for Global Success*, Houston, TX: Gulf Publishing Company, 1993, p. 152.

*313*

being able to save more); professional (the job abroad may have been more interesting, carried more responsibility, or had more diversity); or, personal (old friends may be gone or previous lifestyles changed). Again, problems can be reduced if there is an organized career development program designed to handle repatriation matters (Black and Gregersen 1991b).

According to a 1995 Conference Board (a U.S. business research group) study of 152 medium to large firms (two-thirds of them based in the United States and the remainder in Asia and Europe), U.S. firms were not as effective at repatriation as European and Asian firms. For example, 77 percent of returning expatriates at the U.S. firms surveyed came home to lesser jobs than they had overseas and up to half of them quit after returning home. Only 38 percent of the U.S. firms guaranteed expatriates jobs on their return, while 74 percent of the European firms did (Dobrzynski 1996; Kaufman 1999). One survey indicated that only 22 percent of workers believed that firms rewarded such service with advancement ("Repatriating Workers" 1999). More recent studies indicate that U.S. firms overall continue to handle repatriation poorly (Abueva 2000). This study recommends that the following actions be taken by multinational firms to improve repatriation effectiveness: Write down, in clear terms, what they expect the departing executives to achieve abroad and what they expect them to do when they come back.

One approach used to lessen this problem has been to temporarily assign retired employees overseas (Lublin 1998).

## TRAINING AND DEVELOPMENT

*Training* is instruction directed at enhancing specific job-related skills and abilities. For example, training might concern how to manage cross-cultural teams, how to deal with cultural differences during negotiations, or how to speak a foreign language. *Development* is concerned with preparing managers for new assignments or higher-level positions. For example, a development program might be aimed at improving decision-making skills.

As seen from company experiences, development for international managers can begin during the recruitment and selection phases. This section focuses on formal training methods and tools.

As with staffing, both training (job-related skills and abilities instruction) and development (generally, management education) involve assessing needs (for the training and trainees), selecting methods or approaches, and managing and carrying out the process. A special focus on international operations is needed to prepare managers for international assignments and to prepare workers for assignments to international teams.

### Needs Assessment

Training and developing needs are arrived at through a matching process. For example, first the basic job needs are defined. This was the case with the four qualifications identified for successful expatriate managers.

These success profiles are then matched with individual profiles to determine areas where training is needed. The degree and type of gap between desired qualifications and each individual's skills will determine the amount of training and the methods and approaches used, as well as how the training is managed. Examples of this matching process are given in the following sections.

### Training Methods and Approaches

Training decisions involve several areas: kind and source, content, environment, methods and processes, and tools.

#### Kind and Source

The decision to use programs that are standardized or customized (to meet specific company requirements) can depend on:

- the size of the company and its international operations (large companies, such as Coca-Cola, tend to have their own customized training programs), and
- the content (standardized programs are available for language training, interpersonal interaction, and country-specific familiarization training, for example).

Whether the program will be developed and conducted in-house or outsourced (developed and conducted by someone outside the company) will be decided by the following:

- the training resources available in-house and outside (does the company have facilities appropriate for the program and people qualified to teach it?),
- the financial resources available,
- the perceived effectiveness of each (programs tailored to company needs and conducted by in-house personnel are favored by many),
- the timing, and
- the content to be covered.

*Content*

Both kinds of training—familiarization with the specific country or countries involved and managing or dealing with interpersonal interaction between cultures—are needed for expatriate mangers and technical personnel. The first is generally background for the second.

*Environment*

Training can be conducted on- or off-site, in classrooms or on-the-job, depending on the resources, training level, people, content, and facilities. For example, machine operations is a good area for on-the-job, on-site content training, as seen in the Motorola-Panang study in Chapter 11. In contrast, country-specific information often can be conveyed more effectively in a classroom. Shadowing (working alongside an experienced manager) and mentoring are also effective in management development.

*Teaching and Learning Methods and Processes*

Whether the passive lecturing method or active participative learning approach is used depends on the content and the cultural environment. For example, participative learning methods, such as interactive discussions, work well in the U.S. and Australian cultures. More structured, passive approaches work best in Arab nations. There are exceptions, of course, depending on who is giving or taking the course. Interactive methods seem to work well among more educated and cosmopolitan executives in both China and Russia, even when working through an interpreter.

One approach used at GE in Europe has been to encourage junior managers to mentor senior managers. This reverse-mentoring approach has become important in an age where the speed of technological change, especially that related to the Internet, has been so rapid that younger people often are more abreast of what is currently happening than older managers (Murray 2000). General Motors has a similar reverse-mentoring program (King 2000). Mentoring also has proven effective when working with Asian and Russian managers (Wickman and Sjodin 1997).

*Teaching and Learning Tools*

The selection of tools may depend on the cultures involved. For example, Americans tend to prefer written or oral instruction, while the Japanese prefer group practice sessions and intragroup discussions. The content or subject matter may also dictate the tool. Country-specific information can be learned from readings, lectures, case studies, and presentations, for instance, whereas interpersonal interaction is best learned through active learning tools such as team projects and incident/case studies. Recent studies indicate that almost all large companies now have, or will have, training for every job available on the Internet (Stuart 1999; Taylor 1999).

## MANAGING THE STAFFING, TRAINING, AND DEVELOPMENT PROCESSES

Managing staffing, training, and development involves balancing many situation factors. Cultural factors, reviewed in Chapter 10, may affect these processes. Regardless of the specific training and development goals, techniques must be adapted to the cultural, content, facility, people, resources, and business restraints within the situation. Table 12.2 compares training approaches in three cultures; the approaches shown can range from those involved in the timing of sessions and training materials used, to how the training is conducted. For instance, the Japanese culture favors group work and consensus, as well as protocol and status; therefore, the best teaching methods are intragroup discussions and sharing experiences (but not necessarily with the instructor participating). The management process for training sessions, then, is a familiar contingency one—the methods chosen must be adapted to the audience, subject matter, and objectives.

In the same way, cultural differences impact on other leadership and management tasks, such as motivation. This impact can also be identified and analyzed, as shown in Table 12.3.

An example of such culturally dependent management action is found in the experiences of Electronic Data Systems, Ltd. (EDS), a U. S. company with offices worldwide. The company introduced a new leadership strategy in 1992—a more team-, people-, and vision-oriented strategy. In trying to implement this leadership strategy in Japan, Larry Purdy, former leadership development manager, came to two conclusions after the first year of leadership training. First, he discovered that the Americans and Japanese shared many leadership values. *This core set of values* included team orientation. Second, the company discovered that major cultural differences affected the way in which values were communicated and leaders were evaluated (Purdy 1995). For example, in Purdy's words:

1. As for the ways we teach our values, generally, Japanese workers spend much less time than Americans doing formal classroom training. Japanese workers are educated and developed by giving them frequent new assignments, on-the-job training, and establishing career-long, mentor-like relationships with seniors who will help them assimilate the values and culture of the company. As our training program was based primarily on a classroom, lecture-style format, our Japanese middle managers (almost all of whom have only recently joined EDS from other companies) felt they could have understood

our message more clearly, and put it into practice more effectively, if we had chosen a more culturally appropriate manner of conveying that message.

2. The second aspect of leadership that is culturally dependent concerns how we measure, evaluate, and select leaders in relation to our leadership value model. This involves judging how leaders demonstrate the behaviors associated with the identified leadership attributes or values: strong personal convictions, vision, emotional bonds, inspirational, team-oriented, risk-takers, and drive to excel. For example, EDS expects its leaders to be team-oriented. The Japanese also place great value on teamwork. However, the motivation and the expectations of team members and manifestation of team spirit varies significantly between the two cultures. The Japanese find satisfaction in being anonymous contributors to group goals. Though Americans also value teamwork, they expect recognition for their individual contributions. American management in turn expects individuals to make recognizable, measurable contributions. Japanese managers would place much more emphasis on a team member's ability to harmonize with the group as a whole than they would on evaluating individual contribution and performance.

EDS' experiences illustrate the difficulties involved in balancing the many diverse cultural differences encountered in multinational management situations. First, it is necessary to recognize the similarities and differences to provide a basis for action. Second, it is necessary to reasonably balance differences. For example, EDS used different evaluation criteria to judge leadership performance by two distinct cultural norms within the same worldwide firm. The situation is further complicated by the fact that customs are changing: for example, in the late 1990s, Toyota and other Japanese firms introduced individual merit pay raises based on performance, as in the United States and other Western countries, and abandoned pay raises based on seniority, their long-standing traditional pay practice (Harney 1999).

## COMMUNICATIONS ACROSS CULTURAL BOUNDARIES

Communication skills are especially critical to successful management and leadership in an international enterprise because of the geographic distances and mix of cultures involved. They are, therefore, a key factor in staffing, training, and development. This section discusses available communication tools, including the Internet, and explains how their effectiveness can depend on cross-cultural factors, as well as on other situation factors and the individual media's inherent characteristics (Kessler 1998).

TABLE 12.2. Cultural Contrasts: Training

| | American | Japanese | Arab |
|---|---|---|---|
| Group Composition | Medium-sized; mixed level acceptable | Smallest group; grouped for functional harmony | Largest group; very level-conscious |
| Time | 8-5 with breaks | 9-6 with breaks; may go until 8 or continue informally after hours | 9/10-3 maximum; no lunch break |
| Preparation | Individual reading; written homework | Group orientation | Not necessary or important |
| Getting Started | Self-introductions; randomly or by seating order | Introductions emphasizing company/belonging; senior member going last | Introduction by status; senior member going first |
| International Process | Emphasize "how to" and practical applications; self-reliance; specialization; ample reading | Emphasis on doing/discussion; sharing experiences; intragroup discussion; role play, rotation | Memorizing general skills; coaching; demonstration by leader; minimal reading |
| Training Materials | Written; self-explanatory | Visual with group discussion and practices | Visual; coaching by team leader |
| Tests of Knowledge | Direct questions to individual; spontaneous, open questions | Group questions; intragroup discussions; directed questions | No direct, individual questions; participants need preparation |
| Cultural Values | Self-reliance; competition; time conscious | Relationship; group achievement; group harmony | Seniority; reputation; individual achievement |

*Source:* Adapted from Elashmawi, Fadrid, and Philip R. Harris, *Multinational Management: New Skills for Global Success,* Houston, TX: Gulf Publishing Company, 1993, p. 133.

*319*

TABLE 12.3. Cultural Contrasts: Motivation

| | American | Japanese | Arab |
|---|---|---|---|
| **Management Style** | Leadership; friendliness | Persuasion; functional group activities | Coaching; personal attention; parenthood |
| **Control** | Independence; decision-making; space; time; money | Group harmony | Of others/parenthood |
| **Emotional Appeal** | Opportunity | Group participation; company success | Religion; nationalistic; admiration |
| **Recognition** | Individual contribution | Group identity; belonging to group; group contribution | Individual status; class/society; promotion |
| **Material Rewards** | Salary; commission; profit-sharing | Annual bonus; social services; fringe benefits | Gifts self/family; family affair; salary increase |
| **Threats** | Loss of job | Ouster from group | Demotion; damage reputation |
| **Cultural Values** | Competition; risk-taking; material possession; freedom | Group harmony; achievement; belonging | Reputation; family security; religion; social status |

*Source:* Adapted from Elashmawi, Fadrid, and Philip R. Harris, *Multinational Management: New Skills for Global Success,* Houston, TX: Gulf Publishing Company, 1993, p. 144.

### Media: Types and How to Use Them

Four types of media are discussed here: electronic mail, written (facsimile and postal), telephone, and videoconferencing.

#### Electronic Mail and Computers

E-mail sent over BITNET and the Internet is a familiar type of electronic media. Its main advantages are that it is immediately transmitted, it saves time because it is entered directly, it is generally less expensive than telephone calls, and it enables time/place differences to be bridged. Its drawbacks are that it can be impersonal and terse, and while it is formal (in writing), often it is not carefully written or edited. No visual or verbal feedback exists to verify and refine understanding. As a result, e-mail is often incomplete, inaccurate, and lacking in the nuances necessary for exploring situation contexts and developing close, personal relationships with people from different cultures. Because computers and computer systems are needed at both ends to use it, e-mail (and associated Web pages) are difficult to read and send without some introductory training. In addition, since privacy is lacking, e-mail messages can be read by others.

Given these characteristics, e-mail's effectiveness can be limited. It is, however, effective in communicating simple tasks and uncomplicated information quickly. Examples include communicating technical specs for products, routine changes in assignments, orders that are repetitive or uncomplicated, and any hard data that does not need extensive explanation or feedback to understand.

E-mail usually is not an effective way to initially get to know someone, to amplify contexts of more complex decision and action situations, or to clarify ambiguities. E-mail is most effectively used in situations in which face-to-face trust building has already occurred. However, under special circumstances, for example, when mutual interests are strong, personal relationships can be established through e-mail, just as they can through regular mail.

Language differences can also create problems when using electronic media. To overcome such problems, digital-coding computer software systems are being developed to allow representation in, and translation into any language, from Chinese ideographs and Russian Cyrillic, to Sanskrit. Such software systems will allow the Internet to adapt to, and integrate, a major cultural difference—language.

Other potential problems also exist with electronic mail. For example, many Asian cultures regard off-the-cuff responses and intellectual banter, which are sometimes found in e-mail communications, insulting and rude. Blunt, untempered criticism, which is common on e-mail systems, is particularly offensive in many cultures. Irony and sarcasm can be misconstrued. Moreover, electronic media lack reinforcement from body language, eye contact, or the simple act of "chatting" (Petzinger 1999). Training and use can increase sensitivity to, and handling of, such problems, but electronic media nonetheless have built-in limitations.

In spite of its drawbacks, e-mail and the Internet are indispensable to busy executives. Many top executives of firms in rapidly changing competitive markets—for example, the president of the chemical joint venture in China and the international director at a large multinational consumer products firm—can be reached within hours through their e-mail, which they check many times daily (Mockler 1994-1999). E-mail, computers, and related software, worldwide telecommunications infrastructures, and telephone and fax linkages, link employees online with other company offices and personnel and make it possible to work virtually anywhere in the world as if working from one's own office. That is, these new technologies have made possible the "virtual office" (Caldwell and Gambon 1996).

Many computer-related telecommunications software systems go beyond using electronic media for correspondence purposes. One example is groupware—software systems that enable a group of individuals to interact through computers and the Internet. Because groupware enables exploring, coordinating, and reconciling different viewpoints, it provides a mechanism for developing interpersonal relationships. This can be reinforced by using groupware in combination with teleconferencing in conference room settings (a group of people may sit on one side of a four-sided conference room with television screens on the three other sides of the conference room showing people at similar conference tables in three other worldwide locations, for example). The technology is still in the early stages of development, so its use is limited and costly.

### Written: Facsimile and Postal

Postal communications are the most traditional and familiar forms of written communication. Facsimile machines are essentially faster ways of sending letters and other written communications. However, like e-mail, these communications do not involve face-to-face contact, and share many of the following advantages and drawbacks of e-mail:

- Facsimiles are transmitted instantly, like e-mail, though, they require more time for preparation and sending (e-mail is typed and sent in the same media).
- Facsimiles enable time/place differences to be bridged.
- There is no visual feedback to refine and verify understanding, making facsimiles and postal communications, like e-mail, limited in their effectiveness in developing the personal relationship necessary to work across some cultural boundaries.
- They are effective and efficient in conveying basic information.

There are also differences. Written communications, such as letters and reports, often are more carefully prepared and are considered more formal when sent by fax or post than when sent via e-mail. Because these media are more familiar, they are also easier to use. Faxes are also more versatile than e-mail: any printed material can be sent, including letters, reports, diagrams, spreadsheets, financial statements, etc. Written communications are at times preferred because of their distinctive, personalized impact. The late Roberto Goizueta, former chairman and chief executive of Coca-Cola, reportedly often sent handwritten letters to analysts, both challenging them and stating his position in support of his firm.

Cultural differences also influence the use of written communications. For example, Tellabs found that the Finnish prefer written communications over face-to-face interaction. Consequently, whenever possible when communicating with Finland, Tellabs has used letters or faxes (Solomon 1995a).

## Telephone

Interpersonal oral communications enable organizations and people to work to maintain a balance among global efficiencies, local responsiveness, and rapid new information and technology transfer. The daily and weekly telephone conferences cited in earlier chapters are examples of the need for a continuing oral exchange of information among divisions and with a home office.

Telephone communications have the disadvantages of being ineffective where language differences exist, being more costly, requiring working between different time zones, and lacking the added visual dimension arising from supporting nonverbal communications. It is possible, however, to selectively reduce telephone costs by using the Internet and compatible computer links.

Because telephone conversations involve oral conversations, successfully using them in business interactions requires understanding and being sensitive to the cultural differences described in Chapter 10. Telephone conversations have the advantage over e-mail and other written media in that they provide a means of instantly asking for clarification, amplifying points, and pursuing new ideas that arise during the conversation. In this sense, they can be used more effectively than written communications to develop the personal relationships that provide a basis for working with other cultures. The impact of the cultural factors on oral communications is further explored in the following sections.

## Videoconferencing

Videoconferencing is another way to bridge cultural communication gaps. In contrast to the media already described, it combines vision with interactive voice communications. The format can save considerable travel time and expense in some situations. Videoconferencing is growing in popularity; for example, GE Medical Systems reportedly does 1,000 hours of teleconferencing a year worldwide. Although videoconferencing was originally done over telephone lines, video capabilities have now been built into computers with Internet access.

One problem with videoconferencing, as with telephones, is international time zone differences, since videoconferencing works only when both parties meet at the same time. For example, talking between New York and Singapore (a twelve-hour time difference) requires one party to keep inconvenient business hours. A second problem is availability; at present, facilities are available only in major cities. Although service is increasing, videoconferencing is not yet as widespread worldwide as the telephone. The technology is also relatively new and costly, but the problems may lessen as computer video capabilities are enhanced (Himowitz 1998).

Although inferior to face-to-face exchanges, videoconferencing is superior to telephone, fax/postal, and electronic media because it permits body language communication and enables multilevel interaction, which is important in communicating in some cultures.

### Nonverbal Communication

Nonverbal communication is important in many cultures, especially in those which are more relationship oriented. Since the American culture depends largely on verbal communications, this is an area with which many Americans are unfamiliar.

The Japanese, in contrast, depend not just on words but also on gestures, body language, and the use of silence and personal space to convey information. Information can be conveyed by status in those cultures where status is important. In order to participate and benefit from such information flows, one must first understand them. When Japanese and Americans communicate, for example, it is likely that the Americans will be communicating mostly verbally, while their counterparts will be communicating on many levels.

Differences need to be learned culture by culture. For example, handshakes may be forceful and vigorous in the United States, limp in Asia, and quick in Europe. In Southeast Asia, direct eye contact should be avoided until you know someone well, but the French like to look directly and intently into one's eyes. Mexicans will want to embrace at the end of a successful meeting, as will Central and Eastern Europeans. Touching the side of one's nose in Italy indicates distrust, and in some cultures, beckoning with the palm is considered polite while beckoning with the forefinger is considered impolite.

These are all examples of the messages that nonverbal communication can convey in cross-cultural business situations.

### *Using an Interpreter or Translator*

In situations in which language fluency is insufficient to communicate orally face-to-face, an interpreter is needed. A translator is one who translates written communications.

When affordable, it helps to have an interpreter familiar with your situation. An interpreter can function as a partner in furthering your goals through the subtleties of language handled by one familiar with the other culture. In addition, the interpreter should possess any special skills that may be needed, such as familiarity with the industry or subject matter.

A person communicating through an interpreter should always talk and look directly at the person one is talking with, not at the interpreter. Moreover, speaking in complete units of thought assists the interpreter in communicating (interpreting) the *ideas* behind the words rather than just translating word by word. The most exciting aspect of using an interpreter is the time it gives one to rethink ideas as one observes the listeners' reactions to the interpreter. It is possible to switch paths, rephrase, rethink, and reinforce an idea when the pace is slowed by the interpretation process.

### *Face-to-Face: Negotiations*

Although face-to-face communications are effective and often preferred, they are not always possible due to cost and time limitations. When they are used, careful attention should be paid to cultural differences to maximize the benefits of the meetings. This section will focus on one of the key face-to-face situations during which cultural factors have a major impact and where business is most often affected—business negotiations.

Intercultural negotiation consists of four major processes: preparing for the negotiation; establishing rapport; exchanging information; and persuading. This list is not unlike the negotiating process anywhere in the world. However, the way the process is carried out will vary depending on the cultures, business tasks, time frame and stage of negotiations, and people involved.

The purpose of the negotiation should be determined when *preparing for the negotiation*. Whether the negotiation concerns price, joint ventures, distribution contracts, or any other business purpose, both sides should agree on the objective. During cross-cultural negotiations, subjects should be brought up in a culturally appropriate way. For example, Americans tend to move more quickly than Japanese, who need more time to get acquainted. Negotiators from non-Western cultures may withdraw from negotiations if they interpret the American fast-paced time frame as excessive pressure.

Nonverbal communications are also important. These include seating arrangements, dress codes, and the presentation style—often indicators of status in other cultures. Protocols can communicate messages such as a willingness to make concessions (for example, informal dress communicates this in some cultures). The number of participants and who participates involve other cultural differences—the Japanese tend to prefer larger negotiating teams and often vary the members from meeting to meeting; in the Arab culture, senior members may attend only the first and last sessions.

*Establishing rapport* means different things in different cultures. Americans value directness and are action- and task-oriented. Therefore, they tend to focus directly on the task and give less emphasis to establishing personal relationships. They also consider time schedules important. The Japanese and Latin Americans will spend more time in establishing a relationship, even to the point of mixing socially outside the workplace.

*The exchange of information* will also vary by culture. The Japanese may seek detailed information and ask for in-depth explanation, clarification, justification, and evaluation, and so involve technical people. For others, for example in Latin America, this may be the least important step. Instead, the time will be used to develop personal trust as a contingency base for final decisions.

*Persuasion* is the most important phase for Americans who often present offers directly, with time pressures indicating that the deal is not open-ended but rather will be a lost opportunity if not accepted quickly. The Japanese often work quietly to persuade behind the scenes, not openly.

As seen from these brief examples, different cultures respond in different ways to each negotiation phase. There are many more examples. In Asia, the age of negotiators makes a difference, with younger negotiators automatically considered to be less experienced. Women are not accorded the same respect and position as men in Latin America, Spain, or Arab countries, so they are not good choices to lead a negotiating team in those countries. The list of potential problem areas is long, and the list that applies to the country being dealt with should be studied before negotiations begin.

Everything that has been discussed is well-known to managers. Many people are experienced in these processes, to the point that at times the parties can play roles, manipulate perceived cultural differences, and play off expectations created by just such cultural discussions as the one here. Negotiators will sometimes falsely claim that they lack the authority to make a decision, invent last-minute time restraints to extract last-minute concessions, and provide an unpleasant negotiating environment. These ploys do not have to be accepted or tolerated. Ultimately, each situation dictates its own scenario and breaking rules or calling bluffs as judged appropriate, at times, is the best solution.

## SUMMARY

This chapter has discussed managing human resource enablers—the people and processes that get things done and get results from three perspectives. First, the staffing of an organization was discussed. This major enabler involved: getting people who do the work, triumphing over difficult circumstances, handling emergencies, meeting deadlines no matter what, satisfying customers one by one, adapting to changing competition, and generally making the future happen. Second, ways to support this staff by training and development were discussed from several viewpoints, including training and development methods and environments. Managing these two processes in balanced, contingent ways appropriate for the specific situation at hand was also covered. Third, communications, the lubricant that makes these processes work and helps get these tasks done well, was discussed. Communications is an all-encompassing facility that impacts significantly on leadership and management.

## REVIEW QUESTIONS

1. Discuss the importance of staffing to multinational management.
2. Identify the key factors involved in staffing multinational businesses at all levels of management in both wholly owned subsidiaries and strategic alliances.
3. Describe Gillette's approach to staffing its organization. Compare that approach to those used by other multinational companies. Describe the factors which account for any differences. Describe some of the problems encountered by these companies.
4. From the experiences described in question three, develop some contingent guidelines for which approach works in which type of multinational situation. Pay particular attention to the special factors affecting smaller multinational firms and ways they might be overcome.
5. Discuss the various methods and approaches that can be used to prepare managers for international assignments and workers for assignments to international teams.
6. Describe steps that can be taken to ease the repatriation of a manager who returns from an overseas assignment to work in his or her home country.
7. Describe the different training methods and approaches used and situations in which each is likely to work. Cite specific examples of the ways that training and development approaches are varied from country to country and culture to culture.

8. Describe the different kinds of communication media used and the multinational situations in which they may or may not be effective.
9. Discuss some of the special communication considerations involved in negotiations. Cite specific examples.

### *EXERCISES*

1. Based on your research, select a company which has developed a program for handling multinational staffing situations. Describe their approach and the lessons you learned from it.
2. Select a multinational company that has encountered staffing problems. Identify the situation factors which led to the problems.
3. Using material in Chapter 10, discuss ways in which communication media used will vary in effectiveness by country and culture.
4. Select a company that had problems with one of its strategic alliances and had to renegotiate one or more aspects of the alliance. Describe the experience and how the lessons learned would help in better handling a newly proposed alliance.

# PART IV:
# INTEGRATIVE PERSPECTIVES

# Chapter 13

# Enabling Multinational Strategic Alliances

Because of the difficulties involved in working across cultures, the need for new knowledge and capabilities, and the speed of competitive market change, strategic alliances have become a major enabling mechanism in multinational business (Mockler 1999). Such alliances can involve all of the processes, tasks, activities, decisions, and actions discussed in this book, and therefore, provide an integrative perspective for discussion.

*Webster's Dictionary* defines *strategic* as "important" and *alliance* as "association of interests." In multinational businesses, *strategic alliances,* or important associations formed to further common interests, can include franchising and licensing agreements, partnership contracts, equity investments in new or existing joint ventures, and consortiums.

Strategic alliances are well-known tools widely used by multinational managers. For example, of the more than 167,000 foreign-funded investments in China in the mid-1990s, 64 percent were joint ventures and 15 percent were cooperative partnerships. In the auto industry, more than 250 alliances have been created; in the airline industry, the number exceeds 300. The question is not whether multiple partnerships and joint ventures should be used, but rather how to develop and manage them effectively. Strategic alliances are important both to domestic and multinational firms—firms using them have higher return-on-investment and equity on average, for example (Harbison 1997a,b,c)—and to the economies of the countries involved.

Strategic alliances can facilitate the quicker adaptation of global frameworks to diverse local requirements. For example, Gillette makes and markets some of the world's best-known global brands and products, and has technologically advanced information systems. The desire to expand rapidly worldwide has led Gillette to use strategic alliances, an effective way to move quickly into different countries in an adaptive, flexible way. Hundreds of multinational firms have done the same. Companies often use strategic alliances to quickly establish a comprehensive package of enablers, including marketing and production, organization, financial and accounting, and telecommunications/information systems/Internets, as well as to acquire both knowledge and overseas linkages in these areas.

This chapter discusses the nature and types of strategic alliances; ways in which they are useful in multinational management; how to plan, negotiate, and structure alliances; and ways to organize and manage them successfully over the long-term.

## *NATURE OF STRATEGIC ALLIANCES: CONTINUING PARTNERSHIPS*

The term "strategic alliance" is often used to describe types of cooperative partnerships and joint ventures among firms in different countries (Mockler 1999). Strategic alliances have three distinguishing characteristics.

- Two or more entities unite to pursue a set of important agreed-upon goals while to some degree or in some way remaining independent subsequent to the formation of an alliance.
- The partners share the benefits of the alliance and control over the performance of assigned tasks (perhaps the most distinctive characteristic of alliances, and the one that makes them so difficult to manage).
- The partners contribute on a continuing basis in one or more key strategic (that is, important to them) areas, for example, technology, products, etc.

Although the definition is simple, there are many kinds of alliances and many ways to manage them. When alliances cross national borders, many cross-cultural complexities impact on their effectiveness. Success, therefore, depends on contingent thinking and entrepreneurial skills, as well as personal chemistry, to resolve the many problems that arise. This is especially true as new forms of alliances are created, for example, those involving the Internet and mobile phone technologies.

Understanding strategic alliances also requires understanding what they are not. Mergers and acquisitions are not considered strategic alliances, nor are wholly-owned subsidiaries of multinational corporations, because they do not involve two or more independent firms sharing benefits and control over a continuing time period. An agreement through which a firm grants a license for using technology in exchange for a royalty is not considered a strategic alliance unless there is continuing contribution and control among two or more independent firms.

The essential concept of sharing control and management on a *continuing* basis is what makes managing strategic alliances such a difficult, and demanding task. The concept is relatively new for many firms. Until the 1980s, Borden, for example, generally resisted entering into joint ventures, preferring to retain 100 percent control over overseas ventures. Other companies, such as GM have insisted on retaining majority control, when feasible, to protect technology, facilitate integration, and simplify management and control. Such attitudes have changed dramatically. In the 1980s and 1990s, GM formed many joint ventures and other major auto firms have combined to form hundreds (Betts and Burt 2000; Burt 2000; Del Garda 2000; Meredith 2000).

Although strategic alliances can be an effective way to grow internationally, many firms, such as Siemens, prefer wholly-owned subsidiaries in countries such as Great Britain and Colombia, which allow 100 percent foreign-firm control. Many firms, especially those in the telecommunications area (Sender 2000), use a mixed strategy involving acquisitions and strategic alliances. The decision about when to use alliances instead of wholly-owned subsidiaries or exporting is discussed in Chapter 5.

## TYPES OF ALLIANCES

Major types of interenterprise relationships are outlined in Figure 13.1. The bracket at the bottom of the figure indicates which types are considered strategic alliances.

As seen in Figure 13.1, there are various types of strategic alliances. In 1952, the REFRAC Technology Development Corporation began *licensing* worldwide patented and trademarked technologies for specialized products and manufacturing processes under such names as Heli-Coil and Bellofram. In addition to the existing products, processes, and trademarks that were patented and registered, the agreements included ongoing updating of product technology, as well as assistance with updating manufacturing technology and knowledge—all characteristics of a continuing franchising alliance arrangement (REFRAC 1996).

International airlines have developed *nontraditional nonequity contractual arrangements,* often among competitors. These are continuing contracts and so are considered strategic alliances. *Co-development partnership alliances* have been formed among car manufacturers in developing combined electric/gas autos, and among companies in the biotechnology area. Such partnerships—among competitors, customers, suppliers, and manufacturers—are becoming common.

To enter Asian markets, Mitsubishi Motors used a variety of alliances. In addition to building a dozen parts and assembly plants throughout Asia, Mitsubishi has currently ten joint ventures there, and others in Australia and New Zealand. These *equity investments in joint ventures* ranged from a 6.7 percent stake in Korea's Hyundai Motor Corportaion, a 16 percent stake in Taiwan's China Motor, to a 32 percent stake in Indonesia's Mitsubishi Kram Yudha.

Another venture, Vina Star Motors—formed with the Vietnamese government and Malaysia's state-owned Perusahan Otomobil Nasional (Pro-

FIGURE 13.1. Types of Interenterprise Collaborative Relationships

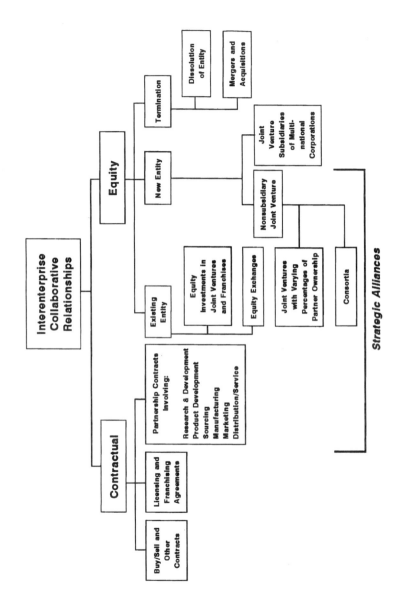

ton)—makes and sells vans in Vietnam. Blockbuster Video has used a *mixed strategy: joint ventures* in countries such as Italy, and *wholly-owned* stores in Britain. Airbus Industrie, described in Chapter 6, is primarily a marketing firm that sells airplanes jointly manufactured by a *consortium of four partners*. The business-to-business (B2B), e-commerce alliances among auto manufacturers to buy parts and supplies discussed later in this chapter is another example of a consortium-type of alliance.

Daewoo's auto group used a different strategy in its effort to become a leading global automaker (in 1994, it ranked twenty-fourth in the world). Between 1994 and 1997, Daewoo moved quickly into Central Europe by investing over $2 billion in *equity-sharing joint ventures*. Daewoo had a *controlling interest* (50.2 to 70 percent) in each of its automobile joint ventures in Poland, the Czech Republic, the former Soviet republics, and Romania. Worldwide, Daewoo had more than 100 alliances with varying interests (ranging from less than 10 to more than 90 percent) in more than forty countries in dozens of industries ("Overseas Projects" 1997). Unfortunately, while its auto group seemed to have survived, Daewoo's other many businesses have not, and the conglomerate was essentially dismantled in late 1999 (Schuman and Lee 1999).

In an effort to penetrate new markets in the former USSR, PepsiCo initially did business through alliances with state-owned firms that controlled production and distribution. In spite of the resulting poor quality products and substandard service, PepsiCo achieved a four-to-one lead over rival Coca-Cola in that region. Since the dissolution of the Soviet Union in 1991, Coke has invested $240 million in Russia. Working through more aggressive local *joint venture* private firms, Coke was able to surpass Pepsi in market share. In 1996, PepsiCo announced plans to invest $550 million in eleven new plants with two private *joint venture* partners to regain its market position.

In 1996, Chrysler entered into a *shared distribution* agreement in Japan. Gillette has entered into many kinds of cooperative distribution/marketing agreements internationally. For example, to reduce national distributor control of pricing in China, Gillette entered into alliances with many regional and local distributors (Mockler 1994-1999).

The final alliance type listed in Figure 13.1 is *dissolution*. Dissolutions occur for many reasons. An alliance begun in 1987 between Ford and Mazda in New Zealand, for example, ended in 1996 because import tariffs declined from 55 percent to 15 percent; cars made in neighboring countries could be made and imported more cheaply than autos made in New Zealand. In addition, the factory in New Zealand needed major capital improvements. At the same time, Ford and Mazda were strengthening their alliances in *parts sharing worldwide* (Nakamoto 1997; Strom and Bradsher 1999). Problems were also encountered in South America where Ford's joint venture with VW was dissolved in part because of the market's growing preference for VW's smaller cars. A major banking alliance in Italy involving Lazard Frères (a French merchant bank) and Mediobank (a Milanese merchant bank) was dissolved in 1999 because of increased competition from international lending firms with superior technology and larger cash reserves (Rossant 1999).

Alliance terminations are not always voluntary. China has moved at times to dissolve alliances in a way that deprived investors of the major investment gains, only returning their original investments plus a small gain (Valance 2000). Political risks are a major factor in determining alliance success.

## THE NEED FOR AND USE OF STRATEGIC ALLIANCES

Strategic alliances are, for many reasons, useful as a method or enabler for multinational growth. First, global competition has increasingly intensified. Meeting rising global competitive demands requires new capabilities, resources, multinational linkages, access to supplies and markets, and knowledge. Second, firms often are restrained by limited resources. Third, the magnitude and speed of change worldwide is accelerating, especially as consumers' tastes change and technologies advance. Fourth, within this global context, diverse multinational factors must be integrated and managed. Fifth, strategic alliances are required by law and are therefore a mandatory method of entering and doing business in many countries. These factors and trends are forcing firms to learn and adapt rapidly, and to develop entrepreneurial approaches to strategic management.

Strategic alliances are one key way to meet changing worldwide competitive market requirements. They can help a firm develop multiple linkages across many countries quickly and simultaneously. As discussed on p. 21 in Chapter 1, Rupert Murdoch, chairman and owner of a 30 percent controlling interest in the Australian-based News Corporation, described his firm's objective as to marry the News Corporation programs with the means to distribute them worldwide.

To achieve this objective rapidly, from 1995 through 1997, Murdoch entered into billion dollar partnerships in the United States, Europe, Latin America, and Asia. In no instance has his company worked alone. If he succeeds with his plan, his worldwide media operation will contribute greatly to the growing globalization trend Murdoch is responding to and taking advantage of.

Airlines, even competing ones, often use strategic alliances. In September, 1995, Delta Air Lines received approval and antitrust immunity to further its partnership with Austrian Airlines, Sabena Airlines, and Swissair. This relationship was expanded in 1997 and 1999 with the addition of Air

France and a joint venture of Swissair's and Sabena's operational departments. In 2000, Delta announced an alliance with Air France, Aeromexico, and Korean Air (Hall 1999; Trivedi 2000). Similar immunity was also granted to an alliance of United Airlines, Lufthansa, Air Canada, Scandinavian Airlines, and Thai Airways International. The immunity allows the airlines to go beyond integrating passengers on selected flights; it also permits them to integrate flight schedules, marketing plans, and sales promotions to compete with major worldwide airlines. At times, major alliances can be the first step toward a merger, as with KLM and Alitalia in 1999 (Skapinger 1999c).

Strategic airline alliances allow the partner airlines to function as one carrier without investing in one another. The firms remain separate. Such alliances are not always easy to manage, however, as seen in the disputes between KLM and Northwest and between KLM and Continental Airlines. Alliances often encounter difficulties arising from government regulations (Skapinger 1999a) and changing company needs, leading to frequent partner changes (Skapinger 1999b). This alliance consolidation activity has raised fears of monopolistic control which could lead to higher prices and diminishing services, and so has caused governments, such as the United States, to explore greater regulation of the industry (Zuckerman 2000).

Automobile firms have formed joint ventures with competitors, noncompetitors, potential competitors, and suppliers. In early 1997, for example, VW and GM announced joint venture plans to make cars in Russia with Central European, Finnish, and Swedish partners. In 2000, GM, VW, Honda, Toyota, Ford, and Fuji Heavy Industries were discussing an Internet-based business-to-business buying alliance which was projected to make $250 billion in purchases annually, a major strategic initiative (Shirouzu 2000; White and Warner 2000).

The Airbus consortium was formed so that European countries could gain the critical resource mass needed to compete with Boeing/McDonnell Douglas. Coca-Cola used joint ventures to establish its position quickly in Russia and Central Europe. In 1999, Deutsche Bank was using strategic alliances with local partners instead of major mergers to expand in Europe to avoid the political backlash generated by aggressive expansion (Harnischfeger 1999). Citigroup bought controlling interest in Poland's top corporate bank, Bank Handlowy, for $1 billion in early 2000 (Wagstyl and Bobinski 2000). In Europe in 1999, smaller telecommunications and media firms scrambled to join alliances to cover the costs of switching to digital and pay-per-view TV, and of marketing integrated bundles of TV, telephone, and Internet services (Tagliabue 1999). Also in mid-1999, the French publisher, Hachette, entered an alliance with Pacific Publications of Australia to publish *Elle* and *Elle Cuisine* (Hachette) in Australia and New Zealand (Robinson 1999).

Governments worldwide have used strategic alliances with multinational businesses in many ways: to privatize state-owned companies while continuing to profit from and to some degree control the businesses; to attract capital while at the same time nurturing local businesses; to bring technology to their country; and, especially in developing countries, to improve overall economic performance quickly without relinquishing control of local businesses to foreign operators.

As an example, in 1997, the Bolivian government privatized SAMAPA, its capital's water supply company, through a joint venture consortium dominated by a subsidiary of Argentina's Comercial del Plata and Lyonnaise des Eaux of France. The new owners invested $360 million in upgrading facilities ("La Paz in Water Sell-off" 1997). Hungary brought in two joint venture partners, Ameritech and Deutsche Telekom, when Matav, Hungary's state telephone company, was privatized. This multibeneficial arrangement enabled Hungary, which retained an interest in the new joint venture firm, to continue to participate in profits from the business, to acquire capital from the percentage of Matav it sold, and to introduce advanced telecommunications technology into the country (Naik 1997).

By 1997, non-Hungarians controlled close to 50 percent of Hungary's state-owned banking assets, and buying was continuing. Belgian, German, Austrian, Irish, American, French, and Japanese financial firms all had established some form of joint venture or equity investment with Hungarian state-owned banks.

> All this foreign money has been a boon for Hungarian consumers and companies, as investors inject fresh capital and know-how into the system, roll out new products and push lending rates to record lows. Compared to the debt-ridden state of most Hungarian banks just five years ago, the transformation is stunning. (Reed 1997, p. A18)

Not all companies or governments need strategic alliances. Citibank, for example, has expanded successfully in Asia on its own, both because of the nature of the banking business and because of its supporting computer and telecommunications technologies. In contrast to Hungary, state-owned banks in Estonia, a Baltic state with little foreign-bank competition, are prospering (over 11 percent annual growth) because a thriving economy is providing a well-regulated, open trading environment (Thornhill 1997). Industry, market, and company requirements, therefore, not only dictate the type of strategic alliances used—they also dictate whether alliances are needed.

Determining whether and how to use multinational strategic alliances, and how best to carry them out, involves many tasks: determining strategic fit; negotiating strategic alliances; selecting compatible partners; determining the type and structure of strategic alliances to enable an effective operational fit; and making multinational strategic alliances work.

## DETERMINING STRATEGIC FIT

As seen from the discussions in the preceding section, each firm has specific needs that dictate whether and how alliances might be useful in implementing its strategic framework. The role of alliances within a firm's strategic framework depends on many factors. For example, strategic alliances played an integral role in Motorola's enterprise-wide strategic framework, which emerged over a twenty-year period as the firm responded to changing market conditions. From its inception in 1928, through 1975, Motorola focused on consumer electronics products such as radios, TVs, and semiconductors. But global competition in the mid-1970s, especially from Japanese firms, made serious inroads into its two core businesses: radio/communications products and semiconductors. Motorola revised its strategy in the late 1970s. First, it decided to become a global company, like its competitors. Second, it decided to move into application areas served by its core businesses.

Motorola's major competitors were diversified and worldwide—Philips, Siemens, and NEC, Toshiba, and Hitachi (Japan) in semiconductors, and NEC, Matsushita, and Fujitsu (Japan) and L.M. Ericsson (Sweden) in communications. Motorola was at a disadvantage because these firms already had major overseas operations and could sell to their own diversified divisions. These competitors also had the resources to develop technologies capable of making Motorola's technologies obsolete. In addition, the market focus for sophisticated high-tech products had shifted to the Far East, so Motorola needed to establish a presence there among major users of its products. These competitive market shifts threatened Motorola's growing product line of microprocessors (a category of semiconductors).

Given Motorola's limited resources, the solution to these competitive disadvantages in design, research, development, and user access was for Motorola to form closer ties with users. The need to move quickly, as well as resource limitations, the high cost of high-tech development, and the need to gain access to the Japanese firms which were major markets for microprocessor and other semiconductor products suggested that alliances would be a key survival strategy. Motorola provides an integrated example of a multinational firm using alliances to leverage resources, enter markets rapidly, gain access to customer markets, meet legal requirements, and acquire advanced technology.

Motorola has used alliances extensively in Japan. In the late 1970s, Motorola had a *licensing agreement* that allowed NEC and Hitachi to build low-end microprocessors using Motorola's technology. This allowed Motorola to enter the microprocessor market in Japan without a large capital investment at a time when Motorola did not have adequate financial resources. The Japanese partners later used Motorola's technology to become direct competitors, an ever-present danger in strategic alliances. This was an expensive learning experience for Motorola about the need to protect technology from competitors' cannibalization.

Because Japan's *keiretsu* system at that time promoted favoritism among domestic companies and often locked out foreign companies, Motorola also entered into several *joint ventures* with Japanese firms to obtain market access to Japanese firms that used its semiconductors. Its most significant joint venture with Toshiba in 1986, was a joint manufacturing firm called Tokoku Semiconductor Corporation. This deal also allowed Toshiba and Motorola to share technologies and the investment burden.

Motorola also *exports* to Japan from the United States, a market-entry strategy that does not necessarily involve strategic alliances. Because of the Japanese market's uniqueness, Motorola also established a *wholly-owned subsidiary* in Japan named Nippon Motorola Ltd. Through this subsidiary, Motorola built a wafer fabrication plant and planned to build a factory to produce logic integrated circuits. Production commenced in 1999.

Motorola's decision to enter another major market, China, was based on the expectation that China's 1.2 billion population will be one of the largest, fastest-growing markets in the twenty-first century. Motorola also has used a variety of alliance and entry strategies there, all tailored to China's market requirements.

Motorola's success in China prior to 1997 was due largely to its superior products and services. Motorola also benefited from its long-term relationship with the Chinese government. For example, when Motorola worked with Chinese suppliers, such as the Tianjin Optical & Electrical Communication Corporation, it spent considerable time helping this firm and other suppliers improve quality and management practices (Guyot 1999). For a short time, Motorola fell behind in product development, but regained its leadership position worldwide by early 2000 (Crockett 2000).

Less rethinking of the strategic framework was needed at Gillette, as its strategic thrust gradually became worldwide. Gillette was a well-focused firm, although it did expand for a time beyond personal-care products. Gillette's strengths were its leading technology, superior resources, and worldwide brand leadership. Alliances were important to Gillette in several areas. First, countries such as China required joint ventures for overseas firms to operate there. Second, joint ventures were becoming necessary for marketing and distribution in many places—the European Economic Union countries, for example. Third, in controlled emerging economies, adequate free-market infrastructures for distribution, promotion, and sales did not exist because governments generally purchased all products.

Alliances were essential elements of Motorola's, Airbus', and News Corporation's enterprise-wide strategies, but in a different way for each company. Alliances for Gillette were, in contrast, effective and necessary business unit enablers (for organizing, marketing, and managing) in selected geographic areas. For example, Gillette's Shanghai joint venture plant, like many of its other plants around the world, has used local cooperative distributor alliances to ensure mass distribution of Gillette's products. In this sense, strategic alliances were used more by Gillette at the business unit level and not as much at the enterprise-wide level as at Motorola. Like Motorola, Gillette learned through experience. On at least one occasion, Gillette found it necessary to restructure a joint venture manufacturing operation because of shifts in market demand and growth patterns. In planning an alliance strategy, therefore, each company should initially reexamine its strategic framework to determine the exact role of alliances, especially in relation to other available market-entry/operating approaches.

In 1996, the Raisio Group, a fifty-seven-year old, farmer-owned firm in a small Baltic Sea village in Finland, was deciding whether and/or how to use strategic alliances to exploit a new margarine it had developed. The margarine, Benecol, contains a pine tree extract that medical testing has determined controls and lowers cholesterol levels in the bloodstream. Demand for the product has been so great that the company built a new factory to increase production and begin overseas sales.

Raisio faced many decisions. First, it had to explore a possible link with a large European or U.S. partner with worldwide marketing capabilities. Second, it had to find new sources of sitostanol, the key ingredient in Benecol, because five tons of waste pulp must be processed at paper mills to distill one pound of the oil that is turned into sitostanol. Third, Benecol would have to undergo testing by regulatory agencies in the United States and in European countries. Fourth, a number of competitive products have been shown to be equally effective.

Within this context, the Raisio Group explored the place of strategic alliances within its existing strategy, and debated how it would structure, negotiate, and manage multinational alliances if it chose to expand overseas with its limited resources (Ipsen 1997). In 1997, the firm announced an alliance with McNeil Consumer Products, a division of Johnson & Johnson (United States), for the use of Benecol in McNeil products (Molvor 1997). In 1997, Raisio announced a joint venture agreement with Westvaco Corporation (a U.S. paper firm) to build a joint venture plant in South Carolina to make sterol, a substance used in paper production and another key ingredient of Benecol (Bloomberg Business News 1997).

Strategic alliances are also important in the e-commerce area, especially when they involve traditional companies which lack the required e-business knowledge and experience. For example, in 2001, Swiss Re, one of the world's largest insurance groups, was exploring plans to enter the U.S. insurance market through Internet-based online selling. To do this, a relatively risky strategy given the difficulty of selling insurance online, Swiss Re would focus on simple strategies and consider working through a joint venture with a firm with technical expertise and experience with insurance selling in the United States.

This type of strategic need is expected to be a dominant stimulator of strategic alliance usage, since they do fulfill a major need of existing traditional companies. Internet companies have extended their presence into traditional businesses in many industries, including retailing, financial services, and mail-order marketing, very often through strategic alliances. In addition, a large number of the business-to-business Internet ventures are essentially domestic and international strategic alliances, as was discussed earlier in this chapter.

A strategic reassessment, similar to those described at Gillette, Motorola, and Raisio, helps companies create a more detailed alliance strategy. Such a reassessment can be done by examining an enterprise's operations from different viewpoints:

- Analyzing and evaluating each of the firm's key activities to determine which ones could safely be done by, or shared with, other firms. In the News Corporation situation, both the programming and broadcasting activities were of value, but could be shared effectively with alliance partners so that each partner could learn from the other.
- Specifying which aspects of the activities could be done through alliances while protecting technologies that were competitive advantages. In Gillette's situation, distribution functions and the manufacturing of cheaper, older model razors and blades could be shared. Because the manufacturing technologies involved in its new Sensor razors and blades were substantial competitive advantages, Sensors were manufactured outside of China and imported for sale.
- Studying ways to leverage other firms' resources synergistically. The capital of four major companies and the influence of major governments were initially required for Airbus to perform the research and development needed to design and manufacture competitive commercial aircraft.
- Preparing for the possibility that an alliance may fail. Mitsubishi, for example, maintained multiple sources of parts supplies so that it did not have to depend on any one.
- Preparing contingency plans for new kinds of alliances that will not be limited by existing alliances. For example, Whirlpool crafted each alliance in a way that enabled it to move into other product and geographic areas.

Strategic management at all levels—including enterprise-wide rethinking, crafting a business strategy and creating an alliance structure, selecting partners, staffing, operational planning, and management and leadership activities—requires situation background studies. In addition to the factors identified in Chapter 4, a number of factors have special relevance for successfully planning and managing multinational alliances. These include:

- The type and structure of the alliance, dictated by the kind of business and the companies involved
- The alignment of strategic frameworks and corporate cultures among partners
- The importance of the alliance to the competitive success of all partners
- The relative contribution of partners
- The compatibility, flexibility, and adaptability of the partners involved
- Clearly defining shared activities and identifying potential conflicts with other business areas of the partners
- Available protection of proprietary knowledge
- The ability to precisely measure each partner's contribution
- The cost and difficulty of measuring and controlling activities and contributions over time
- Comparable levels of management and worker knowledge and expertise of the people involved
- Major cultural differences
- External factors such as government intervention and control, industry practices, local market and competitive differences, government stability, new competition in markets, etc.

The following sections provide additional examples of how these factors can affect strategic alliance decisions and actions, beginning with the negotiation process.

As seen from the company experiences described earlier, a proposed alliance should meet the following criteria:

- The alliance must add value; that is, it must be worth more to a company to enter an alliance than to go it alone.
- The company must learn something from the alliance.
- The company must protect competencies while interacting with the alliance over a continuing period of time.
- The firm must retain flexibility and not be overly reliant on any one partner.

## *NEGOTIATING STRATEGIC ALLIANCES*

An alliance's structure emerges from the negotiation process, which is often complex and can extend over a long time period. For example, the negotiation process GM went through in trying to put together a billion-dollar joint venture in China was long, complex, and without a predetermined script (Naughton, Engardio, and Roberts 1995). GM's China strategy evolved over the years. GM first ventured into China in 1992 (in pickup truck manufacturing) and 1993 (in parts making). GM's strategy was based on the enterprise-wide need to become a major presence in a Chinese market of 1.2 billion people, and to use China as a stepping stone into the rest of Asia (Simison 1999).

In 1996, the firm established a $1 billion luxury car/minivan joint venture with Shanghai Motors. GM was able to make the deal because it agreed to share technology, not just in automobile manufacturing but also in electronics (through its Hughes Electronics division) and in computer technology (at the time, its Electronic Data Systems unit). A similar technology-sharing approach has been used by Motorola, AT&T, and Daimler-Benz. In addition, GM benefited from having a high-level female executive who was born in Shanghai (Stern 1995).

Even with concessions and connections, success is still uncertain. For example, after lengthy negotiations, Chrysler lost a billion dollar deal with the Chinese government to Daimler-Benz, mainly because Daimler-Benz offered to share technology. General Motors had problems with its pickup truck operation when its Chinese partners decided to renegotiate the deal after the plant was completed and operations were about to begin.

In another situation, a major international firm that had one joint venture in China in 1996 was planning four more. Based on its experience, the firm assumed that at least two years would be needed to complete each deal. Complexities arose because the deals involved supply contracts with local companies, facilities that need upgrading, labor contracts that need renegotiation, compliance with worldwide environmental codes and waste disposal regulations, and major labor force reductions. In this situation, technology was not a problem—advanced technologies were not involved, and therefore, plants would be able to use existing technology. After two years of negotiation, American Airlines and British Airways abandoned their proposed alliance due to unresolvable competitor and government objections (Skapinger 1999a).

## SELECTING COMPATIBLE PARTNERS

Selecting a partner for a strategic alliance can involve selecting both the company (private, state-owned, former state-owned, government-linked) and, in some instances, the people, especially where smaller firms are involved. Coca-Cola attributed much of its success in Central Europe to the type of people and firms it had as partners (Nash 1995). The people were relatively honest and forthright, entrepreneurial, and adaptable to free-market business practices in their privately-owned businesses, and they had abundant innovative ingenuity. These joint venture partner characteristics have proved effective in many cultural settings (de Keijzer 1995). Part of Coca-Cola's success was attributed to the fact that Central European countries, such as Hungary, had a relatively free underground economy in the 1980s and the people generally had resisted communist influence.

Cultural differences can make it difficult to evaluate the personality characteristics and chemistry of potential partners. The Japanese culture, for example, is insular and patently self-protective. Westerners are routinely warned that Japanese businesses often appropriate technology unless ironclad protections are built into an agreement. Such preconceptions can make it difficult to develop trust when dealing with individuals (who may or may not conform to the preconceptions)—a problem—because trust is essential to alliance success. In China, trust is most commonly built on close family ties, which makes nurturing trust there a difficult task for foreigners.

Years of state control in China, Central Europe, and other countries have discouraged entrepreneurial thinking. Many state-owned businesses in these geographic areas are major potential joint venture partners. However, their managers cannot be depended on to think entrepreneurially, even though, in general, China has a long history of entrepreneurship which has grown out of its international trading that goes back many centuries to the "silk road."

When selecting partners, therefore, it is important to distinguish among the many personality types and traits in each culture. Traits within each individual involved should be observed and tested formally as well as informally. For example, Arne J. de Keijzer, a consultant, specializes in prescreening individuals and identifying the forthright, entrepreneurial, innovative, honest, and adaptable characteristics that are likely predictors of effective joint venture partners (de Keijzer 1995).

The negotiation period can be used for observing and gaining a feeling for the traits of the potential partners. When appropriate, personal relations and trust can be cultivated and nurtured at this time. Tambrands Inc., an American tampon manufacturer, followed this approach when negotiating a joint venture in Ukraine. Several years of extensive interactive meetings and negotiations were used by participating partner personnel for getting to know each other and developing working relationships (Emmons 1990-1993). These interpersonal exchanges later provided a basis for helping make the alliance work.

The problems discussed so far are less common in developed countries, where cultural and business traditions are more established. For example, reliable information sources are more readily available in Western countries, which have services such as Dun & Bradstreet's credit reports. But even in these countries, cultural and business practice differences exist. Financial information can be difficult to assess because of different accounting approaches and terminology. The problem is especially severe in emerging countries, where accounting systems are often inadequate and credit rating services are rarely available. This lack of basic information makes the partner selection process more complex, and reliance on the personal characteristics of the people involved even more relevant.

## DETERMINING THE TYPE AND STRUCTURE OF STRATEGIC ALLIANCES

Many of the strategic fit, negotiating processes, and partner selection factors affect the type and structure of a strategic alliance. The type of business is a primary consideration in developing alliance type and structure. For example, a U.S. chemical company had an established Chinese chemical firm as a joint venture partner that not only provided manufacturing facilities which had been part of the Chinese partner's existing chemical complex, but also was designated as the local raw material supplier for the new joint venture. The venture was structured to meet these requirements.

The alliance type and structure also depend on the characteristics of the firms involved: their size, location, core competencies, relative contribution to the alliance, corporate culture, and enterprise-wide strategies. Airbus Industrie is a marketing consortium of four firms whose participation percentage is dictated by their contribution based on their core competencies in the aircraft manufacturing operation. As seen in discussions elsewhere in this book, Internet firms have altogether different business needs and so require an entirely different type of structure.

Not only were Motorola's and Mitsubishi's many alliances different from each other, but the structure and type of each alliance also varied, depending on the different businesses and partner companies involved. Motorola, for example, has used many alliance types over the years to balance, supplement, and integrate existing and needed core competencies.

The alliance's strategic importance to each party is another key factor affecting alliance type and structure. For example, in one venture in Shanghai, the Chinese partner (a municipality) was interested in the business mainly for income—not as a means of extending related businesses. It therefore offered its U.S. partner, a global leader in its field, a two-thirds interest in the venture and allowed it to assume operating control, believing that the U.S. firm knew the business better and so would be able to make it more profitable if left in control. In contrast, the structure of the first foreign-controlled power station formed under a build/operate/transfer joint venture agreement was scheduled to end in sixteen years, with eventual control going to the Chinese power authority, a limit dictated by China's desire to maintain control of such basic services as power generation.

The people involved can affect an alliance's type and structure. For example, Rupert Murdoch's personality had a major impact on the speed at which he moved, the price he paid for deals, and his ability to negotiate and structure deals that suited his partners' needs.

Situations in which the potential for misuse of proprietary technology exists and the partners are not well-acquainted call for much more detailed alliance structures. Motorola failed to protect its technology from cannibalization in its initial licensing agreement in Japan—an expensive mistake. Even when an alliance is structured to provide protection of proprietary knowledge and core company competencies, problems can arise.

In the late 1980s, Durawool Inc. (United States) entered into a joint venture with China Metallurgical Zuhai Sez United. Using Durawool's processes, the venture manufactured the shards of steel wool that have replaced asbestos fibers in automotive brake pads. The venture's output was sold in both the United States and Asia. In the early 1990s, the venture's chief engineer, Zhang Ye, who managed the installation of Durawool's steel wool fiber-making process and so knew it intimately, left the venture and started a competing firm, Sunny Steel Wool Co., Ltd. The legal position was unclear under Chinese law, because Zuhai had signed an agreement prohibiting competitive disclosure and use of the process, but Mr. Zhang had not (Holusha 1996). The laws in emerging countries can differ considerably from those in the United States, and it was argued that Zhang had violated no Chinese laws.

Many firms protect their proprietary technology from partners who are potential rivals by using older but adequate technology. As noted earlier, Gillette protected its technological advantage by making only traditional razor and blade models in an alliance in China. Its newer Sensor products are imported. The contingency nature of multinational strategic management requires negotiation of protective alliance structures that are appropriate for the company, market, partners, and products involved.

Conflicts with other business areas of partners can affect an alliance's structure and type. For example, the benefits of the learning potential in the GM/Toyota alliance in Fremont, California, apparently outweighed the fact that the autos produced were to be sold competitively under both the GM and Toyota brands. The deal was structured to terminate in the 1990s, once the shared learning had reached a logical time limit.

When rethinking enterprise-wide strategic frameworks and formulating business unit strategies, a general vision of what is desired and needed often emerges in stages. As structures and deals are negotiated and defined in detail, precise definitions of strategies emerge. This is the first activity described in the strategic management process outlined in Figure 1.3 (p. 9)— knowing exactly what kind of company is envisioned without knowing precisely what it will look like.

The assessment of an alliance, therefore, continues as circumstances change. This assessment can lead to continually modifying the alliance or even at times, as in the Ford/Mazda alliance in New Zealand discussed earlier, to dissolving it.

As the development process continues, additional alliance structure details are defined. These include: percent of ownership; financing mix; each partner's equipment, technology, and other contributions; division and sharing of activities; staffing; location; autonomy; and controls—both for operations and for measuring and controlling each partner's contributions over time. Guidelines for alliance management are also established. Considerable time may be required, therefore, to develop an alliance structure, and often that structure is not simple. For example, the types of structures generally found in the airline industry are shown in Figure 13.2 (Mockler 1999).

A basic process for selecting an alliance type is outlined in Figure 13.3. This outline is only an introductory learning tool, since the actual process can be very complex. In practice, the best type and structure for a specific alliance is the one which is accepted by all concerned parties and enables managers to improve their chances of getting what they want from necessarily ambiguous relationships. The alliance must fulfill the four basic criteria named earlier in this chapter: add value, enable learning, protect and enhance core competencies and competitive advantages, and enable flexibility.

## *MAKING MULTINATIONAL STRATEGIC ALLIANCES WORK: MANAGING AND LEADING*

Planning is useful, but plans do not ensure success because planning involves the unpredictable future, where many uncertain factors affect successful outcomes. Entrepreneurial adaptability, flexibility, and contingency thinking are, therefore, needed to reconcile and balance diverse, conflicting, or even paradoxical forces affecting alliance success, on a continuing basis.

Managing and leading alliances involves many of the tasks outlined in Figure 1.6 (page 25) and described throughout this text, as well as tasks specific to alliances, described in this chapter. Managing and leading also involves the second strategic management activity listed in Figure 1.3 (p. 00): doing whatever is needed to get the job done, within defined strategic frameworks.

Staffing a multinational strategic alliance includes choosing who will manage the venture and who will manage the interaction among the partners and the venture. A joint venture may be managed by expatriates, locals, or some combination of the two. Management may be one or more employees of the partners, or third-party professionals. The choice depends on the situation.

FIGURE 13.2. Strategic Alliance Type and Structure Decision Situation Diagram: Airline Industry Overview of Decisions to be Made

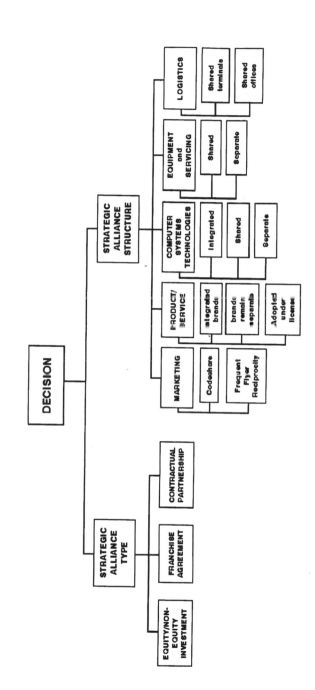

FIGURE 13.3. Decision Situation Overview Diagram: Type of Strategic Alliance

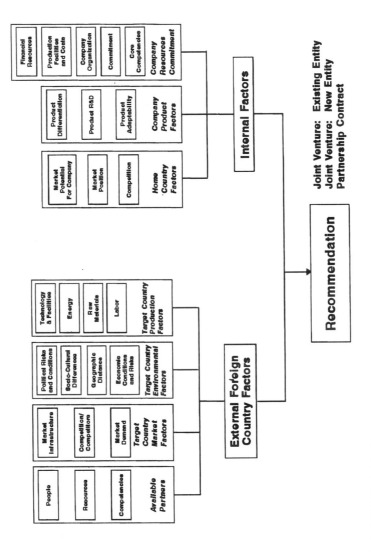

In an optic-fiber venture, the general manager was a newly hired American expatriate with extensive technical experience who had worked overseas and was chosen by the overseas partner; the deputy director (second in command) was chosen by the local partner—its plant manager prior to the venture. In one auto company, two managers, one from the local partner firm and one from the overseas partner, shared decision-making authority. This was done after many problems arose because only one of these managers had previously worked for the overseas partner. Generally, the party with the most expertise in the areas critical to the venture's success will be given the leading management position. Ideally, needs and qualifications should guide staffing choices, and as many locals as possible should be included on the staff. Extended examples of how different firms have handled multinational staffing and the general processes involved in staff selection are discussed in Chapter 12.

When special expertise is needed, many multinational firms form temporary teams. The team's assignment might include, as discussed in Chapters 11 and 12, joint research and new product development, building chemical plants, installing machinery, introducing marketing programs, or initiating training programs.

Communications are important in many strategic alliance management activities. The partners in one manufacturing joint venture had weekly telephone conferences involving the partners and the joint venture management. An agenda and supporting information were circulated a week before each conference. A typical conference lasted about two hours and covered exceptions and special operating problems, as well as progress on planned programs. Annual face-to-face meetings were held in different regions to support and reinforce the almost daily use of e-mail. The communications media available, and additional company experiences in using them, are discussed in Chapter 12.

Integration problems often arise from weaknesses in staffing and communications. For example, in one situation, problems arose when a junior executive was appointed one partner's liaison manager. The problem was resolved when a senior manager with international experience took over the job. In another instance, problems arose during the dealings between the overseas partner's shipping department and the joint venture factory. These problems were resolved after training sessions were conducted and the personnel involved made extended visits to each other's sites.

Top management at each partner needs to carefully introduce the nature, scope, and importance of the alliance to everyone involved. It is also important to identify areas of interaction among the parties and to provide time and money to introduce all parties to the new working requirements. After the merger of two advertising agencies, Publicis (France) and Foote, Cone & Belding (United States), managers devoted two years to continuing top management visits to all branches to explain, promote, and operationally integrate the venture (Applbaum and Yatsko 1993). Even then it failed, largely because of management and client conflicts.

At the same time that management encourages integration, it should also encourage autonomy and independence. For example, two joint ventures initially wanted to have new computer systems installed—systems similar to those at their overseas partner's firms. Each venture also wanted its overseas partner to pay the $5 million installation cost. In both instances, the overseas partner let the joint venture develop its own system and finance the new system out of its own budget. This was done for two reasons: first, it enabled each venture to tailor its system to its specific needs; second, it reinforced the policy that the venture was independent and had to survive on its own.

Managing an alliance involves many activities discussed in this text. For example, joint ventures in China and Russia have been observed to be moving toward adopting current Western interactive organizations and management styles. The flat, circular, interactive organization forms presented in Chapter 9 were drawn from multinational joint venture experiences. These ventures had managers who reinforced the interactive atmosphere on a daily basis. For example, at one joint venture firm, during a session when a new information system was being developed and introduced, the general manager, through a kind of Socratic questioning dialogue, encouraged both the systems developer and the plant manager to participate in developing system interfaces jointly and to come up with their own solution—that is, to take ownership of the system and responsibility for making it work. This was especially important because the plant was in an emerging country where workers were accustomed to hierarchical management styles that allowed for little individual initiative.

Competing in a free-market environment requires individuals to have entrepreneurial initiative to respond to rapidly changing needs. This initiative is developed mainly through daily reinforcement during management/ worker interaction. In this sense, successfully leading multinational strategic alliances requires a change in management mind-set.

Bridging cultural differences is a continuing management activity in strategic alliances, both within the alliance and among alliance partners. It requires collaboration and compromise. Chapter 10 provides additional examples of, as well as practical guidelines for, managing multicultural differences.

Top management—both at the alliance and the partner firms—ultimately has the responsibility to create cooperation and trust, and to provide the enablers needed to make the alliance work. John Mumford, at British Petroleum, and Samuel Hearne, at Shell Italia, have described their experiences in reaching down into the firm to draw out untapped human resources waiting to make major contributions (Forbes III et al. 1995; Murray 1997). Such a process requires someone to keep taking the small success steps that help create momentum using a collaborative leadership style.

At the same time that the free flow of information is encouraged and a supportive enabling environment is fostered through abundant use of electronic media, attention must be paid to controlling the alliance (Das and Teng 1998). For example, the information exchange must be monitored to protect the core competencies of each partner. Technology transfer can be limited by having proprietary products manufactured at non-joint-venture locations, by having older technology installed at the venture, and/or by having procedures, controls, and limitations specified in joint-venture agreements.

The alliance operation itself must always be monitored. Often, integrated reporting systems are required. At one chemical plant, this was relatively simple because the manufacturing systems were very similar to those used by the United States plant. In addition, the product was sold in large lots through controlled distribution channels. The integration of the reporting systems at the alliance with those of the overseas partner was therefore relatively easy to automate.

Monitoring an alliance is often more difficult at consumer products companies because of the large volume of different kinds of unit sales through various sales and distribution outlets. In addition, many joint ventures involve intercompany division transfers, which must be reported separately to government regulatory groups. In one joint venture, a three-person tax accounting group worked solely on reconciling and administering different government tax reporting systems. In this situation, integration was difficult and manual reformulation and reporting of results to the overseas partner were required.

Each partner's contribution to the alliance should also be monitored. Yoshino and Rangan (1995) provide the following guidelines for doing this:

- First, clearly identify what is to be monitored, break it down into identifiable elements, and measure those elements, such as: delivery dates and performance in meeting them, joint research and development output, or quality standards. Adopt a disciplined approach that not only recognizes but ensures ongoing performance consistency by the partner.
- Second, monitor on an ongoing basis, using whatever time period (daily, weekly, quarterly) is appropriate for the element being measured.
- Third, use both formal and informal methods and involve all affected alliance participants in the process.
- Fourth, be prepared to take whatever steps are necessary to correct problems, acting quickly and diplomatically.

In general, such monitoring serves to continually reassess the alliance, both strategically and operationally. Operating adjustments may be made daily to create maximum profit benefits for all involved. Strategically, careful monitoring can lead to rewriting alliance agreements or even to dissolving the alliance.

## SUMMARY

The diversity of alliance types makes it difficult to develop generalities applicable to all of them, or to fully cover the topic in one chapter. This chapter, therefore, has only given a summary review, covering such topics as: the nature and types of strategic alliances; ways in which they are useful in strategic management; how to plan, negotiate, and structure alliances; and ways to organize and manage them successfully over the long-term.

In one sense, this chapter is a capsule summary of the entire subject of this book, multinational strategic leadership and management, because the tasks involved in strategic alliance management parallel those of multinational strategic management in general, as outlined in Figure 1.3. Alliance strategies must be integrated with each partner's enterprise-wide strategies—the strategic fit. Specific business unit strategies, plans, and programs must be formulated for the alliance itself. The operational fit must be determined, and enablers must be put in place in areas such as marketing and production/operations, information systems, finance and accounting, and organization.

Negotiations can be complex and extend over long periods of time as partners are selected and alliances are structured. Finally, the alliance must be managed and led over time.

Managing multinational alliances is a complex and difficult process for many reasons. Such alliances involve diverse partners, some of whom are competitors or potential competitors with different strategic goals. They function in a multicultural environment, and they often are breaking new ground in many areas: distribution, contract law, leading cultural and business practice change, and helping to create free-market economies. All of this must be done within a rapidly changing, highly competitive, uncertain, and risky multinational context. Managing alliances requires adaptability, innovation, balance, creativity, grit, dedication, persistence, hard work, and some luck.

## REVIEW QUESTIONS

1. Describe the importance of strategic alliances in enabling multinational strategic leadership and management. Give specific examples of the different ways in which they can be important enablers.

2. Identify the nature and characteristics of strategic alliances.
3. Identify and describe the different types of strategic alliances used by multinational corporations, and specific company/country situations in which each type has been useful.
4. Describe the uses of strategic alliances, especially focusing on where they may not be appropriate enablers. Cite specific examples.
5. Describe the process of determining the strategic fit of strategic alliances within a company's enterprise-wide strategy, and the ways in which company needs and other situation factors dictate the type of alliance needed.
6. Discuss the experiences of Motorola in using different types of alliances and describe how Motorola has used alliances to enable its strategy implementation.
7. Discuss the differences among Motorola's use of alliances and that of other companies described in the chapter.
8. Identify the four overall criteria that guide alliance strategy development and selection.
9. Discuss the process involved in negotiating alliances and describe some examples of different ways negotiations are carried out in different company situations.
10. Identify major factors affecting partner selection when formulating strategic multinational alliances.
11. Describe what is involved in creating the appropriate type and structure of an alliance. Give specific examples.
12. Why is it so difficult to manage strategic alliances?
13. Describe the activities involved in managing alliances. Give examples of good and bad approaches and practices.

## EXERCISES

1. Based on your research, select a multinational strategic alliance that was successful. Analyze the factors that led to that success. These factors may include strategic fit, negotiation, partner selection, structure and type selection and development, and management.
2. Based on your research, select a multinational strategic alliance that failed. Analyze the reasons for that failure following the guidelines given in Exercise 1.
3. Based on these two experiences and the material in the chapter, develop your own personal set of guidelines for creating and managing multinational strategic alliances.

# Chapter 14

# Managing Integratively in a Multinational Environment

This final chapter not only covers several additional specific aspects and general perspectives of integrative multinational strategic management in rapidly changing markets, it also provides an integrative summary conclusion for this book.

Many aspects of multinational management have been discussed in this book. These range from the leadership task of formulating enterprise-wide strategic frameworks, to the management tasks involved in translating strategic visions into day-to-day operating realities. Such a view of strategic management is becoming common in Western businesses and is being increasingly adapted by firms in other countries.

Multinational strategic management is a context-specific process; that is, it works from situations to solutions. This process is an application of the entrepreneurial focus of this book. Extensive experience and research (Donaldson 1995, 1996) show that this process is a worldwide common contingency framework in business.

Although multinational management can be broken into segments and modeled as a linear process for discussion purposes, in practice it is not so segmented nor linear. Rather, it is a continuing and iterative integrative process.

A central aspect of multinational management is *managing rapid change,* a subject which is briefly reviewed in the first section (to follow) along with privatization, a key change situation worldwide today. Managing change and diversity in a rapidly changing environment often requires skills in *crisis management, improvisation situation by situation,* and *innovation,* which are discussed next. This chapter also discusses ways in which *small companies* can compete with larger firms multinationally, as well as the *long-term future orientation* of multinational management. The chapter discusses the contingency processes involved in multinational management—*managing diversity within general integrative common concepts and frameworks,* the point and perspective at which this book began. The chapter also discusses how to *continue the learning process* started in this book.

## MANAGING CHANGE

This section briefly reviews some of the perspectives on managing change covered so far. It also focuses on a frequently encountered change activity today—privatization.

### Multinational Change Management

The many aspects of managing change that have been covered in this book include:

- becoming a multinational company,
- meeting changing multinational competitive market needs, and
- ensuring an enterprise's long-term, global, future prosperity.

Chapters 1, 2, and 3 described the experiences of many companies wrestling with change management:

- Jack Welch's proactive, engineered change at General Electric, which illustrates how creative destruction can be used to manage change, the so-called "complexity theory" of management (Brown and Eisenhardt 1998, p. 14)
- Airbus' reactive strategies in responding to changing conditions in the worldwide aircraft manufacturing market, the so-called Darwinian evolutionary change path
- UPS's and FedEx's contrasting methods of entering and operating in China
- Sony's diversification responses to changes in the computer and consumer electronics industries

Chapters 5, 6, and 13 described examples of the ways in which companies met the needs of market entries, modified products to meet local needs, shifted supply sources to meet changing trade patterns, etc. Motorola, for example, used many different entry methods in its successful quest to establish strong market positions in China and Japan.

Chapter 7 discussed that management moves that were made to meet the growing opportunities and threats arising from advances in telecommunications and computer information systems technology (such as the Internet) worldwide. Chapter 8 discussed how finance and accounting systems are useful in meeting the challenges of change. Chapter 9 described the experiences of firms such as France's Alcatel Alsthom, which used an accelerated approach in managing the organization changes needed to meet changing market needs in Europe. Chapter 13 explored the ways companies such as Mitsubishi, with its network of alliances in Asia, used strategic alliances to handle diverse and growing markets. Chapters 10 through 12 discussed further examples of change management, especially those involved in working within the diverse needs of different cultures. These included:

- General Electric in Hungary—changing work habits ingrained over years under communism
- Motorola in Malaysia—trying to introduce work structures that would assist in realizing a new vision by the year 2000
- Tellabs in Germany—opening a new operation using culturally appropriate recruiting approaches

The following section goes beyond and adds a new perspective to these and other discussions of change management, describing several experiences in privatization, a major force driving change worldwide.

### *Privatization*

Privatization is the sale of all or part of a state-owned firm to the public, often through a public stock offering. Privatization occurs worldwide: in 1997 through 2000 privatization was reported in China (Lin and Jacob 2000), Czech Republic (Anderson 2000), the Middle East and North Africa ("Survey" 1998), Poland (Tagliabue 2000), South Africa ("The Painful Privatization 1999), Spain (White 2000), and Venezuela (Colitt 1998). In 1997, Hungary neared completion of its privatization program (Beck 1997) and Israel announced plans to privatize thirteen enterprises (World Wire 1997). Brazil planned to privatize $60 billion of state-owned assets by the year 2000 (World Watch 1998). Finland and Italy have also seen a surge in privatizations (Blitz 1999; Essex 1997). In 1999, even the London under ground transportation system was considering going private, and Costa Rica and Beijing were planning to privatize their airports.

One Chinese city, Zhucheng, reported that it had privatized almost all of its state-owned enterprises successfully. Prior to privatization, two-thirds of the state-owned firms were in the red or just breaking even; after privatization, 272 restructured firms (out of the total of 282) were making a profit, with some doubling it each year. In addition, from 1992 to 1995, economic activity in the city surged 87 percent and tax revenues increased 140 percent (Chen 1996). In 1996, after elections of a new government, Mongolia began privatizing 60 percent of all state property, though the move slowed with the reelection of the communists in 2000 (Kynge 2000; Tomlinson 1998).

A World Bank study of 6,000 firms showed that privatization has contributed greatly to increased productivity (three to five times better in privatized firms than in state-owned firms) in Eastern and Central Europe (Done 1997). In Spain, the privatization of Telephonica led to a major international expansion of its telephone business in Latin America very often through joint ventures, and cost billions of dollars (Tomlinson 1999). Two contrasting approaches to managing change in North and South America initiated in 1989 are described as follows: the privatization of a state-owned oil firm in Argentina and the modernization of one in Mexico (Friedland 1999; Solis and Friedland 1995).

In Argentina, Yacimientos Petroliferos Fiscates SA (YPF) was a vast wasteland of patronage when it was wholly state-owned. In 1995, however, two years after a large segment of the company was sold to the public, YPF's workforce had been reduced to one-tenth of the former size and the firm a was gusher of profits.

Many factors contributed to the YPF's success. By the early 1990s, the Argentinian government had deregulated the energy sector (freeing up pricing and domestic oil trading) and the economy as a whole (exploration properties were thrown open to the highest bidder). Although YPF faced increased competition, governmental privatization moves allowed the firm to sell noncore assets and use the proceeds to boost efficiency. The government also quashed inflation.

YPF hired a charismatic manager, Jose Estenssoro. He first brought in a team of U.S. executives from Hughes Tool Co. as consultants. He renegotiated contracts with independent Argentine producers and consumers that were unfavorable to YPF. In 1993, he raised $2 billion by selling off a third of YPF's oil and gas properties and used the money to modernize YPF's facilities and boost its long-neglected exploration and development program.

Steps were then taken to cut the workforce. First, several union leaders were given control of YPF's large shipping fleet. Other nonessential businesses—an air fleet, hospitals, movie theaters, and supermarkets—were sold to employees on favorable terms. Finally, tens of thousands of workers were granted one-year contracts or laid off with generous severance pay. Remaining employees were promised 10 percent of YPF's equity to ensure that they would remain motivated. Since the firm had been used for political patronage and its plants were environmental disasters, it was not difficult to explain to the public why a privatized, professionally managed firm would be best in the long run for customers, suppliers, most employees, and the country.

After the turnaround was underway, 45 percent of the state's stake in YPF was sold to the public in 1993 for $2.5 billion, which was used to repay debts. In mid-1999, Repsol SA, a Spanish oil, natural gas, and chemical firm, offered $3.4 billion to buy the 85 percent of YPF it did not already own (Vitzthum, Torres, and Bahree 1999).

In contrast, Mexico's Petroleos Mexicanos SA (Pemex) was still owned by the government in 1999. Oil reserves were actually declining because the firm lacked the money needed to find new reserves, and imports of natural gas were increasing, even though Mexico's underdeveloped reserves were among the biggest in the world. Ironically, all of this occurred many years into a program to modernize the company's operations.

In contrast to how workers' unions were handled in Argentina, in 1989, Mexico's President Salinas sent in troops to arrest the YPF union's leader on weapons charges. This show of force inaugurated the modernization program. Some progress has been made. The workforce has been cut in half and some private foreign investors have been allowed to build natural gas pipelines. Mexico, however, has maintained a state energy policy heavy with regulation and skittish about foreign capital. Moreover, in Mexico, considerable antiforeign sentiment still exists.

Considerable work has been done to modernize Pemex, such as rebuilding refineries. The overall results have not matched the results of the privately owned YPF in Argentina, however. In 1998, for example, Pemex lost $1.6 billion. Pemex still ran hospitals, pharmacies, clinics, medical offices, and even schools—services normally run by the state. Its problems of poor maintenance, inefficiency, and ecological contamination were evidenced by protests and by accidents which killed hundreds. Although revenues have been high, most of the profits (close to 60 percent) have gone to the government, leaving little for investment in the firm.

Although it has privatized other state-owned companies—$23 billion worth under an earlier administration but only $240 million since 1994—Mexico has been reluctant to privatize Pemex in spite of its poor performance (Anderson 1996; Dillon 1996).

Privatizations have generally been successful, but some attempts have failed. For example, although Poland announced plans in 1995 to privatize 512 state-owned firms, all were still state-owned in 1997 when a new, ambitious privatization plan was announced and pursued (Michaels 1997; Wright and Bobinski 1999). In early 1997 in the Philippines, court challenges were creating problems for the state's privatization program (Marozzi 1997).

## MANAGING CRISES

Crises can occur at any time in a rapidly changing worldwide environment. They may be triggered by economic events, such as the Mexican peso crisis in 1994, the Russian and Asian financial crises in the late 1990s, and the failure of dozens of e-businesses in early 2001. Crises may be technology related accidents, such as at Chernobyl in the Soviet Union in 1986. They may be political, such as the trade disputes between China and the United States, or the Soviet Union breakup in 1991. Or, they may arise from human error, unexpected major competitor moves, or management moves to create a changed environment within a firm.

Change is not always gradual; it is sometimes thrust upon an enterprise in the form of a crisis. Crises must be managed, proactively if possible, first to minimize damage and second to turn adversity into triumph when possible. As described by Laurence Barton in *Crisis in Organizations: Managing and Communicating in the Heat of Chaos* (1993), business crises come in many forms and can be handled in many ways.

For example, by January 1990, the Perrier bottled water company had U.S. wholesale revenues of $640 million. In February of that year, abnormal traces of benzene, a liquid petroleum derivative used for cleaning, were reportedly found in Perrier products. The French-based firm reacted quickly by voluntarily recalling 70 million bottles. It traced the problem to faulty filtering. After completing repairs, shipments of the product resumed three months after the incident with the reintroduced bottles labelled "New Production."

In 1999, Coca-Cola faced a similar crisis in Belgium, France, and Poland, when some contaminated products were alleged to have caused minor illnesses (Hays 1999a,b). Coke's handling of the crisis was weak, with forthright explanations and recalls (the problem was a very contained and minor one) coming ten days after the most publicized incident and almost a month after the first incident, a major failing in crisis management. Their handling of the situation, added to a natural cultural resentment of American dominance in many markets, created a much more damaging situation than warranted by the actual problem.

Crises are not always operational or as nonlife-threatening as at Perrier or Coke. For example, they may be caused by violent terrorism, as was the bombing of a Pan American flight over Scotland in December 1988, an event which eventually led to the airline's bankruptcy. Or, they may be caused by technology failures, such as the Union Carbide disaster at Bhophal, India, which killed more than 3,800 people in 1984, and the nuclear power plant explosion in Chernobyl (Soviet Union) in 1986, which was estimated to have killed or injured several thousand people.

The lessons learned from crises are varied (Barton 1993; Mann 2000):

- *Why do some companies do better than others at containing crises?* Some companies proactively prepare for crises by writing crisis management plans (CMPs) and rehearsing their response to problems well in advance. Others react in a vacuum of information and fail to contain the crisis.
- *Which aspects of management are most helpful in preparing for an inevitable crisis?* Understanding the importance of public opinion in the marketplace is a good beginning. Equally relevant are public-relations skills, understanding organizational behavior, and developing a sense of social responsibility.
- *How can you test crisis skills you have developed on and off the job so they are ready to be used at the company for which you work?* A large

number of corporations, particularly multinational ones, use role-playing scenarios as a crisis management tool. A hypothetical crisis is announced to a group of corporate executives, and for the next several hours, or longer, they are asked to react to and manage the crisis. Throughout this scenario, new information is continually provided by the game organizers, along with realistic surprises and turns in events. Just weeks before Iraq invaded Kuwait in August 1990, for instance, managers at Shell Oil used such a tool to rehearse how their company would respond to a war in the Middle East.

- *What do those managers who have managed a crisis, and who are free to discuss their responses, have to say about the predicaments they faced?* They regret not having been exposed to crisis management when they were formally trained in management. Crises can help the careers of executives whose judgments and actions are proven correct. In many other cases, however, lessons in effective crisis management come much too late and produce a national embarrassment.

- *How can a manager train a team to cope well enough with a crises to minimize damage to the organization's future?* Balance, in terms of background and professional skills, is a good beginning.

- *Why is a crisis management plan important? Why should students pursuing a business management degree, and managers in almost ev ery field of endeavor, care about crisis management?* A single crisis could alter your career and life. A CMP lets you test how you will treat people inside and outside your organization during moments of intense stress. It will challenge you to consider issues and individuals with whom you have had little contact. One day it could be the tool you use to save lives, protect assets, and retain or even enhance your company's image.

Although there is no guarantee that the right answer will be found during training to actually guide action in response to an event in the future, adequate preparation allows managers to plan for and practice responding to such situations. For example, at one company, Gillette, such preparation led to establishing guidelines for handling emergencies. As explained by former Gillette CEO, Colman Mockler:

> whenever a crisis occurs involving a major health risk—for example, a defective product—the objective is to take the initiative and try to have the company be the first to make a public announcement of the problem. At the same time, if possible, the announcement should contain information on how the company has taken care of the problem and its impact, or potential impact, on the public.

This guideline was based on lessons learned from experiences such as Johnson & Johnson's handling of the Tylenol recall in 1982 following the deaths of seven people who took the product (several packages had been tampered with and contained poison). Swift action by the company established a principle for crisis management: by taking the offensive and addressing the concerns, real and imagined, of key audiences, a company is more likely to be viewed as a responsible and responsive citizen rather than as a recalcitrant or indifferent monolith. Plans cannot fully cover all contingencies. An entrepreneurial, situational orientation is needed to respond on short notice to unusual and unexpected accidents, distribution and delivery problems, environmental problems, customer service problems, product defects, manufacturing breakdowns, political upheavals, and crises.

In addition to managing crises as they occur, at times, managers deliberately create crises, These acts of "ethical anarchy" are committed to break the constraints of past successes and renew organizations. One of the best examples of a planned "crisis creation" effort designed to revive a major organization was Jack Welch's attempt to transform GE after he was appointed CEO in 1981 (described in Chapters 4 and 11). One of his first steps was to create a crisis by delayering the management hierarchy, reducing corporate staff, and slashing 100,000 employees to focus on what he believed to be the core elements of the business. He then set about to release the organization's emotional energy and to capitalize creatively on the opportunities resulting from changes in GE's environment. In a sense, Welch used charismatic leadership to move from crisis management to orderly change management, an ideal path in successful change management in the multinational environment.

## *IMPROVISATION, SITUATED ACTION, AND INNOVATION*

Chapters 1 through 4 discussed rational and systematic contingency planning processes at work in multinational management. This is only one level of multinational management—an approach which is sometimes labeled a "Western" or rational planning cultural phenomenon. Other useful concepts in change and crisis management are "situated action," "improvisation," "intuition," and "innovation" (Lave and Wenger 1991; Perry, Stott, and Smallwood 1993). Suchman (1987) draws an analogy with primitive navigators who sailed the seas purposefully—to get to a specific destination—guided by their ability to respond to changing conditions, based on common sense or experience, rather than charts or planned itineraries.

In a similar way, while plans and coordinated efforts underlie most enterprise activities, success can also depend on the ability of managers to take actions within the context of particular, concrete circumstances—so-called *ad hoc* or *situated* actions—in which more than one solution is available.

Multinational management often requires improvisation and innovative situated management action. For example, Gillette's experiences at the inauguration of its new plant in Poland (described in the Preface) demonstrated how planned, creative showmanship and timing, plus entrepreneurial thinking and action, dramatically and effectively achieved business goals when crossing cultural boundaries. Clearly, a combination of purposeful action and innovative entrepreneurial responsiveness to market needs has helped Gillette succeed in its multinational operations prior to its problems in 2001.

During the trade dispute between China and the United States discussed in Chapter 1, entrepreneurial Chinese small business owners quickly moved their production to different markets or through different distribution channels in different countries. The entrepreneurs who started a new cellular telephone company in Tashkent demonstrated considerable innovative and improvisational skills (Chapter 4), as did the managers of the Hungarian telephone company Matav, when setting up their "troika" management structure (Chapter 12).

Such experiences explain in part why it is necessary to have entrepreneurial skills when running multinational businesses—managers face rapidly changing competitive markets and a wide range of unusual incidents and happenings which cannot always be anticipated. Such skills make it possible to be responsive to local needs, whether these needs involve product redesign for a Muslim country, change introduction at a Polish factory, contract negotiations in Japan, or a new plant opening in China.

Steps can also be taken to stimulate innovation, the lifeblood of firms today, especially in the area of technology (Business Value 1997; Quinn, Baruch, and Zien 1997). These steps can involve encouraging individual creativity, not only through leadership initiatives, but also through training (Beich 1997; Tushman and O'Reilly 1997). Putting in place processes and other organization enablers to stimulate and guide innovations that lead to successful cost reductions or product introductions also increase innovation and creativity (Christensen 1997; Peters 1997). For example, Xerox created a new organization that included separate sales forces and development groups to develop, nurture, and market worldwide new digital copier innovations, a high-resolution flat panel computer screen, Internet browser software, and other document-related products (Deutsch 1997). Some leaders have stimulated creativity through a "contrarian" approach, that is, exploring nontraditional approaches that seem to contradict accepted practices (Jenrette 1997). As seen at Xerox, Sony, and other firms, innovation often involves "eating your young," a policy which directs product developers to work on making existing products obsolete starting from the day (or even prior to when) a new product is introduced. Because of cultural differences, the concept of creativity and innovation can vary from culture to culture (Ishida 1994).

The ability to improvise and innovate can also be improved by developing a "learning" organization, that is, an adaptable and flexible organization able to learn and change as situation requirements change. Such an organization is described by Peter Senge in his book *The Fifth Discipline* (1990).

Many other aspects of the learning organization have been discussed in this book. For example, teams can be designed to enable an organization to learn, change, and grow, within a changing environment (Hargrove 1998). Leadership that delegates decision making and learns to listen can help create an adaptable learning organization. Staffing and training can also accomplish this, as seen in the experiences of Gillette in developing its group of 350 experienced expatriate managers. The "learning how to learn" exercise described in the following section and shown in Figure 14.1 is an example of individual professional growth through systematically learning from experience.

Overall, 1998 and 1999 surveys showed that the United States had a slight edge globally in innovation and entrepreneurship, but nations worldwide were gaining ground (Flynn 1999; Yochelson 1999).

## LEARNING HOW TO LEARN: PROFESSIONAL GROWTH

The process involved in systematically thinking contingently is a self-learning one. For example, Warren Buffett (one of America's richest and most successful investors) explained the essence of his success during a workshop at St. John's University: He simply observed and studied successful people and companies (his "heroes") and their experiences. Buffett then identified the qualities they possessed and the business approaches they used (a conceptual model). He then adapted their success qualities in the way he behaved, thought, and worked. In a similar way, he chose firms to invest in by creating models of what he believed to be long-term successful companies. These companies possessed sound core values, good fundamental finances, and the ability to maintain their brand franchise in the marketplace. Buffett constantly updated and refined his "models" based on what worked well for him, as he moved into the insurance business in a major way in the 1990s. Figure 14.1 outlines this learning or professional development process.

The experiences described in the preceding sections are an attempt to put the learning process shown in Figure 14.1 to work in worldwide executive learning programs. These programs focus on helping people learn how to learn—through examining experiences they are familiar with in a systematic way and then developing a model or approach for that kind of situation.

For example, many situation factors are studied in making multinational product decisions. The processes outlined in Figures 1.1, 1.2, and 14.1 were

FIGURE 14.1. Reconceptualization for Professional Growth

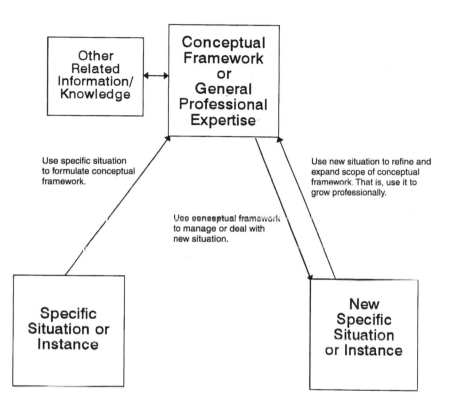

used to develop a general process model for guiding market entry/operating decisions. This model, shown in Figure 5.5 (p. 133), was developed by a young Central European executive working in a multinational company's foreign subsidiary who was involved in market entry/operating decisions while participating in an executive training program. The model was discussed Chapter 5.

Figure 5.5 is not the only way to replicate or model the cognitive processes involved in multinational market entry/operating situations. Readers are encouraged to formulate their own conceptual approaches, as suggested in Figure 1.1. In the words of one training program participant, Figure 1.1 is one way "to be the boss" in any situation encountered.

The reader should keep in mind that Figures 1.2, 1.3, 1.4, and 1.5 are not the *only* or *best* way to model strategic management processes. With some training and practice, most readers could eventually develop as good or better models or replications in areas of interest to them.

Learning how to develop the skills outlined in Figures 1.1, 1.2, and 14.1, three of the many skills needed by multinational managers to survive and prosper, is an essential part of any multinational management book or course. In rapidly developing, diverse, and often paradoxical situations, learning methods and tools used to deal with past situations is not enough. Past solutions, while helpful, do not necessarily provide solutions to new problems. For this reason, Figures 1.1, 1.2, and 14.1 and the skills underlying them are an important focus of this book. Future multinational managers will be required to "break past molds," for example, through exploiting the many seemingly threatening aspects of the Internet as it dislocates and deconstructs past industry strategic patterns by viewing these dislocations as opportunities.

## *SPECIAL MULTINATIONAL MANAGEMENT PROBLEMS FOR SMALL COMPANIES*

It is possible for even small firms to explore multinational markets and become part of international networks (Church 1997; Kanter 1995). Three key areas appear to affect success when introducing and running successful large, medium, or small international operations: concepts (innovative ideas, services, and products—the thinking), competencies (the doing), and connections (working with partnerships, alliances, and networks).

Cohen & Wilks International (CWI), a British apparel manufacturer/supplier with around $30 million in sales, is an example of how partnerships in today's global community can be created and used by a small firm. CWI management oversees the manufacture of two million garments annually in ten factories spanning six countries in Eastern Asia and the Middle East. It is half owned by Mitsui & Co., Ltd. a multibillion-dollar Japanese trading company with 189 offices worldwide and interests in steel, machinery, chemical products, foodstuffs, and petroleum.

Initially, Mitsui's role in CWI was largely administrative and financial. Occasionally, Mitsui performed other tasks, such as enhancing CWI's image by connecting it with an important design firm with which Mitsui had worked in Japan. Mitsui also provided the initial contacts that led CWI to switch nearly all of its trouser manufacturing operations to the United Arab Emirates.

CWI prospered by maintaining a very high competency in production, and by close, on-site supervision of its contract production connections. In addition, it established very close supportive ties with major customers, such as Bhs, a large apparel retail chain (Kanter 1995).

Another small company, TechRidge, specialized in manufacturing identification (ID) cameras and components. TechRidge prospered first by creating innovative concepts in ID cameras which met world-class quality standards. It provided extra services and reliable fast service, including a turnaround time of twenty-four hours for repairs (compared to weeks for competitors). TechRidge formed alliances with suppliers and customers, such as Polaroid, which was located very close to TechRidge. Through these alliances, TechRidge began selling to Mexico and formed other alliances, including one with Kodak in the Dominican Republic and one with IBM (in Mexico) (Kanter 1995).

The businesspeople who started a cellular phone company in Tashkent in Uzbekistan are another example of entrepreneurs who prospered multinationally by specializing in areas of their competencies.

## MANAGING THE LONG-TERM FUTURE

The best measure of a firm's potential for success often is not its past achievements, but how well it manages to keep improving its future prospects. Managing and leading change, therefore, necessarily involves planning for the long-term future (Kotter 1996; James 1996). Earlier chapters, starting with Chapter 1, described the longer-term strategic visions of a number of firms, such as Intel, Hewlett-Packard, IBM, and Microsoft. These firms' longer-term visions are tied to global networks and a wide range of individualized utilities and appliances, very often Internet-related, which enable people to use these networks.

For example, in an effort to manage the realization of Microsoft's long-term vision, CEO Bill Gates has used a variety of techniques (Clark and Rigdon 1995). For example, he wrote the following to his upper-level managers in late 1995 in a memo entitled "The Internet Tidal Wave":

> Now I assign the Internet the highest level of importance. In this memo I want to make clear that our focus on the Internet is critical to every part of our business. The Internet is the most important single development to come along since the IBM PC was introduced in 1981. (p. B1)

The memo argued that all Microsoft products must be modified to exploit the broader Net or else face obsolescence. This was, essentially, a first small step in realizing the emerging vision of networks embraced by major computer companies, a vision which has responded to technological change and increased competitiveness.

The process continued in 1996 when Gates announced that he was reorganizing Microsoft by creating a new division to develop Internet applications and other advanced technologies, and that he intended to take the lead in developing Internet applications (Rebello 1996).

Much of this new thinking and action was triggered by the introduction of the World Wide Web, the graphical portion of the Internet which makes it easy for people to publish information and sell goods and services without middlemen. Because key specifications are openly available, many companies and individuals have developed programs for creating and reading Web pages on different kinds of computer systems. This trend will likely lead to the development of an array of Internet appliances, both computer and other kinds. This expectation was reinforced by a Nielsen survey in late 1995 which indicated that in the United States and Canada alone, already 37 million people aged sixteen and older (17 percent of the population) had access to the Internet. Moreover, 24 million had used the Internet in the past three months and spent an average of five hours and twenty-eight minutes on it per week. Of these users, 34 percent were women, 66 percent reached the Internet from work, and 25 percent had incomes over $80,000 (Dibbell 1995).

Ford's, GE's, and other nontechnical companies' somewhat different enterprise-wide strategic reactions to the Internet's strategic impact were also described in earlier chapters. As has been pointed out earlier in this book, not all companies have been so dramatically affected by the so-called Internet revolution, and for many, the Internet is just another tool with strategic implications in many business areas.

## SUMMARY

A primary focus of this book has been to show how multinational diversity can be managed within common frameworks in multinational enterprises. Contrary to some views, although multinational businesses vigorously pursue global solutions, they also have an interest in encouraging and managing diversity. These and other diverse aspects of multinational management, as well as common frameworks within which they are integratively and synergistically balanced, are discussed in this section.

### Multinational Strategic Management Requires Knowledge Management

Managing knowledge, which is important in multinational management, has developed into a distinct study area (Botkin 1999; "Knowledge Management" 1999). Many aspects of knowledge management have been covered in this book.

The first aspect involves formulating both the structure and content of the strategic framework. These frameworks range from broad, comprehensive ones, such as GE's, to more narrowly scoped ones, such as those at Ciba-Geigy and the pharmaceutical wholesaler described in Chapter 4. This basic strategic knowledge base can be supported by knowledge about the industry, company, customers, and competitors (Torsilieri 1998).

Decisions need to be made as to how other components of this strategic management knowledge base are to be developed. For example, at what business unit and functional level will detailed plans be developed, who will develop them, and how will they be stored and accessed? These decisions and their implementation, which involve knowledge structure, content, and use, are important for two reasons: they affect the quality of the plans and planning, and they affect the depth of "buy ins" by operating personnel, which in turn affects their actual use in running a firm.

The actual use of plans and their impact on a business depends largely on the active participation and support of higher management levels. For example, Jack Welch at GE continually reinforced the planning process, as did Percey Barnevik at Asea, Brown, Boveri (ABB), and Ken Iverson at the Nucor Corporation. As pointed out by successful leaders, such reinforcement is an indispensable way of managing the development, diffusion, and impact of knowledge, especially strategic knowledge.

In addition to establishing the knowledge bases and managing how they are developed and used, access to them must be managed. Access from outside the firm must be limited (access to detailed plans by competitors, for example), and information flows must be directed to appropriate individuals through controlled internal communication channels ("Overload" 1999).

### *Managing and Encouraging Global Diversity: Managing Paradoxes*

Multinational management is, at the core, paradoxical, because it requires dealing with seemingly contradictory factors. This is not unusual, since we live in an age of paradox. For example, social paradoxes occur involving a desire to preserve differences (such as ethnic or personal customs and values) while still having common causes and country goals. In *Global Paradox* (1994) John Naisbitt discusses contrary trends among countries and cultures. For example, on the one hand there exists the search for alliances, such as the European Economic Union and its goal of a common currency. On the other hand, ethnic segments, such as the Slovakians in the former Czechoslovakia who broke with the Czech Republic to form a separate country, are seeking ways to maintain their independent character in spite of the economic hardship. This is only one instance of global paradoxes.

Similarly, multinational management carries the burden of

- the need to integrate some aspects of these diverse elements into a single, successful business enterprise,
- while at the same time recognizing, balancing, and preserving each culture's special interests and needs
- in a way that enables that enterprise to achieve global efficiencies and rapid transfer of new technology
- at the same time it serves the needs of diverse cultures, interests, and rapidly changing markets.

Though not necessarily true of all enterprises, substantial evidence exists that corporate leaders, and their multinational enterprises, are a major social mechanism for both respecting and encouraging diversity. Although multinational firms are interested in global efficiencies, it is also in their interest to maintain a balance and to selectively encourage and manage diversity. This is in their self-interest not only to create market niches, but also because businesses and their products and services need to be different to succeed. Survival of a business depends on differentiation—that is, having a brand, product, or service that is distinctive and differentiated from competitors'. If such differences and diversity did not exist, businesses would have to create them, such as by using strategies involving e-business Internet technologies to encourage individual and cultural differentiation.

The concept of "seeming" contradictions is essential to understanding effective multinational management. What at first may appear or *seem* to be a contradiction, can, from the perspective of common frameworks, combined with integrative management skills, go beyond reconciling differences. If done well, it can produce dynamic synergistic benefits and yield significant competitive advantages.

### *Managing Diverse and Often Paradoxical Factors Within Common Frameworks: A Continuing Integrative Process*

Many integrative common contexts or frameworks at work in multinational management have been discussed in this book:

- Contingency, cognitive, and behavioral frameworks
- Strategic visions of each company
- Global products and services
- Telecommunications and information systems
- The organization and its culture—the company itself
- Accounting and finance systems
- Other human resource management approaches
- Strategic alliances

This book focuses on these common frameworks, which enable managing cultural diversity across and within national borders in a balanced, integrative way. Many aspects of this synergistic balancing of diverse elements—through which the total can equal more than the sum of the parts—have been discussed.

This book began by discussing common frameworks for diversity management, especially contingency management processes. These were discussed in terms of planning, enabling action, and management throughout business enterprises. Examples were given of how planning decision processes use common contingency processes to synergistically reconcile and balance different cultural and other situation factors in both enterprise-wide and operational situations. Some of these contingency processes are given in Figures 1.1 through 1.4 and 1.6.

For example, a subsidiary of a multinational pharmaceutical firm used a well-defined contingency decision process to reconcile and balance different cultural and other situation factors when trying to decide how to introduce a new, differentiated product into Venezuela. This decision framework is shown in Figure 5.5 and discussed in Chapter 5. It is an extension and application of the basic entrepreneurial contingency process outlined in Figure 1.1.

Many of the strategic implications of common technical frameworks, such as global telecommunications and computer information systems, especially the Internet were discussed in Chapter 7 and throughout this book. For example, Gillette's computer system, which calculated the most efficient use of diverse production sources to make the Atra razor, is an example of a common information system enabling framework (discussed in Chapters 1 and 7). The synergy generated through integrative common frameworks can lead to the total solution being greater than the sum of all the parts.

Chapter 8 discussed how global finance, accounting, and control systems have been, and still are, being developed and used to help businesses function more easily across cultural boundaries. Chapter 9 discussed how organizations and their processes and cultures can also enable more balanced management of diverse cultural forces. This was the purpose of Ford Motor Company's reorganization. The collaborative infrastructures (especially the human systems) within the new organization structure—especially cross-cultural teams—were expected to be particularly useful in achieving the synergistic balance on a day-to-day basis and in stimulating the rapid transfer of knowledge. Chapters 10 through 12 extended this discussion to human factor enablers, especially staffing, leadership, and management. Chapter 13 described one of the major integrative enablers in multinational business today, strategic alliances.

Figure 14.2 outlines a general contingency framework useful in creating the enabling mechanisms helpful in implementing strategies and strategic plans, which were discussed in Chapters 5 through 13. It is also an extension and application of the underlying entrepreneurial process shown in Figure 1.1.

The Preface reviewed many popular traditional strategic management tools, none of which is best in all situations. Rather, success will depend on focused, situational thinking and action that will provide the basis for selecting, integrating, and adapting traditional tools and approaches, or developing your own. Readers are urged, therefore, to "be their own boss" and provide their own balance.

Success also depends on being able to creatively and innovatively deal with many situations on an ad hoc basis. It especially depends on interpersonal interaction, communication, staffing and training, and leadership and management action. For example, Gillette hired and trained a group of 350 managers over a twenty-year period to ensure effective diversity management worldwide on a daily basis within a global framework. This is an example of enabling the balance to occur daily throughout the worldwide Gillette organization through a systematic synergistic worldwide staffing/training program, itself a common framework. Even in situations involving ad hoc interpersonal interaction, some common behavioral frameworks can be identified:

- the search for understanding and managing cultural diversity within ourselves and our own origins as a starting/reference point or
- the processes involved in finding the appropriate balance between adapting to, and asserting, differences during one-on-one exchanges.

Based on the experiences studied, the common frameworks discussed in this book are a means of reconciling multinational local differences and still achieving global efficiencies—the essential continuing paradox in multinational management. Emphasis has been given to one strategically useful tool for achieving this balance, the Internet. The Internet allows communication of common cultural perspectives worldwide quickly and cheaply through e-mail, as well as allowing niche groups to form and develop anywhere in the world.

The management processes described in this book are context driven. They are common contingency processes: identify situation requirements, as well as differences and commonalties, and then build appropriate global and locally responsive hybrid solutions. Such entrepreneurial processes are deeply imbedded in all cultures, although not necessarily within every person in every culture. At the core they are human survival processes, and so provide a natural perspective for managing across cultures.

FIGURE 14.2. Strategy Implementation: Developing Enabler Processes (Selective Sample)

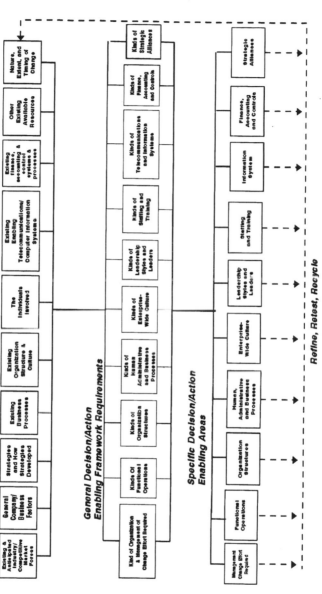

Ultimately, no book can fully articulate the most important skill needed: the individual ability to find appropriate solutions on a minute-to-minute, day-by-day basis—finding just the right balance among the specific (and almost always unique in some aspect) factors faced in each situation. Finding that balance depends on individual skill and, at times, luck.

Because much of this reconciliation of, and respect for, diversity ultimately needs to be done daily on the job, multinational management is a very demanding task requiring a high degree of professional competency. Chapter 1 discussed how to use experiential learning to increase personal professional expertise through the process of learning from experiences and developing and refining professional expertise heuristic models. Figure 14.1 outlines that process.

In all diversity management situations, the individual manager must recognize that balancing seemingly different or conflicting elements in a rapidly changing diverse situation is a continuing process, in business as in life. It is not a finite task that is completed and ends. It never seems to stop. New problems that need solving will arise continuously. The key, then, is to become good at this task and to enjoy it. Creating unity while still preserving diversity in rapidly changing situations can be rewarding, challenging, satisfying, and fun.

## REVIEW QUESTIONS

1. Discuss the ways in which management of change has special relevance in multinational strategic leadership and management. Cite specific examples.
2. Discuss the ways in which a rapidly changing competitive international environment has led to the iterative nature of the strategic management process.
3. Describe the major importance of privatization in international business. In what ways is it increasing the efficiency of international business and increasing competitive pressures? Cite specific examples.
4. Discuss the nature of crises in multinational business, their impact, and the steps that specific companies have taken to reduce the problems crises can create.
5. Describe the importance of entrepreneurial skills in multinational management, especially in relation to innovation and improvisation requirements for success in multinational operations. Give specific examples.
6. Describe some of the ways in which managers can nurture innovation in their organizations.

7. Describe the process of learning from experience covered in this and earlier chapters, and give examples of how you have acquired increased professional skills from your own or others' experiences.

8. Identify the special problems faced by small companies when operating internationally and the steps which can be taken to succeed.

9. Describe the steps companies have taken to create opportunities for the long-term future which are not obvious to others. Draw on examples from this and other chapters.

10. Describe common frameworks that can make managing across borders and cultures more effective and easier. Cite examples from this and other chapters of situation circumstances which may or may not make them effective.

11. Describe some of the steps companies have taken to manage diversity synergistically to produce increased benefits.

12. Describe a key attitude needed for management success in today's rapidly changing multinational environment.

13. Explain your understanding of the learning development process outlined in Figure 14.1 and explained in the text. How do the experiences of Warren Buffett help in understanding this process?

### *EXERCISES*

1. Drawing upon your research, describe the experiences of two multinational managers in managing diversity in a culture other than your own.

2. Referring to the diagram in Figure 14.1, describe how you have grown professionally from studying your own experiences or those of others in the multinational management area.

3. Based on your research, select and describe two contrasting privatization experiences, citing the key factors which contributed to their success or failure.

4. Study a recent international crisis and describe what you learned about handling crises should you be faced with one in business in the future.

# References

## *Preface*

Andrews, Edmund L. 2000. "German Giant Plans Global Phone Strategy," *The New York Times,* July 5, pp. C1, C2.

Baker, Stephen and Kerry Capell. 2000. "Chris Gent, King of the Web?" *Business Week,* February 14, pp. 60, 61.

Burke, James. 1997. Forward and Preface In Peter J. Denning and Robert M. Metcalfe (Eds.), *Beyond Calculation,* (pp. ix-xvi). New York: Springer-Verlag.

Cane, Alan. 2000. "Epicenter of Earth Has Shifted to Europe," *Financial Times,* Financial Times Telecoms Survey, March 15, p. 1.

Denning, Peter. 1997. How We Will Learn In Peter J. Denning and Robert M. Metcalfe, *Beyond Calculation,* pp. 267-299. New York: Springer-Verlag.

Eddy, Kester and Richard Waters. 2000. "Telekom in Hungarian Buy," *Financial Times,* July 4, p. 17.

Maitland, Alison. 2000. "Throw the Rule-Book Out of the Window," *Financial Times,* February 2, p. 14.

Mandel, Michael. 2000. "The New Economy," *Business Week,* January 31, pp. 73-92.

Reed, Stanley, Kerry Capell, Heidi Dawley, and Stephen Baker. 2000. "Ready to Take on the World," *Business Week,* June 12, pp. 70-72.

Shillingford, Joia. 2000. "Towards the Brave New World of Free Phone Calls," *Financial Times,* FT Telecoms, March 15, p. IV.

Vitzhum, Carlta. 2000. "Telefonica's Deals Look Sure Despite Inquiry," *The Wall Street Journal,* June 28, p. A14.

## *Chapter 1*

Ascarelli, Silvia. 1997. "Dell Finds U.S. Strategy Works in Europe," *The Wall Street Journal,* February 3, p. A8.

Banerjee, Neela. 1999. "Russia's Embryos of Enterprise," *The New York Times,* July 30, pp. C1, C23.

Bannon, Lisa. 2000. "eToys' Strategy to Stay in the Game," *The Wall Street Journal,* April 25, pp. B1, B4.

Bannon, Lisa. 2001. "The eToys Saga: Costs Keep Rising But Sales Slowed," *The Wall Street Journal,* January 22, pp. B1, B10.

Barboza, David. 1999. "Pluralism Under the Golden Arches," *The New York Times,* February 12, pp. C1, C7.

Barringer, Felicity. 2000. "Historians Take a Longer View of Net Battles," *The New York Times,* April 10, pp. C1, C4.

Beckett, Paul. 1999. "Citigroup's Web Push to Test Firm's Brand Name," *The Wall Street Journal,* June 23, pp. C1, C2.

Belasco, James A. and Jerry Stead. 1999. *Soaring With the Phoenix: Renewing the Vision, Reviving the Spirit, and Re-Creating the Success of Your Company.* New York: Warner Books.

Boudette, Neal E. and Kevin J. Delaney. 2000. "British Internet Portal Vizzavi Faces Wireless Hurdles," *The Wall Street Journal,* June 21, p. B4.

Brown, Shona L. and Kathleen M. Eisenhardt, 1998. *Competing on the Edge: Strategy as Structured Chaos.* Boston, MA: Harvard Business School Press.

Buckingham, Marcus and Curt Coffman. 1999. *First, Break All the Rules.* New York: Simon & Schuster.

Calbreadth, Dean. 1997. "Management Team To Take Over Budvar As Anheuser-Busch Trademark War Persists," *The Wall Street Journal Europe,* January 23, p. 12.

Chowdhury, Neel. 1999. "Dell Cracks China," *Fortune,* June 21, pp. 120-124.

Claxton, Guy. 1999. *Hare Brain, Tortoise Mind.* Hopewell, NJ: The Ecco Press.

Colitte, Raymond. 1999. "Cola War Stepped Up," *Financial Times,* May 27, p. 19.

Colvin, Geoffrey. 2000. "America's Most Admired Companies," *Fortune,* February 21, pp. 108-117, F1-F7.

Cowell, Alan. 2000. "Unilever Plans Huge Cuts in Jobs, Plants, and Brands," *The New York Times,* February 23, pp. C1, C4.

Daft, Douglas. 2000. "Back to Classic Coke," *Financial Times,* March 27, p. 16.

Daley, Suzanne. 2000. "French Turn Vandal Into Hero Against U.S.," *The New York Times,* July 1, pp. A1, A6.

Dauer, Francis Watanabe. 1996. *Critical Thinking.* New York: Barnes & Noble Books.

Downes, Larry and Chunka Mui. 1998. *Unleashing the Killer App.* Boston, MA: Harvard Business School Press.

Echikson, William and Dean Foust. 2000. "For Coke, Local It Is," *Business Week,* July 3, p. 122.

Faison, Seth. 1996. "Trade Threats? Ho-Hum," *The New York Times,* June 14, pp. D1, D3.

Fisher, Philip. 1999. *Still the New World: American Literature in a Culture of Creative Destruction.* Cambridge, MA: Harvard University Press.

Fleming, Charles. 2000. "In Europe, Buyout Specialists Are Snapping Up Unglamorous Forgotten in Tech Gold Rush," *The Wall Street Journal,* February 14, pp. A13, A14.

Friedman, Thomas L. 1996. "Big Mac II," *The New York Times,* December 11, p. A27.

Graham, Robert. 2000. "Capitalism Fails to Win French Hearts," *Financial Times,* March 6, p. 4.

Greene, Jay and David Rocks. 2000. "Oracle: Why It's Cool Again," *Business Week,* May 8, pp. 115-126.

Gunther, Marc. 1998. "The Rules According to Rupert," *Fortune,* October 26, pp. 92-109.

Guyon, Janet. 1996. "Cellular Start-Up," *The Wall Street Journal,* June 21, pp. A1, A6.

Hays, Constance L. 1999. "This Bud's for Them," *The New York Times,* June 23, pp. C1, C2.

Hof, Robert, Debra Sparks, Ellen Neuborne, and Wendy Zellner. 2000."Can Amazon Make It?" *Business Week,* July 10, pp. 38-43.

Hurst, David. 1995. *Crisis and Renewal.* Boston, MA: Harvard Business School Press.

Kupfer, Andrew. 1999. "Mike Armstrong's AT&T: Will the Pieces Come Together?" *Fortune,* April 26, pp. 82-89.

Landers, Peter. 2000. "In Japan, the Words of Chairman Jack Are Revolutionary," *The Wall Street Journal,* February 9, pp.A1, A8.

Maitland, Alison. 2000. "Catalysts for Change," *Financial Times,* June 26, p. 11.

Manchester, Philip. 1999. "Introducing a Utility Look," *Financial Times,* Information Technology Survey Section, August 4, p. 2.

Maucher, Helmut. 1994. *Leadership in Action.* New York: McGraw Hill.

Mitroff, Ian I. 1998. *Smart Thinking for Crazy Times.* San Francisco, CA: Barrett-Koehler.

Mockler, Robert J. 1994-1999. *On-Site Visits in Europe, Russia, and China.*

Mockler, Robert J. 1999. *Multinational Strategic Alliance.* New York and Chichester, England: John Wiley & Sons.

Nelson, Mark M. 1996. "Treasure Island: Russian Capitalists Use Cyprus as Springboard to Global Marketplace," *The Wall Street Journal Europe,* May 9, pp. 1, 6.

Oliver, Richard. 1999. *The Shape of Things to Come: 7 Imperatives for Winning in the New World of Business.* New York: McGraw-Hill.

Overell, Stephen. 2001. "And Now for Something Completely Paradoxical," *Financial Times,* January 19, p. 10.

Perlez, Jane. 1995. "This Bud's Not for You, Anheuser," *The New York Times,* June 30, pp. D1, D4.

Pfeffer, Jeffrey and Robert L. Sutton. 2000. *The Knowing-doing Gap.* Boston, MA: Harvard Business School Press.

Reinhardt, Andy, Catherine Yang, and Roger O. Crockett. 1999. "The Main Event: Bernie vs. Mike," *Business Week,* October 18, pp. 33-35.

Rossant, John. 2000. "Birth of a Giant," *Business Week,* July 10, pp. 170-176.

Schiesel, Seth. 2000. "For AT&T's Chief, a Redefined Cable Landscape," *The New York Times,* Money & Business Section, January 16, pp. 1, 19.

Slater, Robert. 1999. *Jack Welch and the GE Way.* New York: McGraw-Hill.

Slywotzky, Adrian J. and David J. Morrison. 1997. *The Profit Zone.* New York: Random House (Times Books).

Slywotzky, Adrian J., David J. Morrison, Ted Moser, Keven A. Mundt, and James A. Quella. 1999. *Profit Patterns*. New York: Random House (Times Books).

Spindle, Bill. 2000. "Japan Becomes a Mecca For Venture Capitalists," *The Wall Street Journal,* February 24, pp. A13, A14.

Stewart, Thomas A. 1999. "See Jack. See Jack Run Europe," *Fortune,* September 27, pp. 124-136.

"Survey: Cyprus," 1998. *Financial Times,* April 6, pp. 23-26.

Tagliabue, John. 1996. "Local Flavor Rules European TV," *The New York Times,* October 14, pp. D1, D4.

Tagliabue, John. 1998. "Europe Takes to the Road in a Small Way," *The New York Times,* April 21, pp. D1, D6.

Tran, Khanh T.L. and Keith Johnson. 1999. "Niki Barred by Spanish From Use of Name in Sports Apparel Sold There," *The Wall Street Journal,* September 30, p. A8.

Waters, Richard. 1999. "Case Study: General Electric," *Financial Times,* Autumn 1999 Digital Business Guide, September 30, p.20.

Weber, Thomas E. and Andrea Petersen. 1999. "Big Idea Turns Priceline's Founder Into a Billionaire," *The Wall Street Journal,* April 1, p. B4.

Welch Jr., John F., Paolo Fresco, and John D. Opie. 1996. "To Our Shareholders," *1995 Annual Report,* Fairfield, CT: General Electric Company, February 9, pp. 1-5.

Whittington, Richard. 1999. "The 'How' Is More Important Than the 'Where'," *Financial Times,* Mastering Strategy Section, Part Five, October 25, p. 4.

Willman, John. 1999. "Unilever Thinks 'the Unthinkable' to Accelerate Its Growth Prospects," *Financial Times,* September 24, p. 25.

Wind, Jerry Yoram and Jeremy Main. 1998. *Driving Change.* New York: The Free Press.

Zeien, Albert. 1995. "Gillette's Global Marketing Experiences," *Talk at St. John's University,* New York, February 27.

## *Chapter 2*

Abrahams, Jeffrey. 1995. *The Mission Statement Book.* Oakland, CA: Ten Speed Press.

Aeppel, Timothy and Clare Ansberry. 2000. "When Economies Converge," *The Wall Street Journal,* June 22, pp. B1, B6.

Andrews, Edmund L. 2000. "Streamlining a German Blimp," *The New York Times,* February 29, pp. C1, C25.

Baker, Stephen and Kerry Capell. 2000a. "Chris Gent, King of the Web?" *Business Week,* February 14, pp. 60-61.

Baker, Stephen and Kerry Capell. 2000b. "The Race to Rule Mobile," *Business Week,* February 2, pp. 58-60.

Blackmon, Douglas A. 1998a. "FedEx's Parent, Burned Abroad, Looks to Home Ground," *The Wall Street Journal,* August 31, p. B4.

Blackmon, Douglas A. 1998b. "UPS Net Rises 35% As Gains Are Tied to Lower Cost Base," *The Wall Street Journal,* August 17, p. B4.

Blackmon, Douglas A. and Diane Brady. 1998. "Just How Hard Should a U.S. Company Woo a Big Foreign Market?" *The Wall Street Journal,* April 6, pp. A1, A6.

Blanchard, Ken and Michael O'Connor. 1997. *Managing by Values.* San Francisco, CA: Berrett-Koehler.

Blanchard, Ken and Terry Waghorn. 1997. *Mission Possible.* New York: McGraw-Hill.

Bremmer, Brian, Emily Thornton, and Irene M. Kunii. 1997. "Toyota's Crusade," *Business Week,* April 7, pp. 104-118.

Bremmer, Brian, Emily Thornton, and Irene M. Kunii. 1999. "Fall of a Keiretsu (Mitsubishi)," *Business Week,* March 15, pp. 85-92.

Brown, Eryn. 1999. "9 Ways to Win on the Web," *Fortune,* May 24, 112-125.

Burns, Tom. 1999. "Spanish Operator to Spin Off Media Assets," *Financial Times,* July 1, p. 16.

Burt, Tim. 1999. "Electrolux Sees Future in Fewer, Stronger Brands," *Financial Times,* February 21, p. 23.

Buzzell, Robert D. and Bradley T. Gale. 1997. *The PIMS (Profit Impact of Market Strategy) Principles.* New York: Free Press.

Cowell, Alan. 2000. "Unilever Plans Huge Cuts in Jobs, Plants, and Brands," *The New York Times,* February 23, pp. C1, C4.

Coy, Peter. 1999. "Exploiting Uncertainty: The 'Real-Options' Revolution in Decision Making," *Business Week,* June 7, pp. 118-124.

Davidson, Mike. 1995. *The Grand Strategist.* New York: Henry Holt and Company.

de Kluyver, Cornelis A. 2000. *Strategic Thinking.* Upper Saddle River, NJ: Prentice-Hall.

Deutsch, Claudia H. 1999. "The Handwriting on the Post-It Note: Image and Returns Suffer at 3M." *The New York Times,* July 6, pp. C1, C7.

Donnelly, George. 1999. "Acquiring Minds," *Chief Financial Officer,* September pp. 54-64.

Fleming, Charles. 1999. "Vickers Looks to the Sea for Guidance and a Mainstay," *The Wall Street Journal,* July 8, p. B4.

Hamel, Gary. 2000. "Reinvent Your Company," *Fortune,* June 12, pp. 99-118.

Hansell, Saul. 2000. "Murdoch Sees Satellites As Way to Keep News Corp. Current," *The New York Times,* June 16, pp. C1, C7.

Hax, Arnoldo C. and Nicolas S. Majluf. 1996. *The Strategy Concept and Process,* Upper Saddle River, New Jersey.

Hess, Gregory G. and Alex Miller. 1993. *Strategic Management,* New York: McGraw-Hill.

Iverson, Ken and Tom Varian. 1998. *Plain Talk.* New York: Wiley.

Jackson, Tim. 1997. *Inside Intel.* New York: Penguin Putnam (A Dutton Book).

Kerwin, Kathleed, Maria Stepanek, and David Welch. 2000. "At Ford, E-Commerce Is Job 1," *Business Week,* February 28, pp. 74-78.

Kim, W. Chan and Renee Mauborgne. 1999. "How Southwest Airlines Found a Route to Success," *Financial Times,* May 13, p. 20.

Kotter, John. 1996. *Leading Change.* Boston, MA: Harvard Business School Press.

Landers, Peter. 2000. "In Japan, the Words of Chairman Jack Are Revolutionary," *The Wall Street Journal,* February 9, pp. A1, A8.

Maitland, Alison. 2000. "Throw the Rule-Book Out of the Window," *Financial Times,* February 2, p. 14.

Marsh, Peter. 1999. "Tomkins to Bite the Unbundling Bullet," *Financial Times,* July 12, p. 17.

Marsh, Peter. 2000. "GE's Ambitions For European Sales Online," *Financial Times,* March 24, p. 22.

Reinhardt, Andy. 2000. "The New Intel," *Business Week,* March 13, pp. 110-124.

Rhoades, Christopher and Erik Portanger. 2000. "Burgeoning Internet Enticed Deutsche, Dresdner Into a Marriage," *The Wall Street Journal,* March 9, pp. A21, A22.

Schonfeld, Erick. 1998. "Schwab Puts It All Online," *Fortune,* December 7, pp. 94-100.

Shirouzu, Norihiko. 2000. "Founding Clan Vies With Outside 'Radical' For The Soul of Toyota," *The Wall Street Journal,* May 15, pp. A1, A12.

Slater, Robert. 1999. *Jack Welch and the GE Way.* New York: McGraw-Hill.

Slywotzky, Adrian J. and David J Morrison. 1997. *The Profit Zone.* New York: Random House (Times Books).

Slywotzky, Adrian J., Daniel J. Morrison, Ted Moser, Kevin A. Mundt, and James A. Quella. 1999. *Profit Patterns.* New York: Random House (Times Books).

Sorkin, Andrew Ross. 2000. "Taking Virgin's Brand Into Internet Territory," *The New York Times,* February 14, pp. C1, C17.

Takahashi, Dean. 1999. "Intel Is Exiting Graphic Chips for High End," *The Wall Street Journal,* August 20, p. B3.

Thornton, Emily, Larry Armstrong, and Kathleen Kerwin. 2000. "Toyotal Un-bound,"*Business Week,* May 1, pp. 142-146.

Violino, Bob. 1999. "Banking on E-Business," *InformationWeek,* May 3, pp. 44-52.

Waters, Richard. 1999. "Case Study: General Electric," *Financial Times,* Autumn 1999 Digital Business Guide, September 30, p.20.

Welch, Jr., John F., Paolo Fresco, and John D. Opie. 1996. "To Our Shareholders," *1995 Annual Report,* Fairfield, CT: General Electric Company, February 9, pp. 1-5.

White, David. 2000. "The Acquistor," *Financial Times,* May 20/21, p. 7.

Wilder, Clinton and Maranne Kolbasuk-McGee. 2000. "Putting the 'E' Back in Business," *InformationWeek,* January 31, pp. 45-68.

Willman, John. 1999. "Unilever Thinks 'the Unthinkable' To Accelerate Its Growth Prospects," *Financial Times,* September 24, p. 2.

Woodruff, David. 2000. "France's Danone Advances At Full Speed, " *The Wall Street Journal,* June 23, p. A15.

## *Chapter 3*

Andrews, Edmund L. 2000. "German Giant Plans Global Phone Strategy," *The New York Times,* July 5, pp. C1, C2.

Bahrem, Bhushan. 2000. "BP Expects to Invest Up to $2 Billion in China," *The Wall Street Journal,* March 24, p. A15.

Baker, Stephen and Kerry Capell. 2000. "Chris Gent, King of the Web," *Business Week,* February 14, pp. 60-61.

Banerjee, Neela. 1999a. "From Russia, with Bankruptcy," *The New York Times,* August 13, pp. C1, C17.

Banerjee, Neela. 1999b. "Hoping Bear Will Awaken," *The New York Times,* May 1, pp. C1, C2.

Barham, John. 1999. "Ford Settles on Brazilian Site for New Plant," *Financial Times,* June 17, p. 24.

Bartlett, Christopher A. and Sumantra Ghoshal. 1991. *Managing Across Borders.* Boston, MA: Harvard Business School Press.

Bayart, Jean-Francois, Stephen Ellis, and Beatrice Hibou. 1999. *The Criminalization of the State in Africa,* African Issues Series, Indiana, PA: Indiana University Press.

Betts, Paul. 1999. "Murdoch Enters Italian Pay-TV," *Financial Times,* May 31, p. 13.

Bloomberg. 1997. "Mitsubishi To Write Off Automaker's U.S. Losses," *International Herald Tribune,* April 26, p. 9.

Carreyrou, John. 2000. "Dutch Financial Giant Maps Its U.S. Invasion," *The Wall Street Journal,* June 22, pp. A17, A18.

Chabal, Patrick and Jean-Pascal Daloz. 1999. *Africa Works: Disorder as Political Instrument,* African Issues Series, Indiana, PA: Indiana University Press.

"China." 2000. *The Economist,* Survey, March 8, pp. 3-16.

Colvin, Geoffrey. 2000. "America's Most Admired Companies," *Fortune,* February 21, pp. 108-117, F1-F7.

Davies, Ross and Megan Finney. 1998. "Retailers Rush to Capture New Markets," *Financial Times,* Mastering Global Business (Part Seven): Reaching the Global Customer, March 13, pp. 2-4.

Deogun, Nikhil. 1999. "Made in U.S.A. Deals From Europe Hit Record," *The Wall Street Journal,* October 25, pp. C1-C18.

Deutsch, Claudia H. 2000. "Another Economy on the Supply Side," *The New York Times,* April 8, pp. C1, C4.

Downes, Larry and Chunka Mui. 1998. *Unleashing the Killer App.* Boston, MA: Harvard Business School Press.

Eddy, Kester and Richard Waters. 2000. "Telekom in Hungarian Buy," *Financial Times,* July 4, p. 17.

Fritsch, Peter. 1999. "Besieged Brazilian Tries to Sell Troubled Property," *The Wall Street Journal,* July 7, p. A17.

Govindarajan, Vijay and Anil Bupta. 1998. "Turning Global Presence Into Global Competitive Advantage," *Financial Times,* Mastering Global Business (Part One), January 27, pp. 4-6.

Guyon, Janet. 1996. "Cellular Start-Up," *The Wall Street Journal,* June 21, pp. A1, A6.

Harding, James. 1999a. "End of the China Gold Rush," *Financial Times,* March 25, p. 15.

Harding, James. 1999b. "Foreign Investment Slows in China," *Financial Times,* March 25, p. 6.

"India." 1997. *The Washington Times,* September 20, p. A7.

"Infatuation Ends." 1999. *The Economist,* September 25, pp. 71-73.

Jack, Andrew. 1999. "Foreign Banks Edge Back Into Risky Russian Market," *Financial Times,* July 6, p. 18.

Katz, Jan. 2000. "Adios, Argentina—Hello, Brazil," *Business Week,* January 17, p. 56.

King, Neil. 1998. "A Soviet Defense Giant Saw the Inevitable and Decided: Diversify," *The Wall Street Journal,* January 2, pp. A1, A4.

Krauss, Clifford. 1998. "Foreign Expansion: Well-Planned Or Ill-Timed? Despite Uncertain World Markets, a Big U.S. Retailer Bulls Into Latin America," *The New York Times,* Money & Business Section, September 6, pp. 1, 11.

Kristof, Nicholas D. 1997. "Why Africa Can Thrive Like Asia," *The New York Times,* Week in Review, May 25, pp. E1, E4.

"Lawyers Go Global." 2000. *The Economist,* February 26, pp. 79-81.

Leggett, Karby. 2000. "China Sees Solid Jump in Growth," *The Wall Street Journal,* July 11, pp. A21, A23.

Liu, Melinda and Tony Emerson. 1999. "The Black Hole," *Business Week International,* March 8, pp. 40-41.

McGeehan, Patrick and Andrew Ross Sorkin. 2000. "Swiss Bank Is Acquiring Paine Webber," *The New York Times,* July 12, pp. C1, C21.

Mockler, Robert J. 1999. *Multinational Strategic Alliances,* Chichester, UK, and New York: John Wiley & Sons.

Nakamoto, Michiyo. 1999a. "NTT to Invest in Japanese Satellite Group," *Financial Times,* July 7, p, 14.

Nakamoto, Michiyo. 1999b. "Sony To Quit North America," *Financial Times,* July 8, p. 20.

Owen, David and Michael Peel. 2000. "Consultancy Firms in $11.3 Billion Deal," *Financial Times,* February 29, p. 19.

Owen, David, Samer Iskander, and Andrew Taylor. 1999. "Making a Big Splash," *Financial Times,* August 24, p. 11.

Prasso, Sheri and Larry Armstrong. 1997. "A Company Without a Country?" *Business Week,* May 5, p. 30.

Raghavan, Anita. 2000. "MeritaNordbanken Nears Unidanmark Purchase," *The Wall Street Journal,* March 6, p. A17.

Rangan, Subramaman. 1999. "Seven Myths to Ponder Before Going Global," *Financial Times,* Mastering Strategy Section, Part Ten, November 29, pp. 2-4.

Reed, Stanley, Inka Resch, and Jack Ewing. 1999. "Murdoch: Invading Europe?" *Business Week,* March 15, p. 94.

Romero, Simon. 1999."Mercedes Opens Brazil Plant to Build A-Class Compacts," *The New York Times,* April 24, p. C2.

Rose, Matthew and Daniel Michaels. 1998. "As Crisis in Russia Goes on, Fears Grow of Economic Fallout," *The Wall Street Journal,* September 2, pp. A1, A4, A5.

Rosenthal, Elisabeth. 2000. "At a Beijing Aquarium, Dolphins Are Hostages," *The New York Times,* April 3, p. 48.

Rudolph, Barbara. 1994. "So Many Dreams, So Many Losses: Sony's $3 Billion Hollywood Debacle is the Latest in a Series of Setbacks for Japanese Firms in the U.S.," *Time,* November 28, pp. 42-43.

Schemo, Diana Jean. 1998. "Risking Life, Limb and Capital: U.S. Companies Operate in Columbia, but Very Carefully," *The New York Times,* November 11, pp. C1, C3.

Smith, Craig S. 1998. "In China, GM Bets Billions on a Market Strewn with Casualties, "*The Wall Street Journal,* February 11, pp. A1, A8.

Tagliabue, John. 1998. "A Corporate Son Remakes Danone," *The New York Times,* April 1, pp. D1, D5.

Tejada, Carlos. 2000. "Corona Beer Emerges As Key Model for U.S. Importers," *The Wall Street Journal,* March 8, p. B4.

Torres, Craig. 1999. "Chile Becomes a Hot Market for Deals," *The Wall Street Journal,* April 21, p. A18.

Toy, Stewart. 1996. "The Son Also Rises at France's Danone: As Chairman, Franck Riboud Will Keep Up the Push Overseas," *Business Week,* May 20, p. 21.

Ullman, Owen. 1999. "Japan a Mess. Time to Invest?" *Business Week,* April 26, p. 35.

Wagstyl, Stefan and Christopher Bobinski. 2000. "Citigroup to Pay $1Bn For Poland's Top Corporate Bank," *Financial Times,* February 11, p. 1.

Whalen, Jeanne and Bhushan Bahree. 2000. "How Siberian Oil Field Turned Into a Minefield," *The Wall Street Journal,* February 9, p. A21.

WuDunn, Sheryl. 1999. "Capitalizing on Asian Doldrums," *The New York Times,* September 14, pp. C1, C6.

## *Chapter 4*

Atkins, Ralph. 2000. "Internet Threat to German Shops Law," *Financial Times,* April 8-9, p. 2.

Baker, Stephen and Kerry Capell. 2000. "The Race to Rule Mobile," *Business Week,* February 21, pp. 58-60.

Barnham, John. 1999. "Brazil Rings in Telecoms Competition," *Financial Times,* July 5, p. 18.

Blackmon, Douglas A. 1999. "National Mail Services Foil UPS's Big Strategy for Dominating Europe," *The Wall Street Journal,* January 18, pp. A1, A6.

Chionna, Daniela and Robert J Mockler. 1999. *Telecom Italia.* New York: Strategic Management Research Institute.

Clark, Charles. 1989. *Brainstorming: How to Create Successful Ideas.* North Hollywood, CA: Wilshire Book Co.

Clemons, Eric K. 1999. "Information Technology and Customer Profitability," *Keynote Address,* Information Resources Management Association Annual Meeting, Hershey, PA: IRMA, May 16-19.

Coates, Joseph F. 1996. "Science, Technology and American Business: 2025," *Presentation,* New York, NY: Strategic Leadership Forum, February 13.

Colvin, Goeffrey. 1999. "The Year of the Mega Merger," *Fortune,* January 11, pp. 62-65.

Cooper, Helene and Ian Johnson. 2000. "Congress's Vote Primes U.S. Firms to Boost Investments in China," *The Wall Street Journal,* May 25, pp. A1, A8.

Coy, Peter. 1999. "Exploiting Uncertainty: The 'Real Options' Revolution in Decision-Making," *Business Week,* June 7, pp. 118-124.

Daley, Suzanne. 2000. "French Turn Vandal Into Hero Against U.S," *The New York Times,* July 1, pp. A1, A6.

Del Garda, Desenzano. 2000. "The Global Gambles of General Motors," *The Economist,* June 21, pp. 67-69.

Downes, Larry and Chunka Mui. 1998. *Unleashing the Killer App.* Boston, MA: Harvard Business School Press.

Dugger, Celia W. 2000. "Market Economics," *The New York Times,* June 14, pp. C1, C6.

Fahey, Liam. 1999. *Outwitting, Outmaneuvering, and Outperforming Competitors.* New York: John Wiley & Sons.

Faison, Seth. 1999a. "Even If You Build Them . . . The Chinese May Not Come to Theme Parks," *The New York Times,* August 3, pp. C1, C6.

Faison, Seth. 1999b. "Fearing Deflation, Chinese Set Limits on New Factories," *The New York Times,* August 19, pp. A1, C9.

Friedland, Jonathan. 1997. "Latin American Retailer Fights Giants," *The Wall Street Journal,* September 19, p. A10.

Harnischfeger, Uta. 1999. "Deutsche Bank Treads Gently in Europe," *Financial Times,* July 2, p. 18.

Hiebeler, Robert, Thomas B. Kelly, and Charles Ketteman. 1998. *Best Practices: Building Your Business With Customer-Focused Solutions.* New York: Simon & Schuster.

Kilman, Scott and Helene Cooper. 1999. "Monsanto Falls Flat Trying To Sell Europe on Bioengineered Food," *The Wall Street Journal,* May 11, pp. A1, A10.

Kinzer, Stephen. 1998. "On Piping Out Caspian Oil, U.S. Insists the Cheaper, Shorter Way Isn't Better," *The New York Times,* November 8, p. 10.

Kynge, James. 2000a. "Legend Launches TV-Set Stock Trading in China," *Financial Times,* January 14, p. 17.

Kynge, James. 2000b. "Mongolian Communists Back in Power," *Financial Times,* July 4, p. 4.

Kynge, James. 2000c. "Mongolian's Modern Communists Look to the West For Investors," *Financial Times,* July 1/2, p. 3.

Landler, Mark. 2000. "Rolling With China's Web Punches," *The New York Times,* January 31, p. C10.

McCawley, Tom. 2000. "State Corruption 'Endemic' in Indonesia," *Financial Times,* June 28, p. 6.

Michalko, Michael. 1998. *Cracking Creativity.* Oakland, CA: Ten Speed Press.

Mockler, Robert J. 1999. *Multinational Strategic Alliances.* New York and Chichester, UK: John Wiley & Sons.

Mockler, Robert J. 2000. "SJU Faculty Teaches MBA Course in Costa Rica," *Global Views,* Center for Global Education, St. John's University, March, p. 4.

O'Reilly, Brian. 2000. "The Power Merchant (Enron)," *Fortune,* April 17, pp. 148-160.

Pope, Hugh. 2000. "Corruption Stunts Growth in Ex-Soviet States," *The Wall Street Journal,* July 5, p. A17.

Porter, Michael. 1980. *Competitive Strategy.* New York: Free Press.

Porter, Michael E. 1990. *The Competitive Advantage of Nations.* New York: The Free Press.

Reed, John and Erik Portanger. 1999. "Bribery, Corruption Rampant in Eastern Europe," *The Wall Street Journal,* November 9, p. A21.

Roberts, Dexter. 1997. "Going Toe to Toe With Big Blue and Compaq: Suddenly, Chinese Computer Makers Are Holding Their Own," *Business Week,* April 14, p. 58.

Rohter, Larry. 1999. "A Newsmagazine War in Brazil," *The New York Times,* August 30, p. C11.

Rose, Matthew. 1998. "For a Short Time, U.K. Town's Motto was 'Fish Into Chips," *The Wall Street Journal,* October 20, pp. A1, A6.

Rose, Matthew. 2000. "Chinese Officials Force Magazines To Go Without Famous Names," *The Wall Street Journal,* February 2, pp. B1, B4.

Rosenthal, Elizabeth. 2000. "At a Beijing Aquarium, Dolphins Are Hostages," *The New York Times,* April 3, p. 48.

Schine, Eric and Peter Elstrom. 1997. "The Satellite Biz Blasts Off," *Business Week,* January 27, pp. 62-70.

Schwartz, Peter and Gil Ringland. 1998. *Scenario Planning: Managing the Future.* New York: John Wiley & Sons.

Scott, Mark. 1998. *Value Drivers.* New York: John Wiley & Sons.

Shillingford, Jola. 2000. "Ready to Take Off More Rapidly Than the Internet, *Financial Times,* FT Telecoms Survey (2), March 15, p. 1.

Slywotzky, Adrian J. and David J. Morrison. 1997. *The Profit Zone.* New York: Random House (Times Business).

Slywotzky, Adrian J. and David J. Morrison. 1999. *Profit Patterns*. New York: Random House (Times Books).

Specter, Michael. 1997. "Moscow Journal: Lenin's Palace Survives to Serve the Fittest," *The New York Times,* February 4, p. A4.

Stipp, David. 2000. "Is Monsanto's Biotech Worth Less Than a Hill of Beans?" *Fortune,* February 21, pp. 157-172.

"Survey: Albania." 2000. *Financial Times,* February 23, pp. 11-14.

"Survey: Baltic Countries Investment." 2000. *Financial Times,* May 19, pp. 11-16.

"Survey: Brazil." 1999. *The Economist,* March 27, pp. 1-18.

"Survey: Brazil." 2000. *Financial Times,* April 26, pp. I-VI.

"Survey: Egypt." 2000. *Financial Times,* May 10, pp. I-XVIII.

"Survey: India and Pakistan. " 1999. *The Economist,* May 22, pp. 1-18.

"Survey: Indonesia." 2000. *The Economist,* July 8, pp. 1-16.

"Survey: Nigeria." 2000. *Financial Times,* March 30, pp. I-XII.

"Survey: Poland." 2000. *Financial Times,* April 17, pp. I-VI.

"Survey: Russia." 2000. *Financial Times,* May 10, pp. I-VII.

"Survey: Slovakia." 2000. *Financial Times,* May 25, pp. 9-12.

"Survey: South Africa." 1999. *Financial Times,* September 20, pp. I-IV.

Tagliabue, John. 1995. "Step Right Up, Monsieur!: Growing Disneyfication of Europe's Theme Parks," *The New York Times,* August 23, pp. D1, D8.

"The Fireworks to Come," 1999. *The Economist,* October 2, pp. 17, 18.

Tichy, Noel M. and Ram Charan. 1999. "Do You Have a Teachable Point of View?" *Financial Times,* Mastering Strategy Section, Part Three, October 11, pp. 12, 13.

Tomlinson, Richard. 1998. "Mongolia's Wild Ride to Capitalism," *Fortune,* December 12, pp. 192-200.

Vitullo-Martin, Julia. 1997. "Moscow Entrepreneurs Seize Golden Opportunity," *The Wall Street Journal,* Manager's Journal, January 20, p. A14.

Voyle, Susanna. 2000. "E-Tailers Find Their Perfect Partners on High Street," *Financial Times,* April 7, p. 23.

Williams, Michael and Peter Landers. 2000. "When Keiretsu Lose Their Way, It's Time for a Change," *The Wall Street Journal,* April 27, pp. A1, A12.

## *Chapter 5*

Ascarelli, Silvia. 1997. "Dell Finds U.S. Strategy Works in Europe," *The Wall Street Journal,* February 3, p. A8.

Banks, David. 1999. "Microsoft's Huge Cash Hoard Becomes Big Weapon for Entering New Markets," *The Wall Street Journal,* July 19, pp. A3, A4.

Barboza, David. 1999. "Motorola Rolls Itself Over," *The New York Times,* July 14, pp. C1, C2.

Beck, Ernest. 1999. "Populist Perrier? Nestle Pitches Bottled Water to World's Poor," *The Wall Street Journal,* June 18, pp. B1, B4.

Bowley, Graham. 1997. "Daimler-Benz Halts A-Class for Revision," *Financial Times,* November 12, pp. 1, 12.

Burns, Tom. 1999. "GE Acts As Midwife at Spanish Industrial Rebirth," *Financial Times,* January 21, p. 2.

Chowdhury, Neel. 1999. "Dell Cracks China," *Fortune,* June 21, pp. 120-124.

Collins, Glenn. 1996. "A Coke Coup in Venezuela Leaves Pepsi High and Dry," *The New York Times,* August 17, p. 35.

Cowell, Alan. 2000. "Unilever Plans Huge Cuts in Jobs, Plants and Brands," *The New York Times,* February 23, pp. C1, C4.

Edstron, Jennifer and Martin Eller. 1998. *Barbarians Led by Bill Gates.* New York: Henry Holt and Company.

Egan, Cathleen. 1999. "Pepsi's Funyum's Show Some Brands Can Prosper with Little Marketing," *The Wall Street Journal,* September 22, p. B13.

Fahey, Liam. 1999. *Outwitting, Outmaneuvering, and Outperforming Competition.* New York: Wiley & Sons, Inc.

Foley, John. 1999. "Microsoft Is Trying to Address a New Set of Business Needs With a New Set of Technologies," *InformationWeek,* August 3, pp. 46-74.

Frank, Robert. 2000. "Big Boy's Adventures in Thailand," *The Wall Street Journal,* April 12, pp. B1, B4.

Friedland, Jonathan and Louise Lee. 1997. "The Wal-Mart Way Sometimes Gets Lost in the Translation Overseas," *The Wall Street Journal,* October 8, pp. A1, A12.

Fuerbringer, Jonothan. 2000. "A Miffed Moscow Means Headaches For Ikea," *The New York Times,* Money & Business Section, April 9, p. 4.

Guthrie, Jonathan. 2000. "Size Matters in the Movies As the Wide Screen Gets Bigger and Brashier," *Financial Times,* July 21, p. 11.

Hamm, Steve and Robert D. Hof. 2000. "An Eagle Eye on Customers," *Business Week,* February 21, pp. 67-76.

Harbison, John R. and Peter Pekar, Jr. 1997a. *A Practical Guide to Alliances: Leapfrogging The Learning Curve.* New York: Booz-Allen & Hamilton.

Harbison, John R. and Peter Pekar, Jr. 1997b. *Cross-Border Alliances in the Age of Collaboration.* New York: Booz-Allen & Hamilton.

Harbison, John R. and Peter Pekar, Jr. 1997c. *Institutionalizing Alliance Skills: Secrets of Repeatable Success.* New York: Booz-Allen & Hamilton.

Iskandar, Samer. 2000. "Carrerour Plans Internet Expansion," *Financial Times,* February 25, p. 20.

Jordan, Miriam. 1999. "Pillsbury Presses Flour in India," *The Wall Street Journal,* May 5, pp. B1, B4.

Kapferer, Jean-Noel. 1998. "Making Brands Work Around the World," *Financial Times,* Mastering Global Business (Part One): As Business Goes Global, January 27, pp. 12-13.

Knecht, G. Bruce. 1998. "Bertelsmam Breaks Through a Great Wall With Its Book Clubs," *The Wall Street Journal,* September 18, pp. A1, A6.

Kripalani, Manjeet. 1999. "Unilever's Jewel," *Business Week,* April 26, pp. 114E2-114E4.

Kynge, James. 2000. "Bittersweet Story of Success," *Financial Times*, June 21, p. 10.

Lewis, Peter H. 1999. "It's a Land of the Free (Computer)," *The New York Times*, July 8, p. G1.

Lewis, William, Susanna Voyle, and Richard Revlon. 2000. "Wal-Mart Sparks Europe Revamp," *Financial Times*, January 21, p. 13.

Lohr, Steve. 2000. "Again, It's Microsoft Against the World," *The New York Times*, Money & Business Section, February 13, pp. 1, 16.

Maloney, Janice. 1999. "The E-Trade Stampede," *Time*, September 6, Time Select Business Section.

Markoff, John. 1999. "Microsoft Sets New Internet Strategy," *The New York Times*, September 24, p. C2.

Marozzi, Justin. 1998. "Jollibee Shrugs Off Downturn in Asia," *Financial Times*, February 16, p. 18.

Marshall, Samantha and Steve Stecklow. 2000. "Cambodia's 'Beer Girls' Peddle the Product and Endure the Hassle," *The Wall Street Journal*, May 31, pp. A1, A12.

Matlack, Carol, with Inka Resch and Wendy Zellner. 1999. "En-Garde, Wal-Mart," *Business Week*, September 13, pp. 55, 56.

McKay, Betsy. 1999. "Siberian Soft-Drink Queen Outmarkets Coke and Pepsi," *The New York Times*, August 23, pp. B1, B4.

McNeil, Donald G., Jr. 1996. "Focusing on Black South Africa: Returning After 8 Years, Kodak Runs Into White Anger," *The New York Times*, November 8, pp. D1, D6.

Miller, Scott. 2000. "DaimlerChrysler's Smart Car Roars Back," *The Wall Street Journal*, February 25, p. A17.

Mockler, Robert J. 1989. *Knowledge-Based Systems For Management Decisions*. Englewood Cliffs, NJ: Prentice-Hall.

Mockler, Robert J. 1993. *Strategic Management: An Integrative Context-Specific Process*. Harrisburg, PA: Idea Group Publishing.

Mockler, Robert J. 1996-1998. *On-Site Interviews*, Singapore, China, and Boston, Massachusetts: The Gillette Company.

Moeller, Michael and Linda Himelstein. 1999. "Who Do You Want to Buy Today," *Business Week*, June 7, pp. 32-33.

Newman, Cathy. 1999. "BSkyB to StepUp Free Digital TV Drive," *Financial Times*, July 3/4, p. 7.

Parker-Pope, Tara. 1996. "Challenges Weaken Outlook for Unilever," *The Wall Street Journal Europe*, May 2, p. 6.

Quick, Rebecca. 1999. "Behind Doors of a Warehouse: Heavy Lifting of E-Commerce," *The Wall Street Journal*, September 3, pp. B1, B3.

Robinson, Gwen. 1997. "Shiseido's New Brand Targets Asia," *Financial Times*, July 3, p. 18.

Rose, Matthew. 1998. "For a Short Time, U.K. Town's Motto was 'Fish Into Chips'," *The Wall Street Journal,* October 20, pp. A1, A6.

Sahay, Arvind. 1998. "Finding the Right International Mix," *Financial Times,* Mastering Marketing Section (Part Ten), November 16, pp. 2, 3.

Simonian, Haig. 1997. "Mercedes Smart Car Hit By Safety Worries," *Financial Times,* December 19, p. 1.

Smith, Craig S. 1999a. "Coke Expects Sales in China to Stay Strong," *The Wall Street Journal Europe,* August 28, p. 7.

Smith, Craig S. 1999b. "Volkswagen Plans to Build Low-Price Car To Sell in China," *The Wall Street Journal,* June 30, pp. A19, A22.

"Spin Style," 1999. *The Economist,* August 14, p. 52.

Stevenson, Richard W. 1995. "Smitten By Britain: Thatcherism's Industrial Evolution," *The New York Times,* Business Section, October 15, pp. 1, 10.

Stodghill III, Ron. 1998. "VW's New Bug: Cute But . . . ," *Time,* January 19, pp. 44-46.

Tagliabue, John. 2000. "Now Playing in Europe: Invasion of the Multiplex," *The New York Times,* January 27, pp. C1, C23.

Taylor, Paul. 1999. "BT Offers Free PC in Bid to Win New Users," *Financial Times,* September 15, p. 10.

Thurow, Roger. 2000. "South Africans Who Fought For Sanctions Now Scrape for Investors," *The Wall Street Journal,* February 11, pp. A1, A4.

Tomkins, Richard. 1999a. "Fading Stars of the Global Stage," *Financial Times,* March 5, p. 30.

Tomkins, Richard. 1999b. "Assessing a Name's Worth," *Financial Times,* June 22, p. 12.

Tomkins, Richard. 2000. "Fallen Icons," *Financial Times,* February 1, p. 12.

"Understanding CRM," 2000. *Financial Times,* Special Section, March 15, pp. 1-36.

Voyle, Susanna and Charles Pretzik. 2000. "Interbrew Buys Bass Brewing Arm for 2.3 Billion Pounds," *Financial Times,* June 15, p. 22.

Wallace, James. 1997. *Overdrive: Bill Gates and the Race to Control Cyberspace.* New York: John Wiley & Sons, Inc.

Zachary, G. Pascal. 1996. "Major U.S. Companies Expand Efforts to Sell to Consumers Abroad," *The Wall Street Journal,* June 13, pp. A1, A11.

## *Chapter 6*

Ball, Jeffrey. 1999. "Productivity Improves Among U.S. Auto Makers," *The Wall Street Journal,* June 18, pp. A2, A6.

Barham, John. 1999. "A Leaner, Simpler Production," *Financial Times,* June 11, p. 12.

Beit-On, Harel. 1999. "In the Digital Factory: The Next Generation," *Chief Executive,* Virtual Manufacturing Section, May, issue 144, pp. 54-57.

Bremner, Brian, Larry Armstrong, Kathleen Kerwin, and Keith Naughton. 1997. "Toyota's Crusade," *Business Week,* April 7, pp. 104-118.

Brooks, Rick. 2000a. "FedEx to Launch Service That Allows Small Companies To Sell Online," *The Wall Street Journal,* June 12, p. A3.

Brooks, Rick. 2000b. "UPS in Talks to Buy 2 Logistics Firms," *The Wall Street Journal,* June 12, p. A6.

Burt, Tim. 1999. "Boss of GM Offshoot Wants Lean Machine to Accelerate," *Financial Times,* October 19, p. 11.

Bylinsky, Gene. 2000. "For Sale: Japanese Plants in the U.S." *Fortune,* February 21, pp. 240(B)-240(D).

Chang, Leslie. 1999. "Megabookstores Arrive in China, Courtesy of the State," *The Wall Street Journal,* March 1, pp. B1, B4.

Cordon, Carlos, Tom Vollman, and Jussi Heikkila. 1998. "Thinking Clearly About Outsourcing," *Financial Times,* Mastering Global Business (Part Four): Creating the Global Organization, February 20, pp. 4-6.

Deutsch, Claudia H. 2000. "Another Economy on the Supply Side," *The New York Times,* April 8, pp. C1, C4.

Forest, Stephanie. 1999. "Look Whose Thinking Small," *Business Week,* May 17, pp. 67-70.

Friedland, Jonathan. 1999. "Mexico's Oil Company Becomes Businesslike to Avoid Privatization," *The Wall Street Journal,* May 24, pp. A1, A114.

George, Stephen. 1997. *Uncommon Sense.* New York: Wiley.

Gibson, Ian. 1998. "Outsourcing: Why I Have Reservations," *Financial Times,* Auto Survey, February 23, p. VIII.

Griffiths, John. 1997. "Toyota Announces New Euro-Car," *Financial Times,* May 8, p. 15.

Griffiths, John. 1999. "Daewoo Tops Car Productivity League," *Financial Times,* October 22, p. 8.

Hansell, Saul. 1998. "Is This the Factory of the Future?," *The New York Times,* Money & Business Section, July 26, pp. 1, 12, 13.

Hollinger, Peggy. 1999. "Who's Afraid of Wal-Mart?" *Financial Times,* May 5, p. 15.

Hornblower, Margot. 1997. "Guess Gets Out: The Jeans Company, Beset By Rivals and Union Organizers, Bolts For Mexico," *Time,* January 27, p. 48.

Hult, G. Thomas M., Mark N. Frolick, and Ernest L. Nichols, Jr. 1995. "Organizational Learning and Cycle Times Issues in the Procurement Process," *Cycle Time Research,* Volume 1, Number 1, pp. 25-40.

Jackson, Tony. 1998. "The Eclipse of Manufacturing," *Financial Times,* December 15, p. 17.

Kahn, Jeremy. 1999. "Wal-Mart Goes Shopping in Europe," *Fortune,* June 7, pp. 105-112.

Kline, Maureen. 1996. "Olivetti Undergoes Its Latest Revamping: Staff Cuts, Other Changes Bring Initial Payoff," *The Wall Street Journal Europe,* May 2, p. 4.

Lundegaard, Karen. 2000. "Ford Plant, GM Receive High Marks in Study of Auto Makers' Productivity," *The Wall Street Journal,* June 16, p. A8.

"Manufacturing Survey." 1998. *The Economist,* June 20, pp. 1-18.

Marsh, Peter. 1999a. "Just-In-Time Culture Key For Europe," *Financial Times,* October 18, p. 10.

Marsh, Peter. 1999b. "Step Into the Engine Room of the World," *Financial Times,* September 16, p. 14.

Matta, Khalil F. 1999. "Quality as a Strategic Instrument for Competing in the Automobile Industry," Presentation, Decision Sciences Institute (DSI) 5th International Conference, Athens, Greece, July 4-7.

Miller, Joel. 1999. "Mexico Builds a Home-Appliance Bonanza: GE, Whirlpool Shift Production, Boos Exports to U.S." *The New York Times,* August 23, p. A12.

Mockler, Robert J. 1993. *Strategic Management: An Integrative Context Specific Process.* Harrisburg, PA: Idea Group Publishing.

Moran, Nuala. 2000. "Seductive Software Services on Offer," *Financial Times,* E-Business Survey, May 17, p. I.

Nelson, Emily. 1999. "Wal-Mart's 'Small-Marts' May Make It Biggest Grocer," *The Wall Street Journal,* June 21, p. B4.

Newing, Rod. 1999. "Leaner, Meaner—and More Agile," *Financial Times,* Electronic Business Section, October 22, p. 2.

Parkes, Christopher. 1998. "Boeing Shares Fall 17 percent After Big Drop in Profit Forecast," *Financial Times,* December 3, p. 1.

Pereira, Joseph. 1997. "New Sneaker Superstores Aim to Step on Their Competition," *The Wall Street Journal,* March 10, pp. B1, B5.

Pollack, Andrew. 1996a. "AIWA Plans a Production Shift to Japan: A Weak Yen Makes Home Seem Sweeter," *The New York Times,* August 6, p. D3.

Pollack, Andrew. 1996b. "U.S. and Japan Car Makers Tailor Their Models to Vie for Asia," *The New York Times,* June 6, pp. D1, D7.

Pope, Kyle. 1996. "A Steelmaker Build Up By Buying Cheap Mills Finally Meets Its Match: Global Success of U.K.'s Ispat Helps Little in Kazakstan At a Laughably Bad Plant," *The Wall Street Journal Europe,* May 2, pp. 1, 6.

Raymo, Joshua Cooper and David S. Jackson. 1997. "The Prince of San Mateo," *Time,* May 5, pp. 40-42.

Robinson, Elizabeth, David Wighton, and Andrew Edgecliffe-Johnson. 1999. "Wal-Mart Set to Win UK Group," *Financial Times,* June 15, p. 1.

Romero, Simon. 1999. "2 U.S. Auto Makers Delay New Factories in Brazil," *The New York Times,* April 21, p. C6.

Rundle, Rhonda L. 1997. "Guess Shifts Apparel-Making to Mexico from Los Angeles Amid Labor Charges," *The Wall Street Journal,* January 14, p. A2.

Schemo, Diana Jean. 1996. "Is VW's New Plant Lean, or Just Mean?" *The New York Times,* November 19, pp. D1, D6.

Schuckman, Lisa. 1998. "Toyota Revamps Plants for Shift to Exports If Local Market Fails," *The Wall Street Journal,* October 7, p. A17.

Sharpe, Antonia. 1999. "Body Shop Disposes of Manufacturing Business," *Financial Times*, August 24, p. 19.

Shirouzu, Norihiko. 1999. "An Efficiency Guru Refits Honda to Fight Auto Giants," *The Wall Street Journal*, September 15, pp. B1, B4.

Simison, Robert L. 1999. "Toyota Develops a Way to Make a Car Within Five Days of a Custom Order," *The Wall Street Journal*, August 6, p. A4.

Simonian, Haig. 1998. "Smart Work for Partners," *Financial Times*, Auto Survey, February 23, p. VII.

Stein, Tom and Jeff Sweat. 1998. "Supply Chains," *InformationWeek*, November 9, pp. 36-46.

Steinmetz, Greg and Christopher J. Chipello. 1998. "Local Presence Is Key to European Deals," *The Wall Street Journal*, June 30, p. A15.

Taylor, Paul. 1999. "Passport to Business Integration," *Financial Times*, Enterprise Resource Planning Survey, May 26, p. I.

"The Modular T," 1998. *The Economist*, September 5, pp. 60, 61.

Thornton, Emily and Kathleen Kerwin. 1999. "Can Honda Go It Alone?" *Business Week*, July 5, pp. 42-45.

Tomkins, Richard. 1999. "The Formula to Beat," *Financial Times*, May 5, p. 15.

Uchitelle, Louis. 1996. "Basic Research is Losing Out As Companies Stress Results," *The New York Times*, October 8, pp. A1, D6.

Vlasic, Bill. 1997. "In Alabama, the Soul of a New Mercedes?" *Business Week*, March 31, pp. 70, 71.

Wagstyl, Stefan. 1997. *The Financial Times*, Financial Times Survey, January 7, p. I.

Willcocks, Leslie. 1998. "Reducing the Risks of Outsourced IT," *Financial Times*, Mastering Global Business (Part Four): Creating the Global Organization, February 20, pp. 10-11.

Womack, James P. and Daniel T. Jones. 1996. *Lean Thinking*. New York: Simon & Schuster.

Woodruff, David. 1989. "Adding Some Spice to an Old Formula," *Business Week*, Special Issue, p. 134.

Woodruff, David. 1999. "Carrefour Pushes to Expand Into Japan, Counting on Appeal of Hypermarkets," *The Wall Street Journal*, June 15, p. 1.

World Wire. 1997. "Italian-Japanese Auto Venture," *The Wall Street Journal*, January 29, p. A7.

Zuckerman, Laurence. 1999a. "Airbus Won't Be Transformed This Year, Finance Chief Says," *The New York Times*, March 18, p. C4.

Zuckerman, Laurence. 1999b. "The Jet Wars of the Future," *The New York Times*, July 9, pp. C1, C5.

## *Chapter 7*

"A Survey of Business and the Internet." 1999. *The Economist*, June 26, pp. 1-40.

Akwule, Raymond. 1992. *Global Telecommunications: The Technology, Administration, and Policies*. Stoneham, MA: Butterworth-Heineman.

Baker, Stephen and Kerry Capell. 2000a. "Chris Gent, King of the Web?" *Business Week,* February 14, pp. 60-61.

Baker, Stephen, and Kerry Capell. 2000b. "The Race to Rule Mobile," *Business Week,* February 21, pp. 58-60.

Beckett, Paul. 1999. "Citgroup's Web Push to Test Firm's Brand Name," *The Wall Street Journal,* June 23, pp. C1, C2.

Berners-Lee, Tim with Mark Fischetti. 1999. *Weaving the Web: The Original Design and Destiny of the World Wide Web by Its Inventor.* San Francisco, CA: Harper.

Blumstein, Rebecca and Leslie Cauley. 1999. "Ma Bell's Plan Is to Serve up TV, Phone Via Cable," *The Wall Street Journal,* May 6, pp. B1, B11.

Boudette, Neal E. and Kevin J. Delaney. 2000. "British Internet Portal Vizzavi Faces Wireless Hurdles," *The Wall Street Journal,* June 21, p. B4.

Brooks Rick. 2000. "FedEx to Launch Service That Allows Small Companies to Build Online Services," *The Wall Street Journal,* June 12, p. A6.

Cane, Alan. 2000. "Epicenter of Earth Has Shifted to Europe," *Financial Times,* Financial Times Telecoms Survey, March 15, p.1.

"Cleaner Cars: Pure As the Driven Snow," 2000a. *The Economist,* January 15, p. 86.

Cohn, Linda, Diane Brady, and David Welch. 2000. "B2B: The Hottest Net Bet Yet?" *Business Week,* January 17, pp. 36, 37.

Cowell, Alan. 2000. "Europe Plays Internet Catch-Up," *The New York Times,* March 11, pp. C1, C14.

Dalton, Gregory. 1999. "Globalization," *Information Week,* January 18, pp. 38-62.

Deutsch, Claudia H. 2000. "G.E. Is Planning to Offer Online Banking," *The New York Times,* April 25, p. C2.

"E-Commerce: Survey," 2000. *The Economist,* February 26, pp. 5-54.

Edmondson, Gail and Elisabeth Malkin. 2000. "Spain's Surge," *Business Week,* May 22, pp. 73-60.

Fairlamb, David. 1999. "E-Day: Online Banks Invade Europe," *Business Week,* October 25, pp. 134E6-134E8.

Ferrarini, Elizabeth. 1985. *Informania: The Guide to Essential Electronic Services.* Boston, MA: Houghton Mifflin.

French, Howard W. 1998. "In Africa, Reality of Technology Falls Short," *The New York Times,* January 26, pp. D1, D10.

Golden, Fredick and Michael D. Lemonick. 2000. "The Race Is Over," *Time,* July 3, pp. 18-23.

Gomes, Lee and Thomas Weber. 2000. "Hackers' Weapon Exploits Internet's Open Nature," *The Wall Street Journal,* February 10, pp. B1, B6.

Green, Heather, Mike France, Marcia Stepanek, and Amy Borus. 2000. "It's Time for Rules in Wonderland," *Business Week,* March 20, pp. 83-94.

Greenwald, Jeff. 1994. "Wiring Africa," *Wired,* June, p. 12.

Greenwald, John. 2000. "J'Adore Content," *Time,* June 26, pp. 42-43.

Hall, Stephen S. 2000. "The Recycled Generation," *The New York Times,* Magazine Section, January 30, pp. 30-35, 46, 74, 78, 79.

Hamilton, David P. 2000. "U.S. Service Providers Still Do Mediocre Job of Wireless Access," *The Wall Street Journal,* June 21, p. B1.

Hamilton, David P. and David S. Cloud. 2000. "The Internet Under Siege: Stalking the Hackers," *The Wall Street Journal,* February 10, pp. B1, B6.

Harding, James. 2000. "Reed Elsevier to Invest $1.1Bn in Online Services," *Financial Times,* February 26, p. 15.

Harris, Roy. 2000. "Special Report: E-Banking," *Chief Financial Officer (CFO),* June pp. 99-108.

"Japanese Internet Tsunami." 2000. *Financial Times,* March 3, pp. I-VI.

Johnson, George. 1999. "How Much Give Can the Brain Take," *The New York Times,* Week in Review Section, October 24, pp. 1, 6.

Kahoe, Louis. 2000. "B2B Revolution Set To Reshape the Competitive Landscape," *Financial Times,* March 20, p. 22.

Koretz, Gene. 2000. "E-Shoppers Take a Breather," *Business Week,* March 20, p. 32.

Lemonick, Michael. 2000. "The Geneome Is Mapped. Now What?" *Time,* July 3, pp. 24-29.

Luh, James C. 2000. "A Personal Touch," *Internet World,* June 1, pp. 54-58.

Maitland, Carol and Anthony Bianco. 2000. "Vivendi's Global Grab," *Business Week,* May 8, pp. 66-67.

Markoff, John. 1999. "Tiniest Circuits Hold Prospect of Explosive Computer Speeds," *The New York Times,* July 16, pp. A1, C17.

McCartney, Neil. 2000. "WAP Telephones: Confusion and Excitement In the New Wireless Era," *Financial Times,* FT Telecoms Survey (2), June 21, p. XVIII.

McCartney, Scott. 2000. "Airlines Find a Bunch of High Tech Tricks to Keep Income Aloft," *The Wall Street Journal,* January 20, pp. A1, A6.

McDaniel, George (Ed.). 1994. *IBM Dictionary of Computing,* 10th Edition, New York: McGraw-Hill.

"Now for the Hard Part,"1999. *Chief Executive,* Cover Story, September, issue 147, pp. 36-42.

Nusbaum, Alexandra, Rahul Jacob, John Burton, James Kynge, and Peter Montagnon. 2000. "Asia Plays A Game of Commercial Catch-Up," *Financial Times,* February 23, p. 10.

Parsons, Andrew J. 1996. "Nestle: The Visions of Local Managers—An Interview with Peter Brabeck-Letmathe, CEO elect, Nestle," *The McKinsey Quarterly,* Number 2, pp. 4-29.

Petersen, Andrea. 2000. "DoubleClick Reverses Course After Privacy Outcry," *The Wall Street Journal,* March 3, pp. B1, B6.

Pollack, Andrew. 1999. "Even a Sky Can Have Limits," *The New York Times,* August 4, pp. C1, C9.

Port, Otis. 2000. "A Clean Technology Powers Up," *Business Week,* May 8, pp. 102-105.

Rich, Jennifer L. 2000. "Big Latin Investment by British Telecom," *The New York Times,* April 29, p. C2.

Romero, Simon. 2000. "Millions Phoning Online, Finding Price Is Right Even If Quality Isn't," *The New York Times,* July 6, pp. C1, C2.

Sager, Ira, Steve Hamm, Neil Cross, and John Carey. 2000. "Cyber Crime," *Business Week,* February 21, pp. 37-42.

Schiesel, Seth. 1999. "At Last, a New Strategy for AT&T," *The New York Times,* Money and Business Section, January 17, pp. 1, 13.

Schiesel, Seth. 2000a. "Convergence, The Next Stage in Technology, May Wind Up Being a Different Creature Than Expected, *The New York Times,* May 29, p. C3.

Schiesel, Seth. 2000b. "Vivendi's Vis-a-Vis the Internet," *The New York Times,* June 21, p. C10.

Schlender, Brent. 1999. "The Real Road Ahead," *Fortune,* October 25, pp. 138-152.

Shillingford, Jola. 1999. "Satellite Costs To Total $23 Billion," *Financial Times,* FT Telecoms Survey (2), June 9, p. XVII.

Shillingford, Jola. 2000. "Ready to Take Off More Rapidly Than the Internet," *Financial Times,* FT Telecoms Survey (2), March 15, p. 1.

Stepanek, Marcia. 1999. "How an Intranet Opened Up the Door to Profits," *Business Week, E-Biz,* July 6, EB32-EB38.

Tait, Nikki and Louise Kehoe. 2000. "Motor Giants Unite to Form Online Supplies Exchange," *Financial Times,* February 26, p. 1.

Tedeschi, Bob. 1999. "The Net's Real Business Happens .Com to .Com," *The New York Times,* April 19, pp. C1, C6.

Vogel, Thomas T. and Pamela Druckerman. 2000. "Latin Internet Craze Sets Off Alarm Bells," *The Wall Street Journal,* February 16, p. A23.

Voyle, Susanna. 2000. "E-Tailers Find Their Perfect Partners on High Street," *Financial Times,* April 7, p. 23.

Wagstyl, Stefan. 2000. "Net Fever Spreads East (Eastern Europe)," *Financial Times,* March 3, p. 12.

Waters, Richard. 1999a. "Case Study: General Electric," *Financial Times,* (Autumn 1999 Digital Business Guide), September 30, p. 20.

Waters, Richard. 1999b. "New Communications Industry Takes Shape," *Financial Times,* FT Telecoms Survey (2), June 9, p. XII.

Zimmerman, Ann. 2000. "Wal-Mart to Open Reworked Web Site for SamsClub.com," *The Wall Street Journal,* June 6, p. B8.

## *Chapter 8*

"A Survey of International Banking." 1999. *The Economist,* April 17, pp. 1-26.

Andrews, Edmund L. 2000. "Top German Bank in Talks to Buy Rival," *The New York Times,* March 8, pp. C1, C7.

Beckett, Paul. 1999. "American Express Starts Online Bank," *The Wall Street Journal,* July 23, p. B8.

Betts, Paul. 1999. "Italian Banks Move to Join European Merger Wave," *Financial Times,* March 22, p. 1.

Boland, Vincent. 2000. "World's Bourses Jostle for Position As Upstarts Elbow in," *Financial Times,* Stock and Derivatives Exchanges Survey, March 31, p. I.

Cowell, Alan. 1999. "HSBC To Pay $10.3 Billion for Republic; Biggest Overseas Deal for an American Bank," *The New York Times,* May 4, pp. C1. C6.

"Derivatives." 2000. *Financial Times Survey* Annual Review, June 28, pp. I-VI.

Druckerman, Pamela. 1999. "Do You Want to buy a Phone Company? One Is Going Begging," *The Wall Street Journal,* July 14, pp. A1, A8.

Ewing, Teryak and Silvia Ascarelli. 2000."One World, How Many Stock Exchanges?" *The Wall Street Journal,* May 15, pp. C1, C20.

Fabrikant, Geraldine. 1996. "Murdoch Bets Heavily on a Global Vision," *The New York Times,* July 29, pp. D1, D8, D9.

Fatehi, Kamal. 1996. *International Management,* Upper Saddle River, NJ: Prentice-Hall.

Friedland, Jonathan. 1997. "Argentina Plans $2 Billion Bond Issue, Extending Flurry of Latin Offerings," *The Wall Street Journal,* January 8, p. A18.

Gewitz, Carl. 1997. "Sieman's Issue in 3 Currencies Helps to Shape the Age of the Euro," *International Herald Tribune,* February 10, p. 12.

Iversen, Kathy. 1998. "The Evolving Role of Finance," *Strategy and Leadership,* March/April, pp. 6-9.

Jack, Andrew. 1999. "Foreign Banks Edge Back Into Risky Russian Market," *Financial Times,* July 6, p. 18.

Labaton, Stephen. 1999. "Accord Reached on Lifting of Depression-Era Barriers Among Financial Industries," *The New York Times,* October 23, pp. A1-C4.

Lapper, Richard and Edward Luce. 1997. "Extreme to Mainstream," *Financial Times,* June 9, p. 15.

Logue, Dennis E. 1998. "Managing Currency Risk in a Volatile World," *Financial Times,* Mastering Global Business (Part Eight): Navigating the Tides of Global Finance, March 20, pp. 10-11.

MacDonald, Elizabeth. 1999. "Number of Problems," *The Wall Street Journal,* Global Investing Section, April 26, p. R6.

Mockler, Robert J. 1973. *The Management Control Process.* Englewood Cliffs, NJ: Prentice-Hall.

Mueller, Gerhard G., Helen Gernon, and Gary K. Meek. 1994. *Accounting: An International Perspective,* Third Edition Burr Ridge, IL: Irwin.

O'Brien, Timothy L. 1999. "Follow the Money, If You Can," *The New York Times,* Money and Business Section, September 5, pp. 1, 12.

Owen, David. 1997. "France Telecom Incurs Loss Under U.S. Accounting," *Financial Times,* July 1, p. 17.

Portanger, Erik. 1999. "Barclays Says That It's Signing Up 10,000 a Week for Internet Banking," *The Wall Street Journal,* August 6, p. A8.

Raghavan, Anita. 2000. "MeritaNordbanken Nears Unidanmark Purchase," *The Wall Street Journal,* March 6, p. A17.

Remenzi, Dan and Bill Cinnamond. 1996."Banking 2000? Reengineering at the First National Bank of South Africa To Create a Branch of the Future," *Journal of Strategic Information Systems,* Fall, 5, 293-316.

Rhoads, Christopher, Vanessa Fuhrmans, and Anita Raghavan. 2000. "Deutsche Bank, Dresdner to Unveil $29.74 Billion Merger," *The Wall Street Journal,* March 8, pp. A3, A17.

Ridding, John. 1997. "Want to Buy a City in China?" *The Financial Times,* March 8-9, p. 3.

Schneier Robert and Jerry Miccolis. 1998. "Enterprise Risk Management," *Strategy and Leadership,* March/April, pp. 10-17.

Sesit, Michael R. 2001. "Will Europe's Banks Founder on the Rocks of Telecom Debt?" *The Wall Street Journal,* January 30, p. A6.

Shim, Jae K. and Joel G. Siegel. 1989. *Encyclopedic Dictionary of Accounting and Finance.* Englewood Cliffs, NJ: Prentice-Hall.

Shim, Jae K. and Joel G. Siegel. 1990. *Barron's Accounting Handbook.* Happauge, NY: Barron's Educational Series, Inc.

Simons, Robert. 1995. *Levers of Control.* Boston, MA: Harvard Business School Press.

Siwolop, Sana. 1997. "Online Community," *Information Week,* September 29, pp. 89-90.

Springate, David J. 1990. *Ampak International, Ltd.* Dallas, TX: The University of Texas at Dallas.

"Survey: Birth of the Euro." 1998. *Financial Times,* April 30, pp. I-VIII.

Tett, Gillian. 2000. "Retailer Set to Seek Bank License," *Financial Times,* March 9, p. 15.

Thornhill, John. 1998. "The Bear Takes on the Market: Some of Russia's Largest Companies Are Flagrantly Abusing Shareholder Rights," *Financial Times,* February 16, p. 10.

van Duyn, Bayan Rahman, and John Labate. 2000. "Ten Stock Exchanges Plan to Have 24-Hour Global Trading," *Financial Times,* June 8, p. V.

Violino, Bob. 1999. "Banking on e-Business," *InformationWeek,* May 3, pp. 44-52.

Wagstyl, Stefan and Christopher Bobinski. 2000. "Citigroup to Pay $1Bn for Poland's Top Corporate Bank," *Financial Times,* February 11, p. 1.

Wendlandt, Astrid. 2000. "Winner Gets to Rule the World," *Financial Times,* Stock and Derivatives Exchanges Survey, March 31, p. 4.

## *Chapter 9*

Aeppel, Timothy. 2000. "Young and Old See Technology Sparking Friction on Shop Floor," *The Wall Street Journal,* March 7, pp. A1, A10.

Andrews, Edmund L. 2000a. "Airbus Decides to Make a Bet on a Next-Generation Jumbo Jet," *The New York Times,* June 24, pp. C1, C2.

Andrews, Edmund L. 2000b. "The Metamorphosis of Germany, Inc." *The New York Times,* March 12, Money and Business Section, pp. 1, 12.

Atkins, Ralph and William Lewis. 2000. "Vodafone Wins Takeover Battle for Mannesmann," *Financial Times,* February 4, p. 1.

Ball, Jeffrey. 1999. "Productivity Improves Among U.S. Auto Makers," *The Wall Street Journal,* June 18, p. A2.

"Banking in Europe: Deutsche's Big Gamble," 2000. *The Economist,* March 11, pp. 74-75.

Barrett, Amy. 1999. "How Fred Hassan Rescued Pharmacia and Upjohn," *Business Week,* April 26, pp. 63-66.

Bartlett, Christopher and Sumantra Ghoshal. 1991. *Managing Across Borders.* Boston, MA: Harvard Business School Press.

Buckley, Neil, David Owen, and Robert Corzine. 1998. "Total Set for PetroFina Takeover," *Financial Times,* December 1, p. I.

Cohen, Norma. 1999. "KPMG Withdraws Merger Study," *Financial Times,* November 29, p. 19.

Cowell, Alan. 2000. "Unilever Plans Huge Cuts in Jobs, Plants and Brands," *The New York Times,* February 23, pp. C1, C4.

Cramb, Gordon. 2000. "Philips Rewires Its Structure to Face the Future," *Financial Times,* February 16, p. 18.

Donaldson, Lex. 1995. *American Anti-Management Theories of Organization.* New York: Cambridge University Press.

Donaldson, Lex. 1996. *For Positivist Organization Theory.* Thousand Oaks, CA: Sage.

Dwyer, Paula, Pete Engardio, Zachary Schiller, and Stanley Reed. 1994. "The New Model: Tearing Up Today's Organization Chart," *Business Week,* Special Issue: 21st Century Capitalism, November, pp. 80-90.

Fairlamb, David. 2000. "German Banks Get Religion: Under Pressure, They're Finally Beginning to Restructure," *Business Week,* March 6, pp. 157-160.

Friedheim, Cyrus. 1998. *The Trillion-Dollar Enterprise: How the Alliance Revolution Will Transform Global Business.* Reading, MA: Perseus Books.

Fukuyama, Frances. 1999. "Death of the Hierarchy," *Financial Times,* Weekend, June 12-13, pp. I, IX.

Gillooly, Brian. 1995. "H-P's New Curse," *InformationWeek,* March 20, pp. 45-56.

Griffith, Victoria. 1997. "Teamwork's Own Goals: The Limitations of Applying Teamwork Methods in the Workplace," *Financial Times,* July 18, p. 20.

Guyon, Janet. 1999. "When John Browne Talks, Big Oil Listens," *Fortune,* July 5, pp. 116-122.

Harris, Clay. 1999. "On Course to Topple the Record," *Financial Times,* International Mergers and Acquisitions Section, September 22, p. 1.

Helgesen, Sally. 1995. *The Web of Inclusion: A New Architecture for Building a Great Organization*. New York: Doubleday/Currency.

Ibrahim, Youssef M. 1999. "Importance of Being Persuasive: Daimler-Chrysler Merger Made an Art of Making a Case," *The New York Times,* May 26, pp. C1. C7.

Iverson, Ken. 1998. *Plain Talk.* New York: John Wiley & Sons.

Kerwin, Kathleen and Jack Ewing. 1999. "Nasser: Ford Be Nimble," *Business Week,* September 27, pp. 42, 43.

Kerwin, Kathleen and Kieth Naughton. 1999. "Remaking Ford," *Business Week,* October 11, pp. 131-142.

Kerwin, Kathleen, Marcia Stepanek, and David Welch. 2000. "At Ford, E-Commerce Is Job 1," *Business Week,* February 28, pp. 74-78.

Landler, Mark. 1995. "Alcatel to Be Reorganized Along Product Lines," *The New York Times,* October 6, p. D6.

Liesman, Steve, Carlos Tejada, and Christopher Cooper. 1999. "As Big Oil Gets Bigger, Its Leftovers Provide Feast for Independents," *The Wall Street Journal,* July 1, pp. A1, A10.

Maitland, Alison. 2000. "Throw the Rule-Book Out the Window," *Financial Times,* February 8, p. 14.

Major, Tony and Alexander Nicoll. 1999. "European Aerospace Merger Agreed," *Financial Times,* October 15, p. 1.

Marsh, Virginia, Thorold Barker, and Hillary Durgin. 1999. "BP Amoco Set to Restructure to Meet 'Aggressive' Targets," *Financial Times,* July 16, p. 1.

McDowell, Edwin. 1996. "Changing Course at Cunard," *The New York Times,* August 6, pp. D1, D15.

Meredith, Robyn. 2000. "Autobytel Plans to Sell Cars Directly Over the Internet," *The New York Times,* January 24, p. C2.

Michaels, Daniel. 2000. "Partners Agree on Airbus Incorporation," *The Wall Street Journal,* May 11, p. A21.

Michaels, Daniel and Jeff Cole. 2000. "Airbus Beats Boeing in Jet Orders for the First Time," *The Wall Street Journal,* January 13, p. A17.

Pasternack, Bruce A. and Albert J. Viscio. 1998. *The Centerless Corporation.* New York: Simon & Schuster.

Perlez, Jane. 1994. "GE Finds Tough Going in Hungary," *The New York Times,* July 25, pp. D1, D8.

Pretzick, Charles. 2000. "Cross-Atlantic Consolidation Gains Pace," *Financial Times,* Mergers and Acquisitions Survey, June 30, pp. 1, 2.

Puffer, Sheila M. 1999. "Continental Airlines' CEO Gordon Bethune on Teams and New Product Development," an interview, *The Academy of Management Executive,* August, pp. 28-35.

Rasmusson, Erika. 1999. "An Emerging Success," *Sales & Marketing Management,* October, pp. 62-69.

Rhoads, Christopher. 1998a. "Deutsche Bank to Buy a Unit of French Firm," *The Wall Street Journal,* December 2, p. A15.

Rhoads, Christopher. 1998b. "Deutsche Bank to Give BTR 'No Autonomy'," *The Wall Street Journal,* December 1, p. A3.

Robbins, Harvey and Michael Finley. 1998. *Transcompetition: Moving Beyond Competition and Collaboration.* New York: McGraw-Hill (Business Week Books).

Rossant, John. 2000. "Birth of a Giant," *Business Week,* July 10, pp. 170-176.

Sesit, Michael R. and Anita Raghavan. 1998. "Deutsche Bank Hit Many Costly Snags in Its American Foray," *The Wall Street Journal,* May 4, pp. A1. A12.

Simison, Robert L. 1999. "Toyota Develops a Way to Make a Car Within Five Days of a Custom Order," *The Wall Street Journal,* August 4, p. A4.

Simison, Robert L. 2000. "GM Retools to Sell Custom Cars Online," *The Wall Street Journal,* February 22, p. B23.

Sorkin, Andrew Ross and Melody Petersen. 2000. "Glaxo and SmithKline Agree to Form Largest Drugmaker," *The New York Times,* January 17, pp. A1, A10.

Spindle, Bill. 1999. "Travellers, Nikko Union is Many Things; Easy Is Not One of Them," *The Wall Street Journal,* May 19, pp. A1, A10.

Tagliabue, John. 2000. "Renault Pins Its Survival on a Global Gamble," *The New York Times,* Money and Business Section, July 2, pp. 1, 6.

Treece, James B., Kathleen Kerwin, and Heidi Dawley. 1995. "Ford: Alex Trotman's Daring Global Strategy," *Business Week,* April 3, pp. 94-104.

Zachary, G. Pascal. 1999. "Let's Play Oligopoly! Why Giants Like Having Other Giants Around," *The Wall Street Journal,* March 8, pp. B1,B5.

Zeien, Albert. 1995. "Gillette's Global Marketing Experiences," *Talk at St. John's University,* New York, February 27.

Zuckerman, Laurence. 1998. "The Jet Wars of the Future," *The New York Times,* July 9, pp. C1, C5.

Zuckerman, Laurence. 1999. "How FedEx Made Its Pilots Blink," *The New York Times,* November 24, pp. C1, C2.

## *Chapter 10*

Beck, Ernest. 1996. "Restructured Firm in Hungary Offers Cultural Lessons," *The Wall Street Journal,* June 15, p. A10.

Biers, Dan and Miriam Jordan. 1996. "McDonald's in India Decides the Big Mac is Not a Sacred Cow," *The Wall Street Journal,* October 14, p. A14.

Block, Robert. 1999. "How Big Mac Kept From Becoming a Serb Archenemy," *The Wall Street Journal,* September 3, pp. B1, B3.

Chang, Leslie. 1999. "In China, History Class Means 'An Education in Shame'," *The Wall Street Journal,* June 23, pp. A1, A14.

Chua-Eoan, Howard. 1995. "War of the Worlds," *Time,* August 7, pp. 42-53.

Cook. Joe. 1999. "Muppet Makers Try to Bridge Ethnic Divide," *Financial Times,* August 7-8, p. 2.

Dalcy, Suzanne. 2000. "Europe's Dim View of U.S. Is Evolving Into French Hostility," *The New York Times,* April 9, pp. A1, A10.

Dologite, Dorothy G. and Robert J. Mockler. 1993. *An Information Systems Plan (Strategic and Operational) for the Malaysian Agricultural Research and Development Institute (MARDI)*. Kuala Lumpur, Malaysia: MARDI.

Dunne, Nancy. 1999. "Europe's Fears on Modified Food Cross the Atlantic," *The Financial Times*, October 21, p. 4.

"Enron Can Resume Big Indian Power Project," 1996. *The New York Times*, July 10, p. D19.

"Enron Plans $10 Billion Project in India," 1997. *International Herald Tribune*, February 2, p. 11.

Ferraro, Gary P. 1998. *The Cultural Dimensions of International Business*, Third Edition. Upper Saddle River, New Jersey: Prentice-Hall.

Foster, Dean Allen. 1992. *Bargaining Across Borders: How to Negotiate Business Successfully Anywhere in the World*. New York: McGraw-Hill.

French, Howard W. 1999. "Exam Wars, Prepping and Other Nursery Crimes," *The New York Times*, December 7, p. A4.

French, Howard W. 2000. "Women Win a Battle, but Job Bias Still Rules Japan," *The New York Times*, February 26, p. A3.

Fuerbringer, Jonathan. 2000. "A Miffed Moscow Means Headaches for Idea," *The New York Times*, Money and Business Section, April 9, p. 4.

Gogan, Janis, Shoshana Zuboff, and Gloria Schuck. 1994. *Motorola-Panang*. Boston, MA: Harvard Business School Publishing.

Graham, Robert. 2000. "Capitalism Fails to Win French Hearts," *Financial Times*, March 6, p. 4.

Guha, Krishna. 1999. "'MTV Generation' Helps Transform Indian Retail Culture," *Financial Times*, August 21/22, p. 3.

Guth, Robert A. 2000. "Net Lets Japanese Women Join Work Force at Home," *The Wall Street Journal*, February 29, pp. B1, B20.

Herskovits, Melville J. 1952. *Man and His Works*. New York: Alfred A. Knopf.

Herskovits, Melville J. 1963. *Cultural Anthropology*. New York: Alfred Knopf.

Jordan, Miriam. 1999. "India's Novel Shopping Mall Attracts Throngs," *The Wall Street Journal*, September 22, p. 39A.

Kluckholn, Clyde. 1951. The Study of Culture. In Daniel Lerner and Harold D. Lasswell, *The Policy Services* (p. 86). Stanford, CA: Stanford University Press.

Kripalani, Manjeet. 1999. "Capitalist Generation," and "We Want to Grab the Funky Market," *Business Week*, October 10, pp. 128E2-128E12.

Kristof, Nicholas D. 1997. "A Japanese Generation Haunted by Its Past," *The New York Times*, January 22, pp. A1, A8.

Lohr, Steve. 1992. "Under the Wing of Japan Inc, a Fledgling Enterprise Soared," *The New York Times*, January 15, pp. A1, D5.

Macquin, Anne and Dominique Rouzies. 1998. "Selling Across the Cultural Gap," *Financial Times*, Mastering Global Business (Part Seven): Reaching the Global Customer, March 13, pp. 10-11.

Magnusson, Paul, Ann Palmer, and Kerry Capell. 1999. "Furor Over 'Frankenfood'," *Business Week,* October 18, pp. 50-51.

McKay, Betsy. 2000. "To Fix Coca-Cola, Daft Sets Out to Get Relationships Right," *The Wall Street Journal,* March 23, pp. A1, A12.

Miller, Scott. 1999. "Europe's Auto Market Takes On American Look," *The Wall Street Journal,* September 23, pp. A33, A38.

Morrison, Terri, Wayne A. Conaway, and George A. Borden. 1994. *Kiss, Bow, or Shake Hands, How to Do Business in Sixty Countries.* Holbrook, MA: Adams Media Corporation.

Murray, Sarah. 1999. "It Pays to Respond to Local Traditions," *Financial Times,* September 9, p. 11.

Perlez, Jane. 1994. "GE Finds Tough Going in Hungary," *The New York Times,* July 25, pp. D1, D8.

Strom, Stephanie. 2000. "Rising Internet Use Quietly Transforms Way Japanese Live," *The New York Times,* May 14, pp. A1, A6.

Trompenaars, Fons. 1994. *Riding the Wave of Culture: Understanding Diversity in Global Business.* Burr Ridge, IL: Irwin Professional Publishing.

Warner, Fara. 1996. "So Much for an MTV World: Teens Are Far Apart on Hopes and Values," *The Asian Wall Street Journal,* June 20, pp. 1, 8.

Wartzman, Rick. 1999. "When You Translate 'Get Milk' For Latinos, What Do You Get?" *The Wall Street Journal,* June 3, pp. A1, A8.

WuDunn, Sheryl. 1998. "Learning to Go Against Japan's Corporate Grain," *The New York Times,* Week in Review, March 8, p. 3.

WuDunn, Sheryl. 1999. "The Greatest Leap," *The New York Times,* Magazine Section, May 16, pp. 102-104.

## *Chapter 11*

"A Conversation with Kim Clark." 1995. *Harvard Business School Bulletin,* December, pp. 42-48.

Amelio, Gil and William Simon. 1996. *Profit From Experience.* New York: Van Nostrand Reinhold.

Baker, Stephen and Kerry Capell. 2000a. "Chris Gent, King of the Web?" *Business Week,* February 14, pp. 60-61.

Baker, Stephen and Kerry Capell. 2000b. "The Race to Rule Mobile," *Business Week,* February 21, pp. 58-60.

Beck, Ernest. 1996. "Restructured Firm in Hungary Offers Cultural Lessons," *The Wall Street Journal,* June 15, p. A10.

Bennis, Warren. 1999. "It's All About Relationships, Stupid," *InformationWeek,* June 15, p. 48.

Bernstein, Arron, Susan Jackson, and John Byrne. 1997. "Jack Cracks the Whip Again," *Business Week,* December 15, pp. 34-35.

Blanchard, Ken and Michael O'Connor. 1997. *Managing By Values*. San Francisco, CA: Berrett-Koehler Publishers.

Blanchard, Ken and Terry Waghorn. 1997. *Mission Possible*. New York: McGraw-Hill.

Boudette, Neal E. and Kevin Delaney. 2000. "British Internet Portan Vizzavi Faces Wireless Hurdles," *The Wall Street Journal*, June 21, p. B4.

Bourgeois, L. J., III. and David Brodwin. 1984. "Strategic Implementation: Five Approaches to an Elusive Phenomenon," *Strategic Management Journal*, July-September, pp. 241-264.

Brake, Terence. 1997. *The Global Leader: Critical Factors For Creating a World Class Organization*. Chicago: Irwin Professional Publishing.

Byrne, John A. 1999. *Chainsaw: The Notorious Career of Al Dunlap in the Era of Profit-At-Any-Price*. New York: HarperBusiness.

Calori, Roland and Bruno Dufour. 1995. "Management European Style," *The Academy of Management Executive*, August, pp. 61-77.

CE Roundtable. 2000. "Leadership in the New Economy," *Chief Executive*, July, pp. 63-73.

Charan, Ram and Geoffrey Colvin. 1999. "Why CEOs Fail," *Fortune*, June 21, pp. 69-78.

Colvin, Geoffrey. 2000. "America's Most Admired Companies," *Fortune*, February 21, pp. 108-117, F1-F7.

Covey, Stephen R. 1991. *Principle-Centered Leadership*. New York: Simon & Schuster (Fireside).

Crawford, Leslie. 1997. "Long Reach Opens New Sources of Finance," *Financial Times*, Global Company Section, November 7, p. 1.

Davenport, Thomas H. and Laurence Prusak. 1998. *Working Knowledge*. Boston, MA: Harvard Business School Press.

Day, Charles R., Jr. and Polly LeBarre. 1994. "GE: Just Your Average Everyday $60 Billion Family Grocery Store," *Industry Week*, May 4, pp. 13-18.

Deogun, Nikhil. 1999. "Can Douglas Investor End Coke's Crisis?" *The Wall Street Journal*, June 18, pp. B1, B4.

Fiedler, Fred E. 1967. *A Theory of Leadership Effectiveness*. New York: McGraw-Hill Book Company.

Forrester, Russ and Allan B. Drexler. 1999. "A Model for Team-Based Organization Performance," *The Academy of Management Executive*, August, pp. 36-49.

Fuller, George. 1998. *Win Win Management: Leading People in the New Work Place*. Paramus, New Jersey: Prentice-Hall Press.

Garrat, Bob. 1999. "Never-Ending Challenge of Change," *Financial Times*, FT Director Section, October 1, pp. 1, 2.

George, Jill A. and Jeanne M. Wilson. 1997. *Team Member's Survival Guide*. New York: McGraw-Hill.

Gogan, Janis L., Shoshana Zuboff, and Gloria Schuck. 1994. *Motorola-Panang*. Boston, MA: Harvard Business School Publishing.

Gorden, William I., Erica L. Nagel, Scott A. Myers, and Carole A. Barbato. 1997. *The Team Trainer*. Chicago, IL: Irwin Professional Publishing.

Griffith, Victoria. 1997. "Teamwork's Own Goals," *Financial Times,* July 18, p. 20.

Guyon, Janet. 1997. "Cable & Wireless's American Chief Shakes Up Europe's Telecom Sector," *The Wall Street Journal,* January 20, p. A10.

Hagerty, James R. 2000. "A Free Spirit Energizes Home Depot," *The Wall Street Journal,* April 11, pp. B1, B4.

Heller, Robert. 1995. *The Leadership Imperative: What Innovative Business Leaders Are Doing Today to Create the Successful Companies of Tomorrow*. New York: Dutton (Truman Talley Books).

Helyar, John. 1998. "A Jack Welch Disciple Finds the GE Mystique Only Takes You So Far," *The Wall Street Journal,* August 10, pp. A1, A8.

Hofstede, Geert. 1983a. "National Cultures in Four Dimensions: A Research-Based Theory of Cultural Differences Among Nations," *International Studies of Management and Organisation,* Summer, pp. 46-74.

Hofstede, Geert. 1983b. "The Cultural Relativity of Organizational Practices and Theories," *Journal of International Business Studies,* Fall, pp. 75-89.

Hofstede, Geert. 1984. *Culture's Consequences: International Differences in Work-Related Values*. Beverly Hills, CA: Sage Publications.

Hofstede, Geert. 1992. "Cultural Constraints in Management Theories," Distinguished International Scholar Lecture, Las Vegas, Nevada: 1992 Annual Meeting of the Academy of Management, August 11.

House, Robert J., Paul Hanges, and Michael Angar. 1993. *A Multi-Nation Study of Cultures, Leadership and Organizational Practices*. Philadelphia, PA: The University of Pennsylvania.

House, Robert J., Norman S. Wright, and Ram N. Aditya. 1997. Cross-Cultural Research on Organizational Leadership. In P.C. Early and M Elly, (Eds.) *New Perspectives on International Industrial/Organizational Psychology.* pp. 535-635. San Fransisco, CA: New Lexington Press,

Hurst, David K. 1995. *Crisis & Renewal: Meeting the Challenge of Organizational Change*. Boston, MA: Harvard Business School Press.

Iverson, Ken with Tom Varian. 1998. *Plain Talk*. New York: Wiley.

Katzenbach, Jon R. 1998. *Teams at the Top*. Boston, MA: Harvard Business School Press.

Kim, W. Chan and Renee Mauborgne. 1998. "Building Trust," *Financial Times,* January 9, p. 25.

Kotter, John P. 1996. *Leading Change*. Boston, MA: Harvard Business School Press.

Lancaster, Hal. 1999. "Herb Kelleher Has One Main Strategy: Treat Employees Well," *The Wall Street Journal,* August 31, p. B1.

Landers, Peter. 2000. "In Japan, the Words of Chairman Jack Are Revolutionary," *The Wall Street Journal,* February 9, pp. A1, A8.

Lipnack, Jessica and Jeffrey Stamps. 1999. "Virtual Teams," *Strategy and Leadership,* January/February, pp. 14-19.

Lowe, Janet. 1998. *Jack Welch Speaks.* New York: Wiley.

Lublin, Joann S. 2000. "Building a Better CEO," *The Wall Street Journal,* April 14, pp. B1, B4.

Maitland, Alison. 1999. "A Future Based on Sharing," *Financial Times,* June 11, p. 12.

Maucher, Helmut. 1994. *Leadership in Action.* New York: McGraw-Hill.

McDermott, Lunda C., Nolan Brawley, and William W. Waite. 1998. *World Class Teams.* New York: Wiley & Sons, Inc.

Murray, Matt. 2000. "GE Mentoring Program Turns Underlings Into Teachers of the Web," *The Wall Street Journal,* February 15, pp. B1, B16.

Perlez, Jane. 1994. "GE Finds Tough Going in Hungary," *The New York Times,* July 25, pp. D1, D8.

Raghavan, Anita and Gautam Naik. 1999. "How Lone-Wolf CEO Let Telecom Italia Fall Into Olivetti's Grip," *The Wall Street Journal,* July 12, pp. A1, A10.

Rowe, Alan J. and Richard O. Mason. 1987. *Managing With Style.* San Francisco, CA: Jossey-Bass Publishers.

Segalla, Michael. 1998. "National Cultures, International Business," *Financial Times,* Mastering Global Business (Part Six): Cross Cultural Management and Leadership, March 5, pp. 8-10.

Sherman, Stratford. 1995. "How Tomorrow's Best Leaders Are Learning Their Stuff," *Fortune,* November 27, pp. 90-102.

Sherriton, Jacalyn and James L. Stern. 1997. *Corporate Culture/Team Culture.* New York: American Management Association.

Slater, Robert. 1999. *Jack Welch and the GE Way.* New York: McGraw-Hill.

Snyder, Neil H. and Angela P. Clontz. 1997. *The Will to Lead.* Chicago, IL: Irwin Professional Publishing.

Solomon, Charlene Marmer. 1995. "Global Teams: The Ultimate Collaboration," *Personnel Journal,* September pp. 49-58.

Waters, Richard. 1999. "Case Study: General Electric," *Financial Times,* Autumn 1999 Digital Business Guide, September 30, p.20.

Weaver, Richard G. 1997. *Managers As Facilitators.* San Francisco, CA: Barrett-Koehler Publishers.

Welch, Jr., John F., Paolo Fresco, and John D. Opie. 1996. "To Our Shareholders," *1995 Annual Report,* Fairfield, CT: General Electric Company, February 9, pp. 1-5.

Wellins, Richard S., William C. Byham, and George R. Dixon. 1994. *Inside Teams: How 20 World-Class Organizations are Winning Through Teamwork.* San Francisco, CA: Jossey-Bass Publishers.

Zambrano, Lorenzo. 1995. "CEMEX: An Emerging Multinational," *Keynote Address,* Mexico City, Mexico: Strategic Management Society Conference, October 16.

Zand, Dale E. 1997. *The Leadership Triad: Knowledge, Trust, Power.* New York: Oxford University Press.

Zeien, Albert. 1995. "Gillette's Global Marketing Experiences," *Talk at St. John's University's Annual Colman Mockler Leadership Award Ceremony,* New York, February 27.

## *Chapter 12*

Abueva, Jobert E. 2000. "Return of the Native Executive: Many Repatriations Fail, at Huge Cost to Companies," *The New York Times,* May 17, pp. C1, C8.

Aiello, Paul. 1991. "Building a Joint Venture in China," *Journal of General Management,* Winter, pp. 47-63.

Anfuso, Dawn. 1994. "HR Unites the World of Coca-Cola," *Personnel Journal,* November, pp. 112-116.

Ball, Jeffrey. 1999. "DaimlerChrysler's Transfer Woes," *The Wall Street Journal,* August 24, pp. B1, B12.

Barrett, Paul M. 1999. "Joining the Stampede to Europe, Law Firm Suffers a Few Bruises," *The Wall Street Journal,* April 27, pp. A1, A8.

Beard, Alison. 2000. "Leaders of the Right Stuff in Big Demand," *Financial Times,* June 7, p. 12.

Beck, Ernest. 1996. "Restructured Firm in Hungary Offers Cultural Lessons," *The Wall Street Journal,* June 15, p. A10.

Black, Stewart and Hal B. Gregersen. 1991a. "The Other Half of the Picture: Antecedents of Spouse Cross-Cultural Adjustment," *The Journal of International Business Studies,* Third Quarter, pp. 461-477.

Black, Stewart and Hal B. Gregersen. 1991b. "When Yankee Comes Home: Factors Related to Expatriate and Spouse Repatriate Adjustment," *The Journal of International Business Studies,* Fourth Quarter, pp. 671-694.

Caldwell, Bruce and Jill Gambon. 1996. "Telecommuting: The Virtual Office Gets Real," *InformationWeek,* January 22, pp. 32-40.

Cane, Alan and Louise Kehoe. 1998. "Cable and Wireless Chief Quits to Take Top Job at EDS," *Financial Times,* December 11, pp. 1, 18.

Clark, Tanya. 1995. "Managing China's Challenge," *Industry Week,* July 17, pp. 31-36.

Dobrzynski, Judith H. 1996. "A Study Sees a Down Side to Going Overseas As an Executive," *The New York Times,* August 16, p.D2.

Donkin, Richard. 1997. "The Expatriate Experience," *Financial Times,* November 14, p. I.

Feldman, Daniel C. and David C. Thomas. 1992. "Career Management Issues Facing Expatriates," *Journal of International Business Studies,* Spring, pp. 271-293.

"Global Mobil," 1998. *Chief Executive,* March, pp. 42-45.

Govindarajan, Vijay and Anil K, Gupta. 1998. "Success Is all in the Mindset," *Financial Times,* Mastering Global Business (Part Five): Controlling the Global Organization, February 2, pp. 2-3.

Guyon, Janet. 1997. "Cable & Wireless's American Chief Shakes Up Europe's Telecom Sector," *The Wall Street Journal,* January 20, p. A10.

Harney, Alexandra. 1999. "Toyota Plans Pay Based on Merit," *Financial Times,* July 8, p. 20.

Himowitz, Michael J. 1998. "Long Distance Eye Contact Made Easy," *Fortune,* February 2, p. 137.

Kaufman, Jonathan. 1999. "An American Expatriate Finds Hong Kong Post a Fast Road to Nowhere," *The Wall Street Journal,* January 21, pp. A1, A8.

Kessler, Ian. 1998. "The Art of Employee Compensation: Getting the Right Message Across," *Financial Times,* Mastering Global Business (Part Six): Cross Cultural Management and Leadership, March 5, pp. 4-6.

Kets de Vries, Manfred F.R., with Elizabeth Florent-Treacy. 1999. *The New Global Leaders: Richard Branson, Percy Barnevik, and David Simon (and John Brown).* San Francisco, CA: Jossey-Bass Publishers.

King, Julia. 2000. " 'Personal Coaches' Help Execs 'Get' the Net," *Computerworld,* April 17, p. 16.

Lublin, Joann S. 1998. "Companies Send Intrepid Retirees to Work Abroad," *The Wall Street Journal,* March 2, pp. B1, B2.

McKay, Betsy. 2000. "To Fix Coca-Cola, Daft Sets Out to Get Relationship Right," *The Wall Street Journal,* March 23, pp. A1, A12.

McKibben, Gordon. 1998. *Cutting Edge.* Boston, MA: Harvard Business School Press.

Mockler, Robert J. 1994-1999. "Field Interviews with Companies in China and Italy."

Murray, Matt. 2000. "GE Mentoring Program Turns Underlings Into Teachers of the Web," *The Wall Street Journal,* February 15, pp. B1, B16.

Petzinger, Thomas, Jr. 1999. "With the Stakes High, a Lucent Duo Conquers Distance and Culture," *The Wall Street Journal,* April 23, p. B1.

Purdy, Larry. 1995. "Leadership: Is It Culturally Dependent?," Presentation, Mexico City, Mexico: Strategic Management Society Annual National Conference, October 15-18.

"Repatriating Workers." 1999. *USA Today,* May 17, p. B1.

Schellenbarger, Sue. 1997. "Families Are Facing New Strains As Work Expands Across Globe," *The Wall Street Journal,* November 12, p. B1.

Simison, Robert L. and Scott Miller. 1999. "Daimler to Revamp Management to Spur Profit," *The Wall Street Journal,* September 15, pp. A25, A26.

Solomon, Charlene Marmer. 1995a. "Learning to Manage Host-Country Nationals: Multinationals Are Increasingly Committed to Hiring Local Managers; But the Greatest Challenge Is to Skillfully Link Their Native Expertise to the Company's Strategic Goals," *Personnel Journal,* March, pp. 60-67.

Solomon, Charlene Marmer. 1995b. "Navigating Your Search for Global Talent: International Human Resources Managers Are Learning It Takes Years to Develop a Globally Aware Work Force," *Personnel Journal,* May, pp. 94-101.

Stuart, Anne. 1999. "Corporate Learning: Continuing Education," *Fortune,* September 1, pp. 31-42.

Tagliabue, John. 1999. "Bringing Good Things to Fiat," *The New York Times,* Money and Business Section, September 12, pp. 1, 14.

Taylor, Roger. 1999. "On Target, On Course, and Online," *Financial Times,* September 22, pp. 22.

"The Talent Void: Where Are All the Good Managers?" 1997. Central Europe Economic Review: Special Section," *The Wall Street Journal Europe,* February (January 27, 1997), pp. 1-32.

Violino, Bob and Jennifer Mateyaschuk. 1999. "Labor Intensive," *InformationWeek,* July 5, pp. 34-40.

Wickman, Floyd and Terri Sjodin. 1997. *Mentoring: The Most Obvious Yet Overlooked Key to Achieving More in Life Than You Dreamed Possible.* Chicago, IL: Irwin Professional Publishing.

Wind, Jerry Yoram and Jeremy Main. 1998. *Driving Change.* New York: Free Press.

## *Chapter 13*

Applbaum, Ealman E. and Pamela A. Yatsko. 1993. *FCB and Publicis (A): Forming An Alliance,* A Case Study. Boston, MA: Harvard Business School.

Betts, Paul and Tim Burt. 2000. "General Motors and Fiat Close to Signing Strategic Alliances," *Financial Times,* March 13, p.1.

Bloomberg Business News. 1997. "Raisio to Build Plant in Carolina," *The New York Times,* August 29, p. D2.

Burt, Tim. 2000. "Car Pooling," *Financial Times,* March 13, p. 14.

Crockett, Roger O. 2000. "A New Company Called Motorola," *Business Week,* April 17, pp. 86-92.

Das, T.K. and Bing-Sheng Teng. 1998. "Between Trust and Control: Developing Confidence in Partner Cooperation in Alliances," *Academy of Management Review,* Vol, 23, No. 3, pp. 491-512.

de Keijzer, Arne J. 1995. "Identifying Potentially Effective Joint Venture Partners," *Global Market Conference on China,* Baruch College, New York, November 8.

Del Garda, Desenzano. 2000. "The Global Gambles of General Motors," *The Economist,* June 24, pp. 67-69.

Emmons, Willis. 1990. *Tambrands Inc.: The Remtech Soviet Venture (A),* A Case Study. Boston, MA: Harvard Business School Publishing Division.

Emmons, Willis. 1993. *Tambrands Inc.: The Remtech Soviet Venture (B),* A Case Study. Boston, MA: Harvard Business School Publishing Division.

Forbes III, Theodore M., Lynn A. Isabella, Robert E. Spekman, and Thomas C. MacAvoy. 1995. *Shell Italia (B),* A Case Study. Charlottesville, VA: University of Virginia Darden School Foundation.

Guyot, Erik. 1999. "Foreign Companies Bring More Than Jobs to China," *The Wall Street Journal,* September 15, p. A2.

Hall, William. 1999. "Swissair and Sabena to Merge Departments," *Financial Times,* June 23, p. 22.

Harbison, John R. and Peter Pekar. 1997a. *A Practical Guide to Alliances: Leap-frogging the Learning Curve.* New York: Booz-Allen & Hamilton.

Harbison, John R. and Peter Pekar. 1997b. *Cross-border Alliances in the Age of Collaboration.* New York: Booz-Allen & Hamilton.

Harbison, John R. and Peter Pekar. 1997c. *Institutionalizing Alliance Skills: Secrets of Repeatable Success.* New York: Booz-Allen & Hamilton.

Harnischfeger, Uta. 1999. "Deutsche Bank Treads Gently in Europe," *Financial Times,* July 5, p. 18.

Holusha, John. 1996. "For Steel-Wool Maker, Chinese Lessons," *The New York Times,* May 28, p. D10.

Ipsen, Erik. 1997. "Finnish Firm Redefines Health Food," *International Herald Tribune,* January 9, pp. 1, 15.

"La Paz in Water Sell-Off," 1997. *Financial Times,* July 4, p. 5.

Meredith, Robyn. 2000. "In Policy Shift, GM Will Rely on Alliances," *The New York Times,* January 18, pp. C1, C14.

Mockler, Robert J. 1994-1999. "Field Interviews with Companies in China and Italy."

Mockler, Robert J. 1999. *Multinational Strategic Alliances.* New York and Chichester, England: John Wiley & Sons.

Molvor, Greg. 1997. "US License Deal Boosts Raisio," *Financial Times,* July 16, p. 15.

Murray, Shailagn. 1997. "Back from the Brink, BP Finds Religion," *The Wall Street Journal,* September 17, p. A19.

Naik, Gautam. 1997. "Hungary's Tough Call on Matav Pays Off," *The Wall Street Journal,* August 27, p. A8.

Nakamoto, Michiyo. 1997. "Mazda, Ford to Share Parts," *Financial Times,* April 18, p. 17.

Nash, Nathaniel C. 1995. "Coke's Great Romanian Adventure," *The New York Times,* Business Section, February 26, pp. 1, 10.

Naughton, Keith, Pete Engardio, and Dexter Roberts. 1995. "How GM Got the Inside Track In China," *Business Week,* November 6, pp. 56-57.

"Overseas Projects." 1997. *Corporate Publication,* Seoul, Korea: Daewoo Group.

Reed, John. 1997. "Foreigners Transform Hungary's Banks," *The Wall Street Journal,* September 24, p. A18.

REFRAC Technology Development Corporation. 1996. *Annual Report for 1995,* New York.

Robinson, Gwen. 1999. "Hachette in Australian Magazine Joint Venture," *Financial Times,* July 7, p. 16.

Rossant, John. 1999. "Divorce, Italian-Style," *Business Week,* May 17, pp. 54-55.

Schuman, Michael and Jane L. Lee. 1999. "Dismantling of Daewoo Shows How Radically Korea Is Changing," *The Wall Street Journal,* August 17, pp. A1, A10.

Sender, Henny. 2000. "Telecom Pact Is a Mileston in Asian Market," *The Wall Street Journal,* March 1, pp. A18, A23.

Shirouzu, Norihiko. 2000. "Toyota May Join Ford's Online System," *The Wall Street Journal,* January 25, p. A13.

Simison, Robert L. 1999. "General Motors Drives Some Hard Bargains with Asian Suppliers," *The Wall Street Journal,* April 2, pp. A1, A6.

Skapinger, Michael. 1999a. "American and BA Pull Out of Global Tie-Up Plan," *Financial Times,* July 29, pp. 1, 14.

Skapinger, Michael. 1999b. "Austrian Air Switches Allegiance to Star Alliance," *Financial Times,* September 22, p. 9.

Skapinger, Michael. 1999c. "KLM and Alitalia Likely to Merge," *Financial Times,* July 30, pp. 1, 14.

Stern, Gabriella. 1995. "GM Executive's Ties to Native Country Help Auto Maker Clinch Deal in China," *The Wall Street Journal,* November 2, p. B5.

Strom, Stephanie and Keith Bradsher. 1999. "Wedding or Wipe-Out?" *The New York Times,* Money and Business Section, May 23, pp. 1, 13.

Tagliabue, John. 1999. "A Media World to Conquer," *The New York Times,* July 7, pp. C1, C5.

Thornhill, John. 1997. "Estonian Banks Thrive in a New Economy," *Financial Times,* September 24, p. 3.

Trivedi, Kruti. 2000. "Four Airlines Form an International Alliance," *The New York Times,* June 23, p. C3.

Valance, Nikos. 2000. "Sweet and Sour," *Chief Financial Officer (CFO),* March, pp. 36-38.

Wagstyl, Stefan and Christophe Bobinski. 2000. "Citigroup to Pay $1Bn for Poland's Top Corporate Bank," *Financial Times,* February 11, p. 1.

White, Gregory L. and Fara Warner. 2000. "GM in Talks for Web Plan with Honda," *The Wall Street Journal,* January 12, p. A14.

Yoshino, Michael Y. and U. Srinivasa Rangan. 1995. *Strategic Alliances: An Entrepreneurial Approach to Globalization.* Boston, MA: Harvard Business School Press.

Zuckerman, Laurence. 2000. "A New Math: Fewer Airlines + Higher Profits = More Competition," *The New York Times,* June 22, pp. C1, C12.

## *Chapter 14*

Anderson, Nick. 1996. "Petrochemical Privatization Fires Up Mexico," *Hong Kong Standard,* Financial Review Section, June 13, p. 10.

Anderson, Robert. 2000. "Czech's Pay a Heavy Price for Bank Sell-Offs," *Financial Times,* June 1, p. 3.

Barton, Laurence. 1993. *Crisis in Organizations: Managing and Communicating in the Heat of Chaos.* Cincinnati, Ohio: South-Western Publishing Company.

Beck, Ernest. 1997. "Final Flourish: Despite Some Bumps, Hungary's Privatization Nears an End with . . . with Heaps of Cash," *The Wall Street Journal Europe, Central European Economics Review,* February 1997 (January 27, 1997), pp. 10-13, 28.

Beich, Elaine. 1997. *The ASTD Training Source Book: Creativity and Innovation.* New York: McGraw-Hill.

Blitz, James. 1999. "Italy Set for Enel Sell-Off," *Financial Times,* July 7, p. 16.

Botkin, Jim. 1999. *Smart Business: How Knowledge Communities Can Revolutionize Your Company.* New York: The Free Press.

Brown, Shona L. and Kathleen M. Eisenhardt. 1998. *Competing on the Edge.* Boston, MA: Harvard Business School Press.

Business Value. 1997. "The Art of Innovation," *Information Week,* December 1, pp. 36-64.

Chen, Kathy. 1996. "China City Turns Into a Prototype For Privatization," *The Wall Street Journal,* June 10, p. A14.

Christensen, Clayton M. 1997. *The Innovator's Dilemma.* Boston, MA: Harvard Business School Press.

Church, George J. 1997. "Thinking Big," *Time: Quarterly Business Report,* December 8.

Clark, Don and Joan E. Rigdon. 1995. "Stripped-Down PCs Will be Talk of Comdex," *The Wall Street Journal,* November 10, p. B1.

Colitt, Raymond. 1998. "Venezuelan Sell-Off May Fetch $2.5 Billion," *Financial Times,* January 28, p. 3.

Deutsch, Claudia II. 1997. "Original Thinking for a Digital Xerox," *The New York Times,* April 15, pp. D1, D6.

Dibbell, Julian. 1995. "Neilson Rates the Net," *Time,* November 13, p. 121.

Dillon, Sam. 1996. "Mexico Drops Its Effort to Sell Some Oil Plants," *The New York Times,* October 14, p. D2.

Donaldson, Lex. 1995. *American Anti-Management Theories of Organization.* New York: Cambridge University Press.

Donaldson, Lex. 1996. *For Positivist Organization Theory.* Thousand Oaks, CA: Sage.

Done, Kevin. 1997. "Europe's Privatization Fast Track," *Financial Times,* July 4, p. 10.

Essex, William. 1997. "The Dash from Debt," *Euromoney,* May, pp. 143-146.

Flynn, Julia. 1999. "Gap Exists Between Entrepreneurship In Europe, North America, Study Shows," *The Wall Street Journal,* July 2, p. A10.

Friedland, Jonathan. 1999. "Mexico's Oil Company Becomes Businesslike to Avoid Privatization," *The Wall Street Journal,* May 24, pp. A1, A14.

Hargrove, Robert. 1998. *Mastering the Art of Creative Collaboration.* New York: McGraw-Hill (Business Week Books).

Hays, Constance L. 1999. "Coca-Cola Recalls Water in Poland After Bacteria Are Found," *The New York Times,* June 30, pp. C2.

Hays, Constance L., Alan Cowell, and Craig R. Whitney. 1999. "A Sputter in the Coke Machine," *The New York Times,* June 30, pp. C1, C6.

Ishida, Hiromi. 1994. "Japanese and European Experiences of Creativity Compared: A Personal Case Study," *Creativity and Innovation Management,* December, pp. 233-239.

James, Jennifer. 1996. *Thinking in the Future Tense: Leadership Skills for a New Age.* New York: Simon & Schuster.

Jenrette, Richard H. 1997. *The Contrarian Manager.* New York: McGraw-Hill.

Kanter, Rosabeth Moss. 1995. *World Class: Thriving Locally in a Global Economy.* New York: Simon & Schuster.

"Knowledge Management." 1999. *Financial Times,* Mastering Information Management Section, Part Six, March 8, pp. 1-15.

Kotter, John P. 1996. *Leading Change.* Boston, MA: Harvard Business School Press.

Krauss, Clifford. 1999. "Argentina's Rising Oil Fortunes," *The New York Times,* April 24, pp. C1, C2.

Kynge, James. 2000. "Mongolian Communists Back in Power," *Financial Times,* July 4, p. 4.

Lave, Jean and Etienne Wenger. 1991. *Situated Learning.* New York: Cambridge University Press.

Lin, Ho Swee and Rahul Jacob. 2000. "Chinese Airport Privatisation Weighed Down by Expectation," *Financial Times,* January 14, p.17.

Mann, Roland. 2000. "Wise Prescriptions for a Swift Recovery," *Financial Times,* Mastering Risk Section (Nine), June 20, pp.14-15.

Marozzi, Justin. 1997. "Foreign Investors Warn Philippines Over Privatization," *Financial Times,* February 6, p.16.

Michaels, Daniel. 1997. "For Polish Firms, Mass Privatization Moves Glacially," *The Wall Street Journal,* January 6, p. A7C.

Naisbitt, John. 1994. *Global Paradox.* London: Nicholas Brealey Publishing.

"Overload." 1999. *The Wall Street Journal,* Special Information Technology Section, June 29, pp. R1-R26.

Perry, Lee Tom, Randall G. Stott, and W. Norman Smallwood. 1993. *Real-Time Strategy: Improvising Team-Based Planning for a Fast-Changing World.* New York: Wiley.

Peters, Tom. 1997. *The Circle of Innovation.* New York: Alfred Knopf (A Borzoi Book).

Quinn, James Brian, Jordan J. Baruch, and Karen Anne Zien. 1997. *Innovation Explosion.* New York: The Free Press.

Rebello, Kathy. 1996. "Inside Microsoft: The Inside Story of How Internet Forced Bill Gates to Reverse Course," *Business Week,* October 30, July 15, pp. 58-67.

Senge, Peter. 1990. *The Fifth Discipline: The Art and Practice of the Learning Organization.* New York: Doubleday (Currency).

Solis, Dianne and Jonatian Friedland. 1995. "A Tale of Two Countries," *The Wall Street Journal,* October 2, pp. R19, R23.

Suchman, Lucy. 1987. *Plans and Situated Action.* New York: Wiley.

"Survey: Middle East and North Africa Privatization." 1998. *Financial Times,* March 26, pp. I-IV.

Tagliabue, John. 2000. "French Can Pursue Polish Phone Company," *The New York Times,* May 23, p. C4.

"The Painful Privatisation of South Africa," 1999. *The Economist,* September 11, p. 49.

Tomlinson, Richard. 1998. "Mongolia's Wild Ride to Capitalism," *Fortune,* December 7, pp. 102-200.

Tomlinson, Richard. 1999. "Dialing in on Latin America," *Fortune,* October 25, pp. 259-262.

Torsilieri, Jan. 1998. "Success in Knowledge Management: A Case Study at Booz-Allen & Hamilton Inc.," *Evening Lecture Series,* New York: Stern Business School, December 3.

Tushman, Michael and Charles A. O'Reilly III. 1997. *Winning Through Innovation.* Boston, MA: Harvard Business School Press.

Vitzthum, Carita, Craig Torres, and Bhushan Bahree. 1999. "Argentina's YPF May Be Seeking Sweeter Bid," *The Wall Street Journal,* May 5, pp. A14, A18.

White, David. 2000. "Spain to Spced Utilities Deregulation," *Financial Times,* June 24, p. 2.

World Watch. 1998. "Brazil Outlines Privatization Plans," *The Wall Street Journal,* January 30, p. A10.

World Wire. 1997. "Israel Plans First Yen Bonds . . . and 13 Big Privatizations," *The Wall Street Journal,* January 23, p. A12.

Wright, Robert and Christopher Bobinski. 1999. "Hungary, Poland Choose Privatization Flight Paths," *Financial Times,* September 7, p. 19.

Yochelson, John. 1999. "3rd Annual Competitiveness Survey: Global Innovation," *Chief Executive,* June, pp. 41-47.

# Index

## Order a copy of this book with this form or online at:
*http://www.haworthpressinc.com/store/product.asp?sku=4586*

## MULTINATIONAL STRATEGIC MANAGEMENT
## An Integrative Entrepreneurial Context-Specific Process

_____in hardbound at $89.95 (ISBN: 0-7890-1474-2)

_____in softbound at $49.95 (ISBN: 0-7890-1475-0)

COST OF BOOKS_____

OUTSIDE USA/CANADA/
MEXICO: ADD 20%____

POSTAGE & HANDLING_____
*(US: $4.00 for first book & $1.50*
*for each additional book)*
*Outside US: $5.00 for first book*
*& $2.00 for each additional book)*

SUBTOTAL_____

in Canada: add 7% GST____

STATE TAX____
*(NY, OH & MIN residents, please*
*add appropriate local sales tax)*

**FINAL TOTAL**
*(If paying in Canadian funds,*
*convert using the current*
*exchange rate, UNESCO*
*coupons welcome.)*

**BILL ME LATER:** ($5 service charge will be added)
(Bill-me option is good on US/Canada/Mexico orders only;
not good to jobbers, wholesalers, or subscription agencies.)

Check here if billing address is different from
shipping address and attach purchase order and
billing address information.

Signature _____

**PAYMENT ENCLOSED: $**_____

**PLEASE CHARGE TO MY CREDIT CARD.**

Visa     MasterCard     AmEx     Discover
Diner's Club     Eurocard     JCB

Account # _____

Exp. Date_____

Signature_____

Prices in US dollars and subject to change without notice.

NAME_____
INSTITUTION_____
ADDRESS_____
CITY_____
STATE/ZIP_____
COUNTRY_____ COUNTY (NY residents only)_____
TEL_____ FAX_____
E-MAIL_____
May we use your e-mail address for confirmations and other types of information?     Yes     No
We appreciate receiving your e-mail address and fax number. Haworth would like to e-mail or fax special
discount offers to you, as a preferred customer. **We will never share, rent, or exchange your e-mail address
or fax number.** We regard such actions as an invasion of your privacy.

*Order From Your Local Bookstore or Directly From*
**The Haworth Press, Inc.**
10 Alice Street, Binghamton, New York 13904-1580 • USA
TELEPHONE: 1-800-HAWORTH (1-800-429-6784) / Outside US/Canada: (607) 722-5857
FAX: 1-800-895-0582 / Outside US/Canada: (607) 722-6362
E-mail: getinfo@haworthpressinc.com
PLEASE PHOTOCOPY THIS FORM FOR YOUR PERSONAL USE.
www.HaworthPress.com

BOF02